INTRANET BIBLE

By Lynn M. Bremner,
Anthony F. Iasi,
and Al Servati

JAMSA
P·R·E·S·S
...a computer user's best friend

Intranet Bible

Published by
Jamsa Press
2975 S. Rainbow Blvd., Suite I
Las Vegas, NV 89102
U.S.A.

http://www.jamsa.com

For information about the translation or distribution of any Jamsa Press book, please write to Jamsa Press at the address listed above.

Intranet Bible

Printed in the United States of America.
98765432

ISBN 1-884133-31-2

Publisher Debbie Jamsa	*Technical Advisor* Phil Schmauder	*Director of Publishing Operations* Janet Lawrie
Content Manager Rick Pearson	*Proofers* Lisa Kindsvater Rosemary Pasco Jeanne Smith	*Illustrators* Digital West Media James Rehrauer Nelson Yee
Composition James Rehrauer Nelson Yee	*Indexer* Linda Linssen	*Copy Editors* Heather Grigg Lisa Kindsvater
Cover Design Marianne Helm	*Cover Photograph* O'Gara/Bissell	

Dedications

A special thanks to Susan Vreeland for making a difference.—Lynn M. Bremner

To my mom, Elena Iasi, who bought me my first Apple II computer believing that all I was going to do with it was to balance the family checkbook. Surprise! —Anthony F. Iasi

To my parents for their dedication to our well-being. And to my dear sister Zohreh for her support and contribution. It is the team that makes the difference.—Al Servati

Acknowledgments

It takes many dedicated people to put together a project such as this book. On the front lines were Joel and Libby Keller who supported us on key sections of the book. Joel's expertise allowed us to cover the cost analysis aspect of intranets. We would like to thank Bob Matlin who continues to be an indispensable resource in helping us with our manuscript, Terry Reim who gave us peace of mind by reading our work before the publisher saw it, and Zohreh Servati and Vito Asaro who gave us valuable research assistance and for making suggestions for material important for the book's success. We were very fortunate to have Jim Bremner Jr. develop many of the sample Web pages, graphics, and CGI code. His artistic work is in many corporate Web sites throughout the Internet. Also, Jim Bremner Sr. and Kristine Cole, who spent countless hours capturing the many screen shots and assembling the tons of material needed for the CD-ROM. Finally, Kris Jamsa, who continues to believe in us and provide the support to make this book a success. Thanks everyone for being such a great team!

Contents at a Glance

Contents

V

XVI

USING THE INTRANET BIBLE COMPANION CD-ROM

The CD-ROM that accompanies the *Intranet Bible* contains several utility programs you can use to create HTML documents, convert graphics, and perform other key operations. In addition, the CD-ROM contains a Windows-based electronic version of this book that you can read using your computer's CD-ROM. To install the electronic book on your system, perform these steps:

1. If you are using Windows 95, select the Start menu Run option. Windows 95 will display the Run dialog box. If you are using Windows 3.1 or Windows NT, select the Program Manager's File menu Run option.

2. Within the Run dialog box, type **D:\SETUP**, replacing the drive letter D with the drive letter that corresponds to your CD-ROM. For example, if your CD-ROM is drive E, you would type **E:\SETUP** and press <ENTER>.

3. After the SETUP program completes the software installation, select the *Intranet Bible* icon to run the electronic version of this book. To learn specifics about the software programs the disk contains, print or display the *README.TXT* file that resides in the *Intranet* folder (directory).

Chapter 1

The Internet as a Foundation

In the early 1990s, few people knew about the Internet and the World Wide Web (WWW or Web) did not exist. In less than five years, the Internet's explosive growth has touched each of our lives. Using the Internet's worldwide network of computers, users now exchange e-mail messages, files, and chat with other users around the globe. Likewise, the ever growing World Wide Web lets users access vast amounts of information on an unlimited number of topics. In fact, it is almost impossible to find a magazine, TV show, movie, or business that does not have a homepage on the Web.

Today, a new technology—*intranets*—is poised to change the way a business shares information within itself. In short, an intranet is a network of computers that lets a company's employees share and exchange information, e-mail, and even confidential company documents. Just as the Internet connects users worldwide, an intranet connects employees company wide—regardless of where those employees reside.

At first glance, an intranet may appear as nothing more than a corporate-wide local-area network. In some cases, an intranet is merely a local-area network. However, the employees who connect to an intranet often work at geographically dispersed offices—even offices worldwide. A feature that distinguishes intranets from traditional local-area networks is that intranets are based on the TCP/IP protocol—the collection of software rules that control the Internet. Therefore, to better understand how an intranet can work for your company, you must first grasp the basic technology which has made the Internet so popular. As it turns out, intranets and the Internet fundamentally work the same way. You will discover that the tools which have made the Internet indispensable, such as powerful software, ease of sharing information, and increased communication, are directly applicable to an intranet.

Intranets are low-cost, easy-to-implement solutions that will help companies become more competitive and better armed with the latest information. This book examines how users throughout an organization can gain a productivity advantage by using an intranet. If you are involved in upper-level management, you will find compelling case studies of various organizations which have adopted intranets as an alternative to traditional *groupware* products like Lotus *Notes*. As an Information Systems (IS) manager, this book will introduce you to issues and methods that will help you champion a successful migration plan to an intranet-based solution. As a user, you will discover how an intranet will improve your productivity, simplify your work flow, and help you gain a competitive advantage over those who have yet to learn how to exploit intranets.

This chapter will take you through a brief overview of the Internet and will show you how it has given the power of worldwide information to anyone with a computer. You may appreciate the Internet's applicability in solving today's problems, as well as its flexibility for handling new challenges. These problems and challenges range from empowering you to organize your in-house documentation to simplifying your ability to communicate with others in your company.

Intranets, which present users with a new chapter in the history of the computer, have made their way to your door. It is now up to you to maximize your use of this technology—this book will show you how. By the time you finish this chapter, you will understand the following key concepts:

- A network is two or more connected computers that share resources, such as files and printers, and facilitate user communication.

- The Internet was created because of the need for reliable networks that could span the globe.

- Because of its reliability and ease of implementation, TCP/IP has become the standard language (or *protocol*) of the Internet. TCP/IP defines how programs exchange information over the Internet.

- A network consists of two types of computers: a client and a server. A client computer asks for and uses information that the server computer stores and manages.

- Across the Internet (or an intranet) programs exchange information by breaking the information into small, message-sized pieces called *packets*.

- *Telnet, ftp,* and *gopher* are widely available network programs which help users to connect to specific computers and to transfer files.

- The World Wide Web (or Web) is a collection of related documents that users can access and view using a special software program called a browser, such as the Netscape *Navigator* or Microsoft *Internet Explorer* browser programs.

- HTML, which stands for HyperText Markup Language, defines how designers describe the layout and contents of pages on the Web.

- Java is a new computer programming language that lets users run special programs (called *applets*) from across the network and within a Web page.

- A Network Computer (sometimes called an NC) is a low-cost, specialized computer designed to take full advantage of the Internet, including Java applications.

UNDERSTANDING A COMPUTER NETWORK

A *computer network* is simply two or more computers that can communicate with each other. Such communication may take the form of an e-mail message, a fax, or even the exchange of one or more files.

A computer network can reside in one building, several adjacent buildings, or even in offices distributed across the world. When you hear someone talk about a LAN, they are referring to a *local-area network*. LANs connect computers which are located near each other. For example, connected computers that reside in the same building or business park comprise a LAN.

In contrast, WANs are *wide-area networks* that connect computers separated by very large distances. For example, a multinational corporation with offices in New York and Rome might use a wide-area network. The primary distinction between a LAN and a WAN is the network's geographic spread. No hard-and-fast rule distinguishes when a local-area network becomes a wide-area network, but a LAN is usually limited to several city blocks.

Businesses establish computer networks to let employees exchange documents with other employees within the company. Depending on whether the company is geographically located in one area or spread across the world, its network will either be a local-area network (LAN) or a wide-area network (WAN). Figures 1.1 and 1.2 illustrate a LAN and a WAN, respectively.

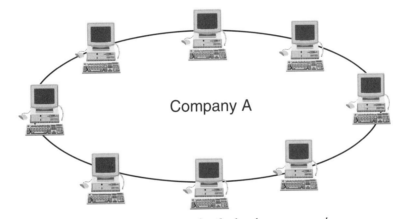

Figure 1.1 An example of a local-area network.

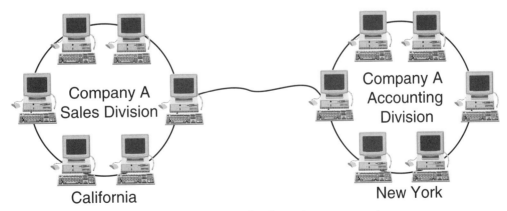

Figure 1.2 An example of a wide-area network.

When another business (a supplier, for example) decides to establish a computer network, that company's employees will be able to send documents or data to other employees within that same company. As shown in Figure 1.3, it is not until individual networks are connected together that companies can send documents or data to each other.

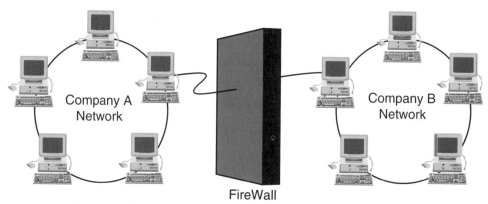

Figure 1.3 Connecting networks to bring multiple companies together.

As you will learn, when two or more companies connect their networks in this way, security becomes a primary consideration. In short, the companies must provide users with the ability to exchange information (such as product and pricing information to a customer) while protecting their data from accidental or intentional security threats.

Connecting two or more networks together in this way is not uncommon. In fact, this type of *internetwork communication* forms the backbone of the Internet and is illustrated in Figure 1.4.

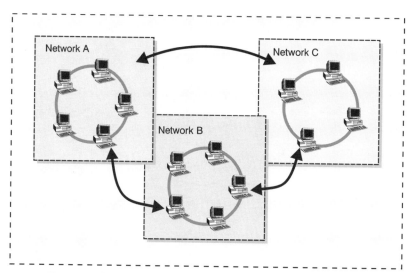

Figure 1.4 The relationship between networks and Internets.

The Internet is a collection of many computer networks—an *internetwork*. Each of these networks can contain as few as two computers or as many as several thousand PCs. The simplicity of connecting networks, coupled with user recognition of the benefits of information sharing, is fueling the explosive growth of the Internet. For example, the ability to send instant electronic mail (or e-mail) to anyone else with a computer is cheaper, quicker, and easier than mailing a letter or making a phone call (and greatly reduces time spent playing telephone tag).

RECOGNIZING THE GROWTH IN INTRANETS

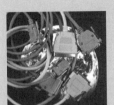

Throughout this book, you will examine ways that the use of intranets will improve a company's productivity and will reduce costs. Today, over 25 percent of Fortune 1,000 companies use an intranet—there were almost no intranets in use in 1994. As the use of intranets continues its explosive growth, analysts estimate that by the year 2000, companies will have 10 times as many intranet servers as they do Internet servers. In fact, Zona Research, Inc. predicts that by the year 1999, the corporate intranet market will reach $28 billion—exceeding the Internet market by 2 to 1. For more details on the forecasted intranet growth, visit the Web site at *http://www.e-land.com/e-stat_pages.*

NETWORKING WITH YOUR HOME COMPUTER

In the previous discussion, you have discovered that computers in a network communicate to other computers in the same network or to computers in different networks. But what about the PC that's sitting on your kitchen counter? At first, it may appear that your computer is not part of any network. However, if your PC has a modem, you can connect your PC to other computers using telephone lines to create a network. For example, you may join the network of an on-line service, such as America Online, CompuServe, or the Microsoft Network (MSN), or you may choose to call your neighbor's computer to create a two-PC network.

Today's personal computers are very easy to network. In fact, the discussion about the Internet and intranets this book presents applies to PCs as well as to their larger Unix-based cousins. In later chapters, you will learn about the differences in networking PCs, Macintoshes, and Unix-based computers. Figure 1.5 illustrates the process of creating a network using your home computer.

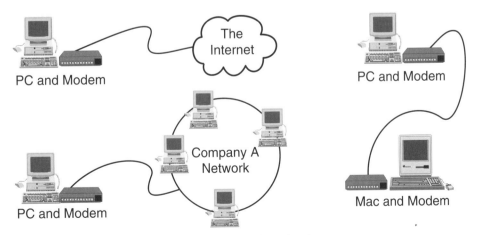

Figure 1.5 Creating a network with a home computer.

THE ORIGIN OF THE INTERNET

To better understand how and why the Internet works the way it does, you need to understand a little about the Internet's history. After reading this section, you will understand how networks can handle heavy communication traffic generated by thousands or, in the case of the Internet, millions of users. In fact, researchers estimate that the number of users connected to the Internet worldwide ranges from 30 to 90 million each day.

A major challenge for the early network pioneers was the problem of coordinating communications between a large number of computers attached to a network. Because a single wire connected the computers, the network designers needed a way to allow the network's computers to share the wire. For example, if just two of the network's potentially large number of PCs were to communicate at the same time, each PC's communication signals would "garble" the signals of the other PC, causing communication to fail. If you have participated in a discussion with a group of people over a speaker phone, you have experienced this frustration. Consequently, imagine being on a conference call with a thousand other people. You probably would not be able to get a word in edgewise! Even if you did, how would anyone know it was you speaking.

In these two situations, either computers in a network or people in a conference call, some type of coordination is needed to prevent losing information. One solution gives the communicating computer the ability to prevent all the other computers from using the network until it is done, as shown in Figure 1.6.

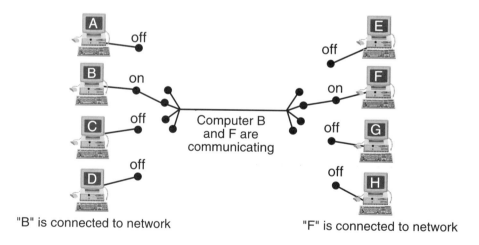

Figure 1.6 Only one computer at a time can communicate in this network.

As you might guess, in such a network one computer could and would monopolize the network. Luckily, network designers came up with a better communication scheme, one that lets each user send small pieces of information, called packets, by sharing the network.

PACKET SWITCHING

In the late 1960s, to allow computers in a network to share transmission lines, network designers proposed *packet switching*—a message passing technique the Internet still uses today. In a packet-switched network, programs break data into pieces, called *packets*, which they then transmit between computers. Each packet contains the sender's address, as well as the destination address, along with the data itself. If you were to send an e-mail message to someone on a packet-switched network, your message would probably be split into smaller pieces. Each of these pieces (or packets) will share the network and intermingle with other packets that other computers are sending. Because each packet has a specific destination address built in to it, the network will eventually route the packet to the appropriate recipient. Figure 1.7 shows you how the network breaks an e-mail message sent from your home computer to your office computer into a series of packets which make their way across the network.

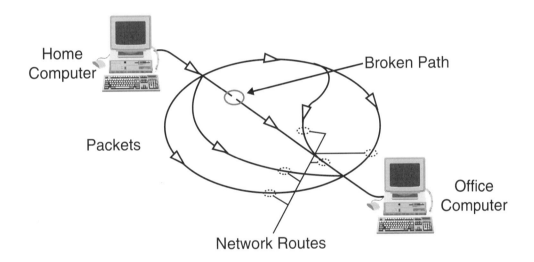

Figure 1.7 An e-mail message traveling along a packet-switched network.

Besides providing efficient network sharing capability, packet switching also lets individual packets take a variety of paths to their final destination. In this way, as a packet travels across the network, the network can route (send) the packet on the next available wire. For example, the packets of your e-mail message may have taken different routes on their way to the recipient because, as the packet makes its way across a network, a *packet switch* (generally another computer running network software) examines the packet's destination address and forwards the packet along an available route.

Should some part of the network become damaged, the packet switch can reroute the packet past the damaged hardware using a different path to reach the packet's destination. At any instant on the Internet, millions of packets are traveling across thousands of different paths.

THE ARPANET STARTED IT ALL

As is the case for many technologies, the Internet and packet-switched networks developed under early government funding and support. The U.S. Advanced Research Projects Agency (ARPA) was an early adopter of the packet-switching theory. ARPA created what was called ARPAnet as a network of key government computers that could survive the kind of network damage that might occur in a war or major disaster.

ARPA's initial efforts, along with the collaboration of several companies and universities, culminated in September of 1969 when a Honeywell 516 minicomputer was delivered to the UCLA campus. This system was the first of four packet switches, also known as *Interface Message Processors* (IMP). Three other packet switches were installed at the University of Utah, the University of California at Santa Barbara, and the Stanford Research Institute. Soon, these computers were exchanging packets with one another over telephone lines, and the father of the Internet, the ARPAnet, was born. Figure 1.8 shows the ARPAnet's original four sites. For over a decade, the ARPAnet grew at the rate of about one new computer every three weeks.

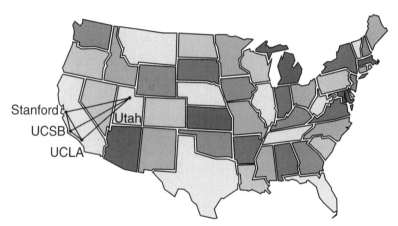

Figure 1.8 The original ARPAnet.

TCP/IP DEFINES INTERNET PROTOCOLS

By the early 1980s, ARPA needed a better protocol (set of rules) for handling packets within its growing variety of networks, which now included satellites and packet radio. Such rules govern how computers place data on a transmission line and how software developers should design software to work with the network. The original ARPAnet protocol was called the *Network Control Protocol* (NCP). The protocol that replaced it in January 1, 1983, and is in use today, is called the *Transport Control Protocol/Internet Protocol* (TCP/IP).

TCP/IP enabled networks to handle different kinds of packets from many different types of networks. In Chapter 19, you will learn about the TCP/IP protocol in more detail. For now, however, when you hear the term TCP/IP, simply think of it as the rules software programs follow to exchange information across the Internet or within a corporate-wide intranet.

TCP/IP AND PACKET SWITCHING DRIVE THE INTERNET

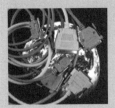

Each day, users around the world exchange e-mail messages and transfer files across the thousands of networks that make up the Internet. To coordinate this vast exchange of information, programs follow a strict set of rules—the TCP/IP protocol.

To send information across the Internet, programs break the information into smaller, more manageable pieces called packets. In short, a program assigns each packet the address of its destination computer and then sends the packet to the network to find its way. Depending on network traffic (other packets that are making their way to a destination), packets which make up the same larger piece of information may travel different paths to reach the destination.

As you will learn, TCP/IP and packet-switched networks are two essential features of the Internet and will prove to be key elements in future intranets. When you hear the term TCP/IP, and you will, simply think of the rules network programs follow to communicate in an orderly fashion.

WHO OWNS THE INTERNET? NO ONE!

By now you may be wanting to buy stock in the Internet. Sorry. You can't—because no single entity owns the Internet. The Internet is a shared collection of computer networks spread among many private and public networks scattered throughout the world.

Each organization that connects to the Internet is responsible for making sure that its network properly communicates with the rest of the Internet. In addition, the organization must pay for its portion of the cost to make that connection. Figure 1.9 shows how the XYZ company connects to the Internet.

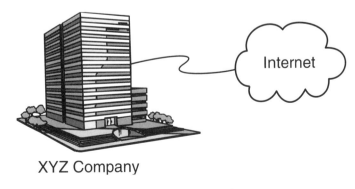

XYZ Company

Figure 1.9 *Connecting to the Internet.*

To connect to the Internet, a company normally connects its network to the closest computer that is already connected to the Internet. The connecting company then pays the cost of installing its portion of the connection (which might be a phone wire connection, a satellite connection, or even fiber optic cable). Figure 1.10 illustrates how a neighboring company, ABC, receives full Internet capability by paying for the connection to the XYZ company.

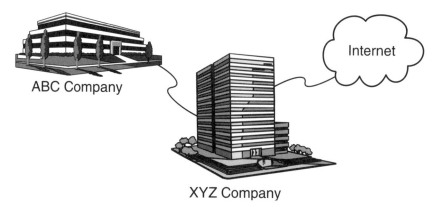

Figure 1.10 Connecting to the nearest Internet-based network.

Understanding the Role of the Internet Service Provider

This "pay for your connection" approach was popular with early adopters of the Internet: universities, large companies, and government. However, the cost to install a special high-speed line (even for short distances) can be prohibitive for a smaller company. Luckily, specialized companies called *Internet Service Providers* (ISPs) solved this problem by becoming the middleman to the Internet.

Internet Service Providers pay for the expensive connection to the Internet, make heavy investments in high-performance servers, data lines, and modems, and then rent time to other users (like you and small companies) who want access to the Internet. Figure 1.11 shows how a small office and a school house can affordably connect to the Internet by using an Internet Service Provider.

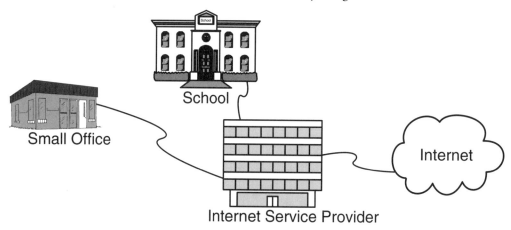

Figure 1.11 Small companies and users gain Internet access through Internet Service Providers.

You should keep two distinctions in mind when considering a connection to the Internet. The first is giving your company a presence on the Internet (in the form of Web pages), and the other is giving your employees access to the Internet so that they can access other companies' Web pages and exchange electronic mail.

A connection to the Internet gives your employees the access to the World Wide Web they need. Your employees simply establish a connection and run special Web navigation software called a *browser.* This is the simplest form of Internet connection. However, for your business or your network to be visible and accessible to the rest of the Internet, you need to have a server (which could be a Macintosh or PC).

A *server* is a computer which dispenses your company's Web pages to anyone on the Internet who knows how to access them. You can either buy and install a server for your company, or you can lease one from an Internet Service Provider. Then, your company can develop and publish Web-page documents and place them on the server for viewing worldwide.

Figure 1.12 illustrates the Web pages for three well-known companies: Microsoft, Netscape, and Intel. These companies use their Web sites to provide company and product information, to recruit new employees, and to provide technical support.

Figure 1.12 Companies with a presence on the Web.

UNDERSTANDING CONNECTION SPEEDS

You have several choices when it comes time to decide how you will connect your company to the Internet. Probably, the two biggest considerations are cost and communication speed. Your Internet Service Provider can offer you a variety of options ranging from a simple dial-up account over phone wires to a leased high-speed line.

A dial-up account is simply an arrangement where you would use your computer's modem and phone lines to call the Provider's computer. Such a dial-up account provides you with a doorway into the Internet. However, your access is only as fast as your modem. Typically, the fastest modems communicate at 33.6Kbps. (*Kbps* measures the data transfer rate and stands for kilobits per second.) A leased line bypasses your modem and, instead, is a special high-speed phone line that connects directly to your network. Data rates over a leased line can be as high as 45Mbps. (*Mbps* is Megabits per second.) Leased lines come in many different configurations with a variety of options. The most common types are ISDN (56Kbps to 128Kbps) which stands for integrated digital services network, T1 (1.4Mbps), and T3 (56Mbps).

If your company only needs to make an occasional connection to the Internet, for example, under 20 to 50 hours per month for all users in your company, you may be able to get by with a dial-up account, which may cost you as little as $20 per month. Some Internet Service Providers offer unlimited connection time for fees in the $250 per year range. In addition, you will incur supplemental charges for disk space on the server if your company needs to publish Web pages.

If your company needs faster data transfer speeds or has several users who all must access the Internet, you should consider a leased line. The monthly charges and special equipment fees can cost your company from $200 to $1,200 per month for ISDN, $1,000 to $3,000 per month for T1, and $2,000 to $10,000 per month for T3.

E-Mail

Perhaps the most basic, yet most essential, of all Internet services is electronic mail, or e-mail. By using e-mail, you can send a message to any other person in the world right from your PC. Generally, your message is delivered in just a few seconds. However, if you are sending a long message across the Internet during mid-day (when network traffic is heavy), the message may take much longer to reach its destination.

Most Internet service providers offer you e-mail capabilities as part of their basic services. If your only goal in connecting to the Internet is to send and receive electronic mail, all you need is the most basic Internet connection. In fact, you can send and receive e-mail across the Internet if you simply subscribe to a commercial on-line service such as CompuServe or America Online. However, as you read through the Internet capabilities this book presents, you will very likely turn to an Internet Service Provider. ISPs are most cost effective for heavy users of the Internet and offer superior features that support your company Web pages.

Why You May Not Need or Want to Use an Internet Service Provider

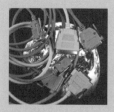
When you are ready to think about building your intranet, you may want to consider against having a direct connection to the Internet. Commercial on-line services such as America Online and CompuServe, for example, provide basic e-mail and Web-browsing capabilities. By using a commercial on-line service instead of an Internet Service Provider, you can save money, but only if your Internet needs are small! For example, consider a doctor's office where scheduling and records are kept on an intranet.

In this case, the staff would probably go out on the Internet only occasionally to access the latest findings in a medical publication. Therefore, an on-line service would be more cost-effective and provide all the capabilities that this particular doctor's office needs.

In addition, depending on the information your company is placing on its intranet, you may find that eliminating a direct connection to the Internet is one way to increase data security. In other words, without a direct connection, other users across the Internet cannot access your company data. To provide your employees with access to e-mail and with the ability to browse the Web, you can let your employees connect to an on-line service such as AOL.

Keep in mind that commercial on-line services do not provide full-featured server capability. If you need to publish a simple Web page that has mostly static graphics and text, the commercial on-line service may work for you. However, if you need advanced features, such as on-line order processing or other interactive features, you will need to contract with a service provider. In Chapter 15, you will learn how to assess your Internet needs and how to balance them with costs, implementation effort, and convenience.

THE WORLD WIDE WEB

As the use of the Internet grew in the late 1980s and early 1990s, it soon became a repository for millions of files. In fact, by 1992, estimates of the Internet's growth placed it at over 75,000 documents per day! Unfortunately, many of these documents remained inaccessible to most users simply because users did not know they existed or how to access them. In short, for the average user, the Internet of the early 90's was a less-than-accessible information highway with few on-ramps. Luckily, however, all that changed with the creation of the World Wide Web.

The World Wide Web (Web or WWW) is a collection of linked documents that sits on top of the Internet. By linking related documents, the Web makes it very easy for users to locate information. Across the Web, there are millions of documents. Each document has a unique name, called a URL (uniform resource locator) or simply, a Web address.

In fact, it is difficult to watch TV news, a sports event, or even a movie without encountering a Web address, such as *http://www.nbc.com*, *http://www.nba.com*, or *http://www.paramount.com*, as shown in Figures 1.13a, b, and c.

Figure 1.13a *http://www.— nbc.com.* *Figure 1.13b* *http://www.— nba.com* *Figure 1.13c* *http://www.— paramount.com.*

As you have learned, programs on the Internet must follow a specific set of rules called protocols to communicate. Web addresses start with the letters *http* because Web software follows the HTTP protocol (hypertext transport protocol). In short, HTTP defines the rules that software programs follow to exchange information across the Web. The Web is so named because it links related documents to form a web of information, as shown in Figure 1.14.

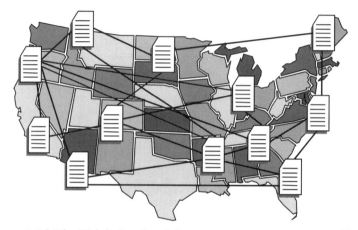

Figure 1.14 The Web links related documents across computers worldwide.

SURFING THE WEB

Over the past two years, the process of moving from one Web document to another has become known as "surfing the Web." For example, assume you are interested in information about the Chicago Bulls basketball star, Michael Jordan. You might begin your search at the NBA Web site *http://www.nba.com*. As you read through the information you find at the site, you will very likely encounter text about the Chicago Bulls. Within that text, you may see highlighted text (usually underlined) that indicates a link to another document. If you click your mouse on the link, your Web browser will retrieve that document. In this case, you might first move to a document similar to that shown in Figure 1.15 that discusses the Chicago Bulls.

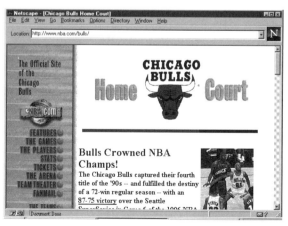

Figure 1.15 The Chicago Bulls homepage.

Next, within the text that discusses the Chicago Bulls, you will likely find a highlighted link for Michael Jordan that takes you to his homepage, as shown in Figure 1.16.

Figure 1.16 Michael Jordan's homepage on the Web.

By allowing users to traverse linked documents in this way (to surf from one document to another), the Web makes it very easy for users to access the information they need.

UNDERSTANDING WEB BROWSERS

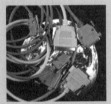

The World Wide Web is a vast collection of files, pictures, sounds, and information stored on a variety of computers throughout the world. To access the Web and to bring all of its features to your computer, you need special software called a *Web browser*.

A Web browser is simply a software program that runs on your computer and lets you traverse and view documents on the World Wide Web. Most browser software is available for free. In addition, your Internet Service Provider (ISP) may also supply a browser for you to use. Commercial on-line services, such as America Online and Prodigy, also supply you with browsers as part of the subscription service.

Today, the two most commonly used browsers are the Netscape *Navigator* and the Microsoft *Internet Explorer*, shown in Figures 1.17a and 1.17b.

Figure 1.17a Netscape Navigator.

Figure 1.17b Microsoft Internet Explorer.

UNDERSTANDING HOMEPAGES

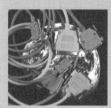

Companies, individuals, and governments that publish information on the Internet usually organize that information into pages, much like the pages of a book or a sales brochure. The first page that people see in a sales brochure is the cover page, which usually summarizes the contents of the rest of the brochure and may contain an index. Similarly, at a Web site, the *homepage* is the first page that users see when they access the site. The homepage is to the Web site what the cover page is to a sales brochure. Both must be appealing, concise, informative, well-organized, and succeed in maintaining the reader's interest.

Imagine that your company is in the business of marketing garden tractors. Your company probably has a sales brochure that it distributes to potential customers. The front page of the brochure would probably have your company's name and logo along with a photograph of a garden tractor. If the company sells a line of tractors, there may be an index on the cover, or perhaps on the next page. If the company were to publish a Web version of this brochure, its homepage would resemble the brochure's cover page. In other words, the homepage tells the visitor to your Web site who you are and what you are offering. Figure 1.18 illustrates the John Deere homepage.

Figure 1.18 The John Deere homepage.

It is important to understand that the homepage is usually what users see first when they visit your Web site. Many companies publish the Internet address (known as a *Uniform Resource Locator*, or URL) of their home pages on business cards, television, magazines, and on radio. Web users type these URLs into their browsers and immediately get a first impression of the company based on its homepage.

You can easily connect to the Web today as long as you have a computer, a modem (or other network connection), and a browser. After you connect to the Web, you can visit an ever expanding array of Web sites, from corporate information pages to searchable databases.

It is important to keep in mind that you will use the same Web browser software and techniques for accessing the Internet as you will to access your company's intranet. The ability for users to move quickly and easily between related documents has led to the Web's success. Rather than reinventing the wheel, most intranets use two proven components of the Web to facilitate information exchange: the HTTP protocol and Web browsers.

COMMON TERMINOLOGY

As you will learn, the Internet and intranets introduce many new terms and, worse yet, many new acronyms. If you are new to the Net (yes, there's even a term for you: newbie), some of these terms may appear intimidating. But, after reading this section, you will have a good general understanding of several key concepts which later chapters of this book will reinforce in detail.

CLIENT PROGRAMS AND BROWSERS

The Internet consists of thousands of computer networks worldwide. However, if you start to think of the Internet in terms of programs and data, the Internet will become much easier to understand.

Across the Internet, information (data) resides on disks at thousands of computers called *servers*. The server computers are so named because, upon request, they serve (or provide) users with information. You can think of a server as nothing more than a special program that runs on a remote computer. In fact, most remote computers run several different server programs, each of which perform a specific task, such as a Web server, mail server, ftp server, and so on.

To communicate with a server, end users run *client programs*—so named because they ask the server for service. In the case of the Web, the client program is the Web browser. All client–server interactions take the same form. To start, the client connects to the server and asks the server for information. The server, in turn, examines the request and then provides (serves) the client with the information. Depending on the information the client needs, the client and server may perform this request-response interaction many times. Figure 1.19 illustrates a client–server interaction.

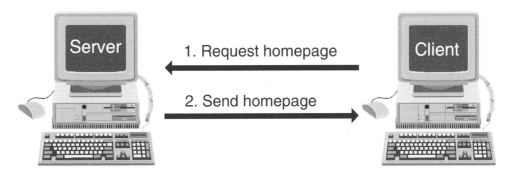

Figure 1.19 A client–server, request–response interaction.

FTP—THE FILE TRANSFER PROTOCOL

As you have learned, there are millions of files across the Internet. In the early days of the Internet, users transferred files using a special program named *ftp*.

The FTP (file transfer protocol) is a standard protocol for copying files from one computer to another computer. Depending on the FTP server's configuration, you may or may not need an account on the remote machine in order to access the system's files using *ftp*. In many cases, using FTP software, you can access a remote computer by logging in with the username of *anonymous*, and entering your e-mail address as the password. Users refer to connecting to a remote *ftp* server in this way as "performing an anonymous FTP operation."

After you log in to the computer, you will see a directory of files the remote computer allows users to access. You can then retrieve the files you want and in some cases you can *upload* (send files) to the remote computer. The remote computer's administrator decides which files you can access. Depending on the remote computer's files, the system administrator may give you a specific username and password you must enter to gain access to the files. In the past, users ran the *ftp* program from a command line. Today, most *ftp* programs support Windows-based versions. Figure 1.20 illustrates a Windows-based *ftp* program accessing files from a remote computer.

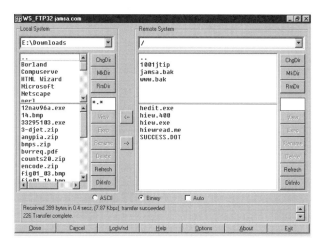

Figure 1.20 Accessing remote files using an FTP client program.

Because of the large number of files dispersed about the Internet, the FTP protocol is an important part of the World Wide Web. In fact, most browsers have the ability to use the FTP protocol to let you access files stored at FTP sites. In this way, you can download files from an FTP site using your browser. To access an FTP site using your browser, you type in the site's FTP address, much like you would type in a Web address. For example, to access the Microsoft FTP site shown in Figure 1.21, you type in the address *ftp://ftp.microsoft.com*.

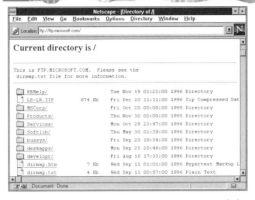

Figure 1.21 Accessing an FTP site using a Web browser.

HOMEPAGE

As you have learned, when a user visits a site on the Web, the first page of information the user sees is the site's *homepage.* In short, the homepage makes the site's all important first impression and either entices a visitor to browse through the rest of the site or to leave in a hurry. You must carefully design your homepage so that it is easy for the visitor to navigate your site and to remain interested in the information your company is presenting.

A visitor typically arrives at a homepage in one of two ways. First, a user may see a URL published somewhere (such as on a brochure or a business card) and type the URL into the browser's address field. Second, as you have learned, Web documents can contain links from one document to another. Therefore, a visitor may simply click the mouse on a link within a document that corresponds to your site's Web address.

A homepage can be as simple as a one page ad for your company's product or more complicated, appearing like a book's table of contents with a list of links to other pages that reside at the same Web site or at a remote site. For example, assume your company publishes a directory of creative service providers in the San Diego area. Your homepage may contain a business listing for each creative provider, which visitors to the Web site can search by category or by company. The visitor can then click the mouse on the category that corresponds to the type of creative service desired. Figure 1.22 shows a sample of a creative directory homepage.

Figure 1.22 The Creative List, an on-line creative directory located at http://www.creativelist.com.

The importance of a well designed homepage cannot be overstated. Whether you are promoting a product or providing some service, you must make it easy for the user to begin on the right foot.

HTML—THE LANGUAGE OF THE WORLD WIDE WEB

As you have learned, the Web consists of millions of interconnected documents. To insure all users can read and view each document's contents, Web designers create the documents using a special formatting language named HTML (as opposed to using a word processor format, such as Microsoft *Word*, that all users may not be able to view, depending on their software).

The Hypertext Markup Language (HTML) is the language of the World Wide Web. Every site across the Web uses HTML to display information. HTML was developed in the late 1980s and early 1990s by a group at CERN, the European Particle Physics Laboratory in Geneva, Switzerland. You can find out more about the birthplace of HTML by visiting the CERN homepage at *http://www.cern.ch/*, as shown in Figure 1.23.

Figure 1.23 CERN, the birthplace of the World Wide Web.

An HTML Web page (sometimes called a Web document) is a plain text file (an ASCII file) that you can read and create with any text editor. A Web document contains a set of HTML instructions that instruct a browser program (like Netscape *Navigator* or Microsoft *Internet Explorer*) how to display the Web page. When you connect to a Web page using your browser, the Web server sends the HTML document to your browser across the net. The power of HTML comes from the fact that any computer running a browser program can read and display it—regardless of whether that computer is a PC running Windows, a Unix-based system, or a Mac.

The HTML text your browser reads includes two types of information:

1. Markup information that controls the document's text display characteristics and that lets the Web designer specify links to other documents.

2. Content information that is the text, graphics, or sound the browser displays.

Later in this book, you will learn that there are many software programs available which convert a variety of document files to HTML equivalents. For example, you might convert a Microsoft *PowerPoint* presentation into a set of HTML files for display on the Web. After you place the HTML files on a Web site, anyone with a browser can view your presentation.

HYPERTEXT AND HYPERLINKS

As you have learned, the Web consists of millions of interconnected documents. Web designers interconnect documents by placing links (called hyperlinks) within one document which points to another document. When you click your mouse on a link, your browser loads the corresponding document, which may reside on the same computer or at a computer on the other side of the world.

Much of the Web's success is due to the simplicity of its point-and-click user interface. You can navigate from one Web page to some other related Web page, perhaps thousands of miles away in another country, simply by clicking on underlined text or a picture.

The HyperText Markup Language (HTML) code, which drives all Web pages, supports what is called *HyperText*, or the creation of multimedia documents that contain pictures, text, animation, sound, and links. Hyperlinks (or simply, links) are the special words or pictures that correspond to some other Web page.

INTEGRATED SERVICE DIGITAL NETWORK (ISDN)

All computers communicate in digital format. When you use a modem to access a remote computer, the modem converts the digital data that comes and goes from your computer to the analog format that it transmits over an ordinary telephone line. When the remote modem receives the signal, it converts the signal back from analog to digital. The modems must perform these conversions to send information across telephone wires which exist to transmit voice data (sound waves easily represented using an analog wave-like format). Unfortunately, the current (low) quality of phone lines limit the speed at which modems can communicate.

Recently, however, ISDN modems (which communicate over a high-quality line) offer high-speed data communication at a reasonable price.

By eliminating the conversion into analog format, it is possible to transmit computer data at a much faster rate. Integrated Services Digital Network (ISDN) is a dedicated telephone line connection that transmits data in digital form. With an ISDN connection, you will not need a modem to convert your computer's signal into analog form. Instead, your computer communicates to other computers in its native digital tongue. ISDN's biggest advantage is that it can transmit data from two to four times the rate of a modem.

SEARCH ENGINE

As you have learned, the Web consists of millions of documents. Often, your challenge is simply finding the documents you need on the Web. Luckily, to help you search for information, several sites now provide special software called a *search engine*. Using a search engine, you type in one or more words that correspond to the topic you desire, such as *Chicago Bulls.* The search engine will display a list of documents that contain the information you desire. Figure 1.24 illustrates Yahoo!, one of the Web's best-known search engines.

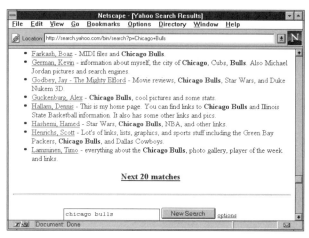

Figure 1.24 *Using the Yahoo! search engine at* **http://www.yahoo.com**.

Across the Web, there are several commonly used search engines. Table 1.1 lists the URL (Web addresses) for these search engines.

Search Engine	URL
Yahoo!	*http://www.yahoo.com*
Lycos	*http://www.lycos.com*
Magellen	*http://www.mckinley.com/*
AltaVista	*http://www.altavista.com*
Excite	*htp://www.excite.com*
Infoseek	*http://www.infoseek.com*
WebCrawler	*http://www.webcrawler.com*

Table 1.1 *Web addresses for commonly used search engines.*

SERVERS AND THE WEB

As you have learned, a server program responds to client requests. For example, when you use a browser to view a Web site, you actually connect to a server. The Web server program sits and waits for a client (a browser) to connect. Next, the browser tells the server the Web document it desires. As shown in Figure 1.25, the server locates the document on its disk and sends the document to the browser.

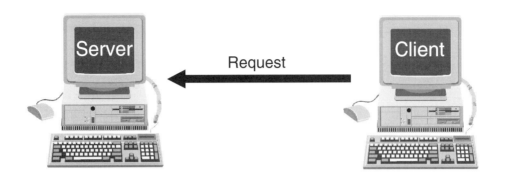

Figure 1.25 Client sending request for data from server.

As you have learned, a Web document uses a special formatting code called HTML (hypertext markup language). As the browser reads the HTML file, it will find references to graphics files or possibly sound files it must request from the server. As previously stated, the browser will send a file request to the server which, in turn, will locate and provide the file to the browser for display. Chapter 7, "A Beginner's Guide to HTML," examines HTML documents and how to create them.

As this request-response interaction occurs, the server logs each request (known as a *hit*) in a file that the site's Web administrator (often called the WebMaster) can later analyze. In fact, most servers have special software to perform this logging feature which records the Internet address of the user accessing your server, as well as the date and time. If, for example, your Web site contains a catalog, you can log the user selections and determine which items users visit most often.

As you have learned, clients and servers work together across a network to give you the ability to navigate the Web. In short, client programs handle the user interaction, displaying the information the user desires. Server programs, on the other hand, are responsible for information retrieval and delivery.

WHERE WEB DOCUMENTS RESIDE

When users publish Web pages for people to view, they actually store those pages as files the server can access. Typically, the Web pages reside on the same computer on which the server program is running, but not necessarily. As you will discover in a later chapter, for security reasons, some information should be available only to certain clients. For example, a sales person may have access to company sales figures and future marketing strategy. Obviously, it might be disastrous if internal data of this sort were made available to the competition. In such cases, the WebMaster can configure the Web server so that it provides confidential information only to specific clients.

By keeping information in one place, the WebMaster has better control over the information while making it easier to log which users are trying to gain access. The WebMaster can control access to a specific server by requiring that the user enter a specific username and password.

24

UNDERSTANDING WEB-SITE HITS

 You may occasionally hear someone talking about how many "hits" their Web site received on any given day. As you learned earlier in this chapter, a server computer responds to a client's request to send it data. A *hit* refers to the number of times a particular client requests data from a server. The more hits a server receives, the more requests are being made by users interested in the Web site. In addition to how many times a client requests data from your server, software on your server is able to record the Internet address of the user accessing it, the date and time, and the specific pages that are being visited.

Measuring hits is a good idea in that it helps you determine if you are effectively promoting your Web site. Promoting a Web site is much like advertising a grand opening sale for a new store. People will not know of the store's existence unless you advertise it. Counting the number of people who walk into the store is a good measure of the effectiveness of your advertising. Likewise, many hits indicate that the Web site is being promoted effectively.

Unfortunately, counting hits to a Web page is not as simple as counting bodies walking into a store. You need to exercise some care in how hits are measured. Technically, a hit is registered every time a client requests a file from the server. Suppose the client requests to view a Web page containing ten pictures. The client will first receive the HTML code of the page itself, followed by ten more transfers—one for each picture contained within the Web page. The server will register a total of eleven hits when only one page was actually viewed.

To give you a better feel for how busy some Web sites are, consider these numbers:

- As of December 1996, Microsoft averages 42 million hits a day

- As of June 1996, Netscape averages 70 million hits a day

- Prior to Super Bowl 30, the site *http://www.Superbowl.com* averaged 1 million hits a day (5 million on game day)

- As of September 1996, the Yahoo search engine averages 14 million hits a day

SLIP AND PPP

The fastest growing segment of Internet users are those who connect to the Internet through an Internet Service Provider via an ordinary telephone connection. There are two major protocols for connecting to the Internet in this way: Serial Line Internet Protocol (SLIP) and Point-to-Point Protocol (PPP).

Both protocols work by allowing your programs to use TCP/IP connections over regular phone lines. SLIP is the older protocol and is in use in many communications packages. The faster PPP is newer; therefore, it is not as widely supported. You should check with your provider to see which protocol they support. They generally will supply you with the SLIP or PPP software. If not, there are several packages available (both shareware and commercial versions).

SURFING THE WEB

In the early years of the Web, universities, government, and big business were its primary users. Access was effectively restricted to these institutions because of the high cost of getting a connection to the Internet. As the Web grew in size, the cost of connecting came down while its diversity in content increased dramatically.

The combination of the Web's diversity of subjects and the instantaneous manner in which a user can navigate from site to site has drawn enthusiasts from all walks of life. Today, just about anyone with a computer can affordably experience the immense variety of Web sites now on the Internet. In fact, many users simply connect to the Web just to randomly explore a new site, much like a hiker would go out exploring a new trail. Such Web users are known as "surfers," and many of them "surf the Web" for the thrill of discovering a hot new site, or visiting pages from a far away country.

The World Wide Web has come a long way from being a tool for reliable communications between big institutions. It has entered the realm of popular culture and has made surfing the Web as appealing to the masses as watching television has been for the past forty years.

TCP/IP

For one computer to communicate with another computer over a network, the software which runs on those computers must adhere to a strict set of rules. By following these rules, computers can share common communication paths among other computers without "garbling" each other's transmissions. TCP/IP or Transport Control Protocol/Internet Protocol defines the set of rules which software programs must follow to exchange information across the Internet. As you will learn, one of the key features that differentiates an intranet from a local-area network is the intranet's use of the TCP/IP protocol.

UNIFORM RESOURCE LOCATOR (URL)

The Uniform Resource Locator is an address browsers use to access Internet information. Across the World Wide Web, there are millions of documents—each with its own Web address. Web users refer to such addresses as URLs (Uniform Resource Locators). Examples of URLs include:

- *http://www.apple.com*
- *http://www.bmwusa.com*
- *ftp://ftp.ncsa.uiuc.edu/Mac/Mosaic*
- *http://www.microsoft.com*

A URL consists of three main parts:

1. A service identifier (such as *http*)
2. A domain name (such as *www.ups.com*)
3. A path name (such as *www.ups.com/tracking*)

The first part of the URL, the service identifier, tells the browser software how to retrieve the file by indicating which protocol it should use. The service identifier can take the following forms:

- *http://* Specifies the connection will use the hypertext transport protocol (HTTP)—the most common type of connection.

- *ftp://* Specifies the connection will use the file transfer protocol (FTP)— typically for a specific file download operation.

- *gopher://* Specifies a connection to a gopher server which will provide a graphical list of accessible files.

- *telnet://* Specifies a connection to a telnet session where you will be able to run programs remotely on the connected computer.

The second part of the URL, the domain name, specifies the name of the system from which you access the data. Essentially, the domain name specifies a specific computer running the server software. An example of a domain name is *www.usatoday.com*.

The final part of the URL, the path name, is optional information, which indicates a directory path name to a specific file you want to retrieve. If the path name is missing, the server will send the default page (typically, the homepage). Large, multi-page Web sites can have fairly long path names. For example, these URLs request specific pages within the Web site.

- *http://www.apple.com/documents/productsupport.html*

- *http://www.bmwusa.com/ultimate/5series/5series.html*

- *ftp://ftp.ncsa.uiuc.edu/Mac/Mosaic*

- *http://www.microsoft.com/Misc/WhatsNew.htm*

JAVA

In the past, Web sites were static and unchanging—much like a slow magazine. To compete with other forms of media, television primarily, developers had to come up with a way to animate a Web's contents.

To improve Web-site presentation, Sun Microsystems released Java, a new programming language that lets programmers create animated Web sites. Using Java, programmers create small applications, called *applets*, which browsers download and run. For example, using Java applets, a Web site might spin a company's logo, play MIDI music or audio clips, or perform other animations. Java is a programming language that closely resembles C++. In the near future, Java will become a household word. To learn more about Java and to see examples of Java's use, connect to Sun's Web site at *http://java.sun.com*.

UPCOMING TRENDS ON THE INTERNET

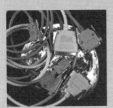

Pick up any trade journal or listen to popular media, and you will find growing recognition that the Internet is becoming an indispensable tool for successful businesses, both large and small. Most of these businesses are well established companies that are supplementing their operations with the Internet's global reach. It is now possible for companies to advertise their products, provide customer service, and market their goods through the Internet. This ground swell of support has technology innovators developing the next generation of Web tools. The first, a new programming language named Java, is already here and is making headlines for a new type of software that can run on any computer. Second, the Network Computer (or NC) is an inexpensive computer that, ideally, everyone can afford.

NETWORK COMPUTER (NC)

Although PCs are becoming more and more common, the number of households with a PC is still only about 1/3 of the number of households with a TV. In short, the PC is still too expensive for the masses.

The Network Computer is a new approach to downsizing the PC. Conceptually, it is an inexpensive (under $500) computer that is designed to be permanently connected to the Internet and to use Java applets as the source for whatever software you may need. The idea behind it is that you will not need to add software to the NC as you must with any PC. In fact, the Network Computer will probably lack a disk drive or CD-ROM drive. Instead, the software will be sent to the NC over the Internet. Furthermore, the NC receives only the software that is needed for the task at hand.

For example, if you need to write a thank you letter to a client, you would need only the simplest features of a word processor. In this case, the NC would load only the features (using a Java applet found on the Web) that you need to complete the letter, like one specific font style, one layout style, and one color. In contrast, to use a PC, you need to buy the entire word processor along with its infinite array of expensive, and often never used, bells and whistles.

Industry prognosticators are saying that the Network Computer will be able to perform all of the tasks of a PC—only at a much lower cost. If successful, the NC computer could reduce the price of computerization to one-tenth the cost of a full-blown PC with its endless expense of software upgrades.

Perhaps one of the most vocal proponents of the Network Computer is Larry Ellison, CEO of Oracle. His company has developed an operating system for an NC that takes up only 1 megabyte of memory versus 8 megabytes for Windows 95. He expects to give the operating system away over the Internet, as well as building it into NCs and other consumer-electronics gadgets. For more information on the Network Computer, visit the Oracle Web site at *http://www.oracle.com* as shown in Figure 1.26.

Figure 1.26 Information on the Network Computer.

In addition, you may want to read about the new JavaStation from Sun Microsystems at *http://www.sun.com/station*, as shown in Figure 1.27.

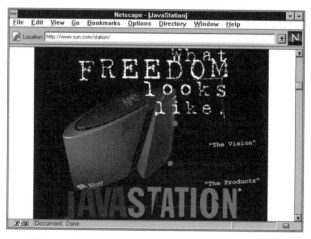

Figure 1.27 Information on Sun's JavaStation.

PUTTING IT ALL TOGETHER

The scale of the Internet is as large as the world. Fortunately, you can find all the pieces which make up this extraordinary resource on your desktop computer. This chapter introduced you to the Internet in very general terms. You can apply the Internet concepts directly to an intranet. In Chapter 2, you will learn more about intranets and how you can replicate all of the power and productivity of the Internet inside your own office. However, before you move on to Chapter 2, make sure you understand the following key concepts:

✓ Two or more interconnected computers, capable of communicating with each other, form a computer network. Two or more interconnected networks form an internetwork—an internet.

✓ Across the Internet, programs exchange information by breaking the information into small, message-sized pieces called packets.

✓ The Internet was created as a way to provide reliable, long-distance connections between computers.

✓ TCP/IP is the standard Internet protocol which defines how programs exchange information with each other over the Internet.

✓ A network consists of two types of computers: a client and a server. A client computer displays information that is stored by the server computer.

✓ HTML stands for HyperText Markup Language and is the standard text-based specification used for describing the layout of Web pages.

✓ Java is a new computer language that makes use of small, Internet-ready programs called applets.

✓ The Network Computer is a low-cost computer designed to take full advantage of the Internet, including Java.

VISITING KEY SITES THAT DISCUSS INTRANETS

The World Wide Web is filled with hundreds of excellent and current articles on all aspects of intranets. Use the following sites as starting points for your Web exploration.

Microsoft Products

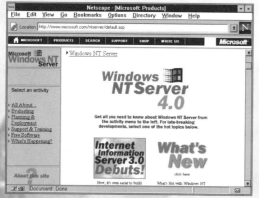

http://www.microsoft.com/ntserver/default.asp

Intranet Forum

http://www.intranet.flashnet.it/

Intranet Demo

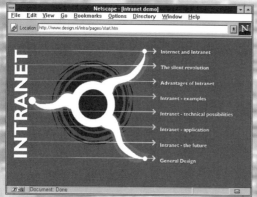

http://www.design.nl/intra/pages/start.htm

Virtual Intranet

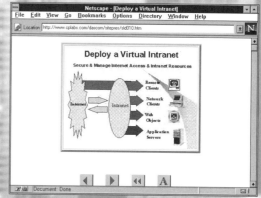

http://www.cplabs.com/dascom/sitepres/sld010.htm

Intranet Resource

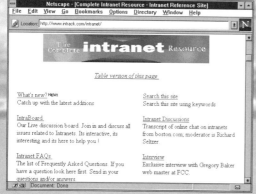

http://www.intrack.com/intranet/

Intranet Technology

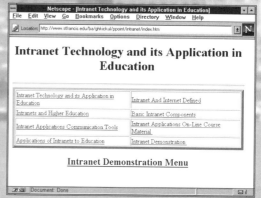

http://www.stfrancis.edu/ba/ghkickul/ppoint/
intranet/index.htm

Chapter 2

Intranets: The Start of a Revolution

The Internet's explosive growth has been widely presented in the news. However, there is an even faster growing use of the Internet technologies that is transforming the way corporations communicate with their employees, customers, vendors, and suppliers: intranets. In short, organizations have discovered that users can employ the same technologies that make the Internet successful to their internal network—their intranet. This chapter introduces intranets. You will not only examine the technologies intranets employ, but you will also read what the experts are saying about intranets, and how they expect intranets to grow over the next few years. By the time you finish this chapter, you will understand the following key concepts:

- An intranet is a company-specific network that uses software programs based on the Internet's TCP/IP protocol.

- Most experts feel that the explosive growth of intranets is just the tip of the iceberg. In fact, by the year 2000, there may be as many as 4 million intranet servers.

- Intranets exploit information sharing, collaboration, fast data access, and many users are already familiar with the software they require.

- Organizations use intranets to publish employee manuals, employee handbooks, company earnings, the CEO's vision, and much more.

- Establishing a functional intranet requires a minor hardware and software investment, the cost of which your company should recoup rapidly after the intranet is in place.

- Introducing an intranet into a large company also introduces short- and long-term challenges.

- Intranets provide many more capabilities than traditional groupware products, such as Lotus *Notes*.

- After the company justifies the cost of an intranet, the company must examine closely the intranet's security issues.

WHAT IS AN INTRANET?

As you learned in Chapter 1, the Internet consists of many networks that are connected together to create a global network. The interconnection of these networks allows computers on different networks to communicate with one another. You also learned that the technology which drives the Internet, TCP/IP, and packet switching are the enabling force allowing different types of computers to share the same information. Simply said, an *intranet* is the application of Internet technologies within an organization's private LAN or a WAN network.

Since the early 1980s, organizations with private networks have struggled with the task of connecting different types of computers, such as PCs, Macintoshes, and Unix-based machines, to share information. In the past, network administrators had to deal with hardware and software incompatibilities. To eliminate these barriers to electronic communication, companies had to standardize specific hardware and software platforms to guarantee seamless connectivity. Even today, if your company uses Macs, PCs, and Unix-based machines, sharing a simple text document can be a challenge. The application of Internet technologies on a private network can solve many of these problems. Figure 2.1 shows the relationship between the Internet and an intranet.

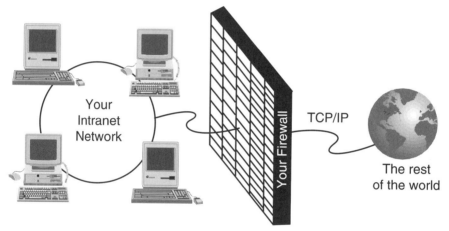

Figure 2.1 *An intranet is a company-wide network that is based on Internet technologies.*

WHAT THE EXPERTS ARE SAYING ABOUT INTRANETS

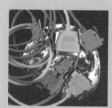
Intranets are quickly becoming valuable solutions to organizations throughout the world. Despite the fact that the concept of intranets is very new and that very little formal information regarding intranets is available, the use of intranets has already blazed a trail of excitement and satisfaction:

- The FedEx package tracking system enables 12,000 customers per day to find information regarding their parcels by computer, instead of calling a human operator for the same information. A manager of Internal Technology for Federal Express said, "We saw the success of the package-tracking site and said, 'Wow, I wonder what we could do on the inside?'" ("Here Comes the Intranet," *Business Week*, February 26, 1996: 76-84.) Today, FedEx has more than 60 Web sites created primarily by and for employees.

- "The intranet is a no-brainer. Go for it." (Richard Karlgaard, Intranets are Real, *Forbes ASAP*, April 8, 1996.)

- By the year 2000, companies will deploy more than 4 million intranet servers compared with less than half a million Internet servers. (Source: IDC, *Forbes ASAP*, April 8, 1996, p.51.)

- The market for intranets will quadruple in 1996 and almost triple the year after. According to forecaster Zona Research Inc., sales of intranet software will hit $448 million in 1996 and $1.2 million in 1997. Based on this forecast, intranet software sales could surpass sales of Lotus *Notes* which International Data Corp. predicts will be $800 million in 1997. (*The Wall Street Journal*, Nov. 7, 1995.)

- "Waves of organizations setting up intranets today are reminiscent of the move from corporate networks to departmental LANs over the past ten years." (Tony Pompili, "Content and Collaboration," *PC Magazine*, April 23, 1996.)

- "From AT&T to Levi Strauss to 3M, hundreds of companies are putting together intranets." (*Business Week*, February 26.)

- "A survey by Forester Research, Inc., of 50 major corporations found that 16% have an intranet and 50% either plan to or are considering building one." (*Business Week*.)

- "Servers started sprouting up all over the place on existing hardware or as departments allocated funding for their own dedicated servers. That broke the dam loose when people found more information on the internal Web than at the local library," said Larry Gutman, Chief Information Officer, Schlumberger LTD. (Joe Mullich, "Schlumberger's self-serve intranet," *PC Week*, May 27 1996, p48.) Schlumberger's CIO also says, "People have to understand they are not only consumers of information, but providers."

- "By eliminating paper systems, I have really seen an increase in the amount of communication between employees," said John Stevens, database administrator at Boeing Co., in Seattle. "We are implementing tons of intranets, probably hundreds." (Torsten Busse, "Intranets flourish due to easy development," *Infoworld*, May 20, 1996, p.35.)

- "TCP/IP is providing us interoperability across platforms and optimizing price-performance for connectivity. Basically the network provides an infrastructure and foundation for people to get to whatever they need on the network," says John Taylor, Du Pont Fellow information technology. "We no longer wanted to rely on proprietary protocols that put users at the mercy of particular vendor's protocols and product strategies," said Taylor. (Saroja, Girishankar, "Du Pont's Network Glue," *Communications Week*, June 3, 1996.)

UNDERSTANDING WHAT'S FUELING THE RAPID GROWTH OF INTRANETS

Ten years ago, personal computers decentralized computing power away from the Information Services Department into the hands of users. Today, intranet technology is taking this concept of putting the information into the hands of the user one step further, giving users even more control of content creation and distribution. The high price-performance of PCs and availability of various productivity tools, such as word processing and spreadsheets, provide companies with a new generation of digital content production. In other words, users within organizations aren't just consuming information, they are producing it (creating the content).

If you consider how difficult it has been for users to share complicated documents in the past, you will appreciate how the intranet has been so quickly embraced. During the early 1980s, employees learned how to type documents, create complicated flowcharts, and analyze financial and scientific data using spreadsheets. Unfortunately, Macintosh and PC software were not compatible—documents created on one machine were difficult simply to view on the other.

At the same time, Unix-based users did not have easy access to these popular Mac and PC-based productivity tools. The products simply did not run on Unix workstations. Instead, Unix-based users were forced to transfer their digital content onto paper and communicate with printed material. The flow of printed material was generally limited to an audience closely tied to a project or to a specific subject.

Compounding the problem of low-quality text-based communications was the e-mail revolution. To ensure all users could read their messages (to ensure compatibility), e-mail users tended to opt for the lowest common denominator for information presentation (such as straight ASCII text). Thus, they seldom used e-mail to send documents that contained pictures, tables, other platform-specific characteristics.

To minimize these compatibility problems, many companies standardized to a single software vendor and computer system. This strategy made many companies dependent on the two giants of the industry for all their personal productivity computing needs: Microsoft and Intel.

Today, on the other hand, the phenomenal growth and popularity of Internet-related solutions has suddenly changed the dynamics of the corporate computing world. Companies no longer must settle on a single operating system. As you have learned in Chapter 1, Internet technologies (such as TCP/IP) are platform independent. Users can choose to work with a Macintosh, PC, or Unix-based computer. Because the Internet (and intranet) supports graphics, all employees can create high-quality graphical documents. For example, a user can create a document with a variety of fonts, graphs, and images on a Silicon Graphics Unix-based computer, which a Mac, or a Windows-based user can easily view. Because of this, many experts believe that the network is quickly becoming a resource more valuable than the computer itself.

Within a traditional multiplatform environment, you unify communications using an intranet. Figure 2.2 shows a Web page whose contents look nearly identical for a PC, Mac, or Unix-based user.

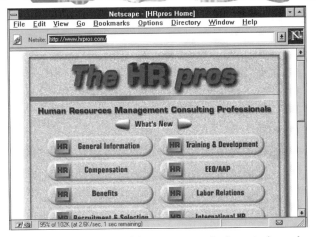

Figure 2.2 A Web-based homepage is platform independent.

UNDERSTANDING THE BENEFITS OF INTRANETS

As the popularity of internal Web sites (that is, intranets) increases, so has the demand for new tools and Web-based solutions. This demand had fueled competition among software manufacturers which, in turn, has resulted in better and cheaper products. For example, consider what has happened to the price of desktop productivity software products (such as word processors and spreadsheet programs) in recent years. The competitive environment of the software industry and the standard nonproprietary architecture of PCs drove down the price of all software and hardware products. In the near future, the same will happen to the price of intranet-based products. Groupware products such as Lotus *Notes* are already dropping in price because of the increasing popularity of intranets.

In short, intranets have brought competition back into the corporate-productivity market, which will help you lower your hardware and software budgets. Similarly, easy-to-use Mac-based servers and the increasing threat of Microsoft's NT operating system are causing the price of high-end Unix-based systems to decrease as well.

Internet technology follows a series of open standards that are well documented and readily available to assist software developers. This, in turn, encourages the development of cost-effective and easy-to-implement intranet solutions. As you will learn, intranet hardware and software require a minimal investment when compared to groupware and other proprietary solutions that are not only expensive, but also require extensive training and support. Within an intranet, you can use universal browsers such as Netscape *Navigator* and Microsoft *Internet Explorer* to perform the following common tasks:

- View documents created on a variety of platforms

- Create and revise content

- Participate in threaded discussions and news groups

- View and interact with multimedia presentations

- Interface with existing legacy data (nonHTML-based data) and applications

- Gain seamless access to the Internet

THE RISING POPULARITY OF NETWORK COMPUTERS—ARE NCS A FAD?

Currently, many companies are working to create a desktop personal computer that will sell for less than $500 and which they can easily attach to a network to take advantage of the power of a distant server. As you will discover, the Network Computer (NC) has great potential as a cost-effective client solution for many small to large sized companies. At $500, the NC will provide your company with a low-cost alternative to a $2,000 PC. In addition, maintenance costs of the simple NC should be dramatically lower than a comparable PC.

The NC does not come with a hard disk, so users must download the programs they want to run from across the network. To use a word processor, the user will download the corresponding program. Likewise, to perform spreadsheet operations, the user will download the spreadsheet program. Because the NC does not have a disk, users will save their files using a remote network-based disk.

Today, many companies depend on users to back up their own data. Often, users either carelessly backup their data or do not back it up at all. In contrast, as discussed, individual NC users will keep their data on a central server where the company's Information Services (IS) group can perform proper archiving techniques. In short, many companies believe that NCs will not only reduce the company's computing budget, they will also reduce the maintenance cost of hardware and software.

However, not everyone is sold on the concept of Network Computers. Because the NC does not have a hard disk, users must continually upload and download programs and documents. In a large company, these file transfer operations will result in a tremendous amount of network traffic, which decreases system performance. In addition, with the cost of full-blown multimedia PCs (which come complete with high-capacity hard drives and fast CD-ROMs) dropping rapidly in price, the $500 NCs are less of a bargain. Worse yet, in a company with 500 to 1000 employees, a network failure can prevent everyone from using a computer! As you can imagine, there is considerable debate over the role and proper use of Network Computers. Stay tuned for more information!

MOVING TOWARD A PAPERLESS COMPANY

Most companies find that because intranets simplify corporate-wide communications, intranets immediately reduce the daily cost of maintaining printed material. In fact, many organizations which have integrated an intranet into their operations are already discovering how the new technologies improve the company's bottom line. For example, consider a company with 10,000 employees. Each year, the company updates and prints its employee manual at a cost of $5 per manual. By placing the manual on an intranet, as opposed to printing the manual, the company can immediately eliminate the $50,000 printing expense. Better yet, by working with an electronic version of the manual, the company can easily keep the manual current. Next, think about similar cost savings in a larger company, one with 100,000 employees.

Placing an employee manual on-line is one simple example of how a company can reduce paper in the office, while saving money in the process. Most companies will find hundreds of paper-based applications they can eliminate using intranets.

LESS PAPER OFTEN MEANS LESS COST

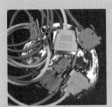 As you are learning, intranets provide instant information access while reducing the amount of paper that travels about and then stacks up within a company. Most companies can immediately benefit from an intranet by starting immediately and starting small. You should begin by putting all of your Human Resource manuals and documents on your internal Web site. The cost to produce, update, and distribute company information directly affects your organization's profit. Putting this information in electronic form immediately reduces this cost. Also keep in mind that information distributed in printed format is frequently out of date by the time it is distributed. In addition, not all recipients need this information; many file it away and never refer to it again.

The implementation of an intranet will bring immediate cost-savings to your company by reducing the need for printed materials and associated distribution costs. It will also make information more accessible to individuals as they need it. A company's cost of printing per employee can easily be as high as $50 to $100 when you include the health-care, 401K benefit packages, and other in-house manuals. Most companies can start an intranet on an initial investment of less than $10,000 and eliminate the need for most of its printed employee manuals and related documentation. Figure 2.3 shows how information can be accessed by anyone within the organization.

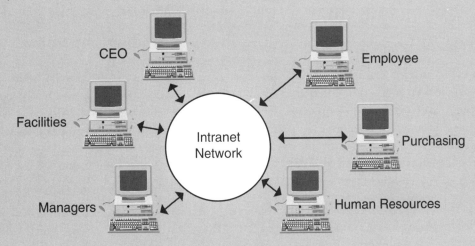

Figure 2.3 Information on demand.

Intranets are not just a trend that is driven by news hype and publicity. Intranets provide many useful applications which can provide the following benefits:

- Reduced operating costs

- Improved productivity

- Quick access to information

- Cross-Platform capability

- Cost effectiveness

- Ease of use

HOW COMPANIES ARE USING INTRANETS

To better understand how your company can benefit from intranet technology, you should examine how other companies have already put intranets to use. Although intranets are a new technology, you will find that companies who are doing well already have intranets in place.

HOW SUNSOFT USES INTRANETS

SunSoft, a subsidiary of Sun Microsystems, uses its intranet to distribute price books to sales representatives worldwide. The sales staff has immediate access to new pricing as soon as it is available. SunSoft has also placed their entire vendor catalog, which includes information on more than 12,000 products from 6,000 vendors, on their intranet. Because Sun still must print, but on a smaller scale, they have established just-in-time demand printing to provide printed versions of the catalog in small quantities on an as-needed basis. In addition, Sun's vendors also benefit from SunSoft's on-line vendor catalog. Sun lets their vendors access sections of the SunSoft's intranet to update their own product information on an as-needed basis. The on-line vendor catalog saves time, money, and improves access to accurate, up-to-date information.

HOW HEWLETT-PACKARD USES INTRANETS

Hewlett-Packard (HP) has also benefited from tremendous cost-savings associated with their intranet and Internet Web sites. Using Internet and intranet technologies, Hewlett-Packard has been able to re-engineer their key business processes, which reduces costs while improving customer relationships and efficiency. For example, HP uses the Internet to distribute software upgrades and support documentation to customers. Customers access a server to download the most current upgrades and related documentation. Users have access to the information when they need it, and HP has eliminated the cost of production and distribution associated with the upgrades.

HP has also been successful in reducing its operating costs associated with internal network support. HP manages and supports more than 82,000 PCs from a central location, which reduces the need for a large support staff to perform upgrades and other support functions. HP's intranet is one of the world's largest and encompasses:

- 400 sites worldwide

- 82,000 PCs

- 23,000 Unix desktops

- 6,000 servers

- 70,000 Netscape *Navigator* desktops

- 2,500 Web servers

How AT&T Uses Intranets

AT&T is one of the world's largest companies, employing over 127,000 persons. Today, AT&T uses intranet technology to manage its Health and Insurance Information Center. AT&T employees can access their intranet from home or the office to manage their own benefits, to access medical-program information, and to fill out forms located on the intranet. Today, AT&T has over 50,000 Netscape *Navigator* users, at least 30 Netscape Communication Servers, 60 Netscape Commerce Servers, and 20 Netscape Proxy Servers. The network applications that AT&T has built include integrated billing services, an interface to its library services, external news feeds, an office-supply ordering system, and an interface to an employee-contacts database containing over 300,000 entries.

How Federal Express Uses Intranets

In many cases, you can measure the benefits of cost reduction that correspond to an intranet. In other cases, the benefits don't easily translate into dollar figures, such as an increase in employee productivity or improved relationships with customers. Intranets have enabled organizations to develop closer relationships with their customers, vendors, and suppliers. For example, Federal Express has developed a Web site (*http://www.fedex.com*) which lets customers access the Federal Express internal database to track packages. Users can enter their air bill number into a powerful search engine to find out the status and location of their package. Customers also have the option to track up to 20 airbills at a time by submitting an e-mail to Federal Express.

Federal Express has plans to offer its many shipping services via the Internet through a program called *FedEx interNetShip*(sm). "The roll-out of *FedEx interNetShip* marks the first time a transportation company has offered its many services within the United States via the Internet. As acceptance grows, FedEx is poised to become one of the Internet's premier providers of electronic commerce services," said Dennis H. Jones, Senior Vice President and Chief Information Officer for Federal Express in a press release distributed on February 29, 1996. "The cost savings alone in customer support, printing, and customer satisfaction are significant."

The Intangible Benefits of Intranets

As you have learned, Hewlett-Packard's intranet has also improved the company's efficiency and productivity, which contributes to the company's rapid growth. For many organizations, having the right information at the right time can make the difference in closing a sale or meeting a deadline. In today's competitive business environment, companies are under constant pressure to improve productivity while reducing costs. To achieve this, companies must work to improve relationships with their employees, customers, vendors, and suppliers.

To remain competitive, organizations need quick access to information on all levels. Many traditional methods of communication are limited by time, need, accessibility, and cost. Using an intranet, individuals can access information when they need it, which will alleviate the time delays associated with information distribution. For example, Hewlett-Packard's Web site, which is linked to its intranet, contains more than 9,000 documents. It has between 30,000 to 40,000 customers looking at these pages every day with an estimated 700,000 pages viewed daily.

In short, intranets increase productivity, reduce costs, and improve an organization's ability to compete in the marketplace.

BREAKING DOWN THE BARRIERS

Many organizations already connect their employees to the Internet. At these organizations, employees have already experienced the benefits of having access to a vast array of information on the Internet. In short, the Internet has changed the way these employees communicate and share information. It won't be difficult for these organizations to sell their employees on the benefits on an intranet.

Within an organization, intranets dissolve the barriers to communication that are created by department walls, geographical location, and decentralized resources. Intranets create global accessibility by bringing together individuals and resources from a distributed environment. Users (which may include employees, customers, or vendors) can access information resources stored at multiple locations through the intranet, as if it were a virtual repository. An intranet allows access to vast amounts of corporate information that has never before been available. By providing information to those who need it, organizations can decentralize resources and flatten the decision making hierarchy while retaining control.

THE TRADITIONAL HIERARCHICAL INFORMATION DISTRIBUTION MODEL

Just about every company has an organizational chart that defines the company's divisions and levels of management. Although the organizational chart is very important for defining employee and supervisor relationships, many companies use the chart to control the dissemination of information. Unfortunately, the organizational chart is not well suited for getting the correct information to the people who need it.

The historical hierarchy model of a corporation is designed to create standard flows for the movement of information. Without an intranet, this standard flow of information traps the free flow of information within a company. Using intranets, an enterprise finally can create an organization where the power of many minds will come together to create a powerful force in the market place.

THE NEW INTRANET-BASED INFORMATION DISTRIBUTION MODEL

Today, technology is changing so fast that every member of an organization needs to be kept abreast of the latest news in the shortest amount of time possible. Companies must let people share their knowledge and findings by publishing on the company's internal Web. Such employee-based contributions will lead to an increased level of personal participation which, in turn, will form the basis of a team-based organization.

Researchers often talk about the concept of the "learning organization" in describing how companies can and should use the power of motivated participants to achieve outstanding team results. The intranet will make the theoretical concepts of a learning organization a reality. Groups that have been geographically separated in the past can finally share a common communication slate. Team members will learn how to depend on each other when faced with difficult tasks. An employee's homepage will become the ultimate garden for growing the seeds of collaboration and knowledge sharing within your company.

An intranet will help dissolve the barriers to communication and will help individuals spend more time focusing on key business strategies. Intranets will flatten the hierarchical structure of your organization, enabling others to participate in the decision making process. Individuals and groups can distribute their ideas to those who need it, without having to go through the departments traditionally responsible for distribution of information.

HELP DESKS—THE IDEAL USE OF AN INTRANET

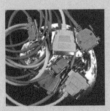

Within most large organizations, you will find a computer support help desk, whose task is to answer user questions, solve user hardware and software problems, and to troubleshoot the wide variety of problems that users can incur. One function of the help desk is to collect information from computer support specialists and to distribute that information to the individuals who need it. In the quickly changing world of information technology and computers, many help-desk staffs cannot keep up with the collection and distribution of information. In every organization, there are many *virtual help desks*, run by those individuals within each department who are the early adopters of new technologies. Employees know who these virtual help-desk staff are, and call them when the help desk is busy or unaware of the new bugs and features of a new product.

An intranet will introduce these virtual help desks to everyone within your organization. How does the intranet do this? When an early adopter of a new technology learns how to perform a task, for example, installing a new printer, he or she could put that information on his or her own personal help page. Others in the organization, including your help desk staff, could easily find this information by automatically searching your entire Web using a ready-to-go search engine. The help desk staff can then copy the information they deem useful for the entire intranet community to the help desk's general help page. As you start to implement an intranet, you will learn that many free consultants are hidden within your organization because the traditional information sharing system inhibits your employees who need assistance from easily identifying the experts.

In an organization empowered by an intranet, every employee will imprint his or her expertise on your internal Web. This is a truly revolutionary phenomenon. This means that the seeds of knowledge can finally grow from the inside of an employee's office and be shared on a common pulpit—your intranet. Your enterprise can finally get what it pays your employees for: knowledge. This knowledge finally becomes available as an ultimate resource that makes your company an information-driven force in the global market place.

The Power of a Knowledgeable Team

As you are learning, intranets place information into the hands of those who need it to solve tasks at hand. Intranets also encourage employees and groups to share their ideas and work collaboratively. At MCI, more than 12,000 IS professionals share their knowledge by storing software code and programming information in a centralized developer's library. This supports their simple company motto "Collaborate, don't duplicate" (*Information Week*, January 29, 1996). You can visit MCI's web site at, *http://www.mci.com* for more information.

Researchers constantly study ways companies can become more competitive. Today, companies who act and perform as a team normally win. For a football team, winning is the result of months of practice, hard work, and coming together as a team. Unfortunately, applying strategies used by football teams to create success within a corporation is quite challenging. Intranets allow you to perform like a winning football team by giving you the ability to constantly monitor your resources, and those of your opponents.

For example, as soon as one of your sales people learns of a new sales lead, he or she can use the intranet to request help approaching the customer. Within hours, new ideas may appear within the sales group's intranet chat room, resulting in real-time reaction to a sales lead—much like the fast response you would see in a football game. Without an intranet, the sales staff may act as individuals and not as a team. True teamwork will spawn better ideas, shared knowledge, and will result in a win.

Threat of an Intranet Culture

With intranets come the birth of a new culture that depends on the free flow of information for its existence. Your development teams, your sales teams, your production teams, and your marketing team all must know about the others' moves to better service the customer. The intranet culture requires your enterprise to seriously examine the way it operates.

To start, because an intranet places information into the hands of your employees, the intranet will cause your company's structure to evolve into a democracy. Your management must be confident enough to listen to and evaluate employee views and address their concerns promptly. Your corporation must realize that to provide the customer with the best possible service, employees must be heard and their opinions considered. The danger of such an "information democracy" is that once you grant information and the ability to respond to your employees, you cannot take it back without seriously damaging cooperation among your employees.

Individuals in an intranet environment must have the power to distribute information, both good and bad. You will discover that training on intranet etiquette and communication must become an important part of your implementation strategy.

RELATIONSHIP MARKETING—GETTING THE CUSTOMERS INVOLVED

Companies such as Sun Microsystems are moving quickly to make their customers an integral part of their intranets. At Sun, different departments are setting up their own servers to service their customers directly. Customers no longer have to go through various layers of organizational hierarchies to get to people who actually build the product or provide the service. Employees can learn first hand how a customer feels about the company's products and services.

Involving key customers with your intranet will help move your company's focus from being product driven to being customer driven. In turn, your focus on the customer will set the stage for your company to develop a long-lasting relationship with your customer. The job of marketing will shift toward establishing a relationship with your customer, rather than positioning and establishing the product. This "hands on" customer approach may require employees in your organization to change their views about the customer. Using intranets, your employees will rediscover customer satisfaction. Figure 2.4 shows the communication flow in a intranet-less organization and how it filters out details as information reaches higher levels. As shown in figure 2.5, the intranet can make your users the center of attention for all departments within the organization.

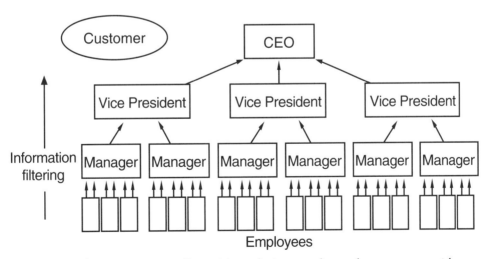

Figure 2.4 Communication flow without the intranet leaves the customer outside.

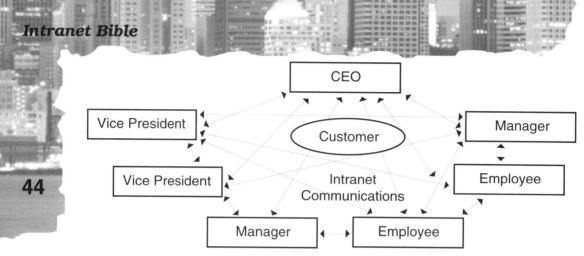

Figure 2.5 Customers are at the center of attention with an intranet.

WHAT YOU NEED TO ESTABLISH A FUNCTIONAL INTRANET

In Chapter 5, "Understanding Intranet Components" you will learn in detail, the hardware and software components you need to establish a functional intranet. If you already use TCP/IP as your network protocol, all you need is a high-end PC or Mac running your favorite operating system. You can even download several powerful Web servers for free. Most commercial Web servers cost $300 to $1,000. A high-end PC running Windows NT will cost about $4,000 to $6,000. You can start your first intranet for 100 to 200 users for less than $10,000 complete.

You will find that setting up most Web servers is easy. Your Information Services (IS) department should be able to quickly set up a Web server. Creating basic content is also easy. You can buy a commercially available HTML editor for less than $100 or download a free upgrade for the latest version of your word processor. In Chapters 5 through 8, you will learn in detail how to setup a Web server, convert text to HTML, convert images, and create dynamic Web pages.

Your first Web site may not necessarily be graphically pleasing. Most IS departments are not trained to use high-end graphical programs such as Adobe Photoshop. However, this should not stop you from starting your first intranet. As long as the site is functionally useful, employees will access it for its utility.

A very popular first project is the company telephone directory. Phone books are often out of date, so employees will find an on-line system convenient. By gradually adding features such as a search engine for names, departments, photos, and other employee related information, you can increase the functionality of your on-line phone book over time. You should apply this method of gradually adding features to your new Web applications because it maximizes employee interest and their skill with the new features of your intranet. As you develop intranet-based applications, you will find that many of the features are reusable. For example, a search engine you created to look up a name in the telephone directory can also be used to look up terms in the employee handbook. In many cases, you can obtain features from other Web sites and reuse them. Figure 2.6 shows a useful corporate intranet Web site.

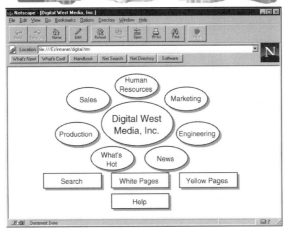

Figure 2.6 *A corporate intranet site.*

WHERE TO GET FREE WEB SERVERS

Across the Internet, you can find several server software programs available for no charge (many of which run for a predefined length of time—a demo period). As you have learned, servers are programs which run on a computer (generally referred to as a server) that sends data to client programs. Keep in mind that, like all free things, these programs may not perform as well as their commercial counterparts. However, they are a good stepping stone towards establishing basic service which you can always upgrade later.

Before you actually obtain your server software, you must first determine which computer you will dedicate as the server. Generally, your server computer should be a high-performance system. In selecting your server, you must also consider ease of set up and security. These are areas that you will learn about in more detail in Chapter 5. The following list identifies Web URLs where you can download server software for free:

For the Macintosh:

- *http://www.starnine.com* (MacHttp or WebStar)

For Windows 3.1:

- *http://www.qdeck.com* (WebServer)

- *http://www.city.net* (httpd)

For Windows 95 or NT:

- *http://website.ora.com* (WebSite server)

- *http://www.cleveland.co.uk* (Quota NT server, 20 day demo)

For Novell based networks:

- *http://www.glaci.com*

For Unix:

- *http://www.spyglass.com* (demo version)

You may also want to visit a search engine, such as *http://www.lycos.com*, and enter compound search keys such as "server free Macintosh download". In this example, Lycos will return a series of URLs that relate to Macintosh servers.

UNDERSTANDING YOUR LONG- AND SHORT-TERM CHALLENGES

As you will learn in Chapter 5, setting up simple HTML pages is not difficult. Your immediate challenge is to sell the idea of intranet benefits to your management. Start with hard numbers that relate to savings in time and money. Then, use real-world examples from companies that already have an intranet. If possible, find out if your competitors have an intranet. (The fact that your competitors have installed an intranet will motivate your management to approve your corporate intranet.)

Next, provide your management with a projected return on investment for the intranet project. Chapter 15, "Return on Investments for Intranets" presents the steps you should follow to determine the return on investment. You might start by asking your Human Resources department how much money they spend on printing every year. Show your management that the break-even point is less than they might expect. Next, you will have a better chance to get approval for your project if you can show them a working prototype. In Chapter 14, "Web Publishing Using FrontPage 97" you will learn how to download and install Microsoft's integrated intranet package called *FrontPage 97* with which you can quickly create a working a prototype.

After you have your management's approval, start simple and move fast. Your first challenge is to get other employees involved. With their involvement, you will can unleash the true power of the intranet—collaboration. Next, your long-term challenges are the following:

- Collecting content from key divisions that you can display on-line

- Integrating your company's legacy content (pre-existing documents) and databases into your intranet

- Training employees on basics of HTML and Web publishing

- Creating and sustaining the fire of distributed information sharing

- Motivating all departments to develop their own sites and to continually update and contribute content

- Transferring the administration of intranet responsibilities to the appropriate organization

- Finding the people with right skill set to carry the company's intranet revolution to the next level—increasing the amount of information available to employees and customers

In Chapters 8 through 11, you will learn how to approach these challenges and how to set up a program that will provide you with long-lasting intranet benefits.

GROUPWARE PRODUCTS VS INTRANETS

 In 1995, Ed McCracken, CEO of Silicon Graphics, Inc. (SGI), addressed a group of local business executives on the difficulties associated with providing information to all employees across a network (*Forbes*, April 8, 1996: 11). SGI had started a number groupware projects, but soon realized the difficulties associated with centralizing information and computer-resource requirements. So, SGI decided to use their own hardware and software in place of groupware products. "Hey, let's eat our own dog food. Let's dump these other groupware projects and use the Internet to share corporate information across the network," said McCracken.

You will notice several key differences between groupware products (namely, Lotus *Notes* from IBM) and intranets. Depending on your needs, company size, budget, and your expectations from a set of tools, you can decide which products can help you be more competitive. The primary difference between Lotus *Notes* and intranets is that Lotus *Notes* uses a proprietary system to distribute and keep track of information. With Lotus *Notes*, you must pay on a per-client basis to bring the groupware technology to everyone. On the other hand, intranets use open systems to distribute information. Integration of tools under an intranet environment may be more difficult for smaller companies. If you have less than 100 employees, it might be more cost effective to go with groupware products. If you are planning for growth, intranets are a better choice. The only per-client cost associated with intranets is the cost of the browsers. The Netscape *Navigator* browser is available for around $40, and Microsoft *Internet Explorer* is currently free.

As you have learned in the previous chapter, the growth of Internet-related technologies, including software and hardware improvements, provides you with a large pool of resources that you can use to develop your own intranet project. Conversely, traditional groupware products have a more limiting array of compatible products, as well as fewer specially trained consultants who can administer your system. In addition to cost considerations, intranets provide easy-to-use tools which encourage everyone in the organization to contribute content.

In recognizing the threat that the intranet has posed to Lotus *Notes*, IBM is adding new intranet-compatible features to its product. For example, the newest release of Lotus *Notes* allows users to view Lotus *Notes* documents from within the Web. In the future, other software manufacturers are likely to make their groupware products compatible with intranets.

Even if your organization has made a commitment to a groupware product, look for the inevitable trend toward intranet friendly products. For more information on groupware and intranets, visit *http://roxa33.cern.ch/www.icptalk/grpware.htm* shown in Figure 2.7.

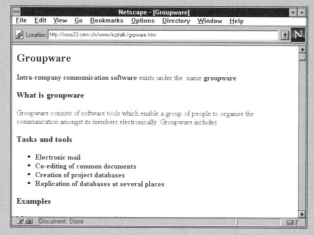

Figure 2.7 Information on groupware and intranets.

SECURITY ISSUES

There several aspects of security that you must consider before you set up your intranet. First, you must consider the security issues that prevent outsiders from tapping into your private intranet without proper permission. Second, you should consider the security issues regarding the illegal transfer of your corporate documents and information to the outside world by your employees. The problem of people penetrating your intranet from the outside is real, but it is being addressed globally by all companies. As you will learn, *firewalls* are software programs that can block intruders from getting to your internal data, marketing reports, employee information, and host of other types of information available on your intranet.

Your biggest problem lies in providing data to people who, until recently, didn't have access to all of the available data. With the availability of removable mass storage units, your employees can easily copy all of your corporate intranet pages on a single floppy and transfer the files to the outside world. Many companies are considering restricting sections of corporate intranets to various groups of employees. This would minimize your security concerns, but could easily hamper the real benefits of intranets: collaboration and information sharing. For example, if you allow your sales staff to engage in a strategy discussion on their intranet server, you probably don't want to restrict access to your engineers. In most cases, the engineers have tremendous product knowledge and can help the sales staff to better understand and present products.

EMPLOYEE TRAINING INCREASES SECURITY

When your company moves to intranet technology, all employees must play an active role in maintaining a secure environment. Thus, it is essential that employee training becomes a key aspect during the initial deployment phase of your intranet. With the new intranet paradigm comes a new sense of responsibility that companies must clearly communicate to their employees. The Human Resources department should conduct training on ethical and legal aspects of transferring corporate confidential data to the outside world.

With proper training, employees will realize that the company's survival in competitive markets depends on trust and respect for the corporate knowledge repository—the intranet. In Chapter 19, "Intranet Security Issues" you will learn in greater detail about firewalls and how you can use them to discourage outsiders from breaking into your intranets.

PUTTING IT ALL TOGETHER

This chapter has introduced you to the intranet and has given you a broad view of some of the issues surrounding intranets. You have discovered that the intranet is an adaptation of an existing set of technologies that make up the Internet. In Chapter 3, you will discover how companies are applying intranets to solve specific problems within various industries. Before you continue with Chapter 3, however, make sure you understand the following key concepts:

- ✓ An intranet is a company-based version of the Internet. Intranets provide an inexpensive solution for information sharing and user communication.

- ✓ Companies that have installed intranets are finding that installation costs are low and versatility high.

- ✓ An intranet makes it easy for users to communicate and share common documents, even if the computers are a mixture of PC's and Macintoshes.

- ✓ Some organizations are expanding their intranet to let customers access the internal databases and documents.

- ✓ Most companies can establish a functional intranet using in-house personnel and minimal new equipment.

- ✓ Your primary challenges in sustaining an intranet include maintaining order and control over content, as well as coping with corporate-wide changes in the corporate culture.

- ✓ Intranet solutions are open and are shaped by competitive forces, whereas groupware products tend to be closed and proprietary.

- ✓ You must design security into all levels of your intranet.

VISITING KEY SITES THAT DISCUSS INTRANETS

The World Wide Web is filled with hundreds of excellent and current articles on all aspects of intranets. Use the following sites as starting points for your Web exploration.

Intranet - Revolution or Evolution

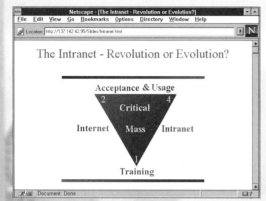

http://137.142.42.95/Slides/Intranet.html

Intranet Career Resources

*http://www.careerexpo.com/pub/docs296/
intranet.html*

Intranet Handbook Page

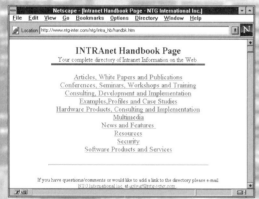

*http://www.ntg-inter.com/ntg/intra_hb/
handbk.htm*

Blenheim Intranet Show

*http://www.netlink.co.uk/users/ploppy/blenheim/
index.html*

Intranet Development Page

http://www.dsdelft.nl/~intranet/index.com

Definition of Intranet

http://www.onsite.net/faq/intranet.htm

Chapter 3

Intranets in Action

In Chapter 2, you learned about several benefits of intranets and how companies are using them to improve productivity. You also learned about the high-level challenges facing organizations deploying intranets. However, because Chapter 2 provided so much macro-level (big picture) information, you may still be asking yourself, what are the real cost savings ideas behind intranets? In the rest of this book, you will learn, in detail, how to set up your first intranet and how to continuously improve it.

In this chapter, you will learn how you can apply an intranet to a variety of functional areas within your organization. An additional goal of this chapter is to help you develop your thoughts so that you can present a strong case and obtain corporate approval for deploying an intranet. It is important to note that this chapter covers functional areas of both manufacturing and service industries. By the time you finish this chapter, you will discover specific applications where an intranet can help your company, as follows:

- ◆ Learn how the Chief Executive Officer can use an intranet to communicate company issues to all employees.

- ◆ Reduce paperwork and documentation that can be maintained electronically in the Human Resources department.

- ◆ Financial and accounting books can be placed within an intranet and made accessible to those who have a need to use them.

- ◆ Your Management Information Systems (MIS) department can supplement user support with an on-line help desk centered within an intranet.

- ◆ Sales, marketing, and customer support departments can leverage an intranet's ubiquitous presence to provide up-to-the-minute information at any location.

- ◆ An intranet can provide manufacturing with automatic production data and performance results.

- ◆ Employees who need to use your company's purchasing, shipping, and receiving departments will be able to transact orders on-line and check for delivery schedules.

- ◆ An intranet can be an effective tool in instituting a corporate-wide quality system.

BUILDING UP YOUR INTRANET

Although not a comprehensive list of intranet applications, the above summary provides you with the beginning of a departmental framework that you can use to derive a variety of intranet homepages. Each department's homepage can be linked to other departments and progressively fuel the growth of your intranet. The technology that makes intranets possible is so flexible that you can start with one department first and not worry about designing the homepages for the other departments all at once.

52

Ultimately, your intranet network can grow outside the borders of one building and expand to your company's other geographical locations. Each of these locations can have its own server computer which will make it easy to support a distributed intranet network. As you have learned in Chapter 1, a wide-area network (WAN) is such a network. Figure 3.1 shows a multi-site intranet arrangement.

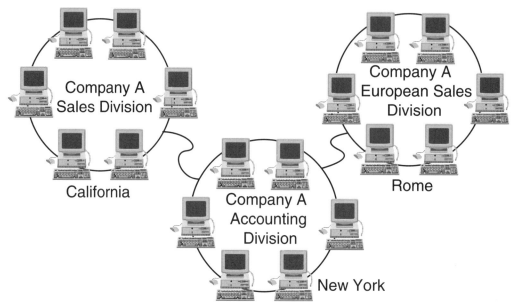

Figure 3.1 A multi-site intranet arrangement.

At first, it may seem that coordinating multiple Web servers across a wide-area network is a daunting task. In fact, this is not the case. Furthermore, you may want to provide separate Web server computers to every department in your company (even if they are located in the same building). In certain high-volume situations (for example, if you have a large sales force all accessing the sales site), you may want to provide an additional server. Multiple servers can also help keep at least part of your business running in case of a failure in one of them.

In short, avoid limiting your thinking to one server per network. You should understand that you may add as many servers and homepages as you need as your company grows. An underlying strategy of this book is that you can start small with an experimental site and carefully build up your intranet's presence. Figure 3.2 shows a network within a company that makes use of two separate Web servers.

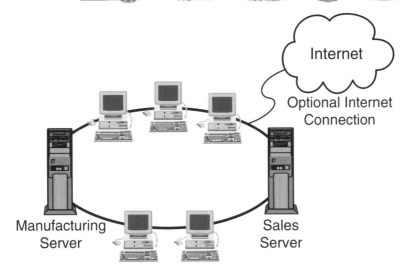

Figure 3.2 A multi-server arrangement.

Besides links to your company's divisions and departments, your intranet pages should provide your employees with links which cross reference other sites on your Web. A *link* is a clickable text or icon on a Web page which connects you to another Web page or location. Links will let your employees quickly go from one Web location to the next, from one department to the next, and from one Web server to the next. As you can see, your users will not need to know how your network is arranged, or whether it has multiple servers, or if it expands outside the continent. Figure 3.3 shows how links on a single Web page can point to completely different locations throughout your intranet.

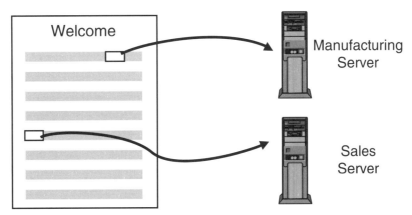

Figure 3.3 Using links to traverse your growing intranet.

As your intranet grows, you will need to update old links or create new ones pointing to new services or departments. The Web page in Figure 3.3 may need a new link if you add another server to your network. Fortunately, keeping Web pages current is not difficult—individual departments can update their own Web sites. Chapter 16 will show you how to maintain and upgrade your intranet.

START WITH THE CEO

One way to introduce an intranet to your organization is by starting at the top. Do you know how many of your employees are aware of your company's vision, mission, and long-term strategy? The CEO of any organization recognizes that communicating corporate objectives to all employees is key to the company's long-term success in the marketplace. As a CEO, an intranet will give you the ability to communicate your ideas, vision, and corporate strategies to all your employees worldwide, on a real-time basis. Using an intranet, a CEO can energize employees about the opportunities of new markets, as well as warn them of the threat of new and old competitors.

Using the multimedia features of an intranet, such as real-time voice and video capability, your CEO can help employees experience the corporate position in ways that were never before possible. The "CEO's Corner" should be a place on your Web where employees go to get assurances about the possibilities of a better and brighter future. In a large organization, the CEO cannot visit every division and have direct contact with every employee on a daily basis. The CEO's Corner could provide employees with the tools to help create a more open and honest corporate culture and provide them with the following information and features:

- The CEO's challenges and accomplishments

- All about the CEO: hobbies and other appropriate personal information

- Corporate vision statement

- Current long-term and short-term financial and productivity goals

- State of the industry and major competitors

- Live chat session with all employees worldwide

You can use a CEO's homepage as a model for setting up departmental and individual homepages. Each employee should be given the opportunity to publish a homepage. You will learn more about the content of a personal homepage later in this chapter.

VISIT WITH CEOS OF VARIOUS COMPANIES

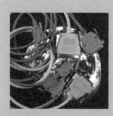

Although the CEO's Corner discussed in this section is geared toward the employees of your company, you can get some ideas from several open-to-the-public CEO pages. Many companies already have internal CEO pages which are shielded from public access, and you may want to follow a similar model. For example, your CEO's Corner could have two sets of Web pages: one for in-house viewing and the other for the general public.

Check out these interesting sites of Chairmen, CEOs, and Presidents:

- Dr. Gilbert Amelio, Apple Computer, Inc (*http://www2.apple.com/leadership*)

- Lew Platt, HP (*http://www.mediacast.com/mediacast/calendar/96-02-14/hp*)

- William Lu, Acer Computer Intl (*http://www.aci.acer.com.tw/william.html*)

- Helen J. Clark, Apollo Trust Company (*http://bankswith.apollotrust.com/~hjc*)

- Gerry Hsu, ArcSys (*http://www.edac.org/ArcSys/gerry.html*)

- Beverly Kolz, WCB Publishers (*http://www.wcbp.com/kolzltr.com*)

- Rodney H. Brady, Bonneville Intl Corp. (*http://www.bonneville.com/pres.html*)

- Charles W. Mueller, Union Electric (*http://www.ue.com/about-ue/mueller.html*)

- Tom Olson, Katz Media Group (*http://www.katz-media.com/olson.htm*)

- Gary A. Dachis, Game Financial (*http://www.gamecash.com/gfininfo/garyd.html*)

- Gilbert J. Barnes, DTS Personnel (*http://www.datatrac.com/bios/gbarnes.html*)

- Ian D. Argranat, Argranat Systems (*http://www.argranat.com/ian*)

- Robert L. Armstrong, Omaha Housing Authority (*http://www.omaha.org/ofn/oha/ofn-10.html*)

HUMAN RESOURCES: AN IMMEDIATE BENEFICIARY OF INTRANETS

As you learned in Chapter 2, intranets provide your organization with both immediate and long-term benefits. The immediate benefit of intranets is that you can replace corporate manuals, policies, and other forms of information that are distributed through printed media with electronic versions at your intranet's Web sites. The problem with printed information is that it is difficult to keep up-to-date. Your organization requires an infrastructure just to print, store, distribute, dispose, and maintain paper documents. The costs associated with printing affect your company's profitability and margins. Your company can benefit more if your staff spends their time training and counseling employees, rather than creating and distributing printed documents, manuals, and announcements.

An important goal of your Human Resources department (HR) is to maximize the utilization of human resources by providing the best working conditions for your employees. However, because companies constantly focus on cutting costs, Human Resources departments are frequently left trying to do too much with too few staff. Historically, Human Resources departments often receive little help to automate their information distribution processes from the Management Information Systems (MIS) group.

Intranets are here to rescue you! The following is a list of some of the documents and manuals that you can immediately put on your intranet with minimal difficulty:

- Organizational chart and directory of job titles
- HR forms, including performance review forms
- Employee policies, EEO policies, and employee handbooks
- 401K forms, fund data, and performance of funds
- List of job openings
- List of upcoming training classes
- Employee related information—picture, telephone number, employee number, years of service, e-mail address, and organizational position
- Upcoming company events and official holidays

If you have the above information in digital form, as in a word processor, then you will find it easy to convert your existing information to HTML format. You will learn about converting text, creating organizational charts, and creating HTML documents in Chapter 6. Figure 3.4 shows how a stack of HR manuals can disappear within an intranet.

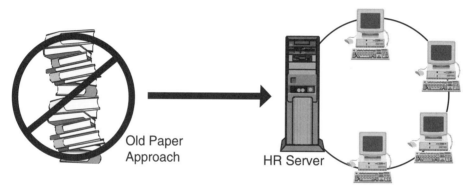

Old Paper Approach

HR Server

Figure 3.4 *Replacing HR manuals with electronic ones.*

Note: You may need to put photographs of events or happenings around the company campus, as well as photographs of your employees on your Web page. In that case, an additional investment you will have to make is for a digital camera to take digital pictures, or a document scanner to scan existing photos. Once you have digitized these photos, it is a very easy job to publish them on your Web page. For example, you may want to provide an on-line version of your organization chart, complete with photographs of each employee.

WHAT IS A DIGITAL CAMERA?

A digital camera is a relatively new product which takes pictures like an ordinary camera. The difference is that instead of exposing a strip of film, the digital camera stores the exposure as picture data in memory or on a floppy disk. You would use a digital camera to produce picture data files that are easily pasted within Web pages. For the most part, you would be able to simply transfer the data file from the camera directly to the server computer (no processing required!).

Digital cameras tend to be very expensive when compared to their film-based counterparts. The photo quality of an $800 digital camera is no better than that of a $20 disposable film camera. If you need quality that approaches your 35mm film camera, you may need to spend as much as $32,000. Fortunately, in most cases, the least expensive digital camera is fine; this is what most Web publishers are using today. For more information on digital cameras, visit the Casio Web site at *http://www.casio.com* shown in Figure 3.5.

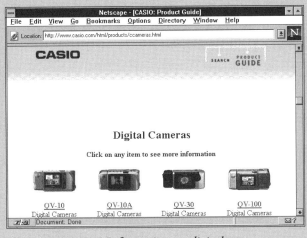

Figure 3.5 Information on digital cameras.

EMPLOYEE'S HOMEPAGE

As you learned in Chapter 2, one of the powerful features of an intranet is its ability to help your employees share their experiences with the rest of the organization. The vehicle for this is your employees' personal homepages. How does a personal Web page do this? A personal Web page is an on-line resume for each employee. Unlike a static resume, a Web page is a dynamic place where your employees have an opportunity to share their work, their hobbies, and their experiences with other employees. An employee's personal Web page may include the following information:

- Work experience and educational background

- Goals for the year

- Current projects and challenges

- Areas of expertise

- Reports and guideline for areas of interest and expertise

- Hobbies and other nonwork related topics

Figure 3.6. shows a sample of an employee intranet page.

Employee Profile

Employee Name:	Jim Bremner
Employee Number:	12545
Address	7704 Rue Michael Falls Church, VA 22043
Phone #:	703-555-1212
Emergency #	703-213-2648
Job Title	Web Site Designer, Programmer
	Complete web production from Art to

Figure 3.6 A sample of an employee intranet page.

Personal Web pages could include a Frequently Asked Questions (FAQ) section where employees go to obtain information quickly. Because the content of personal homepages is accessible by all your employees regardless of their organizational position or geographical location, an employee with a specific problem could search the Web pages for an in-house expert to provide assistance. Not only will problems be solved faster, but teamwork will be fostered among all members of the organization. By making the corporate skill set available to everyone, your company will develop a sense of unity that comes from working together. Figure 3.7 shows how one user can gain access to the rich talents that already exist within your company.

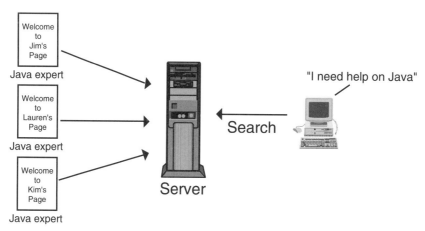

Figure 3.7 Searching personal Web pages for an expert.

Financial and Accounting Information

Unless your company has a completely integrated financial and accounting system, an intranet could offer your finance and accounting department many ways to reduce your operating costs while improving that department's productivity. For example, Sun Microsystems has cut the cost of processing its employees' travel expense reports by a significant amount using an intranet. Just as in the case of the previously discussed HR department, you can start by putting your static manuals, templates, and financial forms on your intranet first.

Consider how much money your company spends on printing weekly financial data for department managers. In many companies, existing legacy systems are good at printing hard copy reports—perhaps too good. These systems are responsible for developing a managerial culture that depends on printed reports for everything. Your intranet will transform your company's culture from a paper-hungry to a paperless organization.

Start by putting your department's weekly, quarterly, and yearly financial reports on your intranet first. In Chapters 8 and 9, you will learn how to convert your spreadsheet data and graphs to a format that your Web browser can display. The following financial data are great candidates for going on your intranet:

- Mission and goals of your department
- Historical income statements and balance sheets
- Weekly, quarterly, and yearly financial measures—inventory turnover, return on equity, gross margins, and return on assets
- Your competitors' financial measures
- Historical inventory levels and product costs
- Cost cutting measures and spending guidelines
- Training manuals for understanding financial measures
- Miscellaneous forms

The information provided by your financial homepage will help your managers and their staff learn how your company generates its revenue and how each employee can affect your company's profitability. Even with the most sophisticated financial and accounting systems, your department will still need spreadsheet programs to track many of its financial measures. Intranet conversion tools make it easy to migrate existing spreadsheet files from your current system to your Web pages. So why not share this information with the rest of the company? Your employees need to know how the company makes its money. You can educate your employees using your intranet and help transform your organization to a world-class profit generating enterprise.

Management gurus argue that you can manage only that which you can measure. By putting your company's financial information on an intranet, it becomes readily accessible and easier to use on a daily basis. Most of your employees correlate the financial health of companies with the value of their stock. Perhaps this is because stock prices are published every day in newspapers. Even though the price of a company's stock is an indicator of the short-term health of a company, your employees need to learn about other financial measures that affect the long-term profitability of companies. These other measures, including gross margins, return on assets, and inventory turnover, can be summarized and presented concisely on a Web page.

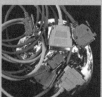

How Big Can Your Intranet Grow?

An intranet can be as large as you need it to be. As you recall from Chapters 1 and 2, intranet technology is the same technology used for the Internet. Furthermore, the Internet supports a continuously expanding audience that by some estimates is growing by more than a million users per month.

Hewlett-Packard's private intranet is one of the world's largest with 140,000 servers. Hewlett-Packard's intranets have allowed the company to eliminate its mainframes and rapidly move most of the company's strategic business processes to this new and flexible technology.

You can start implementing a small intranet with very little planning. It is likely that the companies who originally developed your legacy systems will provide you with the tools to connect them to your intranets. As your company begins to develop an organized intranet migration plan, expanding your intranet should be a smooth operation.

MANAGEMENT INFORMATION SYSTEM (MIS)

An intranet can be very effective when it is applied to solve information support situations. If you look at your computer support expenses, you will realize that the cost of maintaining and supporting each PC could be as high as four times the original cost of the PC hardware. Many of these costs are associated with helping the users solve their PC's hardware problems and helping them use their application programs. As you have learned in Chapter 2, intranets can help you reduce the number of help desk calls and can also help your staff learn from the many power users that are already within your company.

Whether you know it or not, power users are already providing your employees with support that they cannot get from MIS groups. These are the people who have a reputation for solving a particular class of problem or knowing how to configure software, for example. By making these people accessible on your intranet and encouraging them to publish a set of Frequently Asked Questions (FAQs), you will promote better customer service, as well as better use of the power user's time. Remember, if your engineers are helping others to solve their computer-related problems, they are not spending time solving your engineering problems. The cost associated with setting up an intranet is much lower than the cost of paying your engineers to help other employees with computer problems.

Your problems are not different than those of a software company when faced with providing free customer support. Companies such as Apple, Microsoft, and Symantec are providing an extensive library of documentation, software upgrades, and other customer support services on their Internet sites to reduce their cost of after sales support, as shown in Figure 3.8. Many companies also have public bulletin sites where users with problems can post a question and have it answered by one of the many experts that may be reading it. By following a similar model with your intranet, you can have users help themselves while reducing the number of petty calls that go to the MIS department.

61

*Figure 3.8 Microsoft's support online page located at **www.microsoft.com/support/**.*

Another good reason for having an MIS intranet page is to help employees who have the ability to dial into your network. These are employees who work after hours and on weekends when the MIS is not at work to help them with their problems. With an intranet in place, these users can dial in and access troubleshooting hints, read FAQs, or leave a message for someone to call back later. In the near future, your MIS department will be able to create and publish training videos and interactive assistance guides. The following is a list of topics you should consider putting on your MIS homepage:

- Help desk hours and who is responsible for what

- List of available software and hardware upgrades

- List of recommended software and hardware products

- List of frequently asked questions (FAQs)

- List of upcoming computer training classes

- Self-help and troubleshooting sheets

- Forms for reporting computer-related problems

While your power users can provide you with the information you need, the job of organizing and distributing that information cost-effectively and with minimal disruption is still a challenging task. It is important to have an avenue for all employees to get timely assistance with their computer-related problems. In Chapters 10 and 11, you will learn about available, ready-to-go tools that can help you develop help desk features for your intranet. Again, start by putting static MIS help pages on your intranet. After users are accustomed to getting help from your intranet, install more dynamic and multimedia features to enhance your user's experience.

SALES, MARKETING, AND CUSTOMER SUPPORT

Many organizations currently have a homepage on the Internet. The deployment of corporate Internet homepages has commonly been the responsibility of the marketing, sales, and customer support departments. One reason for this is that customers are finally demanding that organizations be more responsive to their support needs. Customers do not want to be put on hold to obtain product information anymore. Support groups that are not directly involved with the outside world often must go through the marketing and sales staff to be in tune with customer needs. Even among sales and marketing personnel, information sharing is not as fluent as it needs to be.

With the help of an intranet, your customers can become the center of attention. How can you do this? Start putting your customers' comments and most frequently asked questions, by product line, on your sales and marketing homepage, as shown in Figure 3.9. That way, everyone within your organization will see and understand what it is that customers are really saying about your company. Do not be afraid to publish the negative comments on your intranet. You need to let everyone in the organization share the frustration of your customers regarding a low-quality product or service. As you learned in Chapter 2, intranets will transform your organization from a product-centric to a customer-centric organization.

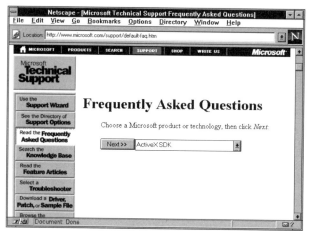

Figure 3.9 A Web page showing frequently asked questions.

Besides customer-related information, your intranet could help you quickly distribute information about your competitor's latest pricing, promotions, and product offerings to your sales staff worldwide. Without an intranet, your staff must wait for a sales meeting to learn about your competitor's latest strategy. The rapid distribution of information to your marketing and sales staff can give you an edge over your competition. If you are a salesperson on the road, you can easily connect to your company's intranet any time and download the latest product sales presentations before seeing your next customer. A centralized repository for sales presentations will help your staff reduce the time necessary for developing sales presentations; consequently, your sales force will spend more time with your customers. The following marketing and sales topics are great candidates for going on your intranet:

- Strategic marketing plans and the general status of market conditions by product line

- Your competitor's strategic updates, press releases, and product introductions

- Competitive analysis reports for your products versus those of your competitors
- Your customers' most frequently asked questions and comments
- Product information and specification sheets
- List of complementary products and services
- Current sales forecast
- List of available sales presentation and training documentation
- Latest sales and marketing help requests

Again, you can see how intranets can decrease your operating costs while increasing the speed of information distribution to your sales and marketing staff worldwide. One of the most dynamic and powerful aspects of an intranet is its ability to expand with changing technology. Unlike your previous information distribution system, your intranet will be able to use the latest technology to help you reduce your sales costs. For example, the future of video conferencing is not as far away as you think. Finally, Internet technology has given telecommunication and multimedia companies a reason to enhance and provide low-priced video conferencing solutions to the masses. In the near future, you will be able to video conference with your sales staff on a worldwide basis. Your intranet will be the storage bank where your sales and marketing staff go to get the latest training materials. No longer will you have to depend on those expensive worldwide sales meetings to communicate your sales and marketing strategy. In addition, you do not have to wait until the next sales meeting to learn what customers in other geographical territories are saying about your products.

INTRANET AND DEVELOPMENT TEAMS

If you thought providing a communication medium for sales and marketing was challenging, you have not spent time in a product development meeting. Companies are spending large sums of money to reduce their product development time in response to shorter product life cycles. With decreasing product life cycles, the success of development teams depends on how well the team members can communicate their needs and problems to one another. In addition to the communication barriers that exist between development team members located across a broad geographical range, your company is also faced with providing a communication medium or forum where team members world wide can get information on demand. Your intranet will help you bring your product development team together quickly and help the team execute on time.

So how can an internal Web do this? Your intranet is the ultimate information bank for your development teams. Team members, through the use of the product development homepage, will have access to old design techniques, as well as the latest technical information. The product development homepage also provides other departments with access to the latest product schedules and requirements. Your product development homepage may have links to the marketing group's homepage so that your team can get the latest competitive data useful in possible product redesign. Your marketing department in return could put a link from their homepage to your product development's homepage so that the sales and marketing staff could stay on top of product design issues. The following information could reside on your product development's homepage:

- Product justification, marketing plan, sales forecast, and competitive analysis information

- Product features and scope of the plan

- Product schedule and resources and their roles

- Product specification and design challenges

- Project milestones and documentation of assumptions

- Ongoing list of issues and concerns resulting from team meetings

- List of receivables and deliverables from and to other departments

- Solutions that worked during the project and those that didn't

How many times during the planning or development phase of a product have you received a call from your manufacturing group asking about a simple attribute of your product? How many times have you had to call your manufacturing organization to get information regarding equipment specifications on the production floor? Your product development's Web page will reduce, if not eliminate, the need for this type of cumbersome information gathering. Again, all of the information listed above could be available in digital form. You will learn in Chapters 8 and 9 how to convert schedules and flow diagrams so that your Web browser could display this information. In the near future, most of the productivity tools will output their content directly to HTML and other standard graphical formats, eliminating the need for many of the current conversion programs.

MANUFACTURING

Often, a manufacturing organization is geographically located far from the research and development centers. Barriers that exist between manufacturing and product development organizations are usually due to the lack of information sharing between the departments. Intranets provide great opportunities to help these organizations share their knowledge with one another and to help decrease the product development cycle time. Using a product development homepage, manufacturing can get involved in the planning stages of a product to optimize its manufacturability. At the same time, development teams can use the manufacturing intranet pages to discover manufacturing problems in advance. Your manufacturing pages could also become the source of information for equipment utilization reports, as well as equipment downtime and maintenance reports.

Currently, most manufacturing organizations depend on hard copy spreadsheet plots and reports to update upper management and other interested parties. These reports are often kept by upper management for future reference. How many times has your manager called you right before an important meeting because he cannot find a specific report? This is when your intranet pages become your most valuable asset. The following list of activity reports could provide your organization with powerful information about your manufacturing capabilities:

- Current production plan

- Product cost variance reports

- Production cycle time per product

- Machine utilization reports

- Shop floor news

- Maintenance activity and machine downtime reports

- Actual throughput versus production throughput

- List of current production training classes

In addition to utilization reports, standard versus actual machine setup and production runtimes will help upper management see what products may be causing your throughput problems. Manufacturing activity reports will provide all of your departments, especially your quality organization, with up-to-date information regarding factors affecting the cost and quality of your products.

PURCHASING, SHIPPING, AND RECEIVING

You often go through the tedious process of purchasing new equipment by calling different departments, obtaining the appropriate forms, filling out the forms, getting signature approvals, giving the paperwork to your purchasing department, and then waiting for the item to arrive. If your company, like many others, does not have an integrated (and expensive) purchasing system, you end up spending days completing this process. When specific items are unavailable or too tedious to order through the in-house purchasing process, you probably short circuit the whole process and buy what you need at the local office supply store.

Yet, buying equipment and services without going through your purchasing department could be quite expensive. By placing the appropriate forms and ordering information on your corporate intranet, you can make ordering easy and convenient, as shown in Figure 3.10.

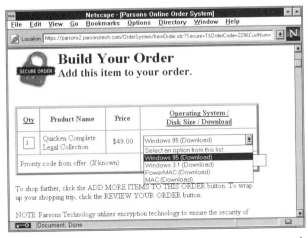

Figure 3.10 A sample of a Web page that demonstrates an intranet purchasing application.

In addition to purchasing information, you can also post your shipping and receiving related information. Shipping departments often look for the best and most affordable carriers to ship documents, equipment, and products. Information regarding the cost of package delivery and pick-up and committed delivery times are appropriate for your intranet page. After putting this static information on your internal Web, you can create a dynamic form to automate the ordering of common products and services. The following items are most suited for your purchasing and shipping/receiving page:

- A list of qualified vendors and consultants
- The process of creating and getting approval for a purchase requisition
- Cost-saving tips
- A list of carriers, pick-up and delivery times
- Various forms

QUALITY

The challenges of producing high-quality, low-cost products and services have made many people re-think the way they perform their jobs. You cannot improve the quality of your services and products with simple inspection plans. Quality has to be ingrained into every aspect of your company's way of doing business. An intranet can help you achieve this by making the quality goals and challenges of the organization available to everyone. Your quality group's homepage should provide the latest quality reports and charts, as well as your competitor's reports and charts.

Your people will respond to your call for continuous improvement and quality initiatives if they can see how the competitor's quality levels compare with their own products and services. In the past, organizations made the task of improving product quality the primary responsibility of quality groups. Using your intranet, your quality group could expand its role by educating all employees on a continuous basis with little cost. Intranets are driving many companies to provide their educational products on-line. Soon your employees will have on-demand access to the latest quality training videos and multimedia products.

However, you do not need to wait for interactive products to start your quality homepage. Begin by putting all of your quality manuals and guidelines on your intranet. Next, add all of your weekly, monthly, quarterly, and yearly quality reports. Currently, your organization may spend thousands of dollars in printing and copying costs to distribute this information to employees. Just look around you, and see how many hard copy quality reports you are sending out every month. Instead of spending your time printing and copying reports, you can convert your charts and graphs directly from your spreadsheet and put them on your intranet homepage. The following is a list of useful topics that you should consider putting on your quality homepage:

- Corporate quality goals
- Periodic quality reports and graphs

- Long- and short-term quality programs

- List of quality related classes and educational guidelines

- Statistical methods and techniques

You should remember that intranets alone cannot improve the quality of your products. Quality must be designed into your product or service. Intranets will provide you with a vehicle whereby you can distribute information to all employees. In the next section, you will learn how intranets can help you implement ISO-9001 standards throughout your organization.

REACHING YOUR ISO-9001 GOALS

Whether your company has a quality system already in place or is considering implementing one, your intranet can make compliance a much easier job. Many companies today are scrambling to beat the competition on the quality front. ISO-9001 certification has become a stated goal for many Fortune 500 companies. For more information on ISO-9001 certification, visit *http://bbs.itsi.disa.mil:5580/E7789T1910,* shown in Figure 3.11.

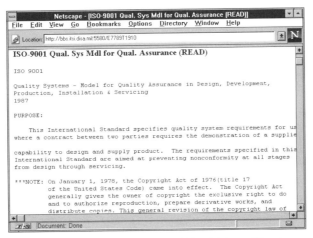

Figure 3.11 Information on ISO-9001 certification.

HOW CAN AN INTRANET HELP?

The ISO-9001 is actually one of several developing standards within the ISO-9000 series which also includes ISO-9002 and ISO-9003. In any of these, there are four major tasks that need to be accomplished:

- Write the quality manual according to ISO guidelines

- Document all ISO required procedures

- Document all work instructions (or "how-to" procedures)

- Provide ready access to the above items

An intranet is an ideal forum for maintaining this type of documentation. Your organization will be able to maintain the latest versions of the quality manual, documented procedures, and work instructions. One way to lose certification is by keeping outdated documentation which could inadvertently be used by someone. Your intranet can be designed so that only the latest approved documentation is made available.

EASING INTO *ISO-9001*

Implementing a quality system like ISO-9001 is a major endeavor requiring months of dedicated commitment from everyone in the organization. Obviously, it is beyond the scope of this book to present this topic other than a brief discussion of its impact on an intranet. If you would like specific information on the ISO standards, please consult:

> American Society for Quality Control
> 611 East Wisconsin Avenue
> Milwaukee, Wisconsin 53202

You may also obtain certification information from:

> National Standards Authority of Ireland
> North American Certification Service
> 5 Medallion Center
> Merrimack, N.H. 03054
> Telephone: 603-424-7070

START THINKING ABOUT AN INTRANET EARLY

The company quality manual is usually the first document that the ISO-bound organization attempts to assemble. This manual addresses the ISO requirements and is subsequently referenced by other departments within the organization. It needs to be maintained by a representative in charge of company quality, and it must be available to all employees.

By publishing your developing quality manual on your intranet, you will be able to encourage employee participation at a very early stage. Successful implementation of ISO-9001 requires the cooperation of all employees, and an intranet can make this aspect much easier to deal with.

Once the company quality manual has been defined, department procedures and work instructions can be derived and published on your intranet. For example, ISO-9001 has specific requirements on how you should document product testing procedures. If your department does testing, the procedures you use must be documented. If you use a piece of equipment, the actions you perform (work instructions) must be posted nearby. All of this documentation can be placed on-line and be ready for immediate access.

WHAT IS ISO-9001?

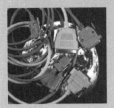 ISO-9001 is a set of standards which must be followed in order to receive an international certification of quality. It attempts to increase product quality by increasing the quality of the processes that produced it. ISO-9001 applies to any industry including hardware and software development, installation, and services. ISO-9001 certification has these principle themes:

- **Records:** Say what you do and record what you do.

- **Responsibilities:** Do what you say.

- **Reviews:** Check and correct what you do.

ISO-9001 certification will give your organization a competitive advantage over other companies which do not have a recognized quality system. In addition, many organizations require that their suppliers and vendors be ISO-9001 certified.

BE READY FOR THE AUDIT

In order to receive ISO certification, your organization needs to be audited by an independent third party certified to perform audits. For example, the National Standards Authority of Ireland travels to a company that is requesting certification and performs a checklist-based verification of compliance. Many companies train in-house auditors to perform preliminary practice audits. By keeping your company's ISO documentation on-line, it becomes much easier to refer to specific procedures and work instructions when requested by the auditors.

During the audit function, it is likely that the auditors will find an instance of noncompliance. An example of noncompliance is missing work instructions for a piece of equipment. The auditor will issue a non-compliance form which itself must be controlled or kept somewhere for easy retrieval. Your intranet again is a perfect solution for placing this documentation on-line.

PUTTING IT ALL TOGETHER

In this Chapter, you have learned how an intranet can be applied to various functional areas within your organization. The key applications that were discussed include:

- ✓ Start with the Chief Executive Officer so that he or she can communicate company issues to all employees.

- ✓ The Human Resources department has a large variety of forms and documentation that can be accessed by all employees via an intranet.

- ✓ Financial and accounting books can be placed within an intranet and made accessible to those who need to use them.

✓ Your Managemnt Information Systems (MIS) department can supplement user support through an online help desk centered within an intranet.

✓ Sales, marketing, and customer support departments can leverage an intranet's ubiquitous presence to provide up-to-the-minute information at any location.

✓ An intranet can provide manufacturing with automatic production data and performance results.

✓ Employees who need to use your company's purchasing, shipping, and receiving departments will be able to transact orders on-line and check for delivery schedules.

✓ An intranet can be an effective tool for instituting a corporate-wide quality system.

VISITING KEY SITES THAT DISCUSS INTRANETS

The World Wide Web is filled with hundreds of excellent and current articles on all aspects of intranets. Use the following sites as starting points for your Web exploration.

INTRANET AUSTRALIA PTY. LTD.

http://www.intra.net.au/

BELL GLOBAL SOLUTIONS

http://www.bellglobal.com/worldlinx.html

INTRANET AUSTRALIA

http://www.intra.net.au/pages/dec_intra.htm

WEBSERVE INTRANET

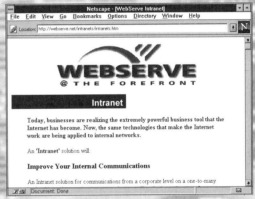

http://webserve.net/intranets/intranets.htm

AT&T INTRANET PROFILE

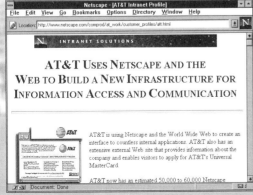

http://www.netscape.com/comprod/at_work/—
customer_profiles/att.html

THE INTERNET COMPANY

http://www.intranet.ca/

INSIDE THE INTRANET

http://techweb.cmp.com/cw/intranet/intranet.htm

BENEFITS OF INTRANET

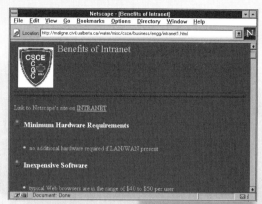

*http://maligne.civil.ualberta.ca/water/misc/csce/
business/engg/intranet1.html*

INTRANET

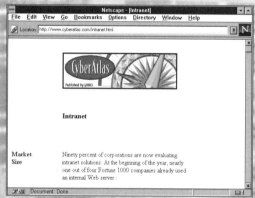

http://www.cyberatlas.com/intranet.html

WINDOWS NT INTRANET SOLUTIONS

*http://www.windowssolutions.com/
WSComm.html*

INTRANET DEVELOPMENT

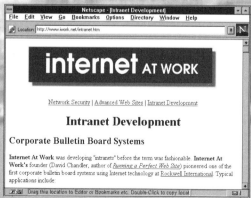

http://www.jwork.net/intranet.htm

BAY NETWORKS

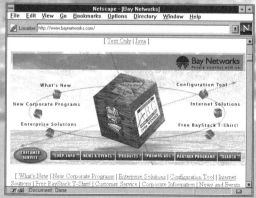

http://www.baynetworks

Chapter 4

Intranets for Your Customers

73

In the previous chapter, you discovered that you can apply intranet technologies to many of your company's internal departments. As a result, those departments can benefit from a more efficient distribution of information and an increased collaboration among various other departments. As you will discover in this chapter, your customers also have much to gain from your intranet. By the time you finish this chapter, you will learn about the following key concepts:

- Your customers may be either internal or external and may have a wide range of skills and expectations.

- By giving customers access to your intranet (or sections of your intranet), you can supplement your customer-support operations.

- There is a fine line between the Internet and an intranet. To provide customers or an outside agency with access to specific data, you can easily expand your intranet to the Internet.

- A *kiosk* is a self-contained browser which can help your customers access your intranet.

- In addition to enhancing customer relations using an intranet, you may improve your supplier and vendor relationships by allowing limited access to your intranet.

- Companies use an intranet as a sales tool in a variety of ways, including kiosks, limited Internet connections, and as a private network for your company's sales force.

WHO IS YOUR CUSTOMER?

Although it is a seemingly obvious step in your intranet development, you must identify your customers before you design the infrastructure to service them. Your intranet will provide an effective tool to your customer only if it fits the customer's needs.

Your intranet may service internal as well as external customers. An internal customer is usually an employee who already has access to your network and is familiar with it. Your internal customers include the CEO, the people in the Human Resources department, managers, and anyone else in the company who depends on the intranet. An external customer is someone with whom your company transacts business. The external customer is a user who may use your intranet only occasionally and may need additional help to get started. Keeping a clear distinction whether a customer is internal or external can help you formulate an appropriate interface to your intranet.

However, throughout this book, we will generally refer to an internal or external customer simply as a customer. As you evaluate your customer, use the following questions to define your user's characteristics:

- What is the level of computing skill you anticipate for an average, high-end, and low-end user?

- Are your customers from a specialized field, or will you have to cater to a wide and varied audience?

- Will your intranet require special codes or passwords for security?

- How familiar are your customers with your company's products and services?

- On average, how often and for how much time will customers use your intranet?

- Will you cater to one-time or long-term users? Or both?

- Will you treat internal customers differently than external customers?

Because your customer will normally access your intranet using a Web browser (such as the Netscape *Navigator*), understanding your typical customer will help you design an effective Web page. The best way to start is to develop a user profile. Your company may already have profile information about your customers, which has been developed over the years from a variety of sources, including questionnaires, surveys, customer studies, as well as statistics on your product categories and who is buying which product.

By anticipating your customer's skill range, you can design an interface that your customer will find familiar and easy to use. For example, you are developing an information kiosk in the main lobby of a children's hospital. Visitors can range from children, to their parents, to medical specialists. In this case, you may want the Web-page layout, as well as its content, to be different, depending on the user. You may want to implement a password system so that a specific set of users can access certain sections of your intranet. The medical specialists in the previous example may need access to medical records and other patient data. By using a password system, you can shield this data from other hospital visitors. Figure 4.1 shows how a variety of different users may want to access the same intranet.

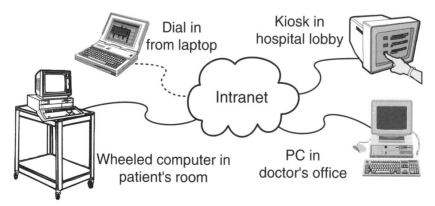

Figure 4.1 *An intranet may need to handle a variety of users.*

A variety of other factors will help you design an effective, customer-friendly intranet. For example, if your typical customer is knowledgeable about your products, you will not need to introduce the user to your products and services. Likewise, busy customers may not be willing to spend time traversing a slow or difficult intranet. If your customers visit your intranet on a regular basis, you may want to give your intranet pages a shortcut key that expert users can use to skip sections they don't need to access.

WHY LET YOUR CUSTOMERS ACCESS YOUR INTRANET?

By letting your customers and other parties access specific areas within your intranet, you can provide them with an immediate level of support for very specific situations. Because intranets work much like the Internet, your customers will have little or no trouble navigating the point-and-click, Web-browser interaction. Although your customers are actually limited to your intranet pages (granted, you may also provide the customer with full Internet access from within your intranet), their experience will be the same as that of surfing the Web. External customers who may need to access your intranet include:

- Customers who physically come to your location and need electronic help or information.

- Vendors who maintain a special account on your intranet to assist in bidding, billing, and advertising new products.

- Buyers who may need regular updates on your inventory levels or latest order fulfillments.

- Service contractors who can use your intranet to log time-and-service charges.

- Visitors and guests who can sign an electronic guest book when entering and leaving your company's "virtual offices."

WHEN YOUR INTRANET GROWS INTO THE INTERNET

Because the hardware and software that runs the Internet is essentially the same as the hardware and software that runs intranets, the line that separates the two easily blurs. As you have learned, the main difference is that the Internet is visible to anyone in the world, while an intranet can only be seen by specific users (generally, employees and customers of the company that owns the intranet).

As you learned in Chapter 1, the computer which maintains your intranet files is a server. For an intranet, the server is normally some computer in your company that is connected to your in-house network, but not necessarily connected to the rest of the world. To convert your intranet to an Internet-accessible network, you must do one of two things: either move your server files to a computer that is capable of communicating to the Internet or, as shown in Figure 4.2, add an additional network card to your current server and connect it directly to the Internet.

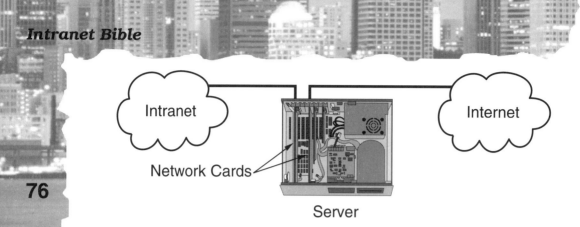

Figure 4.2 Your server acting as a gateway between two separate networks.

Every HTML-based file you create for your intranet will work fine on the Internet. The procedures and techniques your users perform to access your files will not change. Perhaps the only immediate difference is security. After you connect to the Internet, you may want to "password protect" certain material that was previously open to anyone on your intranet. Security is an important topic that you will learn more about in Chapter 19, "Intranet Security Issues."

USING A KIOSK

To access your intranet pages, your customers need access to a computer. In some cases, you may let your customers dial-in to your network over a modem. At other times, the customers who come to your site must use public-access computers that reside on your premises. Depending on your company's customer traffic, you may decide to install a bank of computers and desks in a special visitor's room. Another approach is to scatter special, self-contained systems, called *kiosks*, about your organization. Kiosks are not new; they are used for many applications from selling hot dogs to printing greeting cards. For the purpose of providing your customers with intranet access, a kiosk is a small, free-standing enclosure containing a computer running a Web browser.

The Web kiosk is a terrific solution to the need for delivering intranet access to the general public. For example, as a mall operator, you can place Web kiosks and customer-assistance booths throughout the mall that let you dispense store information. Assume a mall customer is looking for a particular coffee machine. After a few keystrokes, and possibly a few mouse clicks (or screen touches), your intranet will produce a printout of the stores that carry the item. Remember, the software to do this is already available and is very inexpensive to install and maintain.

KIOSKS AND TINY INTRANETS

You can further simplify your kiosk by putting all the server files on the same machine running the browser (that is, the kiosk's computer itself). If the server files are local to the kiosk, you will not need any network for this tiny intranet. Other than a source of electricity to power the system, you don't need a modem or a network connection. Instead, you just wheel the kiosk to a location and plug it in!

Keep in mind that you can connect a kiosk to a network just as you would any computer. Some pros and cons of a network connection to a kiosk include:

- A network connection lets you constantly update server files (such as store information, the office directory, and so on). On the other hand, you must manually update a kiosk that is not connected to the network.

- A network connection provides the option of connecting the kiosk to the Internet, or other networks. You might, for example, connect one mall's kiosk to that of another mall to help customers locate products which the first mall does not carry.

- A kiosk that is connected to a network can continuously send activity reports back to a database which your sales, marketing, and customer service representatives can analyze.

- A network-based kiosk that allows on-line merchandise selling can use software on the network to perform credit-card validation.

You can generally get by with a non-networked kiosk if it is intended to dispense static information only. However, if you need more advanced customer interactions, such as taking orders, interactive help, and so on, you will want to connect your kiosk to a network.

KEEPING THE INTERFACE SIMPLE FOR EVERYONE

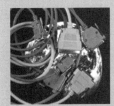

As you have learned earlier in this chapter, having an accurate customer profile can help you design a successful set of Web pages. After you profile your potential customers, you must integrate your findings into the construction of your Web pages. Some interface issues you should consider include:

- Using the same language styles as used by your customer. For example, a Web page designed for lawyers to look up cases should use descriptive language that is typically used by legal professionals. Likewise, a kiosk used to help customers find a music CD within a store might use sound clips.

- If your Web page addresses a variety of skill levels, make sure you provide a skill selector button. Based on the user's skill-level selection, you should adjust your presentation to match the intended audience.

- Regardless of the skill level, your Web site must provide the customer with on-line help. Frustrated customers go elsewhere for solutions.

- Regardless of how simple and trouble free you believe your site to be, you should provide an option that lets customers reach a person when they are having trouble. Your site's "human access" can be as simple as a phone number or directions to a manned help desk within your company.

- As you design your Web pages, ask several of your potential users to help "beta test" the pages. Beta testing is the process of testing an unfinished product to identify errors, as well as areas for improvement.

- As you test your Web pages, make sure your new intranet pages transition and load quickly enough for the planned hardware. If your pages use many images and or perform extensive user interaction, your pages may run annoyingly slow on an older computer.

- Don't overuse cute sounds and loud speaking prompts and announcements. Most users do not like what appears to be a condescending tone. In addition, some users may be embarrassed when spoken to by a machine in a public place.

USING AN INTRANET TO IMPROVE SUPPLIER AND VENDOR RELATIONSHIPS

As briefly discussed, you can and should use your intranet to support company recommended vendors and suppliers. For example, outside vendors who maintain special accounts on your intranet can use your resources to assist them in placing bids for equipment and services, for billing, and for advertising new products, which the rest of your organization may desire.

Assume that your company uses XYZ, Inc. as its office supplies vendor. The XYZ representative might sponsor a special Web page on your intranet that presents XYZ's products and pricing. Your employees, in turn, might use this page to view these products and perform on-line ordering. The intranet could collect the orders and forward them to your purchasing department who, in turn, could forward the orders to XYZ, Inc. Using pages on your intranet, XYZ, Inc. saves money for catalog distribution and selling expenses, while your company benefits from streamlined order processing. Figure 4.3 illustrates an on-line catalog.

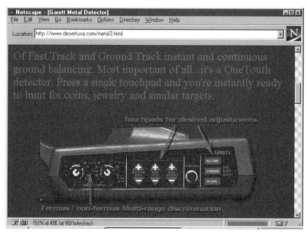

Figure 4.3 A sample of an on-line catalog page.

As more companies put their products and services on the Internet, more electronic catalogs are becoming available. Your vendor may suggest that you link your intranet directly to its pre-existing Internet catalog. You could do this. But if your company is a major account with the vendor, you may convince your vendor to build a custom catalog specifically for your employees. The major benefit of the custom catalog is that your company maintains control of the ordering process by keeping the orders in-house. Other advantages of having an in-house intranet catalog include:

- The in-house catalog is convenient for your employees—available products and services are always a few mouse clicks away.

- Your employees see only the latest price lists.

- Your company can restrict the catalog's contents to only company-approved products and services.

- Your purchasing department can analyze and approve all orders.

- The intranet can automatically generate expense breakdowns by department.

- The intranet can automatically hold small orders until they can be combined with other in-house orders to obtain volume discounts from the vendor.

- Your company's use of the in-house catalog may improve your possibility of obtaining preferred-vendor status.

- The in-house catalog provides the vendor with an opportunity to showcase its products to your employees.

UNLEASH YOUR INTRANET AS A SALES GENERATOR

For certain applications, you can think of a Web kiosk as a vending machine. Customers walk up to a snack machine, press a selector button, authorize payment by entering coins, and receive a product. If your company sells a service or product which customers can order electronically, an intranet kiosk may increase your sales.

Many companies already are trying to sell products over the Internet, but the results have been mostly disappointing. It turns out that customers tend to be shy about ordering over the Internet. It is likely that customers fear that the Net does not safely transfer credit-card numbers. In addition, because anyone can establish a store front on the Internet, some customers may have an uneasy feeling that they are dealing with an unreliable operation.

Unlike an Internet on-line ordering service, customers must physically come to your intranet location to place their order. Because customers can come to your building, they see that your company is real. Your ordering room, for example, might use intranet-based kiosks surrounded by physical samples of the products your customers are thinking of ordering. In this way, your customers can see, smell, and touch products before placing an order.

For example, assume you operate a department store. Using a kiosk, you can spread your store's presence around town by connecting the kiosk to your intranet. A kiosk does not take up much space, and many small business owners welcome the extra traffic and cash that a kiosk rental space provides them. In some cases, your kiosk need not take orders to succeed. You could design the kiosk to show today's special sales and entice customers to come to the main store.

USING AN INTRANET FOR CUSTOMER SUPPORT

In many cases, an intranet has worked so well for employees that the company expanded its intranet to the Internet, allowing customers to benefit from it as well. For example, for many years, companies like UPS (*http://www.ups.com*) and FedEx (*http://www.fedex.com*) have used a network to let their employees track package movement for their customers. When a customer calls asking about a package, a representative simply enters the tracking code into a computer and tells the customer the package location. Today, customers can also use their own computers to access the shipping company's Web site to find out about their packages directly from the shipper's computer.

Another example of using Web pages to provide customer support is the Bank of America Web site (*http://www.bankamerica.com*), as shown in Figure 4.4. At this site, customers can enter their checking account numbers and passwords to get a complete on-line statement, showing cleared checks, payments, deposits, and so on. Although this is an Internet-based system, you could take advantage of the same capabilities within your intranet, except that your customers would come to your physical location to transact their business.

Figure 4.4 *Bank of America's on-line bank.*

Using an Intranet within a Store

Whether your application involves a small mom-and-pop operation or a major multi-national chain store, customer satisfaction remains the key to a successful business. A great way to support your sales force and to make shopping a more pleasant experience is by giving your customers access to your intranet. Your customers may either walk into your store and use a strategically placed Web kiosk or dial into your intranet via modem. In either case, you effectively expand the extent of your sales force, while providing customers with the information that they need.

Customer Satisfaction Surveys

Surveys are notoriously expensive to administer, yet they provide extremely valuable information to any business. Terrific sales last quarter is one measure of running a business correctly, but knowing why your sales were so strong can be elusive. A customer satisfaction survey can tell you why people are coming to your store rather than the competitor's store down the street. Your store may have better parking, friendlier sales people, a safer neighborhood, or perhaps a superior returns policy. Knowing what influences your customers can help you price your products, adjust your services, and increase revenues.

An intranet can collect this information in a direct survey or as a series of optional questions at the end of each on-line order form, as shown in Figure 4.5. A simple question like, "Where did you see this product advertised?" can help you concentrate your advertising dollars in the most effective areas.

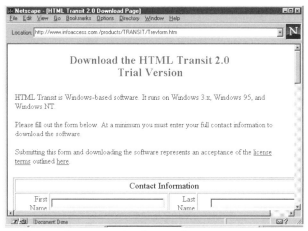

Figure 4.5 *A sample of an on-line customer survey.*

UPCOMING SALES AND SPECIAL EVENTS

You might use your intranet-based kiosk as a bargain hunter's paradise. For example, on your kiosk, you might publish special sales events, special pricing, and even provide coupons which the customer can take to the register. You might also convert the standard flyer that your store mails out to local residences to an electronic form that your kiosk displays. In Chapters 8, 13, and 15, you will learn how to convert your advertising to a format users can view on your intranet.

PRODUCT INFORMATION

Many companies (perhaps yours) use the Internet today to showcase their products and to provide potential customers with detailed product specifications and available services. Your intranet can do the same, using essentially the same Web files and software. Using your intranet, your customers can come into your store and peruse the entire inventory. You can provide search parameters for maximum prices, desired features, desired manufacturers, and so on. For example, consider the customer who walks into an electronics store looking for a fax machine. Your intranet can supplement your sales force by giving the customer the opportunity to pin down the exact model of fax machine he or she wants to buy.

Many larger department stores maintain a bridal registry as a service to their customers. The bride and groom input the items that they need and wish to receive; those attending the wedding simply access this list on your intranet and know both what to buy and what has already been purchased. Your intranet can be easily designed to accept customers' names and the presents they will be bringing to the event. In addition, you can configure the Web page to offer suggestions (especially if the present has already been taken). This is a great time saver to a very specific group of customers. Figures 4.6a, 4.6b and 4.6c illustrate several Web sites that let customers search for the products they desire.

Figure 4.6a *Southwest Airlines.*   **Figure 4.6b** *Domino's Pizza.*   **Figure 4.6c** *Ticketmaster.*

USING AN INTRANET WITHIN A PROFESSIONAL OFFICE

Professional offices, such as doctors' and lawyers' offices, often suffer from paper log jams. As anyone who has been at a doctor's office can see, much of the record keeping still happens on paper. These offices are generally too small to invest in large database servers and typically do not have the expertise to administer such software. Within such an office, an intranet not only stream-lines office operations, but provides customers with service opportunities not previously offered.

CUSTOMER ACCESS TO RECORDS

Storing records electronically provides easy access for customers as well as office personnel. By using an intranet within a professional office, clients can review their own files. For example, rather than waste an attendant's time physically pulling records off a shelf, the customer can make inquiries directly through a dial-in modem or kiosk. Of course, you can limit what information you make available and restrict access through the use of passwords. As more professional offices come on-line, interoffice record sharing will take the place of transporting files by courier.

FEE SCHEDULE AND AVAILABLE SERVICES

In addition to providing customers with access to their records, your office can use the intranet to publish a schedule of fees and services. Providing this schedule for your customers can mini-mize surprises and embarrassment. In addition, you can provide scheduling software that lets customers select appointment times that match your schedule. Using an electronic speaking voice, your intranet can automatically call your clients in advance to remind them of their scheduled appointments. Automating the appointment scheduling function is a time and money saver that will free your staff for other office duties.

TRADE JOURNALS AND NEWSLETTERS

While your in-house staff can certainly appreciate up-to-the-minute trade information, your cus-tomers may enjoy reading your private newsletter. You can publish one over your intranet and have clients read it at their leisure. In fact, depending on the services your business provides, you might use a newsletter as a selling tool, reminding patients of the need to get a flu shot, or inves-tors of the need to update their trust or tax shelters.

USING AN INTRANET WITHIN A SCHOOL

As you may already know, most schools have an Internet site which they use to communicate their course information and school services to both potential and existing students. For example, San Diego State University's Web site, shown in Figure 4.7 provides visitors with information about:

- Campus maps and directories
- Academic programs for each college and department
- Admissions, class schedules, and course descriptions
- Student activities and profiles
- Athletic and social events

Figure 4.7 San Diego State University homepage.

Most schools, including San Diego State University, use the Internet primarily for information distribution in the form of one-to-many. That is, one source of information is disseminated to many recipients. In theory, such educational establishments exist to share information and experience using give-and-take interactions which result from group thinking. An intranet is a perfect medium to extend this experience throughout the campus. By allowing such user interactions, the intranet will transition the current communications model from the one-to-many Internet to the many-to-many intranet.

By moving a school's Internet site toward an intranet, students and teachers can access the information they need, when they need it. For example, teachers must no longer make copies of class materials for distribution. Using the school's intranet, students can access class materials at any time. Professors, in turn, can use multimedia presentation software applications, such as Microsoft *PowerPoint*, to develop their class material and then place the course materials on the school's intranet. In Chapter 9, "Images and HTML," you will learn how to convert PowerPoint presentations to HTML format for inclusion on an intranet.

Extending the concept of information sharing, students can develop a personal homepage and share their ideas and talents with other students and faculty. In Chapter 3, you learned how an employee's personal homepage can be a valuable resource for shared information. Students can use a homepage to promote their skills to potential employers. Using a search engine, employers can search for students that have specific skills. A personal homepage will help students organize an on-line profile and resume that will reap benefits as the world marches towards its dependence on network connectivity.

Another use of school intranets is for student communications involving school issues. Currently, most schools publish a daily newspaper. Intranets will eventually replace a school's daily newspaper. Using school intranets, students can publish articles, search for jobs, use classifieds to buy and sell, and promote their services to other students.

While most schools are moving forward with their Internet projects, there are enormous opportunities for cutting costs in various departments within any school. Schools are in the business of teaching and not of filing forms and processing papers. Given the current pressure to decrease school budgets, schools can aggressively cut printing costs by developing electronic versions of all current paper media.

Another benefit of using intranets is that schools can migrate toward teaching classes over the Internet. Such on-line teaching requires the same steps performed by companies who develop and use training classes across their private intranets. Such on-line classes could provide schools with an additional income stream and reach markets far beyond their traditional boundaries. In the next three to five years, real-time audio and video technology will make intranets an ideal tool for reaching large numbers of students. Students can also engage in discussion over school intranets and participate in lively two-way discussions.

Security is always an issue for intranets, especially if you allow users the ability to review their grades, school standing, or other personal data. Currently, many professors post student grades outside their offices using student identification numbers. One approach to security and privacy is to extend this simple coded method to the intranet. Students would access the professor's grade list and look up their grades listed by student number. The school's intranet should provide students, faculty, and staff with the ability to perform the following operations:

- Distribute school directories, schedules, and forms electronically
- Distribute class notes and study guides electronically
- Create an interactive information sharing environment
- Reduce printing cost in all departments
- Develop off-campus educational courses
- Help students market their skills to companies

USING INTRANETS WITHIN GOVERNMENT AGENCIES

If you have ever surfed the Net, you may have come across the White House site located at *http://www.whitehouse.gov*. Increasingly, government agencies are distributing information on the Internet to reduce costs and improve customer service; however, most government agencies can cut their operational costs by deploying intranets for their internal customers. Like a company, a government agency depends on the collective knowledge of its employees to service the public. When it comes to budgetary pressures, government agencies are more likely to cut their services rather than investing in new technology to cut their expenses. Using intranets, government agencies can process forms automatically to reduce the cost of printing and processing.

After different departments begin using intranets to share information, the departments can eventually open their internal Web sites to the public, allowing people to avoid unnecessary trips to government offices. As it turns out, government has been quick to embrace the Internet for the purpose of information distribution and the posting of forms. Institutions, from state governments to the Federal government (see Figure 4.8) and from the Department of Motor Vehicles to the Internal Revenue Service, all have publicly available Web sites. The following site list defines a few government sites you may want to visit.

Figure 4.8a http://www.—
whitehouse.gov

Figure 4.8b http://www.—
irs.ustreas.gov

Figure 4.8c http://www.—
ca.gov/dmv/dmv.html

Figure 4.8d http://www.ca.gov

Figure 4.8e http://www.census.gov

Figure 4.8f http://www.—
sandiego.org

INTRANETS FOR SMALL OFFICES AND BUSINESSES

If your company consists of fewer than 50 people and they are all located in one office, the usefulness of an intranet may not be as evident as it is for a larger office. For a small office, an intranet may provide an effective interface to various databases, such as customer, vendor, or policy information. As far as making an impact on communications between employees, the benefits increase as the number of employees increase.

If you are a small business that belongs to a larger organization, intranets can greatly help you improve your operation. For example, if you own a franchise store and need to share information with a corporate office, an intranet is your answer. Using intranets, franchise stores can share issues with one another and help the entire enterprise service customers more effectively. As a franchise owner, you can create a homepage and market your products and services to both your internal and external customers. As a corporate marketing executive, you can use your intranet to quickly provide information on the latest products and factors that may affect their profitability to all the stores in your system. Intranets bring the concept of a virtual corporation closer to reality. With intranets, a community of small business owners can develop cooperative strategies to compete against larger corporations and to provide better customer service.

Mail Boxes Etc. Case Study

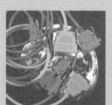 In May 1996, Mail Boxes Etc. (MBE) announced the grand opening of its newly developed World Wide Web site on the Internet. Mail Boxes Etc., located in San Diego, California, is the world's largest franchiser of neighborhood postal, business, and communications service centers. With 3,000 franchise centers worldwide, MBE's corporate headquarters faces the daily challenge of information dissemination to its franchise centers located in close to 50 countries.

In the past, MBE used a combination of printed materials, traditional mail, and a private network system to distribute information and to communicate with its centers. The network system lets MBE centers and headquarters communicate using e-mail and text-based message services. Each time one of the centers dialed in to the network, the center incurred a long distance phone charge. With 3,000 existing centers and approximately 350 new centers opening each year, the need to improve communication while reducing costs became increasingly important to MBE.

MBE decided to establish a Web site on the Internet to provide information and services to its customers and MBE centers. In March of 1996, MBE began the development of its Web site with the help of Digital West Media, Inc., a San Diego-based Web-publishing company. The MBE Web site took two months to produce and spans more than 100 pages. MBE's Web site is maintained on a Windows NT server using Netscape *Commerce Server* software. The server is connected to the Internet with a T-1 line which is located at MBE corporate headquarters. MBE's Web site provides information and services to four distinct groups of customers:

- The MBE franchise network

- MBE customers

- Investors and stockholders

- Potential franchisees

Figure 4.9 illustrates the MBE Web site.

*Figure 4.9 MBE's Web site located at **http://www.mbe.com**.*

MBE's Web site is a marketing tool, as well as an access point for MBE Franchise owners to connect to MBE's intranet. MBE's intranet, called *MBE Web*, is accessible only by MBE franchise owners and approved vendors. The *MBE Web* homepage offers seven categories of information:

- Purchasing

- News and Updates

- Marketing and Public Relations

- Meetings and Conventions

- MBE University

- Center Support

- Human Resources

The MBE Web site is an intranet that contains corporate information, news, marketing materials, convention schedules, and vendor information for approved MBE franchise owners. In addition to the old network system, which provided only text-based information, franchise owners can access *MBE Web* to obtain information that includes pictures, animation, and interactive features. For example, if franchise owners need copies of MBE's logo for a special promotion or copies of the most current press release, they can download the logo or press release from a media library located on *MBE Web*. The media library contains graphics, images, and other media that pertain to the various promotions and campaigns that MBE creates for franchise owners.

Franchise owners access the information on the intranet on an as-needed basis. MBE Headquarters no longer needs to mail or distribute certain information, since the information exists on the Web site and is accessible to all of its franchises.

MBE's intranet also serves as a two-way communication channel between MBE Headquarters and franchise owners. Franchise owners can fill out forms and send messages to the various departments at MBE Headquarters over the intranet. For example, MBE's Marketing Department may want feedback from the franchises on how a specific promotion was received by customers. Franchise owners can use the intranet to provide feedback as soon as they receive it from their customers. This enhances communication between MBE Headquarters, franchises, and their customers. Figure 4.10 shows the main page of the MBE Web.

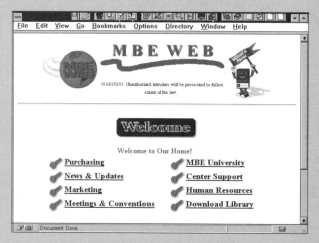

Figure 4.10 The homepage located on the MBE Web.

The public section of the MBE Web site contains a database of MBE center locations that can be searched by customers to locate the MBE centers in their area. Users can search for an MBE center by city, state or zip code, as shown in Figure 4.11.

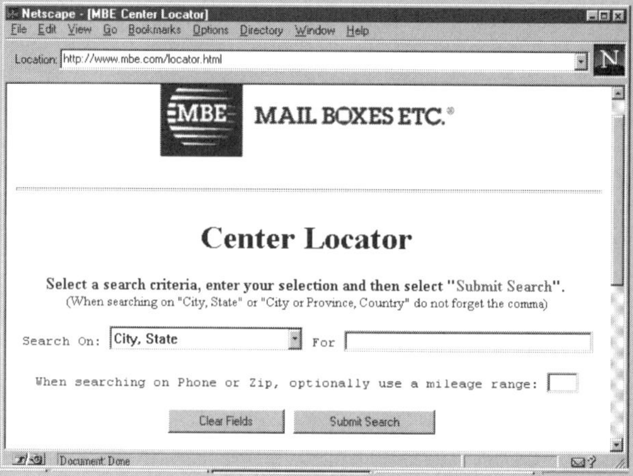

Figure 4.11 The MBE center locator.

Investors can obtain a wealth of information about MBE stock and financial performance from the Investor Relations section of the MBE Web site. The Investor Relations section contains MBE's annual report, financial releases, quarterly reports, and other financial information. You can even click on a NASDAQ link to obtain a current stock quote, as shown in Figure 4.12.

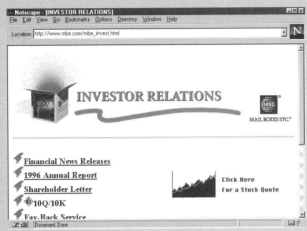

Figure 4.12 The Investor Relations menu located on MBE's Web site.

Individuals interested in owning an MBE franchise can apply for a license directly from the Web site. An e-mail application form is located in the Franchising Opportunities section of the Web site, as shown in Figure 4.13. Franchising Opportunities contains two sections: domestic and international. The international section contains profiles on various countries, including contact information. Some of the international applications are displayed in the country's native language.

According to Eric DeSio, international systems analyst for MBE, "Without advertising or promotional support, the company has received approximately five applications per day from potential franchisees since the site came online in mid-May."

Figure 4.13 Franchising request form.

Customers can learn about the many services offered by MBE Centers throughout the world. The Web site contains information on customer services, corporate services, and current promotions. For example, customers can visit *The Public Eye* section of the Web site to find out if any coupons and specials are being offered by participating MBE Centers. Another valuable feature of MBE's Web site is the Small Office/Home Office (SOHO) resource located under The Customer Services section. The SOHO resource includes information for small business owners, including a description and membership form for the SOHO association, as shown in Figure 4.14.

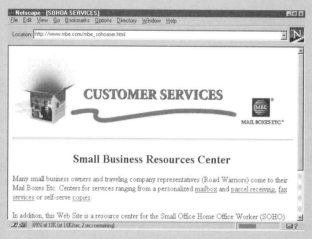

Figure 4.14 *The Small Business Resources Center located on MBE's Web site.*

THE REAL ESTATE INDUSTRY

Another potential beneficiary of intranets are real estate agencies. Using an intranet, a real estate office can provide agents and clients with images and videos of properties across a wide geographical area. Clients can use the private intranet to quickly search for properties that match their criteria. The intranet would also provide agents with the ability to communicate their needs to other agents, which will improve the effectiveness of the sales force.

By providing potential clients with a password, clients can remotely scan private listings of homes at their convenience. An intranet enables a real estate office to differentiate its services from those of its competitors. In addition to information about homes, the real estate office can provide clients with the ability to perform financial calculations on-line, using a mortgage calculator and on-line amortization schedule, as well as the ability to calculate specific purchasing and ownership costs related to any particular home or property.

A growing number of real estate related sites are on the Internet. If you are considering setting up an intranet within your own real estate office, you may want to visit these sites for ideas on services that you can provide to your customers:

- *http://www.coldwellbanker.com*

- *http://www.rextra.com*

- *http://www.listinglink.com*
- *http://www.realtor.com*
- *http://www.hsh.com/today.html*
- *http://www.bankrate.com*

INTRANETS FOR THE HEALTH CARE INDUSTRY

If you have been following the business news, you are probably aware of the pressures on the health care industry to cut costs. The use of intranets will enable a health care organization to process forms electronically, to make patient information available to everyone within the enterprise, and to focus the organization's information flow on the customer. Intranets will allow such organizations to connect their older (sometimes called legacy) systems to PCs, Macs, and other work stations on the network. Using an intranet, doctors can electronically share information (including x-rays, ultrasounds, and EKGs) with other doctors.

In smaller communities, doctors may use an intranet to better compete against larger health care organizations. Today, many independent doctors find it difficult to afford increasing data-processing costs. Using an intranet, doctors can develop universal client-server applications and distribute the cost among a group of doctors. Until now, the incompatibility of computer systems and operating systems has prevented independent doctors from creating such useful collaborative computing systems. With an intranet, doctors can share patient information, make appointments for their patients, help patients with frequently asked questions, and market their specialties more effectively.

USING AN INTRANET WITHIN A THEME PARK

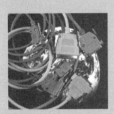 As you have learned, Intranets can be well suited for a wide-variety of tasks, from large organizations, to even theme parks, such as Disneyland. Theme parks are a natural application for intranets. Here, you have a variety of people who at least once during their stay may need information or service. By supplementing your manned information booths with unmanned kiosks, you can increase the presence of your customer service staff.

By setting up a lost and found page, your guests can register lost items and match them with items already found. Even after the guest leaves for the day, you can provide a dial-in line for them to check from home days later.

As guests walk up to kiosks scattered throughout the park, they can sign up for a guided tour. Rather than have preset schedules for tours, you can establish a guided tour when enough customers request one. Your intranet can determine how many customers are signing on and provide a real-time estimate of when and where the next tour will take place.

In addition, your intranet can contain an up-to-date daily schedule of events, last minute closures, and suggestions for alternative attractions. You can also tailor an itinerary, based on each customer's profile, and print it out to guide them during their stay. For example, elderly visitors can be given a schedule which minimizes sun exposure and is timed at a slower pace through specific attractions they may enjoy. Teenagers can be given a fast-paced schedule of suggested attractions and places to stop for snacks.

Your intranet can provide a multimedia combination of sights and sounds showing behind-the-scenes information on every attraction. You can also provide a personal insight of the park's employees and how they help make your park an enjoyable place to visit.

Your intranet can also be a major part of the attraction. The possibilities for prizes and games are endless. You can start by rewarding random users a prize to encourage people to try the kiosk's services. You can also set up special kiosks dedicated for game playing between users of other kiosks within the park. Internet-type games are beginning to appear, and you will be able to apply them to your intranet. Figure 4.15a, 4.15b, and 4.15c illustrate the Web sites for several popular theme parks.

Figure 4.15a http://www.— disneyland.com   *Figure 4.15b http://www.— sixflags.com*   *Figure 4.15c http://4ad— venture.com/*

PUTTING IT ALL TOGETHER

An intranet is a cost-effective way to give your customers the support they need, when they need it. This chapter provided you with an overview of several ways an intranet can enhance the quality of your customer support. As you have learned, intranets are well suited for a wide variety of tasks. In Chapter 5, you will examine the various pieces that make up an intranet. Before you move on to Chapter 5, however, make sure you understand the following key concepts:

✓ Your intranet customers may be internal or external.

✓ To design successful intranet pages, you must first understand your customer profiles.

✓ Successful intranet pages adjust automatically to the user's skill level.

✓ You should make an intranet a vital part of your customer service.

✓ Depending on your needs, you can easily extend an intranet on to the Internet.

✓ Kiosks are free-standing units that house a Web browser. You can use kiosks as a cost-effective and secure way to provide customers access to your intranet.

✓ Intranets may improve your relationship with vendors and suppliers by providing them a convenient forum into your organization.

✓ Many applications exist for intranets, in stores, professional offices, hospitals, schools, government, and more.

VISITING KEY SITES THAT DISCUSS INTRANETS

The World Wide Web is filled with hundreds of excellent and current articles on all aspects of intranets. Use the following sites as starting points for your Web exploration.

FRONTIER TECHNOLOGIES

http://www.frontiertech.com/

3COM

http://www.3com.com/

FIRST WEBMASTER

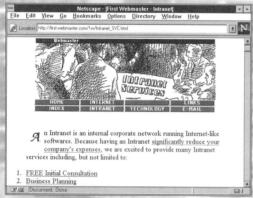

http://first-webmaster.com/1w/Intranet_SVC.html

IBM INTRANET

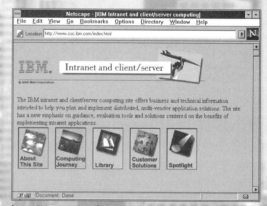

http://www.csc.ibm.com/index.html

JUMP START YOUR I-NETS

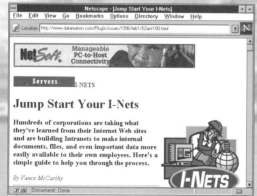

http://www.datamation.com/PlugIn/issues/—
1996/feb1/02ant100.html

AXIS MEDIA GROUP

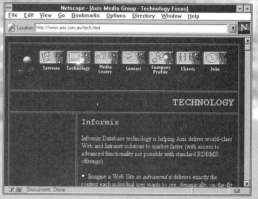

http://www.axis.com.au/tech.html

Chapter 5

Understanding Intranet Components

As you learned in Chapter 1, intranets are based on Internet technology—built primarily around the TCP/IP protocol. Currently, MIS managers must choose between competing technologies that make their company's use of the Internet and an intranet possible. At the heart of these decisions are the issues of browsers, Netscape's *Navigator* versus Microsoft's *Internet Explorer*, and server operating systems, Unix versus NT. In addition, companies must select a network operating system, typically Novell Corporation's *NetWare* or Microsoft Windows NT. Even though the Internet technology is based on open-system standards, the components you choose to build your internal Web affect the overall performance of your intranet.

In this chapter, you will learn how to choose components that will serve both your short- and long-term intranet needs. This chapter's goal is not to teach you everything you must know to select the right software and hardware platform for your intranet. Instead, this chapter builds on the previous chapters to provide you with information you can use to further *evaluate* your company's intranet needs. In addition, this chapter also examines some of the costs associated with various intranet components. In Chapter 15, you will learn how to determine your company's return on investment for deploying an intranet. Therefore, take notes as you go through this chapter and build an inventory of what types of hardware and software your company supports today, and what your company plans to support in the near and distant future. By the time you finish this chapter, you will understand the following key concepts:

- An intranet requires a network operating system (NOS) that supports the TCP/IP protocol.

- Internet server software runs on a variety of hardware platforms.

- You must select a browser that will let users view your intranet's content from Unix-, Windows-, Mac-, and OS/2-based client systems.

- Many Internet-server software packages are available for different computers, servers, platforms, and various operating systems.

- Which intranet components you select will depend on your company's size, level of computer expertise, user needs, and future intranet expansion plans.

AN INTRANET'S BUILDING BLOCKS

As you learned in Chapter 1, the elements that comprise the Internet are the same as those you will use for your intranet. To use the Web, you must have a computer (or computer network) connected to the Internet, as well as a browser. To establish an intranet, you need the following components:

- A computer network for resource sharing.

- A network operating system that supports the TCP/IP protocol.

- A *server computer* that can run an Internet server.

- Server software that supports HyperText Transport Protocol (HTTP) requests from browsers.

- Desktop *client computers* running network software capable of sending and receiving TCP/IP packet data.

- Browser software for various client computers.

Figure 5.1 illustrates these intranet components.

Web Browser	Netscape Navigator Internet Explorer
WEB Client Machines	Unix, PC, Mac
WEB Server Software	Netscape Enterprise Microsoft I.I.S.
WEB Server Operating System	Unix, NT, Netware, Win 95, Mac
Network Protocols	TCP/IP - IPX/SPX
Network Operating System	Unix, NT, Netware, OS/2
Server Hardware	Unix, PC, Mac
Network Technology	Ethernet, IBM Token Ring
Physical Network	Star, Bus, Ring Topologies

Figure 5.1 Intranet building blocks.

In addition to these software and hardware requirements, you must know how to create hypertext markup language (HTML) documents which provide your intranet's content. You will learn how to create HTML documents for your intranet in Chapters 7 through 10. If you decide that you do not want to use an internal server within your company, you can use an Internet Service Provider (ISP) to house your intranet. For example, if you are part of an independent physicians group, you will need the services of an ISP if you do not have a business location where you can locate your intranet server. Normally, the services of an ISP are necessary for various groups and individuals that belong to virtual corporations.

A COMPUTER NETWORK

The first requirement in establishing an intranet is a computer network. A *computer network* is a collection of computers, usually connected by cables. (You can also create a computer network using wireless technologies, but this is much less common.) Today, most computer networks are local-area networks (LANs) which reside within one office building. Most LANs are based on the client–server computing model which uses a central, often dedicated, computer called the server to fulfill client requests.

UNDERSTANDING THE CLIENT–SERVER MODEL

As you have learned, network communication requires a network connection between two or more computers. A network connection consists of the two communicating computers, as well as the path between them. The client–server computing model divides network communication into two sides: the client side and the server side. By definition, the client requests information or services from the server. The server, in turn, responds to the client's requests. At first, you may find it difficult to determine which side of a connection is the client and which side is the server. In many cases, each side of a client–server connection can perform both client and server functions.

Network servers let people share files electronically, send and receive e-mail, and share printers. In addition, network servers normally provide a storage area to backup client files and to run programs that reside only on the server. Server applications provide specific services. Usually, this service is beneficial to all network users or at least to those in a specific industry, business, or group. For example, a distributed database provides airlines with reservation information. The airline reservation system uses a server process that provides access to all distributed databases. This server is useful across the network to the entire airline industry. Likewise, a corporate-wide e-mail system typically uses a server process that is accessible from any computer within the company's network.

A server application (or server process) usually initializes itself and then goes to sleep, spending much of its time simply waiting for a request from a client application. An interactive request from a network computer user usually activates a client application. Typically, a client process will transmit a request (across the network) for a connection to the server, then request some type of service through the connection. For example, the *Telnet* client program will send a request to login to a remote host computer. In this case, the *Telnet* client sends its request to a *Telnet* server application.

CLIENT SOFTWARE ON THE WEB

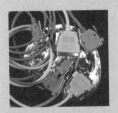

Across the Web, you can find a number of sites from which you can download client software for free. The following sites should provide you with a good start for your collection of Internet and Web software. If you are using Windows 95, use the following site list to download your client software:

ftp client   *http://omni.cc.purdue.edu/~xniu/winsock/ws-ftp.htm*

Internet Explorer   *http://www.microsoft.com/ie/download/*

Netscape Navigator	*http://home.netscape.com/comprod/mirror/—client_download.html*
telnet client	*http://home.sprynet.com/sprynet/voc/yawtel.htm*
whois client	*http://www2.aznet.it/ftp/finger.htm*
ping client	*http://www.ccs.org/winsock/ping.html*
Real Audio client	*http://www.realaudio.com/*

Likewise, if you use a Mac, you can download clients from the following sites:

ftp client	*http://super.zippo.com/appsite/ftpapps.htm*
Internet Explorer	*http://www.microsoft.com/ie/download/*
Netscape Navigator	*http://home.netscape.com/comprod/mirror/—client_download.html*
telnet client	*http://www.ucaqld.com.au/dovenetq/software/—macware.html*
whois client	*http://super.zippo.com/appsite/whofing.htm*
ping client	*http://www.eup.k12.mi.us/support/programs/mac/—mac.html*
Real Audio client	*http://www.realaudio.com/products/player/—download.html*

BUILDING A COMPUTER NETWORK

To build a computer network, you must select various network components that dictate which software and hardware you can use to build your intranet. If you do not have a computer network already, this section should provide you with enough knowledge to start your network development. To begin, you should contact a networking consultant to help you assess your company's networking needs. A computer network is an integral part of your business infrastructure. While an intranet is one application that you will use on your computer network, it should not be the sole factor behind selecting networking components. If you already have a network, this chapter will help you decide what additional hardware and software you need to build your intranet. These intranet components are additions to your existing network and should not force you to drastically change the architecture of your network.

UNDERSTANDING THE PHYSICAL NETWORK CONNECTION

The basic element of every computer network is the physical network connection that connects the network computers. As it turns out, this physical network connection creates a pattern by which network designers describe your network. Common patterns for connecting computers include the star, token ring, and bus topologies. You will learn in detail about each of these network topologies in Chapter 17. Figure 5.2 shows a computer network using a star topology.

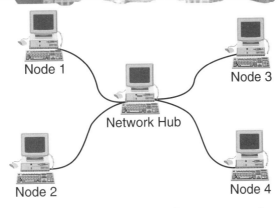

Figure 5.2 A computer network using star topology.

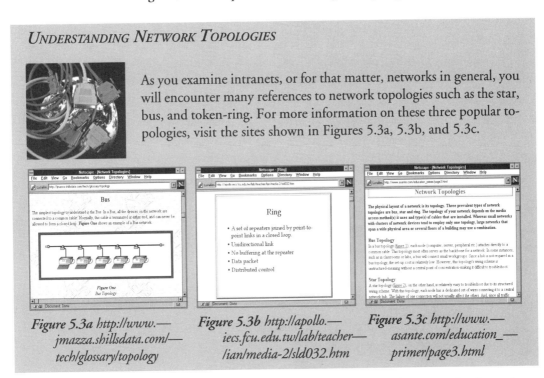

*Figure 5.3a http://www.—
jmazza.shillsdata.com/—
tech/glossary/topology*

*Figure 5.3b http://apollo.—
iecs.fcu.edu.tw/lab/teacher—
/ian/media-2/sld032.htm*

*Figure 5.3c http://www.—
asante.com/education_—
primer/page3.html*

In a star topology, a direct connection between two client computers does not exist. Instead, every client communicates to other clients through the server.

To physically connect computers, you need a network-interface card. The network-interface card resides in your computer and provides a connector into which you plug in the network cable. Depending on your network type, you will connect computers using twisted-pair wiring (much like telephone wiring), or coaxial cable (much like cable-TV wiring). The type of network-interface card establishes the type of network technology you can use. Network designers discuss networks using statements such as, "This is a twisted-pair network," or "The network uses coax (coaxial cable) connections."

INFORMATION ON NETWORK CABLES, CARDS, AND SUPPLIES

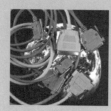

As you discuss your intranet design with your Information Systems staff, you may be overwhelmed by the wide range of network cables, connectors, and related products. To better understand network products, visit the sites shown in Figures 5.4a, 5.4b, 5.4c.

Figure 5.4a http://www.—data.com/tutorials/—mile.html

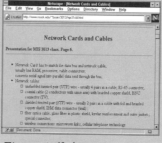

Figure 5.4b http://www.—nsuok.edu/~bosin/3013/—npr31cbl.html

Figure 5.4c http://www.—dataexpresssystem.com/—work2.htm

NETWORK TECHNOLOGY

Each computer on a network contains one or more technology-specific network-interface cards that connect the computer to the network. Currently, the most popular network technologies are Ethernet and IBM Token Ring. Network professionals also refer to network technology as *network architecture.* The Internet is comprised of many Ethernet and IBM Token Rings (and other networks using less common proprietary networking technologies). Network technology establishes the basic rules for data flow and regulates the flow of data by managing data communication between computers on a network. For more information on Ethernet, visit the site *http://www.3com.com/nsc/501403.html* shown in Figure 5.5a. If you are looking for low-level specifics on Ethernet, visit *http://asylum.apocalypse.org/pub/u/paul/docs/ethernet.txt,* shown in Figure 5.5b.

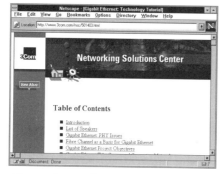

Figure 5.5a Information on the Ethernet technology.

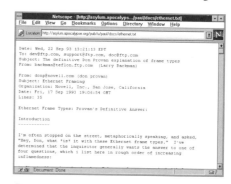

Figure 5.5b Low-level Ethernet specifics.

SELECTING A SERVER

The key computers within a network are the server machines which run the network operating system and control how network computers share server resources. Currently, large businesses (businesses with thousands of users) normally use high-speed Unix-based machines as their primary servers. Small- and medium-sized companies normally use less expensive Intel-based machines. The load (number of users and network traffic) on your intranet server machine will influence your selection of a specific processor type. You will learn more about selecting server machines later in this chapter.

NETWORK OPERATING SYSTEM SOFTWARE

As you have learned, a network consists of one or more computers connected together using one or more network technologies, such as Ethernet and IBM Token Ring. For a suite of protocols to function properly and transfer data between computers on a network, a computer network must run special software called a network operating system. Just as a desktop operating system, such as Microsoft Windows 95, controls how a user runs programs and stores information on a PC, a network operating system controls how different pieces of hardware and software on a network function together.

The most popular LAN–PC network operating systems today are Microsoft *Windows NT Server* and Novell's *NetWare*. Network operating systems function using the client–server network model. As discussed, the client–server network model divides a network application into two sides: the client side and the server side. The client side of a network connection requests information or services from the server side. Figure 5.6 shows a client–server network model.

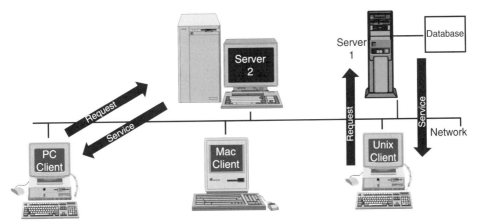

Figure 5.6 A client–server network model of computing.

The network operating system controls the operation of a network server. Network operating systems use one or more network protocols to transfer data to and from clients. For example, *Windows NT Server* can use TCP/IP or IPX/SPX protocols to transfer data. IPX/SPX is *NetWare's* network protocol. IPX is an acronym for Internetwork Packet Exchange, and SPX is an acronym for Sequenced Packet Exchange. Like TCP/IP, the IPX/SPX protocol simply defines a set of rules that coordinate network communication between two systems.

Today, many companies use Novell network products within local-area networks to operate file and print servers. Therefore, it is important you understand how to use Novell's *NetWare* products in an intranet implementation strategy. Later in this chapter, you will learn how you can build an intranet on a *NetWare* network that does not support the TCP/IP suite of protocols. As you will learn, both *NetWare* and Windows NT can connect servers to many different client operating systems. For specifics on Novell servers, visit *http://www.novell.com/intranetware/*, as shown in Figure 5.7a. Likewise, for information on Windows NT servers, visit Microsoft at *http://www.microsoft.com/ntserver*, as shown in Figure 5.7b.

Figure 5.7a Information on Novell servers.

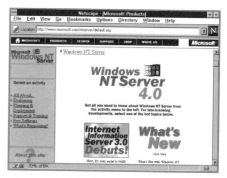

Figure 5.7b Information on Windows NT servers.

CLIENT OPERATING SYSTEM SOFTWARE

As you just learned, the network operating system runs on the network server. Client computers, on the other hand, can run a myriad of operating systems which include Windows 3.1, the Macintosh operating system, OS/2, Windows 95, Windows NT Workstation, and various versions of Unix operating systems. To let the client operating system use the network, you must install special drivers that allow the client computer's network-interface card to communicate with the network. These drivers work much like a printer driver that lets your application programs, such as Microsoft *Word*, send information to a printer. In the case of a network driver, the software lets your programs send and receive information across the network.

CHOOSING A NETWORK PROTOCOL

After you decide the type of intranet network you want to build (such as an Ethernet or token-ring network), you must decide whether or not you want to run TCP/IP on your intranet. If you have a *NetWare* network, you could choose not to provide TCP/IP software to your network clients—instead, you could use the local-area network features provided by the *NetWare* software. However, as you have learned, a true intranet uses the Internet technology, which means you must assign an Internet Protocol (IP) address to each network computer (actually to each network-interface card), and you must use the TCP/IP protocol on the network.

Many computer networks let clients communicate with various servers using different network protocols. For example, you can set up your intranet on a server capable of running TCP/IP and still have your *NetWare* file server on the same machine. Various software products are currently available that translate IPX to IP, making it possible to run an intranet on top of a *NetWare* LAN. In the following sections, you will learn how to set up an Intranet on *NetWare* LANs.

NOVELL NETWARE (IPX/SPX PROTOCOL)

As you have learned, the IPX/SPX protocols are part of Novell's *NetWare* operating system. *NetWare* is a network operating system that provides network-wide file and printer sharing. *NetWare* lets computers in an Ethernet or token ring network communicate using a client–server model. Using *NetWare*, you can create a file server with which employees can share their files. *NetWare* server software runs on all major computer platforms such as Unix, DOS, Macintosh, and Windows. Behind the scenes, *NetWare* sends and receives data packets based on IPX/SPX protocols.

Before a client computer can access the network, you must install *NetWare* client software on the computer. Clients can then share files and printer resources, as well as run a variety of client-server applications using the server. *NetWare* client-side software is also available for Unix, DOS, Macintosh, OS/2, and Windows. Figure 5.8 shows the components of a Novell *NetWare* LAN.

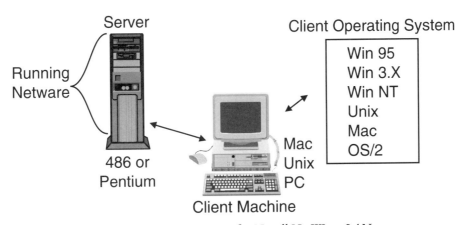

Figure 5.8 Components of a Novell NetWare LAN.

INTRANET ON A NETWARE LAN

To build your intranet on a *NetWare* local-area network, you do not need an IP address for each client. Instead, you use *gateway applications* (special programs) to translate IPX to IP. Then, you must run *NetWare*-compatible Web server software. When you use an IPX to IP translator, you keep your existing LAN infrastructure unchanged. Figure 5.9 illustrates the process of translating IPX to IP (and back again) on a *NetWare* network.

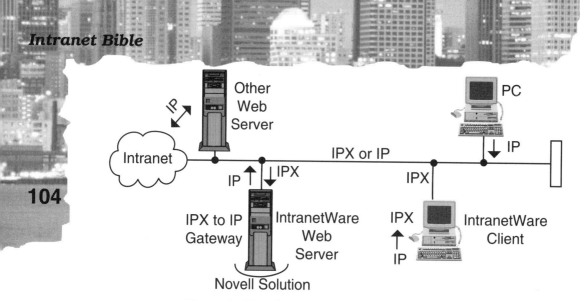

Figure 5.9 *Translating IPX to IP in a NetWare network.*

To create your intranet, you can run the *IntranetWare* server software from Novell on an existing *NetWare* server. Using *IntranetWare*, you do not need to assign an IP address to each client on a network. Instead, you only assign an IP address to the *NetWare* Web server. With your purchase of *IntranetWare*, you will also get software, which performs IPX to IP translation on the client side. You can install the *IntranetWare* server component either on top of an existing *NetWare 4.1* server or on a standalone Web server.

The *IntranetWare* client software translates the TCP/IP protocols generated by a Web browser to IPX protocols. After the protocol translation on the client side, the messages travel across the network until they reach the *NetWare* Web Server. Then, on the *NetWare* server, the *IntranetWare Server* component translates the IPX messages back into TCP/IP and sends them to other servers on the network. For more information on *IntranetWare*, visit Novell's Web site at *http://www.novell.com/intranetware/*, as shown in Figure 5.10.

Figure 5.10 *Novell's IntranetWare Web site.*

As discussed, *NetWare* is primarily a file and print server. It is not a particularly fast or powerful application server. An intranet depends on the client–server computing model within which clients may constantly need the services of the server. By choosing *NetWare*, you limit the types of applications you can provide for your employees. If you have an existing *NetWare* network, you may choose to start your intranet using your *NetWare* server. In the long term, however, you will probably change to a dedicated Web server capable of running the TCP/IP suite of protocols.

INETIX AS AN INTERNET GATEWAY

Another way to create an intranet using a *NetWare*-based local-area network is to use the Internet gateway product *Inetix* from Micro Computer Systems, Inc. *Inetix* runs on *NetWare*, Windows NT, or Unix servers. Using *Inetix*, you do not need to add TCP/IP support to *NetWare* client machines. *Inetix* requires you to assign a single IP address to your intranet Web server. *Inetix* client software lets a Web browser, such as Netscape's *Navigator*, execute on the client side even though the client machine does not have TCP/IP software.

You can download a full-featured evaluation copy of *Inetix* from this vendor's Internet Web site, *http://www.mcsdallas.com/mcs/inetix.htm*, as shown in Figure 5.11. However, as previously discussed, if you will have a large number of intranet users, you may need to establish a separate server, such as an Intel Pentium-class machine running *Windows NT Server* software.

*Figure 5.11 Download an evaluation copy of the **Inetix** software.*

APPLE'S APPLETALK

If your network is Mac-based, you can use *NetWare* for Mac or Apple's proprietary network operating system, *AppleTalk*—a full-featured network operating system. *AppleTalk* is a local-area network protocol and does not support wide-area networks. Unlike *AppleTalk*, TCP/IP supports both LANs and WANs. Like TCP/IP and *NetWare*, you can run *AppleTalk* on Ethernet LANs.

As you may know, Mac computers come with a built-in *AppleTalk* port. However, if you want to connect a Mac to an Ethernet network, you will need an Ethernet network-interface board, which is standard equipment on many Mac models. For more information on *AppleTalk*, visit Apple's Web site at *http://devworld.apple.com/dev/techsupport/insidemac/Networking/Networking-19.html*, as shown in Figure 5.12.

Figure 5.12 Information on AppleTalk.

RUNNING *TCP/IP* PROTOCOLS ON YOUR *LAN*

To establish an intranet that will let employees benefit from current and future Internet technologies, you must install TCP/IP on each client machine. As you learned in Chapter 1, a *protocol* is a set of rules for all data transmission over a network. In Chapter 18, "Getting to Know TCP/IP," you will learn in detail about TCP/IP protocol suites and how network data flows over an intranet. For the purpose of this chapter, you must understand that if your network does not support TCP/IP, you must use gateway applications that can translate TCP/IP to your network operating system protocol.

TCP/IP ON WINDOWS CLIENTS

As you have learned, in a network, two processes (programs) on separate computers exchange packets of data. For messages to flow from one Windows-based machine to another, host computers must exchange data packets using the appropriate network operating system protocol. To use an Internet-based application, such as a Web browser, on a Windows-based machine, you must use special software called the *TCP/IP stack*. Windows 95, Windows NT, and IBM's OS/2 Warp operating systems include the TCP/IP protocol suite. For Windows 3.1, you must purchase TCP/IP software (or download the software from the Web). Most Unix-based systems already use TCP/IP as their main network communication protocol.

USING WINDOWS 3.1 CLIENTS

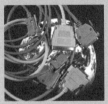

If you are using Windows 3.1 clients, you should consider upgrading the clients to Windows 95 or Windows NT. As you will learn in future chapters, most of the advanced Internet and intranet applications are primarily available for Unix, Windows 95, and Windows NT operating systems. In the meantime, to use Windows 3.1 clients within your intranet, you must install TCP/IP software on each client. One of the most popular TCP/IP software applications for Windows 3.1 is *Trumpet Winsock*, which you can download from *http://nac.kotel.co.kr/~yslim/slipp3/winsock.html*, as shown in Figure 5.13.

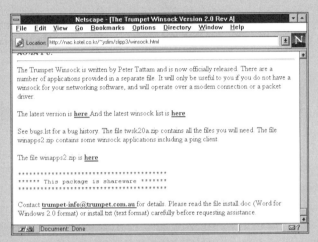

Figure 5.13 Download the Trumpet Winsock for Windows 3.1.

SELECTING A HARDWARE SERVER PLATFORM

Currently, there is considerable debate among computer programmers, network engineers, and intranet designers regarding which is the best intranet hardware server—a Unix workstation, an Intel-based machine, or a PowerPC-based system. In general, your server choice depends on how you plan to use your intranet and your level of familiarity with each of these platforms. Your server hardware selection will also depend on your network operating system.

If you choose a Unix-based server, you will pay more for computing power than you would for an Intel-based machine. Unix machines still carry a price premium over PCs, because most Unix machines use custom-made parts, whereas Intel-based machines use commodity components that are available from many hardware vendors. For example, you can buy a high-end Pentium machine capable of serving more than 1,000 client machines for about $3,000 versus $15,000 to $30,000 for a comparable Unix machine. Mac-based systems are more expensive than comparable Intel-based machines, but less expensive than Unix-based machines.

The decision to use a Unix-based machine versus an Intel-based machine as your intranet server also involves maintenance costs. Maintaining a Unix-based machine takes more resources than maintaining an Intel-based machine. Hardware upgrades are also cheaper for Intel-based machines versus Unix workstations. If you choose a Macintosh server, you will also pay more for hardware upgrades than you would for an Intel-based machine.

The debate over Unix- and Intel-based machines focuses primarily on the performance of these machines as business application servers. For example, companies that use large accounting and financial software packages often use Unix servers. On the other hand, companies that do not want to pay the price premium for Unix machines and are not familiar with hardware configuration of Unix machines often select Intel-based machines as their business application servers.

If you decide to use Intel-based machines, select Pentium-class machines with at least 32Mb of RAM (ideally 64Mb), a 2GB hard disk, and a Pentium 166MHz microprocessor. You can find such a system from many PC vendors for about $2,000 to $2,500. By selecting a Pentium-class machine, you also have access to a vast array of software applications and cheaper server software. Most industry experts believe that Pentium-class machines will take market share away from Unix workstations, which means you will see more and more intranet-based applications for Pentium-class machines in the future.

SELECTING A NETWORK OPERATING SYSTEM

As discussed, the network operating system controls how users access the network. As you have learned, the Internet is a collection of various hardware platforms running various operating systems. In theory, there is no reason why you must stay with one machine type and one network operating system. In practice, however, by using only one network operating system, you will simplify your network maintenance. Unless you have a large support staff, you should standardize your network operating system selection across your company.

Your primary choices for a network operating system are Unix, Windows NT, and Novell *NetWare*. This section examines each of these operating systems and the considerations you should make before choosing a specific system for your intranet. As you visit sites on the Web, you may send the sites e-mail to learn more about the server each uses. As you will find, Sun Microsystems uses Sun Unix machines to run both its internal and external Web sites. On the other hand, Microsoft runs its Web site using Intel-based machines and the *Windows NT Server* network operating system.

As discussed, many larger companies use Unix-based machines as their primary business application server platform. Unix is a proven operating system well suited for the Internet's open system model. If you are familiar with the Unix operating system, you can set up a Web server almost for free. Unfortunately, most users are not "Unix Wizards" and do not find Unix easy to set up and maintain. Also, using a Unix-based machine limits your access to various low-priced software applications which developers will use to create interactive intranets. Most programmers, for example, prefer to develop applications with Windows-based machines using programming languages such as Microsoft's Visual Basic and Borland's Delphi.

Many companies choose Windows NT over Unix because of NT's ease of installation, maintenance, and administration. NT intranet servers are fairly easy to install. Windows NT, like Unix and OS/2, can serve two functions. First, Windows NT can function as a high-performance, multitasking workstation operating system. In addition, it can function as an advanced server. Windows NT has built-in support which let various client operating systems connect to it. Clients such as MS-DOS, Windows 3.1, Windows 95, Windows for Workgroups, Windows NT Workstation, Unix, and even the Mac can easily communicate with *Windows NT Server*. Windows NT also includes built-in support for popular network protocols, such as TCP/IP and IPX/SPX. The latest version of *Windows NT Server* also includes a free *Internet Information Server* (IIS) and a free Web browser (*Internet Explorer*). Microsoft designed the *Internet Information Server*, such that users can install and run the server under Windows NT in less than 10 minutes. The server supports HTTP, FTP, and Gopher.

Another feature of *Windows NT Server* is its built-in Remote Access Services. Using *Windows NT Server*, you can provide employees with the ability to access your intranet by dialing in to the system over standard phone lines. Remote Access gives your sales and field staff the advantage of having the latest sales figures and company information while away from the office. *Windows NT Server* runs on Intel-, Alpha-, and MIPS-based machines. *Windows NT Server* runs most MS-DOS and Windows-based applications. You can purchase a *Windows NT Server* for a 150-user environment for about $5,500.

WINDOWS 95 AS A SERVER OPERATING SYSTEM

Windows 95 has built-in network support for TCP/IP and SPX/IPX protocols. Also, it has built-in support for a few TCP/IP protocols such as Telnet and FTP. If your company wants to use your intranet to publish Human Resource documents and company news and to implement simple interactive forms, Windows 95 may be adequate. However, as soon as you bring your intranet on-line, you will find that users want more functionality, especially connections to various databases. You limit your choice for high-end intranet applications, servers, and various tools if you chose Windows 95 as your intranet Web server. Many companies chose to bypass Windows 95 altogether and transition from Windows 3.1 directly to Windows NT.

WEB SERVER SOFTWARE

In addition to the debate over the right hardware and server operating systems, networking and Web professionals continue to debate over Web server software. As you learned previously, an intranet is based on the client–server model of computing. To have a working intranet, you must have server software that can handle requests from browsers. Figure 5.14 shows how a server handles a Web browser request to access a static HTML page.

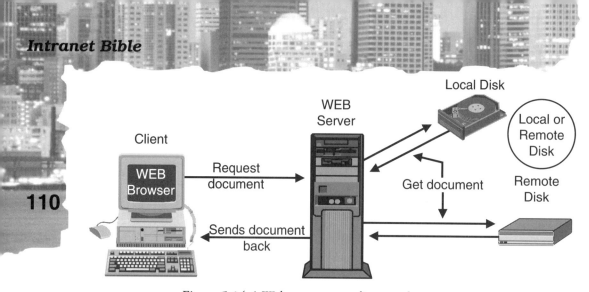

Figure 5.14 A Web server responding to a browser request.

Like the Internet, the intranet client–server operation depends on the Hypertext Transfer Proto-col (HTTP). HTTP defines a set of ASCII-based commands for its command language. Software programs, such as a browser, use these HTTP commands to request services from an HTTP server.

An HTTP transaction consists of four parts: a connection, a request, a response, and a close. In addition to retrieving files, a Web server can run application programs, which perform operations such as searching a database or processing a form that contains user input. In the next two to five years, standalone Web servers will become an integral part of operating systems. Soon, Web serv-ers will handle a large number of specific tasks that require custom programming today. These tasks will include seamless connection to databases, video and audio processing, as well as docu-ment management.

Currently, a number of powerful, free Web servers are available for both Windows NT and Unix. Besides the cost of a Web server, you must consider how the server software supports your Web developers. In other words, the server support must make it easy for you to expand your intranet. In addition to Web servers provided by Microsoft and Netscape, a number of other companies have powerful and inexpensive Web servers, for example, O'Reilly's *WebSite for Windows 95 and Windows NT.*

For the most part, selecting a Web server for an intranet is similar to selecting a Web server for an Internet site; however, Internet servers must handle a large number of requests every day and deal with security issues. On the other hand, most corporate intranet servers will not initially have as much traffic as an Internet server. Therefore, you may first build your intranet with servers that are easy to use and maintain and then move to high-performance servers as your intranet's use increases. Often, the performance of the intranet depends more on the performance of the server machine than the server software itself.

As more departments within your organization request to have their own servers, you will find that you need a simple plan for adding these additional servers. You can easily solve this problem because many companies currently offer free Web servers, which make it easy for you to "test drive" the server. It is not clear how long you can depend on getting free upgrades for these servers; however, at this time, you cannot go wrong selecting a free Web server.

Which Web server you choose is bounded by your choice of server operating systems. In the following sections, you will learn about Web servers for Unix, Windows NT, Windows 95, and Macintosh operating systems.

UNIX WEB SERVERS

One of the best and oldest Web servers for Unix-based machines is the National Center for Supercomputing Application's HTTP (NCSA HTTP) Web Server. Much of the Internet's growth is primarily due to the popularity of this server for Unix-based systems and, better yet, the NCSA HTTP Web server is free.

NSCA is committed to the continued development of this Web server. If you are familiar with Unix-based systems, you should have little problem setting up this server. This Web server provides CGI support and comes with Server Side Includes (SSI) software that increases your server's functionality. For example, if you have visited a Web site that displays a counter showing the number of visitors to the site, you have seen an SSI in action. SSIs are small programs that Web servers run to include dynamic (changing) information within HTML pages.

NCSA also lets you create virtual servers on the same machine, which means you can create multiple Web servers using one system. These virtual servers can have their own universal resource identifiers (URLs). For example, you can assign an IP address to your marketing department and another IP address to your production department, both on the same machine. The ability to create virtual servers is useful for people setting up Internet sites and may not be necessary for setting up intranets, but, as you have learned, it is better to start with a free Web server to establish an intranet presence. This way you can better assess the needs of your users before spending money on a commercially available Web server. In the long run, you will probably have to go with a commercial Web server to gain access to the latest intranet application software.

Currently, the most popular commercial Unix-based Web servers are those developed by Netscape Communications Corporation: *Enterprise Server* and *FastTrack Server*. The *Enterprise Server* software sells for about $1,000 and is designed for companies that plan to develop a large intranet. *FastTrack*, on the other hand, is easier to install but has less functionality. *FastTrack* sells for about $300 and is well suited for companies that plan to build small- to medium-sized intranets. Both of these Web servers are also available for Windows NT. These products also include a copy of Netscape's *Navigator Gold* browser, one of the most popular browsers used today.

WINDOWS NT WEB SERVERS

As you learned in previous section, both Netscape's *Enterprise Server* and *FastTrack Server* are available for Windows NT. You should consider these two servers if you plan to use both Windows NT and Unix-based machines for your Web servers.

If you do not need cross-platform Web server software, consider Microsoft's *Internet Information Server* (*IIS*). This server drives Microsoft's Internet site and, as you might expect, works well for a large organization. Currently, Microsoft offers this server free of charge. Microsoft is also bundling this server with its *Windows NT Server* software. *IIS* is easy to install and provides you with the ability to add users to your intranet without much effort. *IIS* also includes an FTP server.

Another popular Windows NT Web server is *WebSite Professional* from O'Reilly & Associates, Inc. *WebSite Professional* sells for about $500 and is very easy to install. This server has built-in search capabilities, a Web-site management tool, and includes the popular HTML editing tool, *HotDog*. If you want to use the Microsoft NT Workstation operating system rather than the NT Server operating system, you must go with *Website Professional*, because Microsoft's *IIS* only runs on the *Windows NT Server* operating system. Furthermore, *WebSite Professional* is probably the easiest Web server to maintain and is also available for the Windows 95 operating system.

WINDOWS 95 WEB SERVERS

Few high-performance Web servers are available for the Windows 95 operating system. The Web server that you should consider if you are planning to build your intranet on a Windows 95 machine is O'Reilly's *WebSite*. As discussed, if you have a small office, you can create your intranet on a Windows 95 machine. You can download an evaluation copy of *WebSite* from O'Reilly's Internet site at *http://www.ora.com*.

In addition to *WebSite for Windows 95*, Netscape *FastTrack* is also available for Windows 95. You can download a free beta copy of this server from Netscape's Internet site at *http://home.netscape.com/comprod/mirror/server_download.html*. Using *FastTrack*, you can set up various departments to distribute information without the need to purchase a high-performance operating system like Windows NT Workstation or *Windows NT Server*.

MACINTOSH WEB SERVER

As you might have expected, not many Web servers are available for Macintosh computers. The largest market share of the Macintosh Web server market belongs to the *WebStar* server from Quarterdeck Corporation. This server is a mature product and is currently your best bet for a Mac-based Web server. The Macintosh market is not growing, and if you do not have a Macintosh network already, you should stay away from installing a Mac-based intranet server. However, *WebStar* is very easy to install and maintain and sells for about $800.

NETWARE WEB SERVER

As you have learned, *NetWare Web Server* from Novell is, for now, the best choice for companies that already have a *NetWare* network. This server sells for about $1,000. You can, however, download an evaluation copy of this server from Novell's Internet Web site at *http://www.novell.com/catalog/qr/sne34610.html*. *NetWare Web Server* runs on *NetWare version 4.x*. When you use *NetWare Web server*, you must also install IPX to IP translation software on each client machine. By doing so, you do not have to assign an IP address to each client machine.

WEB BROWSERS

The last component you must have to make a functional intranet is a Web browser. Currently, there is considerable debate regarding what is the best browser on the market: Microsoft's *Internet Explorer* or Netscape's *Navigator*. This debate is likely to continue for some time. Because the majority of the Web browser market belongs to Netscape's *Navigator*, Microsoft has made the development of an advanced browser a priority for its entire Internet development team.

Browsers, as we know them today, will not exist in a few years. Instead, Microsoft will integrate the browser's functionality into all of its business application software, such as *Word* and *Excel*, and will make the browser part of the operating system. Figure 5.15, for example, illustrates Microsoft's *Internet Explorer* running within Microsoft *Word* under Microsoft *Office 97*.

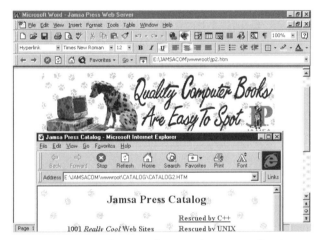

Figure 5.15 Running a browser from within an application program.

On the Unix side, the market will probably continue to belong to Netscape. Microsoft has not chosen to cross over to the Unix platform. Therefore, if you have a network that includes Unix, Macintosh, and Windows clients, and must standardize on one browser, you must go with Netscape's *Navigator*.

PUTTING IT ALL TOGETHER

In this chapter, you examined the basic components of an intranet. This chapter's discussion should help you prepare to plan the implementation phase of your intranet project. As you have learned, the server and browser software market is changing quickly. Fortunately, high-performance servers will be much less expensive in the near future than they are today. A rule you may want to keep in mind is to always buy the latest and fastest hardware, but not necessarily the latest version of server and browser software—it may contain bugs.

As you will learn in the following chapter, planning an intranet implementation is the key to executing your intranet deployment. In the next chapter, you will learn how to put a team together to develop a comprehensive intranet implementation plan. However, before you continue with Chapter 6, make sure you understand the following key concepts:

- ✓ Intranets operate based on the client–server network computing model. The client–server model divides a network application into two sides: the client side and the server side. By definition, the client side of a network requests information or services and the server side responds to a client's requests.

- ✓ The physical network components include network interface cards, cables, and computers.

- ✓ A network consists of one or more computers connected together using one or more network technologies, such as Ethernet and IBM TokenRing.

- ✓ For a suite of protocols to function properly and to transfer data between computers on a network, a computer network must run special software called a network operating system.

- ✓ Suites of protocols, such as TCP/IP and IPX/SPX, manage data communication for various network technologies, network operating systems, and client operating systems.

- ✓ IPX to IP translation programs provide *NetWare* users with the ability to build an intranet without running the TCP/IP suite of protocols on their network.

- ✓ Server machines such as Unix- and Intel-based machines are capable of running various network operating systems and client operating systems.

- ✓ Windows-based intranets are easier and less expensive to deploy than Unix-based intranets.

- ✓ Netscape and Microsoft provide various low- and high-end server software for organizations of different sizes.

- ✓ Netscape's *Navigator* and Microsoft's *Internet Explorer* provide advanced browser features for intranet applications.

VISITING KEY SITES THAT DISCUSS INTRANETS

The World Wide Web is filled with hundreds of excellent and current articles on all aspects of intranets. Use the following sites as starting points for your Web exploration.

Welcome to Livelink Intranet

http://www.opentext.com/livelink/otm_ll.html

Home for Intranet Planners

http://www.kensho.com/hip/

Intranet_index

http://www.webi.co.kr/intranet/

Free Intranet Resource CD

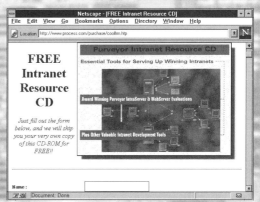

http://www.process.com/purchase/coolfrm.htp

Intranet White Paper

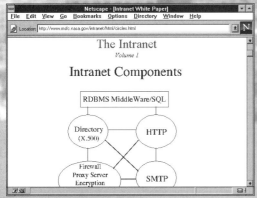

*http://www.msfc.nasa.gov/intranet/html/—
circles.html*

Internet Services Group

http://www.thehost.com/intra01.htm

NETRA I HOME PAGE

*http://www.sun.com/products.n.solutions/hw—/
servers/netrai/index.html*

WAYFARER COMMUNICATIONS

http://www.wayfarer.com/

SURFCONTROL

http://www.intranet.co.uk/

INTRANET INFORMATION MODELS

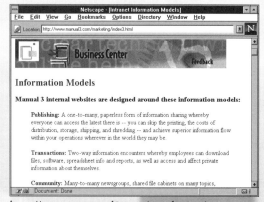

*http://www.manual3.com/marketing/
index3.html*

NATIONAL SEMICONDUCTOR

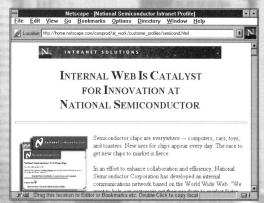

*http://home.netscape.com/comprod/at_work/
customer_profiles/semicond.html*

INTRANET COMPONENTS

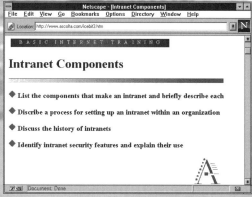

http://www.ascolta.com/icebit3.htm

Chapter 6

Intranet Planning and Management

117

When you design a brochure, write a book, or start a new project, you usually develop an outline or plan before you start. To ensure that your project is successful and meets your needs, you first must define those needs. Then you must determine how you will know when you have met your needs by defining the project's specifications and functionality. As you prepare for your intranet project, you must perform the same type of project planning.

When you undertake the job of developing a plan to implement and manage a corporate intranet, you are actually taking on the job of re-engineering current process flows within your organization. As with any change, you must make provisions to carefully plan and manage those changes. Employees will always appreciate changes that make their jobs easier; however, an intranet may initially seem like an intimidating intrusion of yet more technology. By keeping your employees involved during the intranet's early stages, their transition becomes much easier, and they will sooner recognize the intranet's benefits. In Chapter 5, you learned about the hardware and software decisions you will address during the intranet development process. In this chapter, you will examine the steps involved in the planning, development, and management of corporate intranets. By the time you finish this chapter, you will understand the following key concepts:

- The development of a successful intranet requires planning, goal setting, organizational design, team building, and change management.

- To sell the intranet concept to your company's upper management, you should design a presentation that includes the definition, benefits, and functionality of an intranet, as well as details outlining the company's return on investment.

- To create an intranet plan, you must define the functions and specifications that meet the needs of your intranet customers.

- Winning intranet development teams normally include individuals with complementary skill sets and diverse experience.

- The non-linear structure of Web-based documents links information in a path that enables the readers to explore and browse the information spontaneously.

- An intuitive Web-site design and user interface enable customers to easily locate information on your intranet without getting confused or lost.

- A pilot project based on static HTML pages is a good starting point for the deployment of your intranet.

GAINING SUPPORT FOR YOUR INTRANET PROJECT

The first step to planning the successful implementation of an intranet is to obtain company-wide support that starts with upper management. Often, you must perform research and develop a presentation that sells the concept of an intranet to others in your organization. Managers, for example, will want to know how the intranet will benefit their divisions. As you learned in Chapters 3 and 4, organizations of all sizes and industries have implemented successful intranets. Some benefits of intranets are tangible and easy to measure, while others are not as easy to measure. To sell the idea of an intranet to decision makers, you must show them what an intranet is and how it will benefit the organization. Unfortunately, presenting an intranet can be a difficult task, since most corporate intranets are not available for viewing by the public—which means you can't readily show your organization how others (especially competitors) are using and benefiting from their intranets. Therefore, you may want to create a sample intranet that you can use to let managers take a hands-on test drive of an intranet. Figure 6.1 shows such a demo intranet site.

Figure 6.1 A demo intranet site.

PLANNING YOUR INTRANET STRATEGY

After you have sold your company's upper management on the idea of an intranet, you must start your development of an intranet plan. To do so, you must first define the goals, purpose, and objectives of your corporate intranet. Planning is an essential part of the intranet development process and is critical to the final success of your corporate intranet. Too often, underground (unapproved) development of new systems and technologies crop up within an organization without a plan. As users integrate these unplanned systems within the organization, the systems become an integral part of daily operations. Unfortunately, the systems often become unmanageable and unfocused.

In your intranet plan you must include an overview of the existing organizational structure, as well as a description of the organization's technical capabilities. You must also define the current communication model that controls information distribution and management within your organization. In addition, you should make a list of the communication model's strengths and weaknesses, placing emphasis on workflow processes, document management, training capabilities, and other key business systems. It is important that you understand and define the existing systems within your organization before you implement new systems such as an intranet.

PUTTING TOGETHER AN INTRANET PRESENTATION

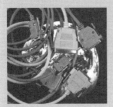

Across the Web, you can find many resources that will provide you with information and ideas on how to put together an intranet presentation. To start, view the sample presentations and related intranet information at the following Internet sites:

Figure 6.2a http://www.cio.com/—
WebMaster/wm_intranet_sites.html

Figure 6.2b http://www.microsoft.—
com/msoffice/intranet/volcano/index.htm

Figure 6.2c http://home.netscape.—
com/comprod/at_work/index.html

Figure 6.2d http://www.acmefruit.com

ESTABLISHING GOALS—THE THINGS YOU WANT YOUR INTRANET TO DO

Before you start your intranet design, it essential that you clearly define your main objectives. To begin, make a list of your customer needs. For example, if your intranet will contain a list of job opportunities available within the organization, your intranet should provide a job application so users can apply for the position on-line. If your intranet has human resources information, users may want the ability to change their 401K information directly from the intranet. Each of these needs is a goal that you can use to shape and define your intranet's functionality.

By interviewing employees and department managers, you can begin to establish a list of goals that will serve as the foundation of your intranet plan. An employee survey is a great way to collect ideas and input from personnel within your organization. Many employees have information and knowledge about processes and procedures with which you may not be familiar. You will find their input necessary to develop the organization, content, and functionality of your intranet.

After you have collected feedback from employees and team members, you must create a list of needs and functionality specifications. Because each employee will be a customer of your intranet, it is crucial that you include their input throughout all phases of planning and production. The following is a list of questions that will help you define customer needs, goals, and design specifications for your intranet plan:

- Will your intranet customers need to access existing (legacy) databases?
- What type of training and support will your intranet customers require?
- Who will manage the intranet's content?
- Who will create and update the content?
- Will individual departments author their own pages autonomously?
- Will there be a central clearing house that manages changes to the intranet's content?
- Do intranet customers need a way to access the intranet remotely?
- Will the intranet need to restrict access to certain content?
- Will there be a Webmaster or a team of intranet managers?
- Will the Information Systems (IS) department install and manage the intranet or will you outsource these operations?

RECRUITING YOUR INTRANET TEAM

To develop your presentation and intranet plan, you will need a team of key personnel—especially if you are not familiar with Internet technologies. You should select a team with representatives from different departments in the organization. It is important that you work with a diverse group of individuals with complementary skill sets and job functions. You will benefit most from a team that incorporates the team member skills shown in Figure 6.3.

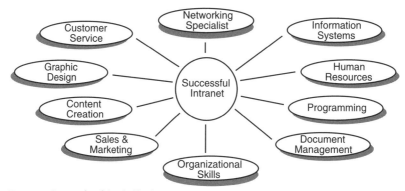

Figure 6.3 Valuable skills that can contribute to the success of your intranet.

It is very important that you involve your Information Systems department early in the planning process. Although the static content of an intranet may not require the assistance of such technical personnel, most intranet projects rely on the organization's existing infrastructure. If your organization does not have an intranet-capable infrastructure in place, you will need the assistance of your Information Systems team to add the appropriate hardware and software. If your organization does not have an IS department or the available resources, hire a consultant or outsource the project to a qualified network vendor.

It is important that you determine whether or not your IS department has the skills and resources to set up and maintain an intranet. Using HTML to create Web documents may be easy to learn, but it is also a new technology, and many IS professionals may not have the expertise to use it effectively. Also, depending on the size of your IS department, management of the organization's current infrastructure may consume all their time—making their participation in the intranet impossible. In such cases, many organizations outsource portions of their intranet projects.

After you select your intranet team, use a skills assessment poll to compare the team member skills to the skills required to develop a successful intranet. Use the skills assessment checklist that follows to evaluate the resources available within your organization. You will need the following skills to put information (your site's content) into a browser-readable format:

Content Development and Design

- Experience in graphic design and content presentation
- Basic understanding of copyright law
- Knowledge of document conversion techniques (to convert spreadsheet data, for example, into a text document for HTML editing)
- Experience in page layout and design
- Experience with Web browsers and HTML document creation
- Knowledge of image-conversion techniques and related software
- Knowledge of programming languages and programming skills
- CGI programming and server interaction

The following lists the technical support skills you will need for your intranet's overall design. You will need people with these technical skills to solve network problems, understand your network design, troubleshoot hardware and software compatibility problems, and implement client–server solutions, such as integrating network databases.

Technical Support

- Knowledge of network hardware and software
- Understanding of TCP/IP and related protocols
- Experience implementing network security

- Knowledge of client-server operations

- Experience with custom programming

- Knowledge of database management

As discussed, you must involve your company's management in the planning and implementation of your intranet. Ideally, the management should have a good understanding of what an intranet offers, as well as related costs and the time frame in which you expect to complete the intranet. Take advantage of your management's skills that relate to quality-control techniques, process-management approaches, and communication patterns, using the following management support skills list. In so doing, your intranet will embody the personality, culture, and business practices of your organization.

Management Support Skills

- Understanding of the organization's document flow

- Experience with the re-engineering process

- Knowledge of quality-control techniques

- Knowledge of the company's informal flow of information

- Experience with training and project coordination

Your organization should have many sources of information: Human Resource manuals, corporate statements, telephone directories, departmental information, ISO-9000 work instructions, equipment calibration records, employee records, and much more. To simplify your content collection, involve those people who are most familiar with the original documentation. For example, ISO-9000 guidelines require certain fields and specific wording in many types of documents. The original authors should work closely with your intranet content developers to ensure that nothing is lost in the translation.

DEVELOPING THE DESIGN AND STRUCTURE OF YOUR INTRANET

Before you create a design for your intranet, you must define its organizational structure, which entails a good understanding of the communication channels within your company. To start, you must decide if you want to use the same information structure for the intranet as is used for existing communication channels within your organization.

You can start building the intranet structure by grouping content into main topics and categories. Then, relate other information by department, function, project, or by a defined order. For example, you might list job opportunities within a Human Resources category. It is important that you involve more than one person in the task of grouping the topics. When an individual selects the grouping, other observers may not relate the data in the same way. By using a team approach to information grouping, you will help keep the groupings user friendly and ensure that they make sense to a wide audience. The following list includes common categories you will find within corporate intranet homepages:

- What's New at Company XYZ
- Corporate Information (history and contacts)
- Help Desk and Technical Support
- Software and Tools Library
- Business Resources
- Sales and Marketing Information
- Product Information
- Human Resources
- In-House Job Postings
- Customer Feedback
- Competitor Data
- Telephone and E-Mail Directory
- Quality System Records
- Plant and Equipment Records
- Finance and Accounting Information
- A Keyword Search/Index Capability

At this stage, you don't have to worry about each topic's exact organization. Instead, you just want to create groupings. When you are designing the pages, you can lay out the exact order of each item.

STRUCTURING INTRANET CONTENT

At this point, you should have grouped your intranet's topics into larger categories. Next, you must structure (layer) the information in a manner users will find intuitive. There are three primary information models you can use to structure your intranet's content: linear, hierarchical, and non-linear. Figure 6.4 shows a linear information structure.

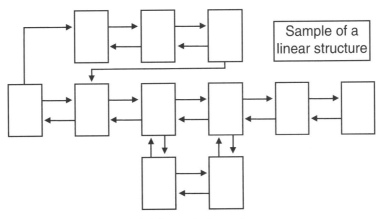

Figure 6.4 A linear information structure.

A linear information structure is similar in layout to a book—the information is linked sequentially, page by page. Linear layouts are very structured and limit the reader from exploring and browsing the content in a nonsequential (non-linear) manner. Most linear information structures let the user search forward and backward with some subtle alternatives.

In a similar way, a hierarchical information structure creates paths that only move up and down, as shown in Figure 6.5. As you can see, the hierarchical information model also uses linear paths.

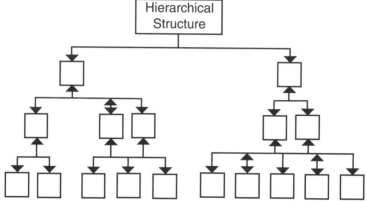

Figure 6.5 A hierarchical information structure.

A non-linear structure, which links information based on related content, has no apparent structure. Non-linear structures let the reader wander through the information spontaneously. A non-linear structure can link information so that the user can move forward, backward, up and down, diagonally, and from side to side. A non-linear structure lets the reader move through the information with complete freedom to change paths. The non-linear structure can be confusing, and readers might get lost within the content. An example of a non-linear information structure is the World Wide Web, which lets users move from one related document to another with ease. A non-linear information structure provides a great way to present information which you want the user to browse freely, as shown in Figure 6.6.

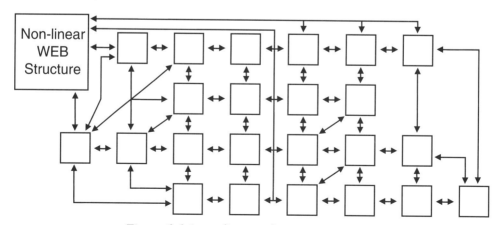

Figure 6.6 A non-linear information structure.

Using a visualization tool, such as a flow-charting program, will help you plan your intranet's content organization. For example, Figure 6.7 illustrates an intranet's content organization.

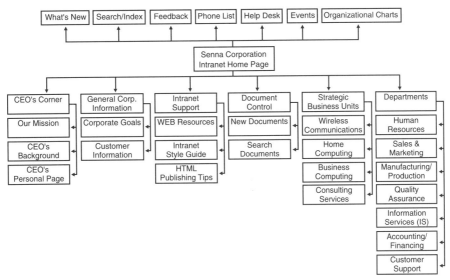

Figure 6.7 A sample flow chart of an intranet's structure.

TOOLS FOR ORGANIZING YOUR INTRANET'S CONTENT

During your intranet's development process, you will change the layout and organization of your intranet content many times. It is important that you use applications that make it easy for you to update your design. There are several good flowcharting applications that automatically update a flow chart when you make a change in the project outline. Some of the Web authoring tools also offer flowchart and organizational tools that you can use to develop an intranet structure. The following sites present a few products that you can use to develop the structure of your intranet:

ALLCLEAR III BY CLEAR SOFTWARE

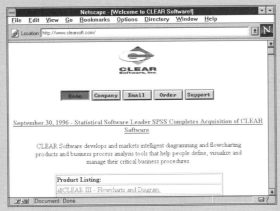

http://www.clearsoft.com

VISIO FOR WINDOWS BY VISIO

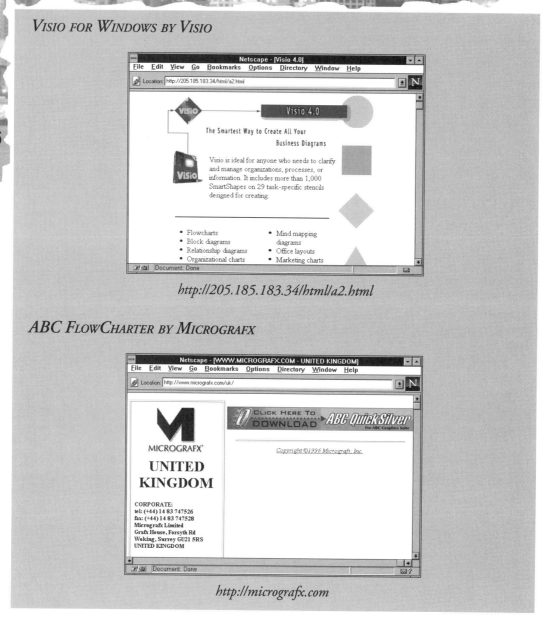

http://205.185.183.34/html/a2.html

ABC FLOWCHARTER BY MICROGRAFX

http://micrografx.com

DESIGNING YOUR INTRANET

After you have defined your intranet's structure, your next step is to define your intranet's design, functionality, and user interface. As you begin, you should tie your intranet design into your organization's existing image using current marketing materials. For example, you can easily include such items as corporate images, logos, icons, and related design themes to add a familiar look and feel to the content. In fact, you should ask your marketing department to assist you with your intranet's design and layout.

Next, you use a technique called *storyboarding* to lay out your content. A storyboard is what film producers, story writers, and comic strip artists use to layout the content sequence and events of their projects. A storyboard depicts the content, images, and links between the pages of your intranet in the form of a rough outline. As shown in Figure 6.8, a storyboard presents a visual concept of how your pages will look and the content they will contain.

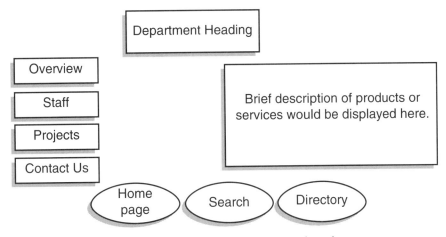

Figure 6.8 A sample intranet storyboard.

You can use software such as Microsoft *PowerPoint* or another similar presentation program to develop your storyboard and sample Web pages. It is also a good idea to test the interface of your intranet design to ensure that the icons, buttons, and navigational tools are logical and intuitive to the user. By building five to ten sample Web pages that include navigational buttons and links, you can test the user interface and content structure.

TESTING YOUR USER INTERFACE DESIGN

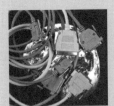

Recruit 10 to 15 employees to interact with the sample Web pages and observe their choices, comments, and reactions to the pages. You must observe without giving the users any directions. By watching the users, you will see which buttons they understand and which ones don't make sense to them. Write a task down on a piece of paper and have each user try to complete the task. For example, a task may read, "Use the intranet to find out which department John Smith works in." It is important that you let the user try to figure out how to perform the tasks that you assign. If the user can perform the task without making any incorrect choices, the user understands your site's interface. If the user pauses often and selects one or more incorrect choices, you may need to redesign your site. By selecting a sampling of employees from various departments and with various levels of computer skills, you will have a good sample of users to observe.

A friendly user interface design and intuitive navigational icons are important elements in the intranet design that you must not overlook. An intranet that does not incorporate an intuitive user interface and navigational tools is like a road without signs. Just as it would be difficult for drivers to find their way from one city to another without the aid of signs, street names, and directional information, your intranet users will find it difficult to retrieve the information that they want without categories, buttons, and links that they understand and can follow. If the intranet's content is not well organized and its structure does not contain intuitive navigational tools, users will get lost.

If your organization has a graphic designer or a marketing-communications person who knows how to create graphics and convert images, you should recruit him or her for your intranet team. All too often, the Information Systems department is given the job of creating the intranet's elements, including the graphics. In most cases, IS professionals are good at working with applications and systems, but most of them don't have experience with graphics or user interface designs. A poor page layout or confusing user interface can make the difference between a successful intranet and one that fails. If you do not have the internal resources available to design the graphics and user interface for your intranet, you may want to consider outsourcing this phase of the project. There are consultants and Web publishing companies that specialize in the design and creation of Internet and intranet Web pages. Figures 6.9 and 6.10 show the difference between a well-designed Web page and one that is poorly designed.

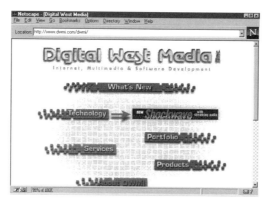

Figure 6.9 A well-designed Web page.

Figure 6.10 A poorly designed Web page.

FREE CLIP ART AND IMAGES

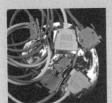

Many icons and navigational tools have become standard directional symbols for Web navigation. These icons are available as clip art in your word processing, page layout, and presentation software programs. A number of Web sites on the Internet contain images and clip art, which you can download for free. When you visit these sites, make sure you read the licensing agreements for each of the resources shown. Some of them have restrictions and requirements for icon usage. The following sites (Figure 6.11a through 6.11f) contain clip art resources you may want to incorporate into your intranet design:

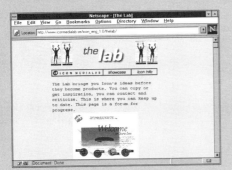

Figure 6.11a A selection of icon ideas.

Figure 611b Free clip art.

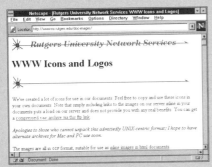

*Figure 6.11chttp://www-ns.rutgers.
edu/doc-images/*

*Figure 6.11dhttp://www.aloha.net/
~jkhanda/images.html*

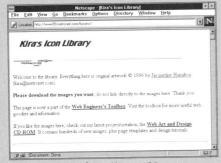

*Figure 6.11e http://www59.metronet.—
com/kicons/*

*Figure 6.11f http://www.earthlink.—
net/webicons*

Designing Functionality into Your Intranet

Before you spend too much time designing the graphics and interface for you intranet, you must define your site's functionality specifications. The functionality and features of an intranet will dictate some of the design and user interface features.

Earlier in this chapter, you learned about the different communication structures organizations use to disseminate information. As you plan your intranet's functionality, one of your goals should be to improve existing systems and infrastructures. Make a list of the strengths and weaknesses of your organization's existing structure. As you examine your organization's current information structure, it may become clear which areas of the structure work well and which ones need improvement. The weaknesses in your current systems should become the areas which your intranet can improve. For example, assume your company sends a weekly or monthly newsletter to its sales staff that provides product updates, as well as sales figures (which the company posts to increase competition among the staff). Although the company gets the information to the sales staff, the week or month delay makes the information less timely. Using the intranet, your sales manager can post daily competitive updates which enable sales representatives to access the competitive information on-demand and within minutes of the information's posting. In addition, using the intranet would also eliminate the cost of print production and distribution.

Workflow processes, document management, and work collaboration are areas of your communication structure which you should strive to improve using your intranet. *Workflow* defines the series of steps, or processes, your organization performs to complete a task. Using an intranet, organizations can speed up workflow timelines by automating certain steps in the workflow process. For example, assume your company uses a research team, which is geographically dispersed. Using the intranet, the researchers can post and update project information as they complete various steps. At any time, team members can visit the intranet page to check the project status.

Document management is another important function that you must address before you deploy your intranet. As your intranet starts to grow, document and content management will become an important task. If your organization already has a document-management system, you may want to adapt that system to work on an intranet.

Your intranet's infrastructure design is also dependent on functionality specifications. You must develop a list of functions that you want to incorporate into the intranet. As you interview employees and managers, ask them what functions they would like to be able to perform on an intranet. Because some individuals may have difficulty understanding how an intranet can be used, you may want to ask them the question, "What tasks would you like changed or improved?" Asking such questions will give you an idea of the functions and tasks that users find time consuming, tedious, or simply wasteful. Make a list of these items to determine which tasks you can apply to the intranet. Use the functionality checklist that follows to define your intranet's specifications:

Functionality Checklist

- The user interface must be intuitive and tested
- The intranet's design must support continuous updates

- The intranet must integrate database management systems to let users access key information (such as customer and product data)

- The intranet should support existing (legacy) applications

- The intranet must provide key directories, such as corporate telephone numbers and e-mail addresses

- The intranet must incorporate groupware applications

- The intranet's design must provide support (or future expansion) for on-line conferencing

- The intranet should provide division-specific and corporate-wide bulletin boards for electronic postings

- The intranet must provide document sharing and management

- The intranet must foster teamwork and collaboration

- The intranet must enhance channels of information distribution

- The intranet should incorporate search engines which simplify a user's ability to locate and access information

- The intranet must support electronic mail

- The intranet's design must provide support (for future expansion) multimedia applications that use text, images, audio, and video

- The intranet's design should support automated real-time Web-page generation

- The intranet's design should not prevent a future interface with factory equipment and other manufacturing devices

- The intranet's design should compliment the organization's quality-system requirements

- The intranet should allow users to automate workflow processes

CONTENT MANAGEMENT

Part of your organization's existing communication structure includes systems for information creation, management, and dissemination. Many organizations struggle with these tasks because they are time consuming and can easily get out of control. The intranet alone cannot solve information-management problems unless you implement specific intranet solutions that address the issues of document management. Integrating a system that provides content management is an important part of your intranet plan. The following list identifies content-management tasks to include in your intranet plan:

- Users must have the ability to add new content

- Users must have the ability to protect their content from changes by other users

- Users must have a way to update existing content

- The intranet must have a content-approval process

- The intranet must provide a way to control document revisions—especially for shared documents

- The intranet must provide an easy way for users to test their Web pages

As you formulate policies and procedures for your content-management system, you must identify and designate responsibilities through all phases of the development process. For example, you must determine who will approve content before it is added to the intranet. If your organization already has an information-approval system, you may want to implement a similar system for the intranet.

You should also develop an intranet style guide that provides guidelines for page layout, design elements, and HTML codes. A style guide will help keep a consistent look and feel throughout the intranet's Web pages. You can either implement your style guide as a printed how-to document, or you can express the guide as a template for a sample Web page. The printed style guide should contain information on where to obtain standard icons, buttons, and graphics, as well as guidelines on page dimension and how to link to other pages.

A template for a Web page is simply a set of HTML files which provide a starting point for anyone interested in adding content to your intranet. Keep in mind that it is very easy to create a working Web page and publish it for mass viewing. Your real challenge is in channeling your user's enthusiasm into the desire to produce a well-conceived Web page which fits into the intranet.

TRAINING AND SUPPORT

After your intranet is up and running, you must focus your efforts on content maintenance and employee training. Part of your plan should include a strategy for content updates and maintenance tasks. The strategy can be part of your document-management system, but you will also need to select content stakeholders. *Content stakeholders* are individuals in different departments or work groups who are responsible for the creation and maintenance of specific content. Stakeholders can be department managers, team leaders, or individuals who are the content authors and publishers.

UNDERSTANDING THE WEBMASTER

Some organizations create a position called a Webmaster, whose job description is to maintain and support a majority of the content on the intranet. The Webmaster works with each department to create, convert, and support the content on the intranet, as shown in Figure 6.12.

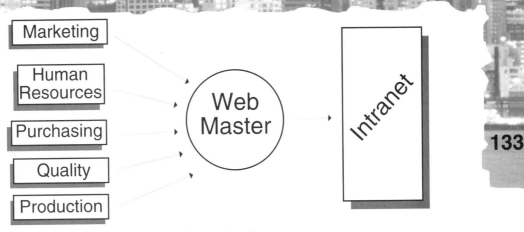

Figure 6.12 A Webmaster's role in your company.

A Webmaster must have a variety of skills to maintain the content and manage the intranet. Use the following list to evaluate possible Webmasters for your company:

- Basic Internet skills including an understanding of e-mail, FTP, and Telnet.

- A thorough understanding of HTML document creation

- Experience with CGI programming

- Programming experience with languages such as Perl, C/C++, and Java

- Experience with content creation and the conversion of text and images

- Knowledge of client–server processing

- Experience with server setup and maintenance

- Knowledge of your organization's structure and inner workings

- Organizational and training skills

If your organization chooses to have individuals from each department or a team of workers maintain your intranet's content, you must train these individuals to handle maintenance issues. You can have the Information Systems department or a vendor maintain the hardware and infrastructure of the intranet and have each department responsible for its own content development and maintenance. In this way, you decentralize the maintenance and support tasks. However, such decentralization requires that more individuals have the skills required to effectively manage the intranet.

Maintenance and support must be an important part of your plan and is necessary to ensure the long-term success of your intranet. As shown in Figure 6.13, a decentralized support structure gives authors and content owners direct access to the intranet to publish and maintain information. With decentralized intranet management, you avoid bottlenecks and improve the availability and timeliness of your site's information.

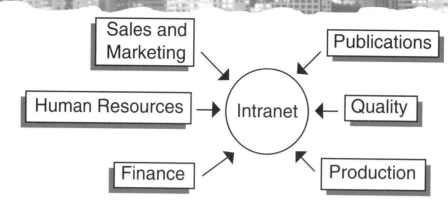

Figure 6.13 Employees can publish and maintain their own pages.

Training for stakeholders, Webmasters, and intranet customers is also an important part of your intranet strategy. Companies lose time, money, and opportunities when employees do not understand or improperly use intranet technology. For example, imagine how much time a company will lose if employees must train themselves how to use the intranet or how to create an HTML document. Employees who train themselves often receive help from coworkers who do not fully understand the concepts and underlying purpose of the technology—which means two employees are now making inefficient use of their time.

You must train intranet customers and content stakeholders with respect to two key elements. First, users must understand the intranet you are introducing and how it will improve the organization and the way your company does business. Second, you must provide users with the skills and knowledge to use the intranet to create, utilize, and maintain content. Companies that invest in the education and training of their employees will have a better chance of creating a successful intranet.

GETTING STARTED

After you have completed your intranet plan, you must start your intranet's development. The first phase of your intranet should include static HTML pages, which provide one or two levels of information. You should start small, with a pilot project based a single department or project and then build from there. As you implement your prototype, get feedback from customers on the user interface and the content structure. Then, make adjustments as needed. It is important that you measure the success of your intranet by keeping track of costs, increases in productivity, and customer responses to the intranet.

During the first phase of your intranet site, you must promote the intranet to employees within your company so they understand what the intranet is, and how they can use it. User training is crucial during the first few weeks of your intranet's release. Make sure that your Web team is prepared to provide the start-up support required to get customers up to speed on the intranet.

After you have successfully released your pilot project, you can expand it by adding content for other departments, including general corporate information. You will learn more about post-release issues in Chapter 12, "Short- and Long-Term Intranet Deployment Challenges."

In this chapter, you examined the planning, development, and management of corporate intranets. In Chapter 7, you will learn how to create basic HTML documents. Before you continue with Chapter 7, however, make sure you understand the following key concepts:

✓ You should include your company's Chief Executive Officer in the intranet planning (make him or her aware of the cost benefits) to ensure you have support throughout the organization.

✓ Your Human Resources department may have a large variety of forms and documentation that is well suited for inclusion your intranet.

✓ Your development of a successful intranet requires planning, goal setting, organizational design, team building, and change management.

✓ To sell the intranet concept to upper management, you must design a presentation that includes the definition of an intranet, the benefits, the functionality, and the details outlining the intranet's return on investment.

✓ Create your intranet plan by defining functions and specifications which meet the needs of your intranet customers.

✓ Successful intranet development teams include individuals with complementary skill sets and diverse experience.

✓ A non-linear structure links information in a path that enables users to explore and browse information spontaneously.

✓ An intuitive intranet design and user interface enable customers to easily locate information on your intranet without getting confused or lost.

✓ A pilot project using static HTML pages is a good starting point for the deployment of your intranet.

VISITING KEY SITES THAT DISCUSS INTRANETS

The World Wide Web is filled with hundreds of excellent and current articles on all aspects of intranets.Use the following sites as starting points for your Web exploration.

INTRANET SOUNDINGS

http://www.intranetjournal.com/ijx/

ISO ONLINE

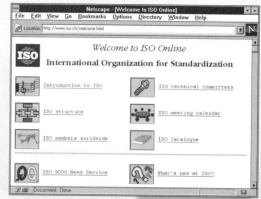

http://www.iso.ch/welcome.html

MARCH INTRANET

http://www.theplanet.net/marchsystems/
INTRANET.HTM

ABITEC, INC.

http://www.abitec.com/home/home.htm

INTRANET PAPERS

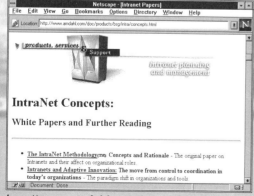

http://www.amdahl.com/doc/products/bsg/
intra/concepts.html

NEUROSYSTEMS INCORPORATED

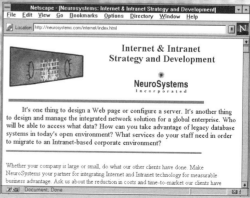

http://neurosystems.com/internet/index.html

Chapter 7

A Beginner's Guide to HTML

As you have learned, across the Web, users create documents using HTML—the hypertext markup language. In Chapter 6, you examined several tools you can use to create your intranet's content. However, you did not learn to create HTML text documents, tables, or images and other data objects that appear on your intranet pages. In the next three chapters, you will learn how to create HTML documents. In addition, if you use Microsoft *Office* products, you will learn how to use Microsoft *Word* to easily convert your existing *Word* documents to HTML.

HTML provides a powerful document-processing language. HTML is not a programming language; thus, you don't have to be a programmer to create HTML documents. Instead, using HTML, you simply embed special symbols (tags), which have specific meaning to your browser, within your documents. For example, the *<B>* and *</B>* tags direct your browser to turn on and turn off the display of text in bold print. Likewise, the *<I>* and *</I>* tags direct the browser to turn on and turn off the display of italics. This chapter examines the use of the basic HTML tags. By the time you finish this chapter, you will have learned the following key concepts:

- To create an HTML document, you need a text editor.
- To view an HTML document, you can use your browser.
- HTML, unlike a word processor, does not create *what-you-see-is-what-you-get (WYSIWYG)* documents. Instead, using HTML, you embed tags within your document that define how your browser will display the document's contents.
- To format an HTML document, you use various tags and elements. You specify HTML tags within left and right angle brackets *<HTML tag>*.
- The power of HTML is its ability to link documents.
- Using an HTML editor, you can create HTML documents easily.

HTML AND WORD PROCESSING DOCUMENTS

As you learned in the previous chapter, HTML stands for HyperText Markup Language. HTML documents are plain ASCII text files. Unlike a word processor, which focuses on the format of a document, HTML focuses primarily on the content. Thus, when you examine an HTML document, you will not see neatly formatted content. Instead, you will see a wide variety of HTML tags enclosed within left and right angle brackets, as shown in the following code:

```
<HTML>
<HEAD><TITLE>Sample Web Page</TITLE></HEAD>
<BODY>
<P>Company Phone: 800-555-1212</P>
<P>Company Web site: http://www.company.abc.com</P>
<P>Company Fax: 900-555-1212</P>
<P>Human Relations: HR@company.abc.com</P>
</BODY>
</HTML>
```

For now, it is not important that you understand any of the entries that appear within this HTML document. Instead, understand that when you create and view an HTML document, you will make extensive use of HTML tags, such as *<HTML>*, which appear at the start of each document. Figure 7.1 illustrates how the Netscape *Navigator* will display this HTML document.

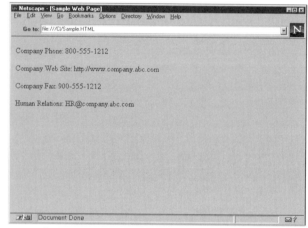

*Figure 7.1 Displaying an HTML document within the Netscape **Navigator**.*

As you have learned, one reason HTML is so powerful is that users, regardless of their hardware and software platforms, can display an HTML document's contents. For example, Mac-, Windows-, and Unix-based users can each display the previous HTML document—something that is difficult to achieve (due to compatibility problems)—with other document types.

HTML DOCUMENTS ARE ASCII FILES

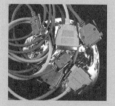

When you create an HTML document, you create an ASCII or text document as opposed to a word processing document. As you know, word processors let you format a document's text using bold or italic attributes and align text along the left and right margins. To perform such formatting, a word processor embeds special hidden characters within the document. Such characters, for example, might direct the word processor to turn on or off the display of the **bold** attribute. Although these hidden characters are meaningful to the word processor, other programs will not understand them. If, for example, you try to display a word-processing document within your browser, the browser would not understand the word processor's special characters and would generate errors.

When you create an HTML document, you must store your document as an ASCII file—in other words, without any special characters a word processor might introduce into the file. If, for example, you create a HTML document using Microsoft *Word*, and then you store that file as a *Word* document, *Word*, unknown to you, will place its formatting characters within the document. If you then try to display the file's contents using a browser, the browser will not understand these characters and errors will occur.

Normally, to create or edit an HTML document, you will use an ASCII-text editor, such as the Windows *Notepad* editor or the MS-DOS *EDIT* command. If you use an HTML editor, such as *HotMetal* or *HotDog*, the programs will store the documents you create as ASCII files. As you will learn, if you install the *Internet Assistant for Microsoft Word*, you can use *Word* to create your HTML documents. The *Internet Assistant for Microsoft Word* lets *Word* store documents in an HTML format.

CREATING AND VIEWING HTML DOCUMENTS

To create and view HTML documents, you need a simple text editor and a browser. If you are currently accessing the Internet or already have an intranet, then you probably have a browser. You need a browser to view your document before making it available to everyone on your intranet. You can use the following text editors to create HTML documents:

- *Notepad* under Windows
- *SimpleText* on the Mac
- *vi* under Unix
- Word processors (You must save your HTML documents as text with line breaks.)

MOST HTML EDITORS ARE NOT WYSIWYG

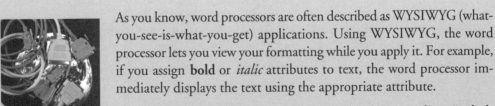

As you know, word processors are often described as WYSIWYG (what-you-see-is-what-you-get) applications. Using WYSIWYG, the word processor lets you view your formatting while you apply it. For example, if you assign **bold** or *italic* attributes to text, the word processor immediately displays the text using the appropriate attribute.

To create an HTML document, you can use any text editor (including your word processor, provided you can save the document as an ASCII text file). To assign text attributes within an HTML document, you must place various HTML tags throughout the document. Because most HTML editors are not WYSIWYG, you won't see your text formatting, such as **bold**; instead, you will see the HTML tags *<B>*bold*</B>*.

As you will learn in this chapter, few HTML editors provide near-WYSIWYG capabilities. Although these HTML editors may not show an exact representation for all HTML tags, you will find the editors much easier to work with than their non-WYSIWYG counterparts.

STAYING CURRENT WITH *HTML*

Like many network standards, the original HTML standards lasted only a short time before they were updated to meet user needs. Currently, you will find several versions of HTML: the original HTML 1.0, HTML 2.0, HTML+ (HTML 3.0), HTML 3.2, and HTML 3.5 (currently under design). Most Web browsers support HTML 2.0 standards. However, popular browsers such as Netscape *Navigator* and Microsoft *Internet Explorer* support most of the HTML 3.0 tags.

The HTML standards are controlled by the W3C consortium. Industry and academic representatives maintain W3C and they are responsible for developing common Web standards by producing specifications and reference software. You can find out more about current W3C activities by visiting their Web site at *http://www.w3.org/pub/WWW/Consortium/*, as shown in Figure 7.2.

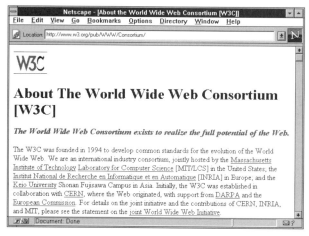

Figure 7.2 The W3C Web site.

In this chapter, you will learn about HTML 2.0 tags, which are currently supported by all Web browsers. The W3C consortium did not support the HTML 3.0 specification because there were significant differences between HTML 2.0 and HTML 3.0 that made standardization and deployment difficult. Instead, HTML 3.2 is now the official, proposed specification by the W3C consortium.

GETTING SPECIFICS ON *HTML*

As discussed, you will find several different versions of HTML, each of which supports different document formatting tags. To get specifics about the various HTML versions, visit the following Web sites as shown in Figure 7.3a through 7.3f.

Figure 7.3a http://www.w3.org/pub/—/WWW/MarkUp/HTMLPlus/—htmplus_1.html

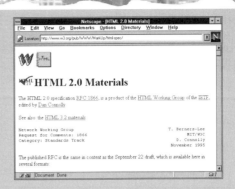

Figure 7.3b http://www.w3.org/pub/—WWW/MarkUp/html.spec/

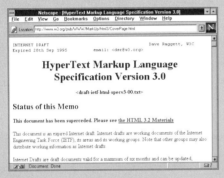

Figure 7.3c http://www.w3.org/pub/—WWW/MarkUp/html3/Cover—Page.html

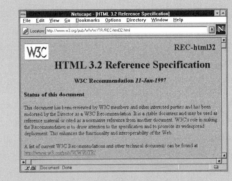

Figure 7.3d http://www.w3.org/pub/—WWW/TR/REC-html32.html

Figure 7.3e http://www.acl.lanl.gov/—HTML_WG/html-wg-95q4.—messages/0001.html

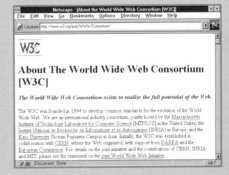

Figure 7.3f http://www.w3.org/pub/—WWW/Consortium/

The Basic Components of an HTML Document

As you have learned, every HTML document consists of tags and elements. An HTML tag identifies the document element to the browsers. HTML tags consist of a left angle bracket, a tag name, and a right angle bracket. For example, the following entry illustrates the *<HTML>* tag which should appear as the first entry in your HTML documents:

```
<HTML>
```

As you will learn, most HTML tags work in pairs; thus, you will use a starting tag and an ending tag. HTML ending tags look exactly like starting tags but begin with a forward slash /. For example, just as the *<HTML>* tag marks the start of the HTML document, the *</HTML>* tag identifies the end of an HTML document, as shown:

```
<HTML>
    Document contents here
</HTML>
```

Every HTML document has two parts: a head and a body. The document's head contains the document's title; the body contains the document contents. To identify to the browser where the document's head begins and ends, you use the *<HEAD>* and *</HEAD>* tags. Likewise, to identify where the document's body begins and ends, you use the *<BODY>* and *</BODY>* tags.

Within the document's head, you specify the document's title which the browser will display within the title bar. To inform the browser where the title starts and stops, you use the *<TITLE>* and *</TITLE>* tags. The following HTML entries illustrate the use of the HTML tags you have examined thus far:

```
<HTML>
<HEAD>
<TITLE> Your HTML Document Title </TITLE>
</HEAD>
<BODY>
    ... Body of your HTML document
</BODY>
</HTML>
```

As you will learn, not all HTML tags are required by a browser. Many tags are optional, and you can omit them from your HTML documents. However, it is a good practice to put each of these HTML tags in a document to maintain consistency. Before you can view your first HTML document using your favorite browser, you must know about the other tags you can use in the body of an HTML document.

Naming Your HTML Documents

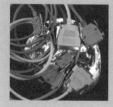
As you store your HTML documents within files on disk, assign meaningful names to your document files that accurately describe the document's contents. For example, if a file contains information on your company's CEO, you might name the document *CEO_Info.HTML*. Likewise, if the document contains marketing

information on your company's new XYZ product, you might name your file *XYZ_Marketing.HTML*. By assigning meaningful names to your HTML files, you can quickly locate the file you need at a later time.

If you are creating documents for several different divisions, you might precede each filename with an abbreviation that corresponds to a specific division. For example, you might start each filename for your Marketing division with the letters *MKT*, such as *MKT_Newsletter.HTML*. Likewise, you might name your company's Human Resources department documents with the letters *HR*.

CREATING AND VIEWING YOUR FIRST HTML DOCUMENT

Now, you are ready to actually create and view your first HTML document. As you learned in previous sections, all you need is a simple text editor to create an HTML document and a browser to view it. To create the HTML document, perform the following steps:

1. Use a text editor, such as Windows *Notepad*, to create a *new document*.

2. Next, type in the following HTML tags into the new document:

   ```
   <HTML>
   <HEAD>
   <TITLE>Your HTML Document Title</TITLE>
   </HEAD>
   <BODY>
   <H1>Your Document Heading</H1>
   <P>Hello, this is my first text HTML paragraph</P>
   </BODY>
   </HTML>
   ```

3. Save the document as *Sample.HTML*.

To view your first HTML document, perform the following steps:

1. Start your browser.

2. Within the URL field, type in the complete path name to the file, replacing the letters *http* (which you normally place in a URL) with *file*. For example, if your HTML file *Sample.HTML* resides in the *TEMP* directory on drive C, you would type *file:///c:\temp\Sample.html*.

The Netscape *Navigator* will display your HTML document, as shown in Figure 7.4.

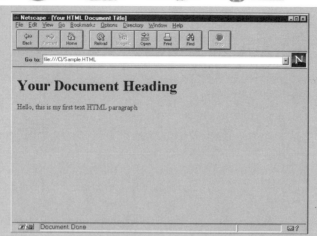

Figure 7.4 The Sample.HTML file within the Netscape Navigator.

If your browser does not display the document as shown in Figure 7.4, use your text editor to examine the contents of your *Sample.HTML* file to make sure the document's entries match those previously shown. Save any changes, then reload the document in your browser. Remember, each time you change your HTML document, you must save your changes to the document's file, and then reload the new document within your browser.

TEXT AND BLOCK LEVEL ELEMENTS

Two types of elements appear within the body of an HTML document: block-level and text-level elements. Within an HTML document, a *block-level element* creates a paragraph break—separating two blocks of text. On the other hand, *text-level elements* do not. Instead, a text-level element manipulates text that appears within a block. For example, you might use a text-level element to bold a sentence or italicize a word which appears within the middle of a paragraph.

FORMATTING TEXT

As you create HTML documents, you will be surprised how little text manipulation you actually perform. In fact, you will most often use the bold and italic text attributes to make text-based changes. To format text within an HTML document, you must specify the two tags that tell the browser where the attribute use begins and ends. For example, to display text using a bold attribute, you use the *<B>* and *</B>* tags, as shown:

```
Displaying this <B>word</B> in bold.
```

In a similar way, to use italics, you use the *<I>* and *</I>* tags, as shown:

```
Displaying this <I>word</I> in italics.
```

At other times, you may want to display text using a mono-spaced (fixed space) teletype font. In such cases, you use the *<TT>* and *</TT>* tags, as shown:

```
<TT>Displaying a sentence using a computer-like font.</TT>
```

The following HTML document, *ShowText.HTML*, illustrates the use of these text-based tags:

```
<HTML>
<HEAD>
<TITLE>Learning HTML</TITLE>
</HEAD>
<BODY>
<H1>Document Heading</H1>
<HR>
<P>This is a Normal text</P>
<P><B>This is a Bold text </B></P>
<P><I>This is a Italic text </I></P>
<P><TT>This is a Teletype text </TT></P>
</BODY>
</HTML>
```

Using your editor, create the *ShowText.HTML* document and then use the Netscape *Navigator* to display the document's contents, as shown in Figure 7.5

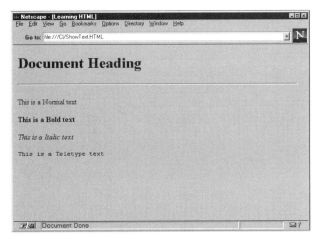

Figure 7.5 Displaying text-based attributes using ShowText.HTML.

Table 7.1 briefly describes the HTML text-based tags.

Tag	Purpose
<B></B>	Turns on and off the display of bold text
<EM></EM>	Turns on and off browser emphasis of specific text
<I></I>	Turns on and off the display of italic text
<KBD></KBD>	Turns on and off the browser-specific attribute the browser uses to display text the user would normally type at the keyboard

Table 7.1 HTML text-based tags. (continued on next page)

Tag	Purpose
`<SMALL></SMALL>`	Turns on and off the browser's use of a small font
`<STRIKE></STRIKE>`	Turns on and off the display strike-through text
`<STRONG></STRONG>`	Turns on and off the browser emphasis of specific text
`<TT></TT>`	Turns on and off the display of teletype text
`<U></U>`	Turns on and off the display of underlined text

Table 7.1 HTML text-based tags. (continued from previous page)

VIEWING HTML DOCUMENTS FROM YOUR DISK

As you create and test your own HTML documents, most browsers make it easy for you to view the document files from your hard disk. To view an HTML document that resides on your disk, start your browser (you don't need to be connected to the Internet). Next, within the browser's address field, type the letters *file:///* followed by a complete pathname to the file, such as *C:\test\MyDocument.HTML*. In other words, you replace *http://* with *file:///* (note the three slashes—although some browsers only require one or two), as shown in Figure 7.6.

Figure 7.6 Displaying an HTML document that resides within a file on your disk.

DISPLAYING SPECIAL HTML CHARACTERS

Within HTML documents, the left and right angle brackets (<>) have specific meaning. Browsers look for these characters to determine how to display a document's text. Depending on your document's contents, there may be times when you need to use these characters within the body of your text—as part of the text itself. For example, programmers often use the symbols > (greater than) and < (less than) in their computer code. For times when your text requires these characters, you can tell the browser to ignore the character's special meaning by placing the following replacement characters within your documents:

Character	Replacement Characters
<	&lt
>	&gt

For example, assume that you need to represent the following expression within an HTML document:

```
if revenues > expenses and net_income < 0 then
```

To display the expression, you must replace the symbols > and <, as shown here:

```
if revenues &gt expenses and net_income &lt 0 then
```

UNDERSTANDING BLOCK-LEVEL TAGS

As briefly discussed, HTML block-level tags separate two or more blocks (such as paragraphs) of text. Within an HTML document, text blocks include headings (which are similar to the headings that appear within the pages of this book), paragraphs, tables, lists, and so on.

UNDERSTANDING HTML HEADINGS

To improve the organization of a large document, you can group your document into related sections. At the beginning of each section, you can place a heading that tells the reader the content that the section contains. For example, within a book, an author divides the content into chapters. Then, within each chapter, the author uses headings to organize the chapter's contents. For example, this section of the book uses the heading *Understanding HTML Headings*.

Within an HTML document, you can use six different heading levels to indicate the size of the headings. The heading tags are: *<H1>*, *<H2>*, *<H3>*, *<H4>*, *<H5>*, and *<H6>*. The *<H1>* tag produces the largest heading. The headings get progressively smaller at each level, ending at *<H6>*, the smallest heading. Normally, you use an *<H1>* tag to identify a main topic, and use the other tags such as *<H2>* and *<H3>* to further divide the topic's contents.

As you have learned, you specify most HTML tags in pairs, and that is also true for heading tags. For example, to create an *<H1>* heading, you must tell the browser where the heading's text starts and stops, as shown in the following statement:

```
<H1>This is a Main Heading</H1>
```

The following HTML document, *Headings.HTML*, illustrates the use of HTML heading tags. Using your text editor, create the file, *Headings.HTML*, which contains the following entries:

```
<HTML>
<HEAD>
<TITLE> Your HTML Document Title </TITLE>
</HEAD>
<BODY>
<H1>Your Document Heading</H1>
<H2>Your Document Heading</H2>
<H3>Your Document Heading</H3>
<H4>Your Document Heading</H4>
<H5>Your Document Heading</H5>
<H6>Your Document Heading</H6>
<P>Hello, this is my first HTML paragraph</P>
</BODY>
</HTML>
```

Then, using the steps previously discussed, view the document's contents using your browser. Figure 7.7 illustrates how the Netscape *Navigator* displays the document's contents.

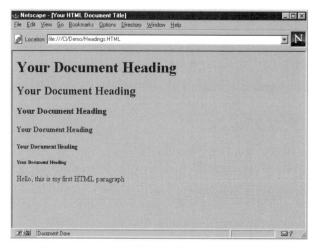

*Figure 7.7 Displaying the contents of the file **Headings.HTML** with the Netscape **Navigator**.*

As you have learned, when you use HTML tags within a document, you instruct the browser how you want to display the document's contents. Notice that the browser ignores the HTML tags and displays only the content that is between the tags—formatting the content as you have specified. As you will learn, some browsers ignore the following attributes within an HTML document and do not display them:

- Many browsers ignore multiple spaces between words, displaying only one space
- Many browsers ignore indentation you place before and after tags
- Many browsers ignore blank lines that appear between tags
- Many browsers ignore line breaks within a paragraph

As you create your HTML documents, you will want to test the document's display using multiple browsers. Although a document may display correctly within your browser, there is no guarantee that the users who visit your Web site will use the same browser. At a minimum, you should always test your HTML documents using the Netscape *Navigator* and Microsoft *Internet Explorer*.

VIEWING A DOCUMENT'S *HTML* ENTRIES

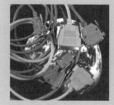

As you view a Web site, most browsers let you view the site's HTML entries. For example, if you are using the Netscape *Navigator*, you can view the current site's HTML entries by selecting the View menu Document Source option. Likewise, if you are using the Microsoft *Internet Explorer*, you select the View menu Source option.

When you examine a site's HTML entries in this way, you cannot change the entries; you can only view them. In other words, you cannot edit an HTML document from within your browser. However, you can copy and paste the file's contents into a text editor within which you can modify the entries as you see fit. As you examine the entries at other Web sites, you may notice HTML is not case sensitive—you can write the head tag as *<head>*, or *<HEAD>*, or *<Head>*.

DEFINING PARAGRAPHS WITHIN AN HTML DOCUMENT USING <P>

As briefly discussed, HTML supports block- and text-based elements. For example, the HTML heading elements are block elements that create line breaks. In a similar way, the HTML paragraph element, *<P>*, forces a line break. The following HTML document, *Paragraphs.HTML*, illustrates the use of the *<P>* and *</P>* tags:

```
<HTML><BODY><H1>Naming Your HTML Documents</H1>

<P>As you store your HTML documents within files on disk, assign
meaningful names to your document files that accurately describe the
document's contents. For example, if a file contains information on
your company's CEO, you might name the document <I>CEO_Info.HTML</
I>. Likewise, if the document contains marketing information on your
company's new XYZ product, you might name your file
<I>XYZ_Marketing.HTML</I>. By assigning meaningful names to your
HTML files, you can quickly locate the file you need at a later
time. </P> <P>If you are creating documents for several different
divisions, you might precede each filename with an abbreviation that
corresponds to a specific division. For example, you might start
each filename for your Marketing division with the letters <I>MKT</
I>, such as <I>MKT_Newsletter.HTML</I>. Likewise, you might precede
your company's Human Resources department documents with the letters
<I>HR</I>. </P> </BODY>
```

Figure 7.8 illustrates how the Netscape *Navigator* will display the document's contents.

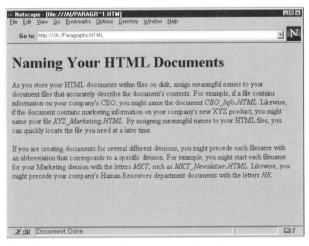

*Figure 7.8 Displaying the contents of **Paragraphs.HTML** with the Netscape **Navigator**.*

DISPLAYING PREFORMATTED TEXT USING <PRE>

As you have learned, the browser has considerable control over how it displays the contents of an HTML document. There may be times, however, when your document contains content that you have preformatted, perhaps using tabs and specific spacing. In such cases, you can use the <PRE> tag to preserve your formatting; however, you cannot insert different font sizes within a pair of <PRE> tags. By using the <PRE> and </PRE> tags, you can preserve blank lines, tabs, and extra spaces. The following HTML document, *Preformat.HTML*, illustrates the use of the <PRE> and </PRE> tags:

```
<HTML>
<HEAD>
<TITLE>Learning HTML</TITLE>
</HEAD>
<BODY>
<H1>My document heading</H1>
<PRE>
First line of text in paragraph 1.
 Line 2 of paragraph 1.
   Line 3 of paragraph 1.
     Line 4 of paragraph 1.
       Line 5 of paragraph 1.
</PRE>
<P>
Compare the font used in the above 5 lines with the font used in
this paragraph.
</P>
</BODY>
</HTML>
```

Figure 7.9 illustrates how the Netscape *Navigator* will display the contents of the file, *Preformat.HTML*.

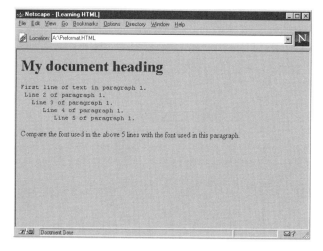

Figure 7.9 Displaying preformatted text.

FORCING A LINEBREAK USING

As you learned in previous sections, you can force a line break anywhere in HTML text by using the paragraph tag <P>. However, you also learned that in addition to forcing the line break, the <P> tag directs the browser to display a blank line. Depending on your document's contents, you want to insert one or more line breaks without inserting blank lines. In such cases, you can use the line-break tag <BR>. The following document, *Break.HTML*, illustrates the use of the <BR> tag:

```
<HTML>
<HEAD>
<TITLE>Learning HTML</TITLE>
</HEAD>
<BODY>
<H1>This document's heading</H1>
<P>
Paragraph 1, Line 1.<BR>
Paragraph 1, Line 2.<BR>
Paragraph 1, Line 3.<BR>
Paragraph 1, Line 4.
</P>
<P>Paragraph 2.</P>
</BODY>
</HTML>
```

Figure 7.10 illustrates how the Netscape *Navigator* will display the contents of the *Break. HTML* document.

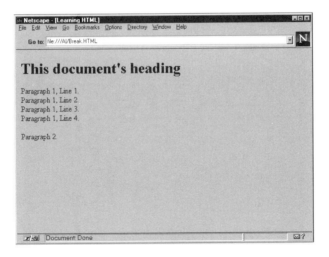

Figure 7.10 Using the <BR> tag to force a line break.

HTML List

If you only had HTML paragraph tags to work with, you could not force browsers to display your HTML documents with the formatting quality of a word processor. Luckily, the HTML creators knew this and have provided you with additional formatting tags. Using these tags, you can create numbered and bulleted lists. Using these two list types, you can make your HTML documents look like a word processing document. HTML list tags, like paragraph tags, are part of the block level category of tags—their use causes a paragraph break. HTML supports two types of lists: a numbered or ordered list and an unordered or bulleted list.

As you will find, the browser controls the format and display of HTML lists; thus, you cannot change the indentation or the numbering scheme of your list as you can with a word processor. To create an ordered (numbered) list, you use the *<OL>* and *</OL>* tags. Within these tags, use the *<LI>* list-item tag to define a list entry:

```
<OL>
<LI> First item of an ordered list
<LI> Second item of an ordered list
</OL>
```

Likewise, to create an unordered list, you use the *<UL>* and *</UL>* tags, as shown here:

```
<UL>
<LI> First item of an unnumbered list
<LI> Second item of an unnumbered list
</UL>
```

Figure 7.11 shows how the Netscape *Navigator* will display these lists.

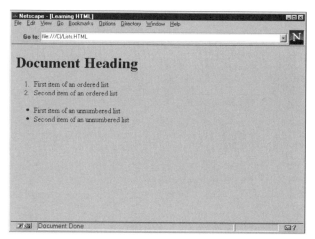

Figure 7.11 Displaying an ordered and an unordered list.

Depending on your document's contents, there may be times when you need to nest (insert) one list within another. To do so, you must make a nested list. For example, the following HTML document, *NestedList.HTML*, nests an unordered list within an ordered list:

```
<HTML>
<HEAD>
<TITLE>Learning HTML</TITLE>
</HEAD>
<BODY>
<H1>Document Heading</H1>
<OL>
<LI> first item of outer list
    <UL>
        <LI> first item of an unnumbered nested list
        <LI> second item of an unnumbered nested list
    </UL>
<LI> second item of the outer list
</OL>
</BODY>
</HTML>
```

Figure 7.12 illustrates how the Netscape *Navigator* will display these two lists.

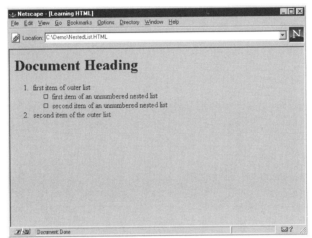

Figure 7.12 Using Netscape **Navigator** to display nested lists.

DEFINITION LISTS

In addition to numbered and unnumbered lists, you can also use the definition list tag, *<DL>*, to list items in your HTML document. Definition lists differ from unordered and numbered lists in that they consist of two parts, and they do not display a bullet or a number in front of list items. Within a definition list, you place terms (using *<DT>*) and definitions (using *<DD>*). For example, the following statements illustrate a simple definition list:

```
<HTML>
<HEAD><TITLE>Definition List</TITLE></HEAD>
<BODY>
<DL>
<DT> Definition Term Name
<DD> First Definition Term's definition
<DD> Second Definition Term's definition
</DL>
</BODY>
```

Figure 7.13 shows how the Netscape *Navigator* will display the definition list.

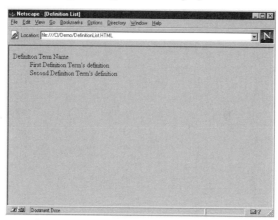

Figure 7.13 Displaying a definition list.

CREATING HORIZONTAL LINE BREAKS USING <HR>

As you visit sites on the Web, you encounter pages that display a horizontal line across the window. Webmasters often use such a line to divide their content into specific sections. To create the horizontal line, you use the *<HR>* tag. The following HTML document, *Horizontal.HTML*, illustrates the use of the *<HR>* tag:

```
<HTML>
<HEAD>
<TITLE>Learning HTML</TITLE>
</HEAD>
<BODY>
<H1>Document Heading</H1>
<HR>
<P>This text is in-between the lines</P>
<HR>
</BODY>
</HTML>
```

Figure 7.14 shows how Netscape *Navigator* uses the *<HR>* tag to create a horizontal line.

Figure 7.14 Displaying a horizontal line within Netscape Navigator.

LINKING HTML DOCUMENTS

In previous sections, you learned how to create simple HTML pages. As your documents become more complex, there will be many times when you will want to link one document to another. A key feature of HTML is that HTML makes it easy for you to link documents.

When a browser displays an HTML document, the browser underlines text within the document to indicate that the text is a link to another HTML document or another object, such as a sound file. Within an HTML document, a link consists of the following:

- The HTML start anchor tag *<A>*

- The name of the document to which you are linking

- The text (hypertext) that the browser underlines to indicate the link

- The ending anchor tag *</A>*

To create complete link tags, you also must place the hypertext reference (HREF) attribute at the start anchor tag. For example, assume you have an HTML document that contains employee phone numbers, named *Phone.HTML*, which you want to link. To link the document, you use the following tags:

```
<A HREF="phone.html">Display Phone List</A>
```

The following HTML document, *Anchor.HTML*, illustrates the use of the link:

```
<HTML>
<HEAD>
<TITLE>Intranet Top Page</TITLE>
</HEAD>
<BODY>
<H1>Company XYZ Intranet Main Page</H1>
<H2>Welcome to our Intranet</H2>
<P>Click <A HREF="phone.html">Display Phone List</A> to view the
employee phone listing</P>
</BODY>
</HTML>
```

To better understand how the link works, create the following simple HTML document, *Phone.HTML*, which you place in the same directory as *Anchor.HTML*:

```
<HTML>
<HEAD>
<TITLE>Phone Listing</TITLE>
</HEAD>
<BODY>
<H1>Company XYZ Employee Phone Listing</H1>
<P>John A (3321)</P>
<P>Lisa B (3322)</P>
<P>James C (3323)</P>
<P>Alfanso D (3324)</P>
```

```
<P>Mark E (3325)</P>
<P>Bob F (3326)</P>
<P>Click <A HREF="Anchor.HTML">here</A> Return to Main Page.</P>
</BODY>
</HTML>
```

As you can see, this HTML file provides a link back to the main intranet page which is contained in the file, *Anchor.HTML*. By clicking on the document links, you can move quickly between the two documents.

In Chapter 6, you examined linear and non-linear links. In most cases, it is much easier for a document's readers to follow a linear, sequential set of pages. Your job, as an HTML document developer, is to direct your readers in such a way that they can follow a clear path in their search for information. So, when you use HTML links, apply your best judgment, and do not let the HTML linking capabilities make you create documents that are hard to follow.

RELATIVE VERSUS ABSOLUTE ADDRESSING

As you create links within your HTML documents, you must specify the location of the file you are linking to the document. If the document resides on the same computer as the current document, you can use an absolute (complete) or relative pathname to specify the document's location. For example, assume your intranet's primary page resides in the directory, *C:\INTRANET*, and the HTML document that contains your company's phone list resides in the directory, *C:\INTRANET\EMPLOYEE*. You can link the pages using either relative or absolute addressing.

When you use absolute addressing, you must specify the complete pathname of the destination file within the link's tag. The problem with absolute addressing is that it makes it difficult for you to move files. Each time you move documents, you must update every absolute address. You may find that using relative addresses simplifies your process of moving files. When you use relative addressing, you specify document locations (their directories) relative to one another. Table 7.2 shows the difference between absolute and relative addressing.

Path Name	Addressing Mode and Description
"Phone.HTML"	Relative addressing. The destination file name for this link is in the same directory as the source HTML file.
"Employee/Phone.HTML"	Relative addressing. The destination file name for this link is in the *Employee* subdirectory which resides beneath the current directory.
"../Anchor.HTML"	Relative addressing. The destination file for this link is the directory above the current directory.
"C:\Employee\Phone.HTML"	Absolute addressing. The destination file for this link is in the *Employee* directory on drive C.

Table 7.2 Relative versus absolute addressing.

In most cases, you should use relative addressing. Relative addressing lets you easily copy your entire document from one directory to another directory, or from one drive to another drive, or from one platform to another platform.

Besides linking one file to another file, you can link a file to another Web site. For example, you can put a link from your intranet to Microsoft's home page using the following tag:

```
<P>Click<A HREF="http://www.microsoft.com">here 1</A> to go to
Microsoft's home page.</P>
```

LINKING TO SPECIFIC SECTIONS OF ANOTHER *HTML* DOCUMENT

In the previous section, you learned how to link an HTML page to the top of another HTML document. However, in some cases, you may want to link to a specific section within another document. To do this, you must first create an anchor within the destination document. An anchor simply identifies a specific location within that document. To understand how anchor tags work, modify the paragraph that contains Bob F's phone number in the document *Phone.HTML*, as shown:

```
<P><A NAME="phonebob">Bob F (3326) </A> </P>
```

In this case, the anchor simply defines a label or location within the document that you have named *phonebob*. As you can see, using the *NAME=* attribute to create an anchor is similar to using the *HREF=* attribute to create links. After creating the anchor tag, add the following line to the *Anchor.HTML* document to create a direct link to Bob's phone number within the *Phone. HTML* document:

```
<P>Click <A HREF="phone.html">here </A> to go to top of Phone.html</
P>

<P>Click <A HREF="phone.html#phonebob">here </A> to go to Bob F's
phone number in Phone.html</P>
```

In this case, to use the anchor, *phonebob*, you simply append *#phonebob* to the link. If you had created an anchor named *dogs* within the *Phone.HTML* document, you would reference the anchor as shown:

```
<P>Click <A HREF="phone.html#dogs">here </A> to go to dogs anchor </
P>
```

LINKING TO SPECIFIC SECTIONS OF THE SAME *HTML* DOCUMENT

In many cases, it is not necessary to create multiple HTML documents. Instead, you can simply create one document (instead of many small HTML documents) which you divide into sections. As you will learn, creating one document makes it easier for users to print the document's contents. If you have ten one-page HTML documents, users must print ten documents.

To divide a document into different sections, you simply create anchors (named locations) throughout the document to which you can define links. The following document, *TwoAnchors.HTML*, uses two anchors. The first anchor is named *Top* and the second, *phonebob*:

```
<HTML>
<HEAD><TITLE>Intranet Top Page</TITLE></HEAD>
<BODY>
<H1><A NAME="Top">Company XYZ Intranet Main Page</A></H1>
<P>Click <A HREF=#phonebob>here</A> to see Bob F's phone number </P>
<HR>
<P>John A (3320)</P>
<P>Lisa B (3321)</P>
<P>James C (3322)</P>
<P>Alfanso D (3323)</P>
<P>Mark E (3324)</P>
<P><A NAME="phonebob">Bob F (3325)</A></P>
<P>Click <A HREF=#Top>here</A> to go back to the top of this page.</
P>
</BODY>
</HTML>
```

So far, you have learned how to create HTML files manually. If you are familiar with computer programming, you can easily create HTML files manually. For nonprogrammers, creating HTML documents can be challenging. In the following sections, you will learn how to create HTML documents without having to learn everything about HTML.

USING INTERNET ASSISTANT FOR MICROSOFT WORD

In most corporations, the bulk of the content that users will put on an intranet resides in word-processing, spreadsheet, and presentation-program files. To help you convert your existing documents to HTML, many software developers now offer add-on upgrades that you can use to convert existing documents to HTML automatically. One such tool is *Internet Assistant for Microsoft Word*.

Recently, Microsoft has released several free add-on programs to help Microsoft Office users automatically create or convert their existing documents to HTML format. You can download *Internet Assistant for Microsoft Word* from the Web at *http://microsoft.com/msword/internet/ia/*, as shown in Figure 7.15.

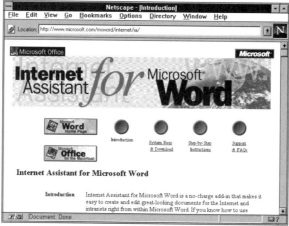

Figure 7.15 Internet Assistant for Microsoft Word.

Internet Assistant is add-on software for Microsoft *Word*. If you are familiar with *Word*, you can learn how to use *Internet Assistant* in a few minutes. In the following two chapters, you will learn how to use *Internet Assistant* to create HTML tables, forms, charts, and graphs. In this section, you will learn how to create HTML text as well as links using *Internet Assistant*.

To begin, you must download and install *Internet Assistant* from the Microsoft Web site. The software is easy to install, but downloading the file may take a while, depending on your modem speed. After you install *Internet Assistant*, you can either create new HTML documents or convert your existing word processing documents to HTML.

159

CREATING A NEW HTML DOCUMENT

To create a new HTML document using *Internet Assistant*, perform these steps:

1. Select the File menu New option. *Word* will display the New dialog box.

2. Click on *HTML.dot* to create a new document. *Word*, in turn, will open a new HTML document.

3. Select the "Heading 1,H1" entry with the dropdown Style list. Next, type the text "This is Heading 1 line" and press ENTER. *Internet Assistant* will automatically change the style back to "Normal,P."

4. Type "This is a paragraph" and press ENTER. *Internet Assistant* will move the cursor to the next line.

5. From the Style list, select "List Number,OL." *Internet Assistant* will indent and number the line as 1.

6. Type the text "This is the first line of a numbered list" and press ENTER. *Internet Assistant* will indent the next line and will number it as 2.

7. Type "Second line of numbered list" and press ENTER. *Internet Assistant* will indent the next line and will number the line as 3.

8. From the Style Menu, select "Normal,P." *Internet Assistant* will clear the number and move the indent back.

9. Type "Ending paragraph" and press ENTER.

10. From the File menu, select "HTML Document Info." *Internet Assistant* will display HTML Document Head Information.

11. Type the document title as "Internet Assistant document title" and click OK.

12. Select the File menu Save option. *Word* will display the Save As dialog box.

13. Type in the file as IAfile. Within the Type list, select HTML Document (*.htm) and click *OK*. Word will save the file as *IAfile.HTM*.

You just created your first HTML document without typing any HTML tags. *Internet Assistant for Microsoft Word* also provides you with the ability to view your document source file.

As you create complex HTML documents, you may find that *Internet Assistant* does not support all HTML tags. Within your HTML document, you can simply type in the HTML tags that *Internet Assistant* does not support.

Within *Internet Assistant*, you can view the document's HTML tags by selecting the View menu HTML Source option. Also, from within your *Internet Assistant* document, you can open a browser window to see how a browser will display your HTML document. To view your current document within a browser window, select the View menu Preview option.

CONVERTING EXISTING WORD DOCUMENTS TO HTML DOCUMENTS

Internet Assistant makes it easy for you to convert your existing *Word* documents to HTML. To convert a *Word* document to HTML, perform these steps:

1. Select the File menu Open option and open the existing document.

2. Select the File menu Save As option. *Word* will display the Save As dialog box.

3. Within the Save As dialog box Type list, select HTML Document (*.htm) and click *OK*.

4. *Word* will save the file, opening it within the *Internet Assistant* for editing.

PUTTING IT ALL TOGETHER

Across the Web, almost all documents make extensive use of HTML. In this chapter, you learned the basics of HTML editing. In Chapter 8, you will learn how to create HTML tables, and import and place preformatted text, such as financial data, into a document. In addition, you will learn how to convert an *Excel* spreadsheet into an HTML document. Before you continue with Chapter 8, however, make sure you understand the following concepts:

✓ To create an HTML document, you must create an ASCII-text file that contains your HTML entries.

✓ Most HTML editors do not support WYSIWYG (what you see is what you get) capabilities, which means you cannot view your document's true format as you create the document.

✓ Currently, you will find several versions of HTML: the original HTML, HTML 2.0, HTML+ (HTML 3.0), HTML 3.2, and HTML 3.5.

✓ To view HTML documents, you need a Web browser. By replacing the letters *http* within the browser's URL field with the letters *file*, followed by a complete pathname, you can use your browser to view HTML documents that reside on your disk.

✓ HTML documents consist of block-level and text-level elements.

✓ HTML lets you create links to locations within the same document or to other documents, which lets users move quickly to the information they need.

✓ If you have installed the *Internet Assistant* add-on program for *Word,* you can convert existing *Word* documents into HTML format by using the File menu Save As option.

VISITING KEY SITES THAT DISCUSS INTRANETS

The World Wide Web is filled with hundreds of excellent and current articles on all aspects of intranets. Use the following sites as starting points for your Web exploration.

WebSite Central

http://website.ora.com/

Intranet and Internet Publishing

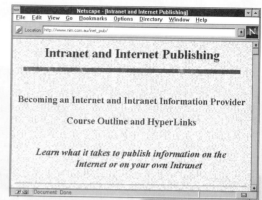

http://www.nim.com.au/inet_pub/

Internet World Online

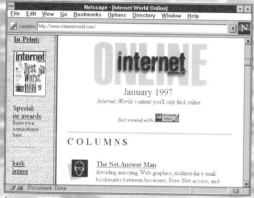

http://www.internetworld.com/

Internet Product Site

http://tips.iworld.com/_frames.shtml/main.html

Help for Web Developers

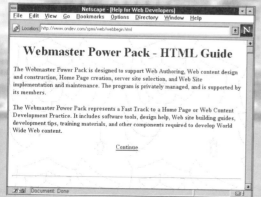

http://www.ondev.com/spmi/web/webbegin.html

HotDog Professional

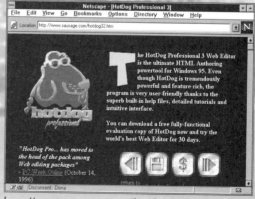

http://www.sausage.com/hotdog32.htm

Chapter 8

HTML Tables and
Special Formatting

163

As you learned in Chapter 7, converting existing data into HTML format can be time consuming and costly. As you build Web pages, another challenge you will face is how to create tables using HTML. As you move your company's financial data to your intranet, you will encounter many documents that require tables. For example, documents such as annual reports, quarterly reports, and retirement policies contain financial information in table format.

Although tables are a common element in many Web pages, tables are not easy to create using HTML. As discussed in this chapter, HTML ignores multiple spaces and tabs within a document, which makes text alignment difficult. In this chapter, you will learn how to create tables using HTML, and how to convert tables from existing programs such as *Word* and *Excel*. By the time you finish this chapter, you will understand the following key concepts.

- Within a Web page, tables let you group and display related data.

- HTML tables consist of a caption, headings, cells, and data.

- To create a table using HTML, you use the *<TABLE>* and *</TABLE>* tags.

- You divide an HTML table into rows using the *<TR>* and *</TR>* tags.

- Within each row of an HTML table, you define cells using the *<TD>* and *</TD>* tags.

- Using *Internet Assistant for Microsoft Word*, you can convert *Word* or *Excel* tables into HTML tables.

BASICS OF *HTML TABLE COMMANDS*

In Chapter 7, you learned how to create Web documents using HTML tags. You also learned how to use Microsoft *Internet Assistant* to convert *Word* documents into HTML format. In this chapter, you will learn how to create tables within an HTML document. If your intranet users are using Netscape *Navigator* or Microsoft *Internet Explorer*, they should have no problem viewing tables within a Web page. On the other hand, if your users have different browsers, you may want to avoid using tables—not all browsers can display tables correctly.

Web pages use tables that require a special format to display information, such as financial data. As you have learned, HTML does not let you format text using tabs and spaces. Figure 8.1 shows how Netscape *Navigator* will display a table within a Web page.

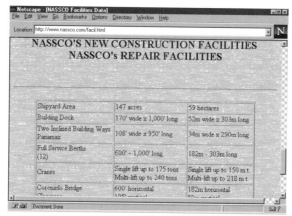

Figure 8.1 An example of a table within the Netscape Navigator.

HTML TABLES

HTML tables consist of a caption, headings, rows, and cells. To specify each part of a table, you use a specific HTML tag. To define the table itself, you use the *<TABLE>* and *</TABLE>* tags. Within these two tags, you will place other tags that define the table's caption, rows, and cells, as shown:

```
<TABLE>
   Other tags here
</TABLE>
```

DEFINING A TABLE'S CAPTION USING THE *<CAPTION>* AND *</CAPTION>* TAGS

The HTML *<CAPTION>* and *</CAPTION>* tags let you define a table's title—which, by default, your browser will display centered at the top of the table. Using the *ALIGN* attribute, you can instruct the browser to position the title in a different location. For example, if you include the *ALIGN=BOTTOM* attribute within the *<CAPTION>* tag, the browser will place the title at the bottom of a table. The following HTML entry illustrates how you create a table caption:

```
<CAPTION ALIGN=BOTTOM>Company XYZ Financial Data</CAPTION>
```

DEFINING A TABLE'S ROWS USING THE *<TR>* AND *</TR>* TAGS

Tables consist of rows, which you further divide into data cells. Within an HTML table definition, you use the *<TR>* and *</TR>* tags to define each row, as shown:

```
<TABLE>
<TR>. . . Row one's entries are here . . .</TR>
<TR>. . . Row two's entries are here . . .</TR>
<TR>. . . Row three's entries are here . . .</TR>
</TABLE>
```

Rows in an HTML table consist of data cells. You define a table cell using the *<TD>* and *</TD>* tags.

DEFINING A TABLE CELL USING THE <TD> AND </TD> TAGS

Within each row of an HTML table, you must define one or more data cells. To define a data cell, you use the *<TD>* and *</TD>* tags. For example, the following HTML entries create three table cells, which contain the values One, Two, and Three:

```
<TABLE>
<TR><TD>One</TD><TD>Two</TD><TD>Three</TD></TR>
</TABLE>
```

Most browsers will not display cells that do not contain any data. If you need to display a blank cell, place a non-breaking space within the entry, as shown:

```
<TD><BR></TD>
```

DEFINING A TABLE HEADING USING THE <TH> AND </TH> TAGS

Most tables use a row of headings that describe a column's contents. For example, a stock information table might contain each company's stock-market symbol, low price, high price, and ending price. Using the *<TH>* and *</TH>* tags, you can create a heading within a table. The *<TH>* tag is quite similar to *<TD>*, except that the *<TH>* tag directs the browser to use a bold font and to center align the cell's contents:

```
<TABLE>
<TR><TH>Company Symbol</TH><TH>Low Price</TH><TH>High Price
</TH><TH>Closing Price</TH></TR>

<TR><TD>ABC</TD><TD>15</TD><TD>16</TD><TD>15.5</TD></TR>
<TR><TD>DEF</TD><TD>5</TD><TD>7</TD><TD>6</TD></TR>
<TR><TD>EFG</TD><TD>20</TD><TD>21</TD><TD>21</TD></TR>
</TABLE>
```

Figure 8.2 shows how the Netscape *Navigator* will display this table's contents.

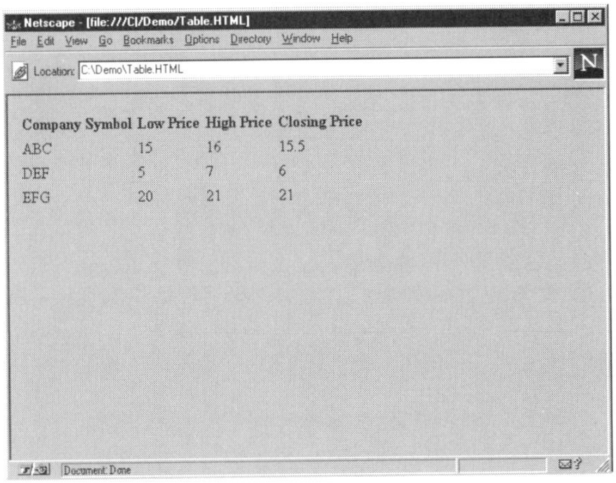

*Figure 8.2 A table of stock prices within Netscape **Navigator**.*

USING TABLE ATTRIBUTES

As you create HTML tables, you can use attribute settings to improve the table's appearance. The following sections examine several of the attributes you can use to format your tables. For more information on HTML tables, visit the site *http://www.erin.gov.au/www-standards/www-authoring/html3/tables.html*, shown in Figure 8.3.

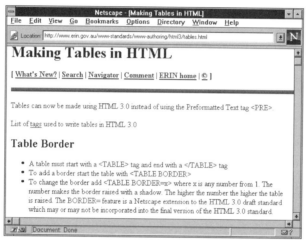

Figure 8.3 Additional information on HTML tables.

DISPLAYING A TABLE BORDER USING THE BORDER ATTRIBUTE

By default, browsers do not display a border around tables. Using the *BORDER* attribute, you direct the browser to display a border around the table as well as the individual cells.

The following HTML entries illustrate the use of the *BORDER* attribute. Figure 8.4 shows how the Netscape *Navigator* will display the table's border:

```
<TABLE BORDER>

<TR><TH>Company Symbol</TH>
<TH>Low Price</TH>
<TH>High Price</TH>
<TH>Closing Price</TH></TR>

<TR><TD>ABC</TD><TD>15</TD><TD>16</TD><TD>15.5</TD></TR>
<TR><TD>DEF</TD><TD>5</TD><TD>7</TD><TD>6</TD></TR>
<TR><TD>EFG</TD><TD>20</TD><TD>21</TD><TD>21</TD></TR>

</TABLE>
```

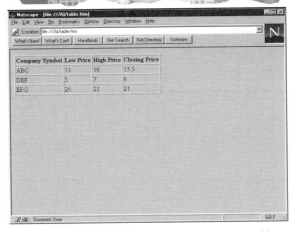

Figure 8.4 The effect of border value on a table.

By default, browsers leave a space between table cells and the border. If you omit the *BORDER* attribute, the browser still leaves the same space between the table cells and the table's invisible border. Therefore, a table with and without the *BORDER* attribute will have the same width. Figure 8.5 illustrates the same table with and without a border.

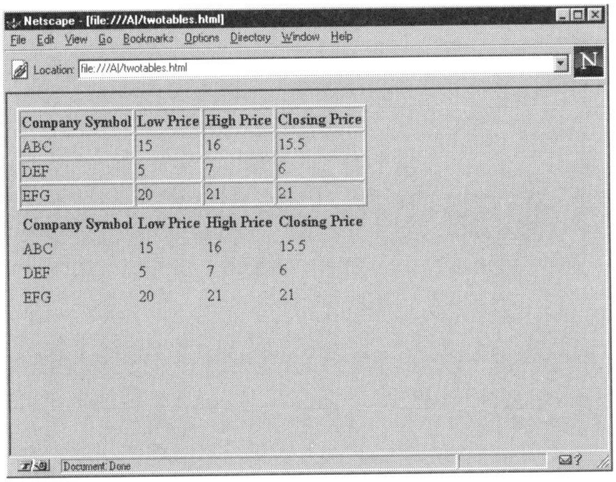

Figure 8.5 A table with and without a border.

ALIGNING TABLE ELEMENTS USING THE *ALIGN* ATTRIBUTE

Within a table's caption, rows, headings, and cells, you can use the *ALIGN* attribute to control where the browser displays an item or how the browser aligns text. For example, within a table's caption, you use the *TOP* or *BOTTOM* attribute values to direct the browser to display the caption at the top or bottom of the table:

```
<CAPTION ALIGN=Bottom>Company XYZ Financial Data</CAPTION>
```

Within a row, heading, or cell, you can use the *LEFT, RIGHT,* and *CENTER* attribute values to control the horizontal alignment. The default alignment value for a cell is *LEFT.* If you specify the *ALIGN* attribute for a row within the *<TR>* tag, the browser will apply your alignment to each of the cells within that row.

CONTROLLING A TABLE'S VERTICAL ALIGNMENT USING THE *VALIGN* ATTRIBUTE

Just as the *ALIGN* attribute lets you specify horizontal alignment, the *VALIGN* attribute lets you specify vertical alignment. You can use the *VALIGN* attribute with the *<TR>, <TH>,* and *<TD>* tags. The values you assign to the *VALIGN* attribute are *TOP, MIDDLE,* and *BOTTOM.* As before, if you specify the *VALIGN* attribute for a row, the browser will apply the alignment to each cell within that row.

USING THE *ROWSPAN* AND *COLSPAN* ATTRIBUTES

Depending on your table's contents, there may be times when you want a column or row entry to span multiple cells. For example, Figure 8.6 illustrates a table that displays the heading *Stock Information* across 4 columns.

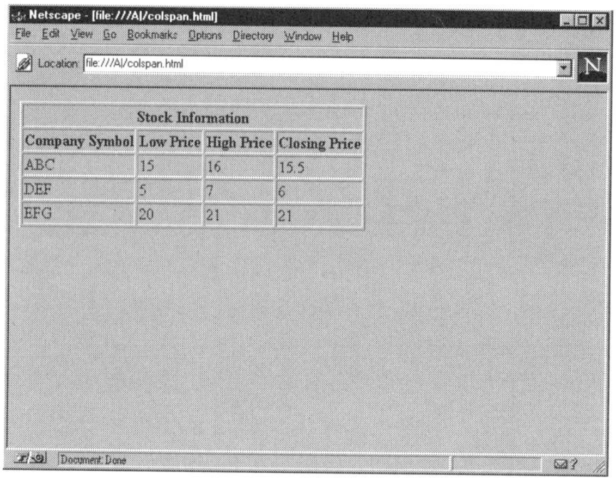

Figure 8.6 A table heading that spans four columns.

To span multiple rows or columns within a table, you must use the *ROWSPAN* or *COLSPAN* attributes within the *<TH>* or *<TD>* tags. To span the current cell across two rows within a table, you assign the value 2 to the *ROWSPAN* attribute, such as *ROWSPAN=2.* Likewise, to span the current cell across 3 columns, you would use *COLSPAN=3.* The following HTML entries use the *COLSPAN* attribute to create the table title shown in Figure 8.6:

```
<HTML><BODY><TABLE BORDER>
<TR><TH COLSPAN=4>Stock Information</TH></TR>

<TR><TH>Company Symbol</TD><TH>Low Price</TH><TH>High Price
</TH><TH>Closing Price</TH></TR>
<TR><TD>ABC</TD><TD>15</TD><TD>16</TD><TD>15.5</TD></TR>
<TR><TD>DEF</TD><TD>5</TD><TD>7</TD><TD>6</TD></TR>
<TR><TD>EFG</TD><TD>20</TD><TD>21</TD><TD>21</TD></TR>
</TABLE></BODY>
```

CONTROLLING SPACE USING THE *CELLSPACING* AND *CELLPADDING* ATTRIBUTES

Depending on your table's contents, you may want to control the thickness of the cell borders or the amount of space the browser displays between the cell's contents and border. The *<TABLE>* tag *CELLSPACING* attribute lets you control the thickness of the border lines that separate the cells. Most browsers use a default setting of two. By increasing the value of the *CELLSPACING*, you can increase the border thickness. For example, the following HTML entries illustrate the use of the *CELLSPACING* attribute:

```
<HTML><BODY><TABLE BORDER CELLSPACING=10>
<TR><TH COLSPAN=4>Stock Information</TH></TR>
<TR><TH>Company Symbol</TD><TH>Low Price</TH><TH>High
Price</TH><TH>Closing Price</TH></TR>

<TR><TD>ABC</TD><TD>15</TD><TD>16</TD><TD>15.5</TD></TR>
<TR><TD>DEF</TD><TD>5</TD><TD>7</TD><TD>6</TD></TR>
<TR><TD>EFG</TD><TD>20</TD><TD>21</TD><TD>21</TD></TR>
</TABLE></BODY>
```

Figure 8.7 illustrates how the Netscape *Navigator* will display the thicker cell borders.

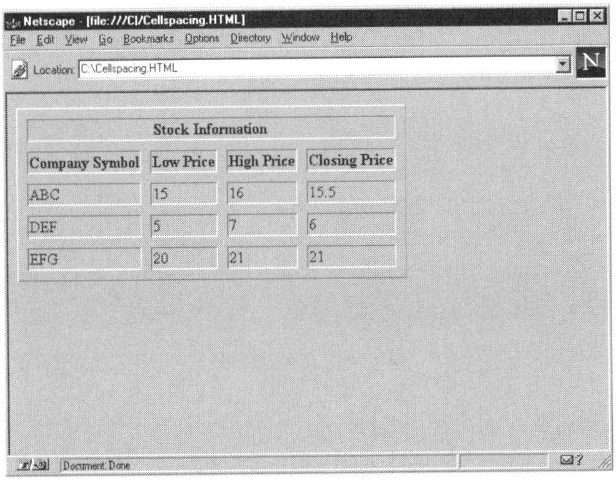

Figure 8.7 Adjusting the cell-border thickness.

The *<TABLE>* tag *CELLPADDING* attribute lets you specify the amount of space between a cell's border and content. Most browsers use a padding of one pixel. The following HTML entries use the *CELLPADDING* attribute to increase the padding to 20 pixels:

```
<HTML><BODY><TABLE BORDER CELLPADDING=20>
<TR><TH COLSPAN=4>Stock Information</TH></TR>

<TR><TH>Company Symbol</TD><TH>Low Price</TH><TH>High Price</
TH><TH>Closing Price</TH></TR>
<TR><TD>ABC</TD><TD>15</TD><TD>16</TD><TD>15.5</TD></TR>
<TR><TD>DEF</TD><TD>5</TD><TD>7</TD><TD>6</TD></TR>
<TR><TD>EFG</TD><TD>20</TD><TD>21</TD><TD>21</TD></TR>
</TABLE></BODY>
```

Figure 8.8 illustrates how the Netscape *Navigator* will display the cell padding.

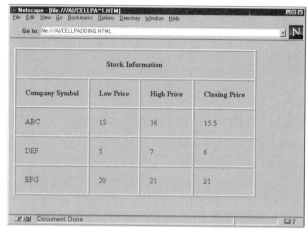

Figure 8.8 *Adjusting the cell padding.*

CONTROLLING TABLE AND CELL WIDTH USING THE *WIDTH* ATTRIBUTE

Depending on your table's contents and the layout of your Web page, you may need to control either your table's width, or the width of specific cells. The *WIDTH* attribute lets you specify a fixed number of pixels or a fixed percentage for your table or cell width. For example, the following entry directs the browser to use 75 percent of the page width for the width of the table:

```
<HTML><BODY><TABLE BORDER WIDTH=75%>
```

Figure 8.9, for example, illustrates how the Netscape *Navigator* will display the table of stock market entries if you use a table width of 75 percent of the page size.

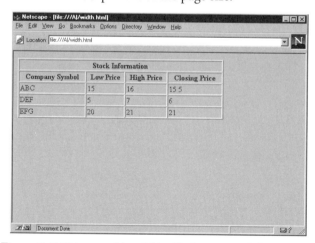

Figure 8.9 *Using a table width of 75 percent of the page size.*

Within each table cell, you can use the *WIDTH* attribute to specify the cell width in pixels or as a percentage of table size.

STORING IMAGES AND OTHER DATA WITHIN A TABLE'S CELLS

As your Web pages become more complex, you may want to expand your table content. Besides placing simple text, such as financial data, within a table, you can also use table cells to hold lists or images. For example, Figure 8.10 shows table cells that contain lists and images.

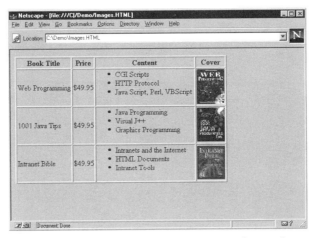

Figure 8.10 A table with both images and a text list.

To create a table with cells that contain a list, you simply define the list entries within the cell data, as shown here:

```
<HTML><BODY><TABLE BORDER=>
<TR><TH>Book Title</TH><TH>Price</TH><TH>Content</TH></TR>

<TR><TD>Web Programming</TD><TD>$49.95</TD>
<TD><UL>
    <LI>CGI Scripts</LI>
    <LI>HTTP Protocol</LI>
    <LI>Java Script, Perl, VBScript</LI>
</UL></TD></TR>

<TR><TD>1001 Java Tips</TD><TD>$49.95</TD>
<TD><UL>
    <LI>Java Programming</LI>
    <LI>Visual J++</LI>
    <LI>Graphics Programming</LI>
</UL></TD></TR>

<TR><TD>Intranet Bible</TD><TD>$49.95</TD>
<TD><UL>
    <LI>Intranets and the Internet</LI>
    <LI>HTML Documents</LI>
    <LI>Intranet Tools</LI>
</UL></TD></TR>
</TABLE></BODY>
```

Figure 8.11 illustrates how the Netscape *Navigator* will display these HTML entries.

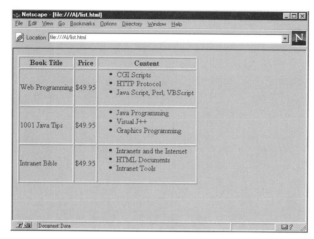

Figure 8.11 *Displaying a list of items within a table.*

Likewise, to create a table with cells that contain images, you simply use the *<IMG>* tag within the cell definition, as follows:

```
<HTML><BODY><TABLE BORDER>
<TR><TH>Book Title</TH><TH>Price</TH><TH>Content</TH><TH>Cover
</TH></TR>

<TR><TD>Web Programming</TD><TD>$49.95</TD>
<TD><UL>
    <LI>CGI Scripts</LI>
    <LI>HTTP Protocol</LI>
    <LI>Java Script, Perl, VBScript</LI>
</UL></TD><TD><IMG SRC="WEBCVR.GIF"></TD></TR>

<TR><TD>1001 Java Tips</TD><TD>$49.95</TD>
<TD><UL>
    <LI>Java Programming</LI>
    <LI>Visual J++</LI>
    <LI>Graphics Programming</LI>
</UL></TD><TD><IMG SRC="JAVACVR.GIF"></TD></TR>

<TR><TD>Intranet Bible</TD><TD>$49.95</TD>
<TD><UL>
    <LI>Intranets and the Internet</LI>
    <LI>HTML Documents</LI>
    <LI>Intranet Tools</LI>
</UL></TD><TD><IMG SRC="IBCVR.GIF"></TD></TR>
</TABLE></BODY>
```

WORKING WITH NESTED TABLES

A nested table is a table that contains one or more tables within a cell. Indeed, experts may even dub you an "HTML Table Master" after you learn to create a table within a table. Figure 8.12 shows an example of a nested table.

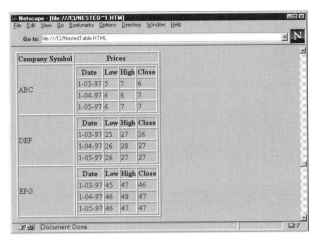

Figure 8.12 An example of a nested table.

To create a nested table, you simply define a second table within a cell definition, as shown here:

```
<HTML><BODY><TABLE BORDER>
<TR><TH>Company Symbol</TH><TH>Prices</TH></TR>
<TR><TD>ABC</TD><TD>
        <TABLE BORDER><TH>Date</TH><TH>Low</TH><TH>High
</TH><TH>Close</TH>
        <TR><TD>1-03-97</TD><TD>5</TD><TD>7</TD><TD>6</TD></TR>
        <TR><TD>1-04-97</TD><TD>6</TD><TD>8</TD><TD>7</TD></TR>
        <TR><TD>1-05-97</TD><TD>6</TD><TD>7</TD><TD>7</TD></TR>
        </TABLE>
</TD></TR>

<TR><TD>DEF</TD><TD>
        <TABLE BORDER><TH>Date</TH><TH>Low</TH><TH>High
</TH><TH>Close</TH>
        <TR><TD>1-03-97</TD><TD>25</TD><TD>27</TD><TD>26</TD></TR>
        <TR><TD>1-04-97</TD><TD>26</TD><TD>28</TD><TD>27</TD></TR>
        <TR><TD>1-05-97</TD><TD>26</TD><TD>27</TD><TD>27</TD></TR>
        </TABLE>
</TD></TR>

<TR><TD>EFG</TD><TD>
        <TABLE BORDER><TH>Date</TH><TH>Low</TH><TH>High
</TH><TH>Close</TH>
```

```
            <TR><TD>1-03-97</TD><TD>45</TD><TD>47</TD><TD>46</TD></TR>
            <TR><TD>1-04-97</TD><TD>46</TD><TD>48</TD><TD>47</TD></TR>
            <TR><TD>1-05-97</TD><TD>46</TD><TD>47</TD><TD>47</TD></TR>
            </TABLE>
    </TD></TR>
    </TABLE></BODY>
```

Using Microsoft Word to Create Tables

In Chapter 7, you learned how to convert your existing *Word* documents to HTML using the Microsoft *Internet Assistant*. As you might guess, using *Word* to create your tables is faster and easier than using HTML. After you complete a table using *Word*, you can use the *Internet Assistant* to convert the table to HTML. Figure 8.13 illustrates a simple table created within *Word*.

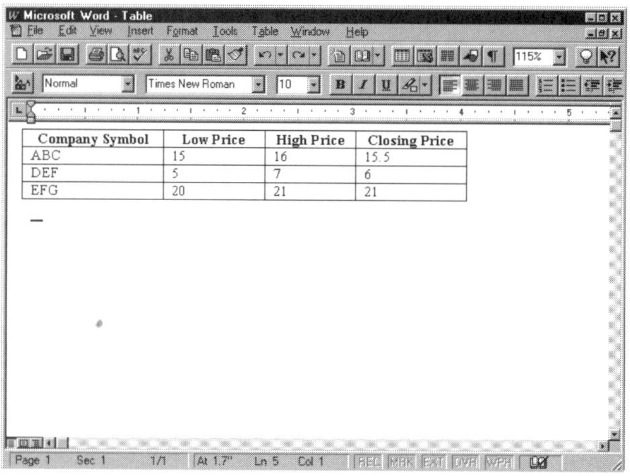

Figure 8.13 A table within Microsoft Word.

Internet Assistant will convert the preceding table to HTML, as shown:

```
<HTML><HEAD>
<TITLE>Table</TITLE>
</HEAD>
<BODY>
<H1>Table</H1>
<!— The following table has been generated by the Internet
Assistant Wizard for Microsoft Excel. You can find this add-in on
"http://www.microsoft.com/msoffice/freestuf/msexcel/index.htm" —>
<!— ——————— —>
<!— START OF CONVERTED OUTPUT —>
<!— ——————— —>

<Table border>
<TR ALIGN="center" VALIGN="bottom"><FONT FACE="Arial">
<TD><B>Company Symbol</B></TD>
<TD><B>Low Price</B></TD>
```

```
<TD><B>High Price</B></TD>
<TD><B>Closing Price</B></TD>
</FONT></TR>

<TR VALIGN="bottom"><FONT FACE="Arial">
<TD ALIGN="left">ABC</TD>
<TD ALIGN="right">15</TD>
<TD ALIGN="right">16</TD>
<TD ALIGN="right">15.5</TD>
</FONT></TR>

<TR VALIGN="bottom"><FONT FACE="Arial">
<TD ALIGN="left">DEF</TD>
<TD ALIGN="right">5</TD>
<TD ALIGN="right">7</TD>
<TD ALIGN="right">6</TD>
</FONT></TR>

<TR VALIGN="bottom"><FONT FACE="Arial">
<TD ALIGN="left">EFG</TD>
<TD ALIGN="right">20</TD>
<TD ALIGN="right">21</TD>
<TD ALIGN="right">21</TD>
</FONT></TR>
</Table>

<!-- ----------------- -->
<!-- END OF CONVERTED OUTPUT -->
<!-- ----------------- -->
<P>Last Update: 1/28/97
<P>Name: Jamsa Press
</BODY></HTML>
```

Figure 8.14 illustrates how the Netscape *Navigator* will display the table.

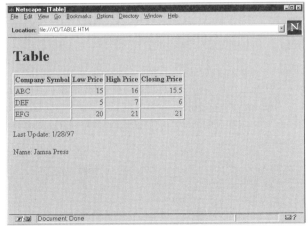

Figure 8.14 Displaying a Word-converted table within Netscape Navigator.

Using Microsoft Excel to Create Tables

Just as you can use *Internet Assistant for Microsoft Word* to convert your *Word* documents to HTML, you can also use *Internet Assistant for Excel* to convert your spreadsheet documents. You will find the software and instructions on how to install *Internet Assistant for Excel* at Microsoft's Web site located at *http://www.microsoft.com/msoffice/msexcel/internet/ia/*. After you install the add-on software, you can save your *Excel* documents in HTML format.

Figure 8.15 illustrates a simple table within *Excel*.

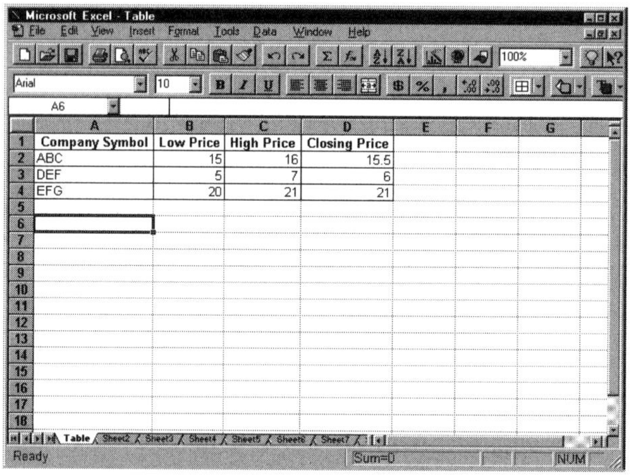

Figure 8.15 A table within Excel.

To save the table in an HTML format, perform these steps:

1. Within *Excel*, select the cells that contain the table data.

2. Select the Tool menu Internet Assistant Wizard option. Excel, in turn, will start a Wizard which will walk you through the steps you must perform.

3. Within the Wizard, click on the Next> button. The Wizard will then display the Step 2 dialog box.

4. Within the Step 2 dialog box, you must decide if you want the Wizard to place the HTML output into an existing file or if you would like to create a new file. For now, place the output in a new file by selecting the Create option—which results in an independent, ready-to-view HTML document that contains your data.

5. Click on the Next> button. The Wizard will display the Step 3 dialog box. Within this dialog box you can enter a header, footer, and other document information.

6. Click on the Next> button. The Wizard will display the Step 4 dialog box. In this dialog box, you must specify if you want the Wizard to convert just the data or to convert data while maintaining the color, font, and text formatting of the cell. Click on the "Convert as much of the formatting as possible" option.

7. Click on the Next > button. The Wizard will display the Step 5 dialog box. Type in the name of the file within which you want to store the HTML code.

8. Click on the Finish button.

The *Internet Assistant* will create the following HTML entries:

```
<HTML><HEAD>
<META HTTP-EQUIV="Content-Type" CONTENT="text/html; charset=ISO-
8859-1">
<TITLE>Company Symbol</TITLE>
<META NAME="GENERATOR" CONTENT="Internet Assistant for Microsoft
Word 2.04z">
</HEAD>

<BODY><TABLE BORDERCOLOR=#000000 BORDER=1>
<TR>
<TD WIDTH=127><CENTER><B><FONT SIZE=2>Company Symbol</FONT></B>
</CENTER></TD>
<TD WIDTH=92><CENTER><B>Low Price</B></CENTER></TD>
<TD WIDTH=80><CENTER><B>High Price</B></CENTER></TD>
<TD WIDTH=98><CENTER><B>Closing Price</B></CENTER></TD></TR>

<TR>
<TD WIDTH=127>ABC</TD>
<TD WIDTH=92>15</TD>
<TD WIDTH=80>16</TD>
<TD WIDTH=98>15.5</TD>
</TR>

<TR>
<TD WIDTH=127>DEF</TD>
<TD WIDTH=92>5</TD>
<TD WIDTH=80>7</TD>
<TD WIDTH=98>6</TD>
</TR>

<TR>
<TD WIDTH=127>EFG</TD>
<TD WIDTH=92>20</TD>
<TD WIDTH=80>21</TD>
<TD WIDTH=98>21</TD>
</TR>
</TABLE>
<P>
</BODY></HTML>
```

Figure 8.16 illustrates how the Netscape *Navigator* will display the table.

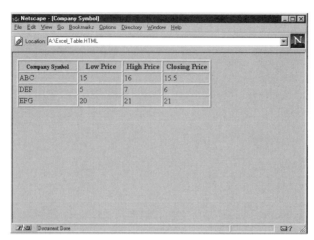

*Figure 8.16 Displaying an **Excel**-converted table within the Netscape **Navigator**.*

OTHER EXCEL TO HTML CONVERSION TOOLS

In addition to the *Internet Assistant* from Microsoft, you can also use the following tools to convert *Excel* spreadsheets to HTML.

- *XL2HTML* is a freeware macro that does an excellent job of translating *Excel* spreadsheet data to HTML. This product is easy to install and use. However, this product is not supported. You can find this freeware tool at *http://www710.gsfc.nasa.gov/704/dgd/xl2html.html.*

- *XTML* is a shareware product, which costs approximately $7, and supports both the Mac and PC platforms. You can find this product at *http://members.aol.com/ksayward/index.html.*

- *Excel to HTML* is a freeware product that supports both the Mac and PC platforms. You can find this product at *http://www.nar.com/~sib/excel-to-html.html.*

PUTTING IT ALL TOGETHER

Within a Web page, tables provide an excellent way to group and display related information. In this chapter, you learned how to use HTML tags to create tables. In addition, you learned how to use the *Internet Assistant for Microsoft Word* to convert *Word* and *Excel* tables to HTML format. In Chapter 9, you will learn how to convert images for use on your intranet pages. In addition, you will examine the HTML tags you must use to place and format images within a Web page. Before you continue with Chapter 9, however, make sure you understand the following key concepts:

✓ HTML does not let you use tabs or spaces to format content.

✓ Tables help you organize and display related information.

✓ Within your company, you should standardize the browsers your intranet users have to ensure that all users can view the content you create—some browsers do not support all of the HTML 3.0 tags.

✓ To define a table using HTML, you start with the *<TABLE>* and *</TABLE>* tags.

✓ You divide an HTML table into rows using the *<TR>* and *</TR>* tags.

✓ You further divide the rows of an HTML table into cells using the *<TD>* and *</TD>* tags.

✓ Using the *Internet Assistant for Microsoft Word*, you can convert your *Word* and *Excel* tables into HTML format.

VISITING KEY SITES THAT DISCUSS INTRANETS

The World Wide Web is filled with hundreds of excellent and current articles on all aspects of intranets. Use the following sites as starting points for your Web exploration.

INTRANET POSSIBILITIES DIAGRAM

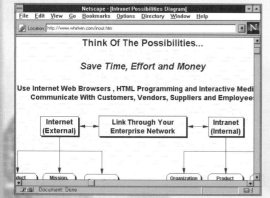

http://www.whirlwin.com/inout.htm

DSP GROUP, INC.

http://www.dspg.com/internet.htm

i WORLD: INTERNET PRODUCT SITE

http://tips.iworld.com/_frames.shtml/main.html

REALAUDIO

http://www.realaudio.com/intranet/examples.html

WEB CROSSING

http://lundeen.com/

VIRTUAL CORPORATIONS

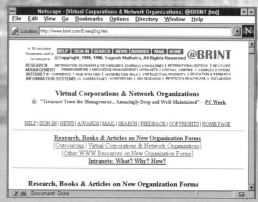

http://www.brint.com/EmergOrg.htm

Chapter 9

Images and HTML

The development of the World Wide Web and the graphical Web browser fueled the growth and popularity of the Internet. The Web's hypermedia capabilities have changed the way users access information on the Internet. In Chapter 1 you learned that the *Hypertext Transfer Protocol* (HTTP) defines the rules software programs follow to exchange information across the Web. You also learned how hypertext links connect related documents together to form a web of information which users can easily navigate. Across the Web, hypermedia documents contain images, video, sound, and even animations.

Without the use of images, Web pages would be plain and lack the pizzazz that makes the Web such a popular medium for information distribution. For example, many manufacturers use Web-based catalogs and marketing materials that include product images and descriptions. Without graphics and other media capabilities, the Web would not function as an effective marketing channel. In Chapters 7 and 8, you learned how to create basic HTML pages and convert tables and spreadsheets. In this chapter, you will learn how to convert images for use on your corporate intranet. By the time you finish this chapter, you will understand the following key concepts.

- The two types of image formats users place in HTML documents are JPEG and GIF.

- Image interlacing and the use of transparent backgrounds are two ways designers change the way an image looks.

- To place an image within an HTML document, you use the *<IMG>* tag.

- An image map defines the areas of an image upon which the user can click the mouse to select a specific operation. Designers use image maps in two ways: client-side and server-side image maps.

- Using the *Internet Assistant for Microsoft Word*, you can convert *Excel* graphs into GIF images, which you can display using HTML.

- Across the Web, you can find several software programs you can use to convert images into GIF and JPEG file formats.

USE VISUALS TO ENHANCE YOUR SITE'S INFORMATION PRESENTATION

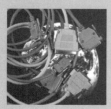

Most Web pages you encounter on the Internet include some images, which may be simple buttons and navigational tool bars, or colorful product photographs and backgrounds. Many of these images function as navigational icons or tools that help users find the information they seek. By clicking on such images, users can quickly navigate through Web pages. Web sites also use images to enhance the site's information and presentation.

When used effectively, visual images are a powerful communication tool. Within your Web site, it is important that your visuals have meaning and add value to your content. Do not use visuals that are confusing or unnecessary. Some Web pages contain icons and images that are not intuitive (easy for the user to immediately understand). Figures 9.1a through 9.1f illustrate sites that make excellent use of visual aids.

Figure 9.1a http://www.mtv.com/index2.html.

Figure 9.1b http://www5.zdnet.com.

Figure 9.1c http://www.3com.com

Figure 9.1d http://www.http.Adobe.com

Figure 9.1e http://www.sgi.com

Figure 9.1f http://espnet.sportszone.com/

The Difference Between *GIF* and *JPEG* Image Formats

In Chapters 7 and 8, you learned how to create HTML documents. You also learned how to create and convert spreadsheets and tables. In this section, you will learn about the different types of images you can include in an HTML document. You will also learn how to convert and incorporate images for use on your corporate intranet Web pages. You can use two types of images within an HTML document: GIF (pronounced like *jiff*) and JPEG (pronounced like *jay - peg*) images.

GIF Image Format

The GIF image format is the Web's most common graphics format. GIF (Graphics Interchange Format) was developed by CompuServe, so developers sometimes refer to it as CompuServe GIF. As you become more familiar with the GIF image format, you may encounter the term GIF87, which corresponds to the original format, and GIF89a, which supports transparency and interlacing (discussed later in this chapter).

Across the Web, GIF is the file format of choice for line art, graphics, and simple images. Complex images, such as photographs and images with a lot of detail, do not work well in GIF format. GIF files are limited to 256 colors, so skin tones and other subtle shades don't reproduce well in GIF format. Instead, you should use the JPEG file format for photographic and other high-quality images which require more than 256 colors. Figure 9.2 shows GIF images on a Web page.

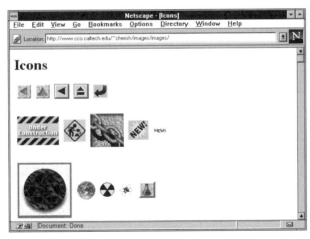

Figure 9.2 GIF images on a Web page.

JPEG Image Format

JPEG images are the second most common type of file format. The Joint Photographic Experts Group (also known as JPEG) specifically developed the JPEG image format for photographic patterns. The JPEG file format compresses 24-bit photographic-quality images, which may require any number of colors. The JPEG compression technology creates smaller-sized files for photographic images than does the GIF technology. However, JPEG technology does not reproduce solid colored areas, line art, and graphics as well as it does photographic patterns. Figure 9.3 shows JPEG images on a Web page.

Figure 9.3 JPEG images on a Web page.

LEARNING THE SPECIFICS ABOUT GIF AND JPEG TECHNOLOGIES

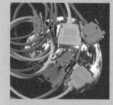

As you design and build Web sites, you will make extensive use of GIF and JPEG images. If you are interested in the details behind these two technologies, visit the Web sites shown in Figures 9.4a and 9.4b.

Figure 9.4a http://www.adobe.com/—studio/tipstechniques/—GIFJPGchart/main.html

Figure 9.4b http://www.adobe.com/—newsfeatures/pallette/main.html

UNDERSTANDING HOW COMPUTERS DISPLAY COLOR

Computer monitors display color by mixing a combination of intensities for three colors: red, green, and blue. Some monitors display up to 256 different intensities (and hence, saturations) for each of the three colors. Such monitors (and video cards) measure intensity values using

8-bits of information for each color (a total of 24-bits for all three colors). Table 9.1 shows how the number of bits the monitor uses to represent colors relates to the number of colors the monitor can display.

Bit Depth	Number of Colors
2	4
3	8
4	16
5	32
6	64
7	128
8	256
16	65,536
24	16 Million

Table 9.1 *How the number of color bits relates to the number of colors a monitor can display.*

While JPEG only works for 24-bit images, you can use GIF files for images that are 8 bits or less. As you will learn, the fewer bits the image uses to display colors, the smaller the image's corresponding file. The advantage of smaller files is that they download faster across the net. While file size and number of colors are important, you must also consider the computer display that your customers use to view the images. Because JPEG files are 24 bits, they are best viewed using a monitor that supports 24-bit colors. Unfortunately, across the Web, users have a wide variety of monitor types. Therefore, you have no guarantee as to your user's monitor quality. When a user displays a 24-bit (16-million colors) JPEG photographic image on a monitor that supports only 8-bit (256 colors) images, the monitor will *dither* the image.

Your system dithers when its video card or monitor cannot handle the number of colors an image contains. In such cases, the system replaces colors using its own smaller color palette. For example, imagine that you must create a picture of a purple balloon using only red and blue pens. To create the purple color, you must blend red and blue dots. Your system performs a similar process to replace colors when it cannot handle a color using its own palette. Although the dithering process lets your system display the image, the process may make the image look blurry or muddy.

Again, not all users have systems that can properly display 24-bit images. Many video cards and monitors can display only 8-bit or 16-bit images. To be safe, you should use GIF images in your Web pages unless your customer base supports and requires 24-bit color, and your images are well suited for JPEG format. Figure 9.5 shows GIF and JPEG images on Adobe's Web site.

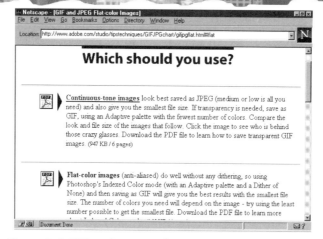

Figure 9.5 GIF and JPEG information at Adobe's Web site.

WORKING WITH IMAGES AND HTML

By now, you should have a good understanding of how to create HTML pages. In this section, you will learn how to incorporate images into your HTML pages. As you will learn, HTML editors are good at converting text into HTML format which makes it easy for you to place images within an HTML document. However, most HTML editors do not include many image-placement options.

In general, HTML editors let you position an image within an HTML page on the left margin, right margin, or center of the page. Usually, your document's text will fall above or below the image, as shown in Figure 9.6. To position images and text more precisely, you must use additional HTML tags. Most of the image tags you will examine are "Netscape extensions" to HTML or part of the HTML 3.0 (or higher) specification. As you will learn, not all browsers support these tags, so it is important that you make sure that your intranet customers have browsers that are compatible with the tags you plan to use within your intranet Web pages.

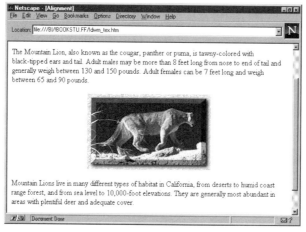

Figure 9.6 An image centered on a Web page.

USING THE *HTML 2.0 <IMG> TAG*

To place an image within an HTML document, you use the *<IMG>* tag. The standard HTML 2.0 image tag consists of three different attributes: *SRC, ALT,* and *ALIGN*. As you learned in Chapter 7, the *
*, *<HR>*, and *<IMG>* tags do not require ending tags (such as *</BR>*).

USING THE *<IMG> TAG SRC ATTRIBUTE*

To display an image within an HTML document, you must specify the name of the file that contains the GIF or JPEG image. To specify the image file, you use the *<IMG>* tag *SRC* attribute. Using the *SRC* attribute, you specify a pathname or URL that corresponds to the image file. For example, the following *<IMG>* tag directs the browser to load and display the graphic image contained in the file, *Globe.GIF*:

```
<IMG SRC="Globe.GIF">
```

In a similar way, the following *<IMG>* tag uses a URL to specify the location of an image file:

```
<IMG SRC="http://www.jamsa.com/Globe.GIF">
```

USING THE *<IMG> TAG ALT ATTRIBUTE*

In the past, some browsers did not support the display of images. Therefore, to improve performance by eliminating image download times, many users turned off the graphics display within their browser and surfed the Web in text mode. The *<IMG>* tag *ALT* attribute currently lets you specify text that the browser displays when it cannot display (or possibly download) the corresponding image. For example, the following *<IMG>* tag uses the *ALT* attribute to direct the browser to display the message "Image of Store Locations" in place of the image contained in *Globe.GIF*:

```
<IMG SRC="globe.gif" ALT="Image of Store Locations">
```

THE *ALIGN ATTRIBUTE*

When you place images on your page, there may be times when you place images within lines of text as shown in Figure 9.7.

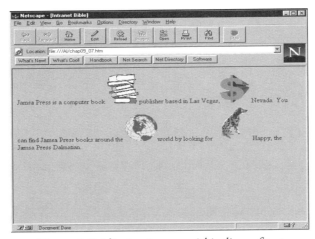

Figure 9.7 Aligning images within lines of text.

The following HTML entries use the <IMG> tags to place the images within the text:

```
<HTML><HEAD><TITLE>Intranet Bible</TITLE></HEAD>

<BODY>Jamsa Press is a computer book <IMG SRC="books.gif">publisher
based in Las Vegas,<IMG SRC="money.gif"> Nevada. You can find Jamsa
Press books around the <IMG SRC="globe.gif">world by looking for
<IMG SRC="happy.gif">Happy, the Jamsa Press Dalmatian.
</BODY></HTML>
```

Depending on the images you are placing within the text, there may be times when you need to move the image up or down to better align it with the text. To specify the image alignment you desire, use the *<IMG>* tag *ALIGN* attribute. The *ALIGN* attribute *TOP, MIDDLE* and *BOTTOM* attributes let you position an image with respect to the text:

ALIGN=TOP	Directs the browser to align the top of the image with the top most part of the line.
ALIGN=MIDDLE	Directs the browser to center the image on the baseline of the text.
ALIGN=BOTTOM	Directs the browser to align the bottom of the image with the baseline of the text.

The following HTML entries illustrate the use of the *ALIGN* attribute:

```
<HTML><HEAD><TITLE>Intranet Bible</TITLE></HEAD>

<BODY>This square is TOP aligned.<IMG ALIGN=TOP SRC="square.gif"><P>
This square is MIDDLE aligned.<IMG ALIGN=MIDDLE SRC="square.gif"><P>
This square is BOTTOM aligned.<IMG ALIGN=BOTTOM SRC="square.gif">
</BODY></HTML>
```

Figure 9.8 illustrates how the Netscape *Navigator* will display the aligned images.

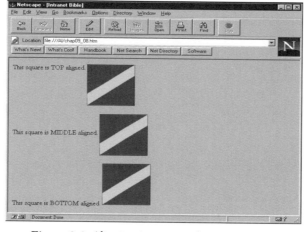

Figure 9.8 Aligning images with respect to text.

If you are working with large images, there will be times when you will want to place the image flush against the left or right margin. To place an image against the margin, you assign the <IMG> tag *ALIGN* attribute the *LEFT* or *RIGHT* values:

ALIGN=LEFT   Directs the browser to align the image against the   left margin.

ALIGN=RIGHT   Directs the browser to align the image against the   right margin.

When you place images against the margin in this way, the browser will flow text around the image as shown in Figure 9.9. The following HTML entries use the ALIGN attribute to align text to the left and right margin:

```
<IMG ALIGN=RIGHT SRC="image.gif">
```

Figure 9.9 illustrates how the Netscape *Navigator* will display these HTML entries:

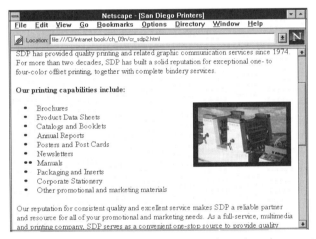

Figure 9.9 Flowing text around images aligned to the margin.

When you align text to the margin, the browser will flow text around the image. If you want the text to fall below the image, place a <BR> tag before the <IMG> tag *CLEAR* attribute to push the text below the image. When you use the CLEAR attribute, you can assign the following values to control where the browser places the text:

CLEAR=ALL   Directs the browser to start the text at a location at which neither the left or right margin have an image.

CLEAR=LEFT   Directs the browser to start the text at a left-margin location that does not contain an image.

CLEAR=RIGHT   Directs the browser to start the text at a right-margin location that does not contain an image.

The following HTML entries illustrate the use of the <*BR*> tag *CLEAR* attribute:

```
<BR CLEAR=LEFT>
<P>The browser will move this text to an empty left margin</P>
```

USING THE <*IMG*> TAG *VSPACE* AND *HSPACE* ATTRIBUTES

When you place images within a document, you may find you want to frame the image, leaving space between the image and its surrounding text. In such cases, you can use the <*IMG*> tag *VSPACE* and *HSPACE* attributes to define the pixel space the browser will place around the image. The *VSPACE* attribute specifies the pixel space above and below an image. Likewise, the *HSPACE* attribute specifies the pixel space to the left and right of the image. The following <*IMG*> tag uses the *VSPACE* and *HSPACE* attributes to place a 20-pixel frame around an image:

```
<IMG SRC="cactus.gif" VSPACE=20 HSPACE=20 ALIGN=MIDDLE>
```

DEFINING IMAGE DIMENSIONS FOR THE NETSCAPE BROWSER

Depending on a user's browser, you may speed up image-download operations by including the image's dimensions within the <*IMG*> tag. Using the <*IMG*> tag *HEIGHT* and *WIDTH* attributes, you can specify the image's pixel height and width. As the browser reads the image's dimensions, the browser can reserve space on the Web page for the image, allowing the browser to format text accordingly. If the <*IMG*> tag does not provide image dimensions, the browser must load and examine each image before it can accurately format text within the page. If the <*IMG*> tag *HEIGHT* and *WIDTH* attributes are different than the actual dimensions of the image, the browser may scale the image to fit the given dimensions. Most browsers that do not support the *HEIGHT* and *WIDTH* attributes will simply ignore them. The following <*IMG*> tag illustrates the use of the *HEIGHT* and *WIDTH* attributes:

```
<IMG SRC="thin_bar.gif" WIDTH="443" HEIGHT="37" ALIGN="BOTTOM">
```

USING IMAGES AS LINKS

Many Web documents use images to represent links to other documents. To create an image link, you place the <*IMG*> tag within an anchor, as shown:

```
<A HREF="Index.HTML"><IMG SRC="People.GIF"></A>
```

In this case, if the user clicks the mouse on any location within the *People.GIF* image, the browser will jump to the linked file, *index.HTML*.

USING THE <*IMG*> TAG *BORDER* ATTRIBUTE

When you use an image as a document link, you may want to place a border around the image to inform the user that the image provides a link. Using the *BORDER* attribute, you specify a pixel value that defines the border size. If you specify *BORDER=0*, the browser will not display the border. The following HTML entries illustrate the use of the <*IMG*> tag *BORDER* attribute:

```
<HTML><HEAD>
<TITLE>Intranet Bible</TITLE>
</HEAD>

<BODY>
<H1>Welcome to Jamsa Press</H1>
<IMG SRC="happy.gif">
<IMG BORDER=5 SRC="happy.gif">
</BODY></HTML>
```

Figure 9.10 shows how the Netscape *Navigator* will display these entries.

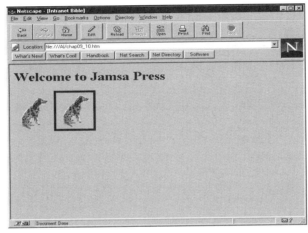

Figure 9.10 An image link with a border.

UNDERSTANDING IMAGE MAPS

Whether you are in a shopping mall, on a road trip, or on a university campus, a map can provide you with a navigational tool to help you find unfamiliar locations. Likewise, an image map provides you with a tool within a Web site that can link parts of an image to specific Web pages or to another Web site. For example, assume your site displays a map of the United States. Using an image map, you can link each state to a specific document containing information about that state.

An image map specifies a set of image coordinates that correspond to a specific link. When the user clicks the mouse within the map's image coordinates, the browser will jump to the corresponding link. You can use two different approaches to create image maps: client-side and server-side maps. Both types of image maps contain a set of coordinates which identify the image area that is clickable. When you create an image map, you must associate each set of coordinates with the URL for a specific Web page.

The difference between client-side and server-side image maps is where coordinate processing takes place. A server-side image map processes the task on the server and returns the requested page to the user's computer. For example, if the user clicks on a specific section of an image map, the browser sends a request across the Internet to the server. The server then processes the request by matching the coordinates to the map and identifying the required URL. After the server determines the corresponding URL, the server sends the corresponding document back to the browser.

There are drawbacks to server-side image maps that make them less attractive to use in comparison with client-side image maps. To use a server-side image map, the browser must contact the server before processing the user's request, which can cause a delay and tie up the server's resources. In addition, server-side maps do not provide any alternative operations for text-based browsers.

The alternative to server-side image maps is client-side image maps, which solve the limitations mentioned above. Rather than sending the coordinates to the server, the browser itself can process client-side image maps, which results in faster processing and easier maintenance. In addition, when you use client-side image maps, you can provide a default text the browser displays when it does not support or cannot process the image map.

Creating a Client-Side Image Map

When you create a client-side image map, you place the mapping information within your HTML document using the *<MAP>* and *</MAP>* tags. Client-side image maps are part of the HTML 3.2 specification and not all browsers support them. To ensure that all Web site visitors can use your image maps, you should use both client-side and server-side image maps. If a user's browser does not support the client-side image map, the browser will ignore the tags and read the server-side image map instructions.

Because your document may have multiple images and multiple image maps, you must assign each image map a name. The format of your image map entries are as follows:

```
<MAP NAME="UniqueImageMapName">
   Area tags that define the maps
</MAP>
```

An image map consists of a set of coordinates and a link you want to associate with those coordinates. When you define an image map, you associate a link to specific pixel regions within the image. Normally, you will specify a rectangular region within your image. However, as you will learn, you can also specify a circular region, a specific point within the image, or even a custom polygon shape.

To specify the shape of your image map, you will use the *<AREA>* tag *RECT, CIRCLE, POINT,* and *POLY* attributes. To specify the coordinates for a rectangular map, you specify the coordinates of the rectangle's top-left and bottom-right corners. For a circle, you specify the coordinates of the circle's center and a radius. To assign a link to a specific point within image, you specify the point's coordinates. Lastly, for a polygon, you specify the coordinates of each line segment.

To map coordinates to the link, you use the *<AREA>* tag. The following HTML entries define a client-side image map named *MyFirstMap*:

```
<MAP NAME="MyFirstMap">
<AREA SHAPE="RECT" COORDS="24,10,82,30" HREF="index.html">
<AREA SHAPE="CIRCLE" COORDS="200,200,50" HREF="flow.html">
<AREA SHAPE="POINT" COORDS="300,300" HREF="whnew.html">
<AREA SHAPE="POLY" COORDS="400,400,450,450,350,450" HREF="tri.html">
</MAP>
```

The *<MAP>* and *</MAP>* entries define an image map. To use the image map, you must place a *USEMAP* attribute within the *<IMG>* entry. For example, the following entry directs the browser to use the image map *MyFirstMap* with the image *MySite.GIF*:

```
<IMG SRC="MySite.GIF" USEMAP="#MyFirstMap">
```

The pound sign (#) that precedes the image map name (*#MyFirstMap*) tells the browser that the image map is defined within the HTML and that the browser should perform client-side image mapping.

CREATING A SERVER-SIDE IMAGE MAP

As you have learned, when you define a server-side image map, the server must process user mouse clicks within an image to determine whether or not the user has clicked on a link. The disadvantage of server-side image maps is that they place additional processing overhead on the server and because the browser and server must communicate each time the user clicks the mouse within an image, the user's performance will decrease. The advantage of server-side image maps is that most browsers support them.

To create a server-side image map, you must create a file that defines the coordinates and their corresponding links. As was the case with client-side image maps, the region you map must be a rectangle, circle, point, or polygon. The format of the server-side image map differs slightly from a client-side image map. To create a server-side image-map file, you do not use an *<AREA>* tag. Instead, you simply place the coordinate shape, the link, and the coordinate points within the file, as shown here:

```
RECT   /Subdirectory/Path/index.html 24,10,82,30
CIRCLE /Subdirectory/Path/flow.html 200,200,50
POINT  /Subdirectory/Path/whnew.html 300,300
POLY   /Subdirectory/Path/tri.html 400,400,450,450,350,450
```

Note that the server-side image-map file specifies a complete pathname to each HTML file. By specifying a complete pathname, you ensure that the server can locate the files. Also, note that the order of the server-side image-map entries differs from the order of attributes within the *<AREA>* tag.

You should store your image-map entries within a file that uses the MAP extension, such as *MyServerImageMap.MAP*. Like the *<AREA>* entry, the server-side image-map file simply defines the image map. To use the image map, you must combine the *<A>* and *<IMG>* entries, as shown here:

```
<A HREF="/Subdirectory/Path/MyImageMap.MAP">
<IMG SRC="MySite.GIF" ISMAP></A>
```

Within the *<IMG>* tag, the *ISMAP* attribute tells the browser that the image uses server-side image mapping and that the browser should pass user mouse clicks through to the server. Note that the *HREF* attribute uses a complete pathname to the image-map file. By using a complete pathname, you ensure that the server can locate the image map file.

SPECIFYING A DEFAULT URL

The *DEFAULT* attribute defines the reference the server or browser uses when the user clicks on a location within the image that does not correspond to a mapped region. The following entries illustrate how you would use the *DEFAULT* attribute within a client-side map:

```
<MAP NAME="MyFirstMap">
<AREA SHAPE="DEFAULT"HREF="default.html">
<AREA SHAPE="RECT" COORDS="24,10,82,30" HREF="index.html">
<AREA SHAPE="CIRCLE" COORDS="200,200,50" HREF="flow.html">
<AREA SHAPE="POLY" COORDS="400,400,450,450,350,450" HREF="tri.html">
</MAP>
```

Likewise, the following entries illustrate the use of the *DEFAULT* attribute within a server-side map:

```
DEFAULT /Subdirectory/Path/default.html
RECT /Subdirectory/Path/index.html 24,10,82,30
CIRCLE /Subdirectory/Path/flow.htl 200,200,50
POLY /Subdirectory/Path/tri.html 400,400,450,450,350,450
```

CREATING A HYBRID CLIENT- OR SERVER-BASED IMAGE MAP

Ideally, you want the browser to handle image mapping. Unfortunately, because some browsers don't support client-side image mapping, you have to take steps to provide server-side image maps. However, by including an image map within the HTML document and on the server, you can achieve the best of both worlds. If a browser supports client-side image maps, the browser will perform the processing. Otherwise, the browser will hand off the image-map processing to the server. The following entries illustrate how you support client- and server-side image maps:

```
<A HREF="/Subdirectory/Path/MyImageMap.MAP">
<IMG SRC="MySite.GIF" ISMAP USEMAP="#MyFirstMap"></A>
```

In this case, if the browser supports client-side image mapping, the browser will locate the image map within your document named *MyFirstMap*. Otherwise, the browser will direct the server to use the image map contained in the file *MyImageMap.Map*.

MORE INFORMATION ON IMAGE MAPS

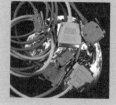

Across the Web, you will find several sites that provide detailed instructions on how to build image maps. There are also a number of image-map programs you will find useful as you create image maps. For more information on image maps, visit the sites listed in Figures 9.11a through 9.11d.

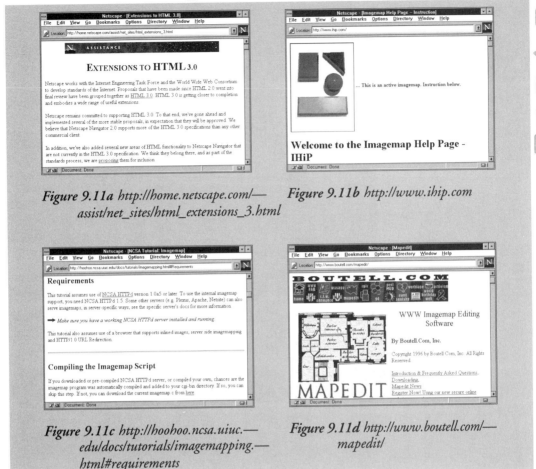

Figure 9.11a *http://home.netscape.com/— assist/net_sites/html_extensions_3.html*

Figure 9.11b *http://www.ihip.com*

Figure 9.11c *http://hoohoo.ncsa.uiuc.— edu/docs/tutorials/imagemapping.— html#requirements*

Figure 9.11d *http://www.boutell.com/— mapedit/*

CONVERTING IMAGES FOR USE ON YOUR INTRANET

One of the largest tasks in developing an intranet is to collect and then convert existing data into HTML format. As you perform this task, you may face files that users created on various platforms with a number of applications. It is important that you develop a system to manage your data conversion.

As you will learn, most employees within your organization will not have the tools or skills they need to create or convert images into a format suitable for use with HTML. As a result, you will spend considerable time training employees how to best perform these operations. In the following section, you will learn how to convert images and other files into HTML format. You will also learn about the different types of image formats and the special effects you can apply to images.

INTERLACED IMAGES AND TRANSPARENT BACKGROUNDS

As you will learn, image interlacing and the use of transparent backgrounds are two ways you can change the way an image looks. Interlacing is a GIF-file option that changes how the browser downloads and displays the image. Browsers display interlaced images in sections, which causes the image to appear blurry or faded at first, and then come into focus as the browser continues the image download. In contrast, browsers display non-interlaced GIF images line-by-line while the browser downloads, as shown in Figure 9.12. There is a similar feature for JPEG format called *Progressive JPEG*, which is similar to interlacing.

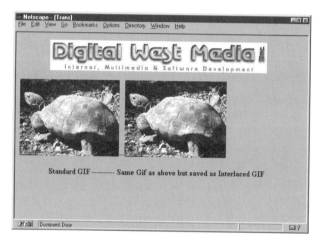

Figure 9.12 A non-interlaced GIF file and an interlaced GIF file.

Webmasters use interlaced images because users perceive the download time to be less than that of a line-by-line, non-interlaced image. For small images, you will not notice much difference between the download times for interlaced and non-interlaced images. But for larger images, the interlaced format provides the user with a blurry preview of the image. This preview lets users stop the download if they are not interested in the final version, or allows users to click on the preview if it corresponds to a link.

USING PROGRESSIVE JPEG IMAGES

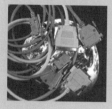

As you just learned, interlaced GIF images let the browser display a preview of an image as it downloads the image contents. If you are using JPEG images, you can use progressive images whose contents the browser displays "progressively" as it downloads the image. For more information on progressive JPEG images, visit the Web site at *http://ww.myna.com/~stan/internet/pjpeg.html*, shown in Figure 9.13.

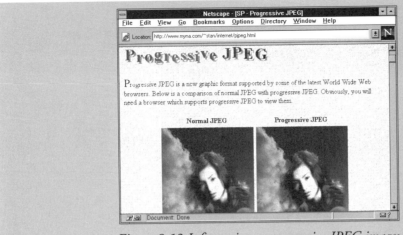

Figure 9.13 Information on progressive JPEG images.

USING TRANSPARENT BACKGROUNDS

The image transparency feature changes the way an image looks by blending the image with the Web page's background. Thus, an image with a transparent background has an invisible background. When you place an image with a transparent background in an HTML document, the Web page's background color shows through the transparent portions of the image background, as shown in Figure 9.14.

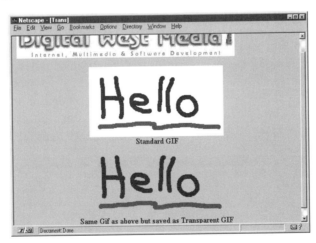

Figure 9.14 A transparent image and a non-transparent image on a Web page.

To create an image with a transparent background, you need an image-editing program that supports transparent backgrounds. The transparency feature works well with images that have only a single background color. If the image has multiple background colors, you must edit the background and make it a single color. Most image-editing programs let you select the background so you can then manipulate its color. Some image-editing programs offer both interlacing and transparent background features. The following list provides a few image-editing programs you can use to create, edit, and convert images.

- Adobe *Photoshop*   *http://www.adobe.com*
- *PaintShop Pro*   *http://www.digitalworkshop.co.uk/psp.htm*
- Equilibrium *DeBabelizer*   *h t t p : / / w w w . e q u i l i b r i u m . c o m / — SoftwareDownload.html*

WHERE YOU STORE IMAGES IMPACTS CACHING

When a user visits your Web site and downloads a page, the user's browser loads the page's contents (graphics and text) within a special storage location on the user's system called a *cache*. By caching the site's content in this way, the browser reduces the number of download operations it must perform if the user leaves and later returns to the site. When the user returns to the site, the browser can use the cached contents rather than downloading the content again, which saves considerable time.

For example, assume that your Web site makes extensive use of a special graphic, such as your company's logo. If you store multiple copies of the image on your Web site, perhaps a copy of the logo within each directory that contains the content for a specific page, the browser must download the logo image each time it requests a Web page that contains the image. In contrast, if you only store one copy of the logo file on your disk and reference that location within every *<IMG>* tag, you increase the likelihood that the browser will locate the image within its cache, which lets the browser eliminate the image download operation.

CONVERTING GRAPHS, DRAWINGS, AND OTHER GRAPHICS

In Chapter 8, you learned how to use Microsoft *Internet Assistant for Excel* to convert spreadsheet tables into HTML. In addition to placing spreadsheet data on your intranet pages, you may also want to include *Excel* graphs. Unfortunately, Microsoft *Internet Assistant for Excel* does not convert *Excel* graphs into an HTML-compatible format. However, you can use *Internet Assistant for Microsoft Word* to convert *Excel* graphs, or other types of graphics, into an HTML-compatible GIF format. Figure 9.15 shows an *Excel* file which includes both data and a graph.

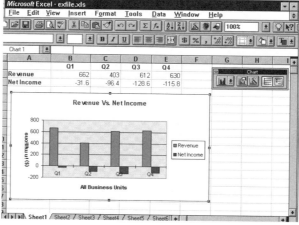

Figure 9.15 An Excel file with a graph.

In the following sections, you will learn how to convert your *Excel* graphs, *Word* drawings, and other graphics into GIF format for use in HTML documents.

CONVERTING AN EXCEL FILE INTO GIF FORMAT

To convert your *Excel* graph into GIF format, you must first copy the *Excel* graph into a *Word* document by performing these following steps:

1. Open the *Excel* document that contains the graph.

2. Click your mouse on the graph to select it. Then, select the Edit menu Copy option to copy the graph to the clipboard.

3. Next, you must create a new document in *Word*. To create a new document, start *Word* and select the Edit menu New option.

4. Position your cursor at the start of the new *Word* document and select Edit menu Paste. *Word* will place the graph at the start of your *Word* document.

To convert a *Word* document to HTML, you must save the document as an HTML document. As you learned in Chapter 7, to save a *Word* document in HTML format, you must select the "HTML document" type in the Save As dialog box.

CONVERTING GRAPHS IN A WORD HTML DOCUMENT

Often, you may want to graph and display data on your intranet. In such cases, you can simply open *Excel*, create a graph, and then perform the steps you examined in the previous section. However, there is an easier way. You can create a graph from within a *Word* HTML file by performing these steps (providing you are using *Word for Office 95*, or later):

1. Create a new document in *Word* by selecting the File menu New option.

2. Select the Insert menu Object option. *Word* will display the Object dialog box.

3. Select the Create New tab and choose Microsoft Graph 5.0. *Word* will display a graph and a datasheet containing the graph data.

4. After you edit the data, click your mouse anywhere within the *Word* document. To complete this process, you do not need to change the default data. *Word* will display the graph without any borders. You can modify the attributes of this graph like any *Excel* graph.

5. Before you convert this file, save it as a standard *Word* document by selecting the File menu Save option and using the filename, *WORDGRAPH.DOC*.

6. After you save the file, select the File menu Save As option and save the file as an HTML document. Then, *Word* will convert the embedded graph into a GIF file named *IMG0000.GIF*.

You can also use *Internet Assistant for Microsoft Word* to convert drawings, graphs, and other graphics into GIF-file format.

CONVERTING MICROSOFT PROJECT FILES INTO HTML FORMAT

Microsoft *Project* is a popular tool for creating project schedules and tracking projects. If your organization uses Microsoft *Project*, you will probably want to use some of the schedules and project tracking tools in your intranet pages. You will now learn how easy it is to convert your Microsoft *Project* files into an HTML compatible format for use on your intranet. You can use *Internet Assistant for Microsoft Word* to convert *Project* files into GIF files. Figure 9.16 shows a Microsoft *Project* file.

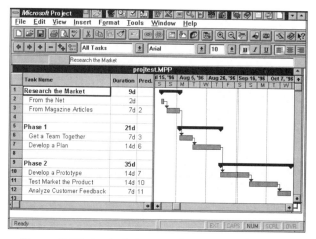

Figure 9.16 *A schedule created in Microsoft* **Project**.

To convert a Microsoft *Project* file to GIF format, perform the following steps:

1. Using Microsoft *Project*, open the project you want to convert and highlight the tasks you want to appear in the graphic. Click your mouse on the task or tasks you want to select.

2. Select the Edit menu Copy option. *Project* will copy your document's contents into the clipboard.

3. Next, start *Word* and use the File menu New option to create a new document.

4. Within *Word*, select the Edit menu Paste Special option. *Word*, in turn, will display the Paste Special dialog box.

5. Within the Paste Special dialog box, click your mouse on the Paste and Picture button. *Word* will insert the clipboard's contents into your document as a picture.

6. Select the File menu Save As option and save the document as an HTML document. *Word*, in turn, will convert all the elements in the *Word* file into HTML or GIF-file format.

CONVERTING DRAWINGS AND GRAPHICS INTO GIF FORMAT

As you learned in previous sections, *Internet Assistant for Microsoft Word* is a powerful, add-on tool that lets you convert *Excel* and Microsoft *Project* graphs into GIF format. There may be times when you need to create and convert drawings or other graphics into GIF format for use on your intranet. In most cases, you can easily convert such drawings using *Word*'s drawing tools. All you must do is create a simple drawing in *Word*, and then convert it into GIF format using the same steps described earlier in this chapter for converting *Excel* graphs into GIF format.

201

PUTTING IT ALL TOGETHER

This chapter introduced you to a number of tools and techniques that will help you create great looking images for your intranet Web pages. In Chapter 10, you will learn more about ways to create and manage content for you intranet. You will also learn about HTML editing and Web site management tools that you can use to develop and manage your intranet. However, before you move on to Chapter 10, make sure you understand the following key concepts:

✓ Across the Internet, GIF files are the file format of choice for line art, graphics, and simple images.

✓ You should use JPEG images for photographic images and images that require more than 256 colors.

✓ When you select an image format, you must consider the video card and monitor types your users may use to view your images.

✓ An interlaced image is a GIF image the browser can download and display in sections. Web sites use interlaced images because users perceive their download time as shorter than non-interlaced images.

✓ When you place an image with a transparent background within an HTML document, the browser displays the page's background color through the transparent portions of the image's background.

✓ An image map defines a set of coordinates within a graphic upon which the user can click a mouse to jump to a corresponding link.

✓ Web pages can use client-side and server-side image maps. The difference between the two types of image maps is where the coordinate processing takes place.

✓ *Internet Assistant for Microsoft Word* can convert *Excel* graphs or other graphics into GIF format, which is compatible with HTML.

VISITING KEY SITES THAT DISCUSS INTRANETS

The World Wide Web is filled with hundreds of excellent and current articles on all aspects of intranets. Use the following sites as starting points for your Web exploration.

MPEG POINTERS

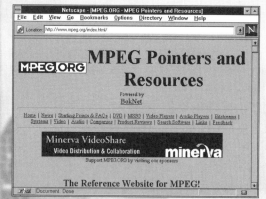

http://www.mpeg.org/index.html/

REAL-TIME VIDEO AND AUDIO

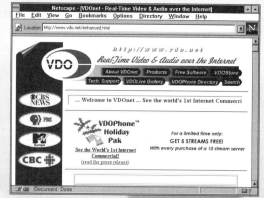

http://www.vdo.net/enhanced.html

ONLINE WORLD

http://203.63.164.17/

ADOBE ACROBAT

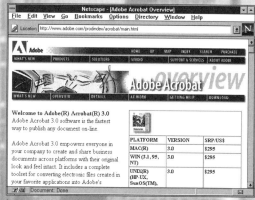

*http://www.adobe.com/prodindex/acrobat/
main.html*

XING TECHNOLOGY CORPORATION

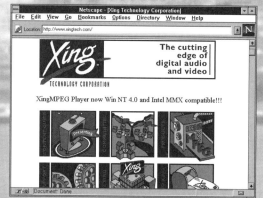

http://www.xingtech.com/

WORLD WIDE WEB CONSORTIUM

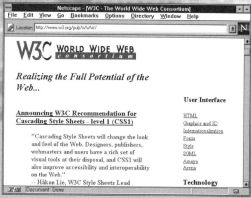

http://www.w3.org/pub/WWW/

Chapter 10

Creating and Managing Content

Creating content for an intranet is similar to building a house. You must first create a sturdy foundation and frame before you can build the walls and put a roof on the structure. After you build your structure, you must then install the windows, doors, floor coverings, and fixtures. Finally, you can put on the finishing touches such as paint, window coverings, and landscape. Developing your intranet content requires a similar set of tasks. In Chapter 6, you learned how to create an intranet plan. In Chapters 7, 8, and 9, you learned how to create HTML documents using raw, text-based HTML tags and various Microsoft *Office* HTML add-on programs. In this chapter, you will learn about several commercial tools you can use to assist you with your Web-page conversion and programming. As you will find, the tools this chapter presents are inexpensive, or free, so you can provide them to a large number of people within your organization. By the time you finish this chapter, you will understand the following key concepts:

- ◆ To provide users with the right HTML-authoring and conversion programs, you must assess their short- and long-term needs.

- ◆ Free (add-on) software packages are available for existing desktop productivity software with which you can convert your exiting documents for Web use without knowing HTML.

- ◆ With advanced editors, you can create new HTML documents using a near WYSIWYG development environment.

- ◆ To track and maintain documents on your intranet, you will need site-management tools.

- ◆ Several programs are available to convert images for use within HTML documents.

- ◆ To create dynamic content for your intranet, you will need multimedia-authoring tools.

THE ELEMENTS AND STRUCTURE OF A WEB DOCUMENT

As you learned in previous chapters, Web documents are similar to printed documents with a few exceptions. Printed documents contain text and graphics. Web documents contain not only text and graphics, they also contain elements that make them interactive, such as links, multimedia objects, and interactive forms. Within a Web document, text and images are very similar to their printed-document counterparts. The only difference is that with a Web document, you can link text and images to specific locations within the same or a different document.

As you have learned, browsers such as Netscape *Navigator* and Microsoft *Internet Explorer* read an HTML document and, based on the document's tags, format and display its content. In Chapters 7 and 8, you learned how to use many HTML formatting tags. As you will learn in this chapter, new software tools eliminate the need for most people in your organization to learn how to create HTML documents using a plain-text editor. In fact, if you expect people in your organization to create HTML documents using plain-text editors, you will end up with a limited amount of content for your intranet and reduce productivity among your staff.

As discussed, companies benefit most from their intranet when everyone in the organization participates in creating content. Knowing that most people in your organization are probably not programmers, this chapter's main focus is to help you learn about commercial Web-page development tools available for the Windows and Mac platforms. In addition, for those of you in a Unix environment, this chapter lists several free tools you can get from sites across the Web.

SELECTING YOUR WEB AUTHORING TOOLS

As you will learn, a wide variety of Web-authoring tools are available. Unfortunately, you may find selecting the right program to meet your specific needs is overwhelming. Most of the authoring programs support WYSIWYG (what-you-see-is-what-you-get) processing, which lets you display many formatting attributes as you apply the attributes within your documents. However, as you experiment with different tools, you will find that most are not one-hundred percent WYSIWYG because some HTML tags are browser specific.

As you evaluate Web-authoring tools, make sure the authoring tools let you create documents using the HTML version you require. As you have learned, most browsers support HTML 2.0. Therefore, make sure your authoring tools let you create HTML 2.0 documents. If you use an editor that supports a later version of HTML, such as 3.0 or 3.2, you may create documents withcontents not all browsers can display.

It is important that your intranet team standardize a specific browser and set of authoring tools as soon as possible. In this way, you increase the likelihood that all of your employees can view the HTML documents your team creates. Before you purchase a Web-authoring tool, use the following questions to define your Web-authoring needs:

- On which platforms will you perform your Web-authoring tasks?
- What are the file formats of your existing files?
- Will you need to convert spreadsheets or tables?
- How many users do you expect to create content for your intranet?
- Do you need to convert a large number of existing documents?
- Will you need to convert existing images, pictures, and drawings to HTML formats?
- Do you plan to use multimedia elements such as audio, video, or animation within your Web pages?
- Will you create interactive Web forms?
- Which Web browsers will users employ to view your intranet documents?

After you establish your authoring needs, you can review the multitude of authoring tools available and select one or more that meet your requirements.

MANAGING AND CONVERTING A LARGE NUMBER OF DOCUMENTS

 A major challenge you will face as you start to distribute information on your intranet is your need to convert a large number of existing documents. For example, many of your current Human Resources documents and other company manuals probably exist in page-layout or word-processing files. Converting large documents such as these may prove a difficult and time-consuming task.

205

Most Web-authoring tools let you convert documents only from specific document formats. For example, to convert a *Word* or *Excel* document to HTML, you can use Microsoft *Internet Assistant*. However, if your existing documents are in a format not supported by the Web-authoring tool, you may have to perform several conversions of the document's contents until you achieve a format the tool understands. For example, if you have a 350-page product manual that was created in *PageMaker*, you might need to save the document using *Rich Text Format* (RTF) which *Word* understands, and then use the *Internet Assistant* to convert the document to HTML.

After you convert the document's pages, you will need to edit the documents to adjust styles and specify links. If the document contains images, you must convert the images into JPEG or GIF format. After you have successfully converted the document to HTML, you can post the document for distribution on the Web. If your manual has quarterly revisions and updates, you will need to repeat this time-consuming process at those times.

As you can see, the conversion of large documents to HTML is complex and time consuming. If you are responsible for document control, content creation, or content conversion, you need tools that will help you automate much of the document-conversion process. Before you choose to convert a document to HTML rather than distributing the document in another format (such as on paper), you should consider the following:

- How difficult is it to convert the file into HTML? How many images must you convert?

- How frequently must you revise the document? What is the normal extent of such revisions?

- Can future updates occur within the HTML document only, or must you first update other documents which you then convert to HTML?

- Do you need to distribute the document's content in formats other than HTML, such as a paper-based manual?

As you plan your intranet, announce to all employees in detail which document formats you will support. By limiting the number of document and image formats you will support, you will greatly improve your ability to manage and control the documents that make up your Web.

MICROSOFT'S INTERNET ASSISTANT ADD-ONS

As you learned in Chapters 7, 8, and 9, by using the Microsoft *Internet Assistant* products, you need to learn only HTML basics. Therefore, the *Internet Assistant* add-on products are ideal for most employees because the add-ons require little training, and your employees can use the software with programs they already know, such as *Word* or *Excel*. In fact, most of the employees who create content for your intranet will need the Microsoft *Internet Assistant* products only to create their HTML documents.

Your Information Systems group should install these add-on programs for your employees. Instead of teaching employees advanced HTML, teach them the HTML basics and how to use the *Internet Assistant* tools. You can download the free *Internet Assistant* products for *Access, Excel, PowerPoint, Word*, and *Schedule+* from the Microsoft Web site at *http://www.microsoft.com/msdownload/*.

LOTUS SMARTSUITE 96 SOLUTION

Like Microsoft, Lotus also provides its customers with free add-on HTML conversion programs. Specifically, Lotus has built HTML publishing capabilities into both Lotus *1-2-3* and Lotus *Word Pro 96*. Also, like Microsoft *PowerPoint*, Lotus *Freelance Graphics 96* can convert presentation files into HTML documents. The *Freelance* HTML conversion utility provides a table of contents from which users can go directly to a specific page within the converted *Freelance* presentation. To find out more about Lotus *SmartSuite 96*, visit the site at *http://www.lotus.com/smartsuite/2116.htm*, as shown in Figure 10.1.

*Figure 10.1 Information on Lotus **SmartSuite**.*

COREL WORDPERFECT SUITE 7 FOR WINDOWS 95 SOLUTION

WordPerfect users can now depend on Corel Corporation, maker of *Corel Draw*, to provide them with an integrated office productivity suite with built-in HTML editing and conversion capabilities. The latest version of Corel *WordPerfect Suite 7 for Windows 95* (comprising *WordPerfect 7, Quattro Pro 7*, and Corel *Presentations*) lets you convert files to and from HTML automatically within the applications. In addition, the software lets you place links within your documents which correspond to files that reside within your intranet or at sites throughout the Internet. For more information on this software, visit the site at *http://www.corel.com/products/wordperfect/cwps7/index.htm*, as shown in Figure 10.2.

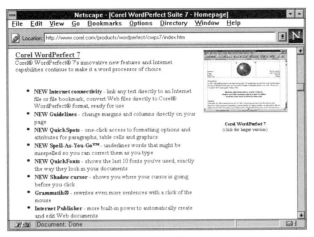

*Figure 10.2 Information on **WordPerfect Suite** 7 at Corel's Web site.*

STANDALONE AUTHORING TOOLS FOR ADVANCED USERS

As you learned in previous sections, add-on tools for desktop productivity software programs provide an easy and inexpensive way to enable a large number of people in your company to create HTML pages. These programs, however, are not as powerful as standalone HTML-authoring programs. Often, you will find that at least 10 percent of your HTML content developers will need additional tools to create advanced HTML pages. Normally, these users are the ones who take the initiative to design attractive features into their pages.

For these users, you may need to buy tools that let them easily create original HTML documents or convert complex existing documents to HTML. In the following sections, you will examine three top Web-authoring programs.

HotDog BY SAUSAGE SOFTWARE

You might not have guessed from the name that *HotDog*, by Sausage Software, is one of the best standalone HTML authoring tools available today. *HotDog* has consistently received rave reviews from both users and experts. *HotDog* supports the Netscape extensions to HTML, as well as W3C's proposed HTML 3.0 elements.

HotDog supports drag-and-drop operations with which you can insert links, images, and text files into an HTML document. Currently, two versions of *HotDog* are available for Windows-based systems: *HotDog Professional* ($99) and *HotDog Standard Web Editors* ($30). The professional version includes a built-in viewer and a spell checker. You can download these two products from *http://www.sausage.com.au/dogindex.htm* and evaluate them for 30 days. Figure 10.3 shows an HTML document within *HotDog*.

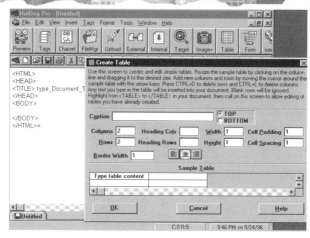

*Figure 10.3 An HTML document within **HotDog**.*

KENN NESBITT'S WEBEDIT

Kenn Nesbitt's *WebEdit* is another top-rated Web-page authoring tool for Windows. *WebEdit* provides a WYSIWYG editor with which you can create HTML pages. *WebEdit* supports both HTML 3.0 tags, as well as the HTML 2.0, and both Netscape *Navigator* and Microsoft *Internet Explorer* 2.0 extensions. *WebEdit* has a built-in image-map builder, an integrated preview capability, and a spell checker. *WebEdit* sells for about $79. You can learn more about this product at *http://www.nesbitt.com*, shown in Figure 10.4

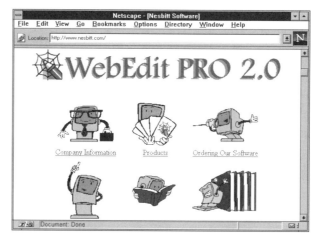

*Figure 10.4 Information on **WebEdit**.*

WebEdit PRO 2.0, which is available for Windows 95 and Windows NT, lets you create forms and manage a number of documents as a group. Like *HotDog*, you can download this product free for 30 days and test-drive the software to ensure it meets your needs.

NETSCAPE NAVIGATOR GOLD

Netscape *Navigator Gold* combines an HTML-authoring tool and a Web browser for the Windows platform. Netscape *Navigator Gold* does not have all of the features provided by *HotDog* or *WebEdit.* For example, the Netscape *Navigator Gold* editor does not support tables, forms, or image mapping. *Navigator Gold* does, however, support *frames,* a feature that lets designers split Web pages into multiple windows with individual scroll bars, as shown in Figure 10.5.

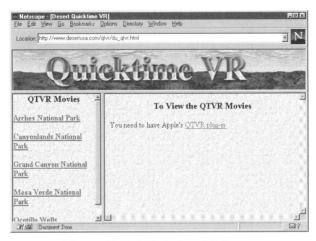

Figure 10.5 *A Web site with frames.*

Navigator Gold also supports real-time objects and in-line viewers for Apple *QuickTime* and Macromedia *Director* movies. The movie viewers let users view movies while scrolling through the Web pages without first having to download large video or movie files, as shown in Figure 10.6.

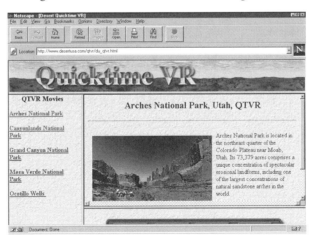

Figure 10.6 *A Web page with an in-line viewer for Apple* **QuickTime Virtual Reality***.*

ADOBE PAGEMILL

Adobe *PageMill* is another popular Web-authoring tool for Mac systems and is soon to be released for Unix and Windows. *PageMill* provides a WYSIWYG interface and supports drag-and-drop features. *PageMill* supports many of the same style tools users find within their word processor.

For example, using *PageMill* you can easily stylize text by highlighting the text and then selecting a style from an options menu. You can also easily insert images and graphics into a *PageMill* document. Linking documents within *PageMill* is easier than most other editing programs because you do not need to enter the linked document's URL. Instead, *PageMill* lets you drag-and-drop to link the document, as shown in Figure 10.7.

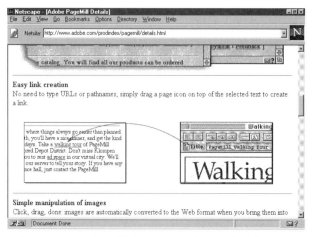

Figure 10.7 PageMill's drag-and-drop link feature.

As shown in Figure 10.8, *PageMill* also provides an extensive tool set that makes it easy for you to build HTML-based forms that contain buttons and text fields.

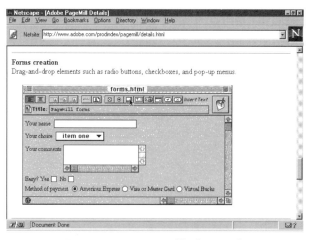

Figure 10.8 PageMill's form tools.

PageMill version 2.0 offers additional features that further enhance your creation of dynamic Web pages—without requiring you to be a programmer. With *PageMill version 2.0*, you can flow text around images which makes your Web pages look more like printed documents. In addition, the software lets you scale and color individual characters as opposed to entire lines or paragraphs. Using the built-in spell checker, you can catch most spelling errors before your Web pages go on-line. *PageMill version 2.0* supports multimedia plug-ins for *QuickTime* movies, Macromedia

Shockwave files, animated GIF files, and Adobe PDF files. The software also provides a library of format converters for popular spreadsheet, word-processing, and database applications. For more information on *PageMill*, visit the site at *http://www.adobe.com/prodindex/pagemill/main.html*, as shown in Figure 10.9.

Figure 10.9 Information on PageMill.

DOCUMENT CONVERSION USING HTML TRANSIT

HTML Transit is a Web-authoring tool specifically designed for the conversion of documents that require frequent revisions or that contain substantial content. *HTML Transit* is a Windows-based application that automates the process of HTML conversion by using standard and custom templates. Its template-based architecture enables you to select a standard template or customize a template before converting content to HTML. The software also lets you convert more than one file at a time—even if the files have different source formats.

HTML Transit version 2.0 provides advanced table conversion and formatting directly from other document files. It has additional table features that let you specify default table cell width and border thickness. You can also specify table background colors, text, and placement of the table on the page. The software is compatible with all major word processing and graphics formats. The program supports HTML 2.0, HTML 3.0, and both Netscape *Navigator* and Microsoft *Internet Explorer* extensions.

The major difference between *HTML Transit* and standalone products, such as *HotDog*, is that the standalone programs are manual-authoring systems that work best when you create customized HTML pages, whereas *HTML Transit* is an ideal complement to your existing word processors.

To best meet your needs, you probably want both *HTML Transit* and a standalone program, such as *HotDog*. *HTML Transit* is available for Windows 3.1, Windows 95, and Windows NT. You can download an evaluation copy of *HTML Transit* at *http://www.infoaccess.com/products/transit/htframe.htm*, as shown in Figure 10.10.

Figure 10.10 *Information on HTML Transit.*

DOCUMENT CONVERSION USING ADOBE ACROBAT

In previous sections, you learned that you need a variety of tools to convert your existing documents to HTML and to convert images to standard formats, such as GIF and JPEG. In reality, most companies cannot convert all of their existing documents and forms to HTML without spending a lot of money and time. In some cases, because of HTML's limitations, making an HTML document look like an existing form may be impossible. Therefore, you may need to convert some existing forms and documents to a format that users can view using special viewers.

There are a number of special viewers currently available. The most popular special viewer is Adobe *Acrobat*. Using *Acrobat*, you can easily convert documents that contain complex formatting, such as tables, figures, and images, to a non–HTML readable format called *Portable Document Format (PDF)*. PDF is a universal electronic-file format that lets users view the document in their browsers using a free copy of Adobe *Acrobat Reader*. For example, the U.S. Government uses PDF files for the tax documents they distribute on the Internet, as shown in Figure 10.11. As you can see, the tax forms are complex and require a specific and uniform structure to enable efficient processing.

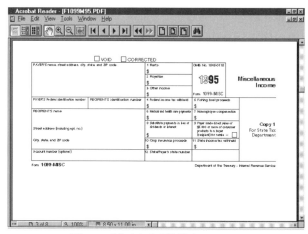

Figure 10.11 *A PDF document.*

CONVERTING FILES TO ADOBE ACROBAT PDF

To convert your documents to PDF format, you need Adobe *Acrobat 3.0*, which is available for Windows, Unix, and Mac platforms. Using *Acrobat 3.0*, you can create PDF files from your existing business applications, such as word-processing and spreadsheet programs. In addition, you can also convert *PostScript* language files into PDF using *Acrobat Distiller*, which is part of *Acrobat 3.0*. *Acrobat Distiller* lets you create PDF files from your drawing, image-editing, and page-layout programs. *Acrobat 3.0* also lets you build navigational links into PDF files. Figure 10.12 shows a Government Web page from which users can download PDF files.

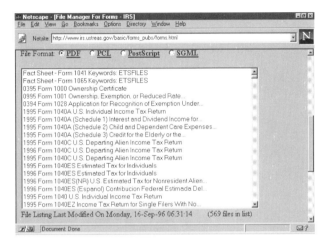

Figure 10.12 A Government Web page from which users can download PDF files.

For information on Adobe *Acrobat 3.0*, visit Adobe's Web site at *http://www.adobe.com/prodindex/acrobat/details.html*, as shown in Figure 10.13.

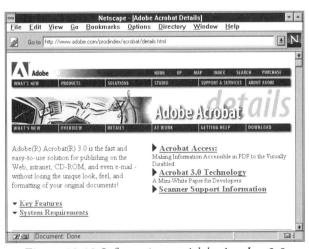

Figure 10.13 Information on Adobe Acrobat 3.0.

How to Download and Install Adobe Acrobat Reader

Adobe *Acrobat Reader* is free and you can download it from Adobe's Web site at *http://www.adobe.com*. After you download the program, you run the *Acrobat Installer* application, contained in the file *ACROREAD.EXE*. The *Acrobat Installer*, in turn, will install the *Acrobat Reader* program on your hard disk within the directory *C:\ACROREAD*.

After you install the *Acrobat Reader*, you must configure your browser so it will know how to display PDF files. For example, Netscape *Navigator* does not have the built-in capability to read PDF files. To display PDF files within your browser, you must tell *Navigator* to use Adobe *Acrobat Reader* to handle the PDF files. To enable *Navigator* to use the *Acrobat Reader* to display PDF files, perform these steps:

1. Start Netscape *Navigator*.

2. Select the Option menu and choose General Preferences. *Navigator* will display the Preferences dialog box.

3. Within the Preferences dialog box, select the Helper tab. *Navigator* will display the Helper dialog box, as shown in Figure 10.14.

*Figure 10.14 Netscape **Navigator** Helper dialog box.*

4. Within the Helper dialog box, click on the New Type button. *Navigator* will display the Configure New Mime Type dialog screen.

5. Within the New Mime Type dialog box, type "application" in the Mime type files and type "pdf" in the Mime subtype field.

6. Click on OK. *Navigator* will display the Helper dialog box again.

7. Within the Helper dialog box, type "pdf" in the File Extentions field.

8. Within the Helper dialog box Action choices, select the Launch the Application button.

9.   Click on the Browse button and locate the Adobe *Acrobat Reader* application which you just installed on your disk.

10. Click on OK.

WEB-SITE MANAGEMENT TOOLS

Successful Web sites are dynamic—constantly changing with new content, images, and input from users. Such Web sites require extensive management to ensure accurate and functional Web pages. Unlike print documents, Web sites require constant maintenance. Maintaining current Web page links is one of the most challenging tasks you will face as you deploy your intranet. As users move or rename files, you must update existing links to the files.

You can manage a small intranet with good organization and planning. Maintaining medium and large Web sites, on the other hand, requires more than just good organizational skills—you will need software tools to help you. Several software companies now differentiate their HTML-authoring programs from their competition by integrating site-management features into them. Two such products include *FrontPage 97* from Microsoft and *SiteMill* from Adobe Systems.

MICROSOFT FRONTPAGE 97

FrontPage 97 (or simply *FrontPage*) is an integrated server, authoring, and site-management tool rolled into one software program. *FrontPage* includes a *Personal Web Server*, an HTML-authoring program, and a site-management program. With *FrontPage*, you don't have to be a programmer to build and manage a Web site. Using the tools built into *FrontPage*, you can integrate threaded discussion-groups and on-line search capabilities into your Web site. As shown in Figure 10.15, *FrontPage* also provides tools to help you track and repair broken links.

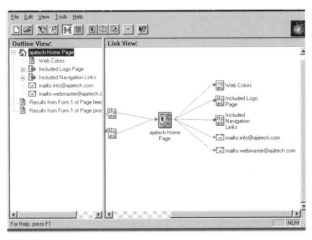

*Figure 10.15 A Web site in **FrontPage** 97.*

FrontPage Explorer provides you with a variety of ways to view your intranet. For example, you can view a graphical representation of how your site's documents relate (how documents are linked), or you might view a summary list that describes your intranet pages.

Using *FrontPage*, you can provide each of your departments with the ability to easily create, develop, and test complete Web documents before transferring the documents to your main Web site. In Chapter 14, "Web Publishing Using FrontPage 97," you will learn how to use *FrontPage* to create dynamic intranet Web sites. The site-management tools available in *FrontPage Explorer* let you assign members of a team to work on a site simultaneously. As you will learn, *FrontPage* has a To Do List feature that makes it easy for you to track the development of your intranet content.

FrontPage 97 also provides a library of wizards—programs that automate the task of building Web pages and Web sites. For more information on *FrontPage*, visit the Microsoft Web site at *http://www.microsoft.com/frontpage/*, as shown in Figure 10.16.

*Figure 10.16 Information on **FrontPage** 97.*

ADOBE SITEMILL

Adobe *SiteMill* is a Web site-management tool for Mac systems, which also includes the *PageMill* HTML editor. One of *SiteMill's* strengths is its automatic link repair, which repairs links (updates the links within documents to point to correct locations) when a user changes or updates a file or Web page. *SiteMill* also contains a site-view mode which lets you view your site's content, as shown in Figure 10.17.

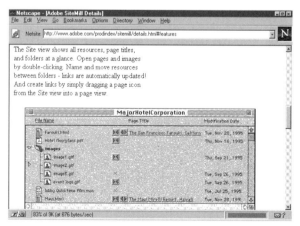

*Figure 10.17 A Web site in **SiteMill's** view mode.*

As shown in Figure 10.18, *SiteMill's* site view also lets you view all of the links into and out of a Web page, including external references to other Web sites.

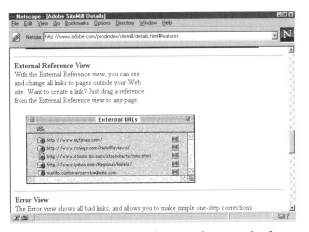

Figure 10.18 *Viewing a Web site with external references.*

Using *SiteMill's* display of external references, you can often detect broken links which are the result of a URL change at a remote site.

EVALUATING WEB SITE AUTHORING TOOLS

This chapter has introduced a variety of Web-authoring tools. As you evaluate various tools, consider the tool's support for the following features:

- The ability to create forms and to convert existing forms

- The ability to create tables and to convert existing tables

- The ability to construct a table of contents and an index

- Automated find and replace operations (throughout multiple documents)

- Graphics conversion (GIF, JPEG, and animated GIF)

- The ability to create new HTML documents and convert existing documents to HTML

- Integration of wizards and templates

- An icon and clipart library

- Support for key programs, such as *Word, Excel,* and *PowerPoint*

- Provides a built-in spell checker

- Support for link management

- The ability to create and edit image maps

- Support for scripting languages, such as JavaScript and VBScript

- Support for CGI programming

- Level of HTML support (2.0, 3.0, 3.2)

- The ability to manage documents (and control document revisions)

- Support for on-line testing

- Support for multimedia objects, such as video and sound

PUTTING IT ALL TOGETHER

This chapter introduced you to several tools you can use to create and manage your intranet's content. In Chapter 11, you will learn about intranet software packages that provide advanced document management and communication features. You will also learn how these tools can enhance your productivity and add functionality to your intranet. Before you continue with Chapter 11, however, make sure you understand the following concepts:

✓ Web sites are dynamic and require extensive management to ensure accurate and functional Web pages.

✓ By using HTML-editing tools that add-on to software that your company already uses, you can minimize employee training costs.

✓ It is important for your intranet team to standardize a specific browser and set of authoring tools to ensure that your employees can view all the HTML documents your company creates.

✓ To better control your document management and revisions, you should standardize the set of file formats employees can submit for use on your intranet.

✓ Most older Web-authoring programs serve as manual conversion tools, with which you can only create or convert one document at a time and possibly from only a limited number of document formats.

✓ To meet your user needs, you will need a Web-authoring tool with which users can create HTML documents from scratch, as well as conversion tools with which users can convert their existing document and image files.

VISITING KEY SITES THAT DISCUSS INTRANETS

The World Wide Web is filled with hundreds of excellent and current articles on all aspects of intranets. Use the following sites as starting points for your Web exploration.

WEBMASTER

http://www.cio.com/WebMaster/wm_irc.html

MANAGING WEB TECHNOLOGY

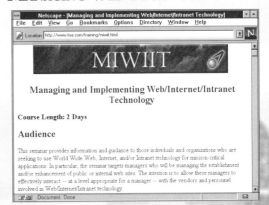

http://www.toa.com/training/miwiit.html

INTRANET PUBLISHING

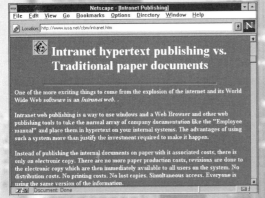

http://www.iusa.net/cbm/intranet.htm

INTRANET DEVELOPMENT

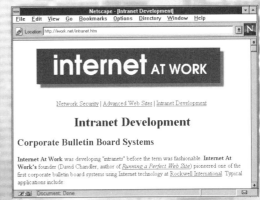

http://iwork.net/intranet.htm

NETFRAME

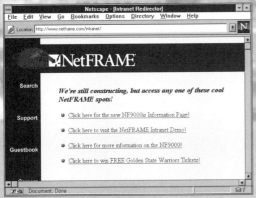

http://www.netframe.com/intranet/

COLD FUSION

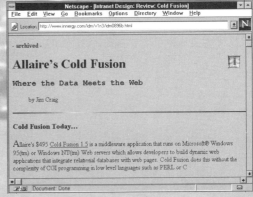

*http://www.innergy.com/idm/v1n3/
idm0896b.html*

INTRANET APPLICATION DEVELOPMENT

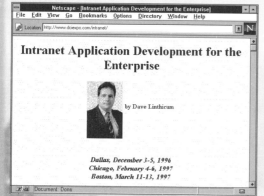

http://www.dciexpo.com/intranet/

ONLINE

http://203.63.164.17/

BUILDING AN INTRANET

http://www.ishops.com/softpro/internet-intranet.html

NOTES AND THE INTRANET

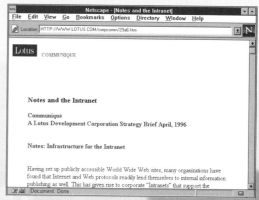

http://WWW.LOTUS.COM/corpcomm/29a6.htm

CORPORATE INTRANET

http://www.4expertise.com/minicat/im012.htm

INVENTING AN INTRANET

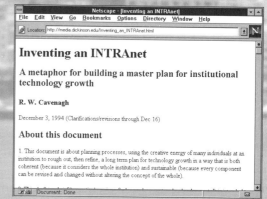

http://media.dickinson.edu/—inventing_an_INTRAnet.html

Chapter 11

Forms and CGI Programming

221

As you have learned in previous chapters, the user's ability to interact with your Web pages enhances the functionality of your intranet. Different methods are available for you to use to extend the interactive nature of your intranet, such as Java applets, ActiveX objects, or CGI scripts. Today, the most common way developers create interactive pages is by using CGI scripts. Normally, sites use CGI scripts to create an interactive form that the user completes and then submits to the server for processing. In addition to CGI, Web-site developers use Server Side Includes (SSI), Application Programming Interfaces (API), and Java applets to create interactive objects. In this chapter, you will learn how to use CGI scripts to create interactive forms. In Chapter 20, you will learn more about using Java applets to create dynamic pages.

In general, the use of CGI scripts requires the user to interact with the browser to complete a form, and then the browser must interact with the server to process the form's contents. For example, after a user fills out and submits a form, the browser will send the information to a server which, in turn, executes a script (set of programming instructions) to process the form's contents. Depending on the script's processing, the server may send a response back to the browser, which will display the result to the user. This chapter examines the steps you must take to create a form and to process the form's contents using a server-based program. By the time you finish this chapter, you will have learned the following key concepts:

- By adding interactive capabilities to your intranet, you make it easier for your employees and customers to utilize your organization's knowledge base.

- In addition to responding to browser requests for Web pages, a Web server oversees CGI operations. The Web server passes information, such as a form, to a program that processes the form's content.

- A Web client can request a server to locate a document, to query a database, or to perform a specific task that requires the server to run a related program.

- Web developers use Common Gateway Interface (CGI) scripts to let users communicate with an application, such as a database program, that normally resides on the Web server.

- When a user connects to a page that contains a CGI script, the browser uses the script's contents to build forms. When the user completes and submits the form, the server passes the form's contents to a program which processes the data.

- ◆ HTML forms include two main parts: an HTML document and a CGI script.

- ◆ HTML documents can contain more than one form.

- ◆ You can create HTML forms using standard HTML document and form tags.

UNDERSTANDING THE USER'S NEED TO INTERACT WITH YOUR SITE

Providing the user with the ability to interact with your intranet pages will enhance your intranet's functionality by allowing the site to better service your customers. The user's ability to interact with your site may reduce costs by allowing you to automate functions that were previously time or labor intensive. For example, an organization that wants to implement a customer survey may use one of following methods:

- Hire a telemarketing company to interview customers through a phone survey, then enter the survey results into a database for analysis.

- Print and mail a survey form to customers, which the customers must complete and mail back to the organization. Again, the company must enter the results into a database for analysis.

Both of these methods require labor and capital. One method includes the cost of hiring additional labor, and the other requires additional labor, production, and distribution to implement the survey. In contrast, if the company posts the same survey on a Web site, customers can complete the survey and submit their responses to the company's database directly. Using this type of survey, companies eliminate all additional labor costs and the production and distribution costs of a direct mail survey. In addition, using the on-line survey, the company can eliminate the time and labor needed to enter the survey's results into a database.

You can use a CGI script to create an on-line survey. Your browser uses the CGI script to build the form that the user will complete. Before you examine CGI scripts, and how to create HTML forms, you must first understand how clients and servers communicate.

CLIENT AND SERVER COMMUNICATIONS

As you have learned, a Web server is a program that processes client requests, such as a request for the server to provide a specific HTML page. Clients, such as a Web browser, send their requests to the Web server. When the Web server receives a request, the server first checks if the client has access to the data it is requesting and, if so, the server processes the request. A client may request that the server provide an HTML document, query a database, or store information within a database that resides on the server computer.

For the client and server to communicate, both must use a protocol, such as HTTP (HyperText Transfer Protocol). As you learned in Chapter 1, a protocol is a set of rules the client and the server follow as they communicate. Client and server communication consists of three parts:

1. **Request:** The client sends a request to the server using a protocol, such as HTTP.

2. **Receipt:** The server receives the request and verifies the client has access to the information.

3. **Response:** The server sends its response back to the client.

UNDERSTANDING CGI SCRIPTS

As you know, Web browsers are a great tool for viewing and traversing HTML documents. Browsers, however, are not well suited for many network operations, such as database operations, on-line ordering, and other operations that require extensive interaction with the user. CGI scripts provide a bridge for users to perform these operations within their browsers. In short, a CGI script sits between the browser and other applications on your system, such as an employee database. The CGI script converts data (such as employee records) into a format the browser can understand (HTML) and user input from an HTML form into a format the application (such as the database) can understand.

As briefly discussed, a CGI (Common Gateway Interface) script is a software tool that Internet and intranet developers use to create interactive pages. For example, a company can use a CGI script to let employees and customers link to corporate databases, place orders, obtain real-time financial reports and manufacturing data, and perform many other functions. In short, a CGI script allows the user to become involved with the client–server exchange by completing an on-line form.

When the user submits a CGI-based form, the server executes a related program to process the form's content. For example, using CGI, a server can create an HTML-based form, and send the form to the user via the user's Web browser. When the user completes the form, the server normally runs a specific program to process the form's content. Depending on the form's purpose, the program might query a database and send the results back to the client. CGI scripts provide users and Web designers with a tremendous degree of functionality. Unfortunately, each CGI-based operation requires a programmer to create a custom program to process the CGI-based data.

Programmers can write CGI in a number of different script and programming languages, such as C++, Java, and Perl. The process the server performs to execute a CGI script is more complicated than the steps it performs to service a simple document request. To understand how a CGI program works, you must understand the following sequence of events that take place between a user, a browser, a server, and a CGI script:

1. A user clicks on a URL link in a Web document to initiate a request to the server.

2. The Web browser requests the URL from the server.

3. The server verifies that the client has permission to access the document.

4. The server downloads the document to the browser.

5. The browser displays a form.

6. The user completes and submits the form.

7. The browser sends the form to the server, specifying the URL of a server-based program.

8. The server runs the specified program, passing to the program the form's fields as environment entries.

9. The program processes the form's content.

10. Depending on the form's content and purpose, the program creates an HTML-based result, which the program instructs the server to return to the browser.

11. The server passes the HTML-based result back to the Web browser which, in turn, formats the result and displays it for the user.

Figure 11.1 shows the CGI transaction process.

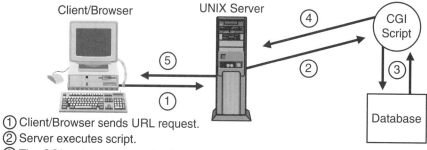

① Client/Browser sends URL request.
② Server executes script.
③ The CGI script accesses database to retrieve information that was requested.
④ CGI retrieves data and sends it back to the server to pass the information on to the browser.
⑤ Server sends requested information to the browser.

Figure 11.1 The process of executing a CGI request.

The following HTML entries illustrate a link to a CGI script named *HelloCGI*. As you can see, the entries use a URL to specify the script to the server.

```
<HTML><TITLE>CGI Script</TITLE>
<H1>This page contains a link to a CGI script</H1>
<P><A HREF="http://www.servername/cgi-bin/HelloCGI">Click here to
execute a CGI script</A>
</HTML>
```

In this case, when the user clicks the mouse on the link, the server will use the URL to determine if the user has selected a CGI script. The server, in turn, will run the specified program.

The following statements use the Unix C-Shell to create the simple *HelloCGI* script. A Unix C-Shell script is similar to an MS-DOS batch file in that the script contains a list of commands (but the C-Shell script processor is much more powerful):

```
#!/bin/csh
echo Content-type: text/plain
echo "Hello from the CGI script. You just executed the CGI script!"
```

This script simply uses the Unix *echo* command to send text messages back to the server, which the server, in turn, sends back to the browser. The script's first line tells Unix that this document contains entries that Unix should process using its C-Shell. The second line specifies the type of content the document contains. The browser uses the content description to identify how it should display that content. The third line is a simple *echo* command that tells the browser to display the text inside the double quotes on a new Web page.

225

When the browser receives the results, it processes the information and then displays a new Web page, as shown in Figure 11.2.

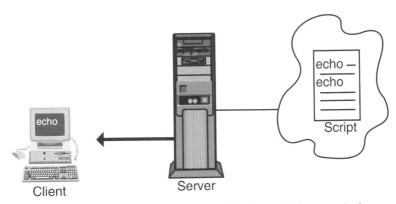

Figure 11.2 The Web page that the CGI script sends back to the browser.

In this case, you can use the *HelloCGI* script only if you have a Unix-based server that supports C-Shell scripts. If that is the case, place the *HelloCGI* script within a directory named */cgi-bin* on your server and try it out. If you are not using a Unix-based server that supports C-Shell scripts, do not worry. You will learn how to create Perl-based scripts later in this chapter which you can run using the Perl software provided on this book's CD-ROM. For now, simply understand that a browser can direct the server to run a program to process a form's data using CGI. You, or a programmer you hire, must write this program using a language such as Perl.

CONFIGURING CGI ON A SERVER

For a server to process CGI scripts, you must first properly configure the Web server to support CGI-based programs. To configure your server to support CGI operations, turn to the documentation that accompanied your server.

As you will learn in Chapter 19, "Intranet Security Issues," many security issues related to CGI scripts exist. For security reasons, your company's server may not allow CGI access, or it may allow only limited access for certain users. For additional information on CGI security issues, visit the Web sites at *http://www.cerf.net/~paulp/cgi-security/safe-cgi.txt* and *http://hoohoo.ncsa.uiuc.edu/cgi/security.html*, shown in Figures 11.3a and 11.3b.

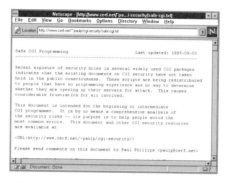   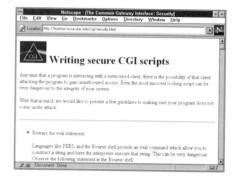

Figure 11.3a Information on CGI security.   *Figure 11.3b More CGI security issues.*

CGI SCRIPT INPUT AND OUTPUT

When a user completes a CGI-based form, the user assigns values to various fields within the form. Each field has a unique name. When the browser submits the form to the server, the server assigns each form's value to an environment variable that corresponds to the field name. For example, if a form has three fields, Name, Company, and City, the server will create three environment variables with the same names. Then, the server will assign the user's value to each variable, creating entries similar to the following:

> Name=William Gates
>
> Company=Microsoft
>
> City=Redmond

Next, the server will run a program that processes the user's entries by accessing its environment variables. If you are not familiar with environment variables, do not worry. You can think of environment variables as memory with named storage locations within which the server passes the form's field values to the CGI-based program. The server passes input to the CGI script. This input usually includes information about the server, the client, and the data the user entered into an HTML-based form.

For additional information on the various environment variables a server passes to the CGI-based program, visit the Web site, *http://hoohoonsca.uiuc.edu/cgi/env.html*, shown in Figure 11.4.

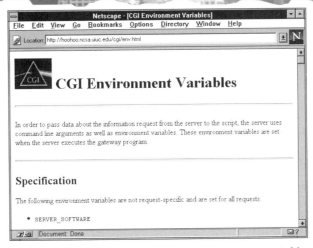

Figure 11.4 Information on CGI environment variables.

LOOKING AT CGI-SCRIPT OUTPUT

As it turns out, depending on how the programmer designed the CGI script, the server can pass the HTML-form data to the script using environment variables or the program's standard input (stdin) device. You will learn more about these two methods of data passing later in this chapter. After the CGI script processes its data, the script may generate output which it intends the browser to display to the user. The output the CGI script returns to the server must be in a format which the server and the browser (to which the server sends the script's output) can understand. Most CGI programs send their output to the server (by way of the script's standard output device) as HTML.

The first item within a CGI script's output is a special one-line header that informs the server, and eventually the browser, of what type of information it should expect to receive. The script will output a line similar to the following:

```
content-type: text/html
```

In this case, the content-type entry informs the server that the CGI script is going to send HTML and text-based data. Table 11.1 contains a list of other common formats and their CGI content types.

Format	Content-Type
Text	text/plain
HTML	text/html
JPEC	image/jpeg
GIF	image/gif
MPEG	application/postscript
PostScript	application/postscript

Table 11.1 Common data formats and their content types.

Following this content information, the CGI script's output will normally contain standard HTML entries which the browser can format and display to the user.

UNDERSTANDING THE PERL PROGRAMMING LANGUAGE

Currently, programmers create most CGI scripts using the Perl programming language. Perl is powerful, yet easy to learn. You can use Perl on Unix, Windows, and Mac-based machines. The following sections will introduce you to Perl. The chapter's intent is not to teach you everything you need to know about Perl, but rather, how to use Perl to get started with CGI programming. For more information on Perl as well as CGI programming, turn to the book *Web Programming*, Jamsa Press, 1996, or visit the Web site at *http://www.teleport.com/~rootbeer/perl.html*, shown in Figure 11.5.

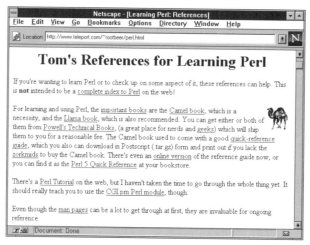

Figure 11.5 Information on Perl programming.

INSTALLING PERL ON YOUR SYSTEM

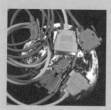 If you are using a Windows-based system, you can install Perl from the companion CD-ROM that accompanies this book. The file *PERL5.ZIP* contains the zipped (compressed) Perl software distribution (the compiler, debugger, and so on), as well as sample scripts. Because some of the Perl 5 files use long filenames, you must unzip this file using WinZip (which you can download from *http://www.winzip.com*). If you encounter error messages while unzipping *PERL5.ZIP*, make sure you are using WinZip version 6.1 or later (and also check the Use Folder Names checkbox).

Perl is a command-line program that you must run from a system prompt. If you are using Windows 95, you can get to a system prompt by selecting the Start menu Run option. Windows 95, in turn, will display the Run dialog box. Within the Run dialog box, type *Command* and press Enter. Then, use the CHDIR command to select the directory within which you installed Perl (probably C:\PERL). Within that directory, you can edit your Perl programs and run the programs by running Perl from the command line, as shown here:

```
C:\PERL> perl  Filename.pl  <ENTER>
```

When you start, most of the Perl scripts you create will simply use the Perl *print* function to display a message. If you examine the message, you will find that its contents look very much like HTML. That is because many of your early Perl programs will simply build HTML documents on the fly, which the server returns to the browser and the browser then displays. For example, the following Perl script, *Date.pl*, uses the Perl *print* function to create an HTML document that displays today's date:

```
#!/usr/local/bin/perl
print "Content-type: text/html", "\n\n"" ;
print "<HTML>", "\n" ;
print "<HEAD><TITLE>Today's Date</TITLE></HEAD>", "\n" ;
print "<BODY><H1>Today's date is </H1><B>","\n"
print "/usr/bin/date"
print "</BODY></HTML>", "\n"
exit(0)
```

The script's first line instructs the server to use the Perl interpreter to execute the CGI script. The second line informs the server of the content type the CGI script will output. You must follow the content-type information with a blank line. The symbols "\n" within a Perl *print* statement direct Perl to output a carriage-return and linefeed.

The remaining print statements create HTML tags that define a document's title and header. The script runs the Unix *date* command to print the day's date. The last line, which contains the *exit* function, terminates the Perl script. For users to execute this script, place the script within the *cgi-bin* directory on your server. Then, create an HTML document that contains a link to the script which users can select to run the script.

If you are not using a Unix-based server, create the following Perl script, *Hello.pl*, which simply displays, "Hello there from Perl" to the user, and does not rely on the presence of the Unix *date* command:

```
print "Content-type: text/html", "\n\n"" ;
print "<HTML>", "\n" ;
print "<HEAD><TITLE>Hello Perl</TITLE></HEAD>", "\n" ;
print "<BODY><H1>Hello there from Perl </H1><B>","\n"
print "</BODY></HTML>", "\n"
exit(0)
```

CREATING HTML FORMS

Across the Web, sites use HTML-based forms to collect information from users, to request data from servers, to process orders, and much more. HTML-based forms let users submit data from a Web site. Each HTML form has a set of fields within which users type related information. The

HTML document that contains the form also includes a link to a CGI script that resides on a Web server. Each of the form's data fields has a *name* and a *value*. A *name* identifies the field to the program that processes the data. The field's *value* contains the user's input.

To execute a CGI program, the user clicks on a link that corresponds to the program itself. The browser sends the link information to the server, along with the form's data. The server, in turn, passes the data to the CGI script through the use of environment variables. The CGI script processes the information and provides a response, or result, to the server, which the server then sends back to the browser. This process may result in an HTML document the CGI program created on the fly. Finally, the browser displays the results it receives from the server.

As discussed, the starting point of a user's interaction with a CGI script is an HTML-based form. The following section discusses how you create a form using the HTML *<FORM>* and *</FORM>* tags.

UNDERSTANDING THE ELEMENTS OF AN HTML FORM

The forms you view within a browser consist of two main elements: an HTML document and a CGI script link. The document used in an HTML form is similar to a standard HTML document. To create the form, the HTML document uses the *<FORM>* and *</FORM>* tags. When you build an HTML form, you will use many of the same tags you learned about in Chapters 7 and 8. The other element in an HTML form is a CGI script link, which is a standard HTML link that contains the program's URL.

DEFINING A FORM USING THE *<FORM>* AND *</FORM>* TAGS

Within an HTML document, the *<FORM>* and *</FORM>* tags group the elements you use to create the form's fields, as shown:

```
<FORM> Define the form fields here </FORM>
```

An HTML document can have more than one form, but you cannot build a form within another form. The form tag has two attributes: *METHOD* and *ACTION*. The *METHOD* attribute specifies how a server sends the form's data to the CGI program. The two values you can assign to the *METHOD* attribute are *GET* and *POST*. The *GET* method directs the server to retrieve the specified resource. For example, a browser sends a server a *GET* method to request a specific HTML file. In contrast, when the browser must send information such as a form to the server, the browser uses the *POST* method. The *ACTION* attribute specifies the URL address of the CGI program.

The following HTML entry, for example, uses the *POST* and *ACTION* attributes to send the form's contents to a Perl script named *instrasur.pl*, which resides on the server:

```
<FORM METHOD="POST" ACTION="intrasur.pl"></FORM>
```

UNDERSTANDING HOW THE BROWSER ENCODES A FORM'S CONTENTS

Before you examine CGI scripts, you must understand how the browser encodes a form's contents before it passes the form to the server. As you will learn, each field within a form has a name and a value. The browser passes the form's contents to the server using name and value pairs. To pass a name and value pair to a server, the browser encodes each pair by separating pairs of values with an ampersand (&) and by replacing spaces and special characters using a special format known as *URL encoding*. For example, the following statement illustrates how a browser might encode two fields, one named *FIRSTNAME* and the second named *SEX*:

```
FIRSTNAME=John&SEX=Male
```

As you can see, the browser uses an equal sign (=) to associate a field's name and value. Likewise, you can see that the browser uses the ampersand to separate fields.

USING THE *<INPUT>* TAG TO CREATE AND INPUT FIELDS

Within a form, you must define one or more input fields in which the user will type text, select a button, or check a checkbox. To create an input field, you use the HTML *<INPUT>* tag. The *<INPUT>* tag's two primary attributes are the *TYPE* and *NAME* attributes. The *TYPE* attribute defines the field's type, such as a text box, checkbox, or radio button. The *NAME* attribute specifies the field's name. As you will learn, the <INPUT> tag also supports the *VALUE*, *SIZE*, and *MAXLENGTH* attributes.

USING THE *TYPE* ATTRIBUTE TO SPECIFY A FIELD'S TYPE

As you have learned, the *<INPUT>* tag *TYPE* attribute specifies the field's type, such as a radio button, checkbox, or a text box. The default field type is a text box, as shown in the following code:

```
<INPUT TYPE="text">
```

The *<INPUT>* tag supports the following TYPE attribute values, as shown in Table 11.2:

Attribute	Function
Text	Creates a text box
Password	Creates a text box within which the browser displays an asterisk (*) for each character the user types
Check	Creates a checkbox
Radio	Creates a radio button
Reset	Creates a button that, when selected, directs the browser to reset variables to their default values
Submit	Creates a button that, when selected, directs the browser to send the form's contents to the server for processing

Table 11.2 Values for the <INPUT> Tag TYPE attribute. (continued on following page)

Attribute	Function
Hidden	Creates an invisible element whose values the browser sends to the server for processing (as a named field) when the user submits the form

Table 11.2 *Values for the <INPUT> Tag* **TYPE** *attribute. (continued from previous page)*

CREATING A TEXT BOX

As briefly discussed, a text field creates a box within which the user can type in text that consists of letters, numbers, and even punctuation symbols. Using the *SIZE* attribute, you can specify the text box size, which specifies how many characters the text box can display (not how many characters the field can contain). To specify the maximum number of characters the text field can store, use the *MAXLENGTH* attribute. The following HTML entries illustrate the use of text boxes:

```
Name: <INPUT TYPE="text" NAME="name" SIZE=40>
Company: <INPUT TYPE="text" NAME="compname" SIZE=40>
E-mail address: <INPUT TYPE="text" NAME="email" SIZE=50>
```

Figure 11.6 illustrates how the Netscape *Navigator* will display these text boxes.

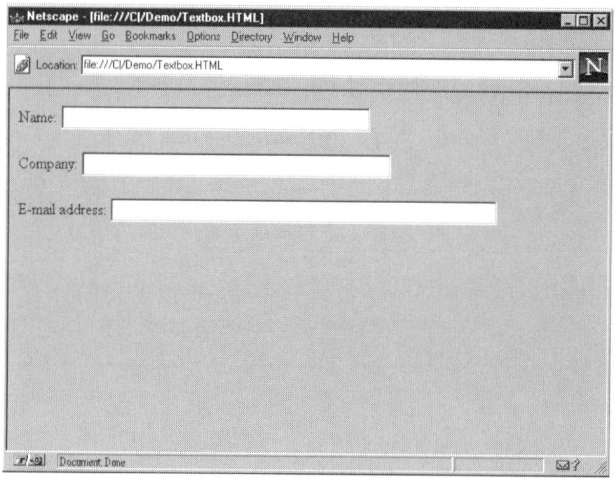

Figure 11.6 *Text boxes within the Netscape* **Navigator***.*

CREATING A PASSWORD BOX

Depending on a form's purpose, you may want users to type in a password before they can use the form. As users type their passwords, you do not want other users, who can see the screen, to view the password. Within a form, a password field creates a text field within which the browser represents each character the user types as an asterisk. The following HTML entry illustrates the use of a password field:

```
Enter your password? <INPUT TYPE="password" NAME="password" SIZE=20>
```

CREATING A CHECKBOX

Within a form, a checkbox field lets users select an option by placing a checkmark within the box. If users do not want to select the option, they simply remove the checkmark. Within a form, users can select more than one checkbox. The following HTML entries illustrate the use of checkbox fields:

```
Which products or services would you like more information on?
(check all that apply)

<INPUT TYPE="checkbox" NAME="Webdev" VALUE="Webdev"> Web Site
Development

<INPUT TYPE="checkbox" NAME="Webcon" VALUE="Webcon"> Web Site
Consulting

<INPUT TYPE="checkbox" NAME="Cuspro" VALUE="Cuspro"> Custom  Pro-
gramming

<INPUT TYPE="checkbox" NAME="Multidevel" VALUE="Multidevel"> Multi-
media Development
```

If you display these HTML entries within the Netscape *Navigator*, the browser will display the checkbox fields, as shown in Figure 11.7.

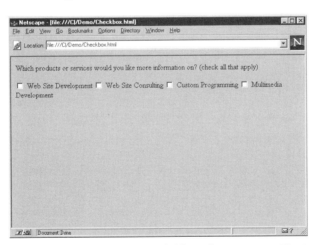

*Figure 11.7 Displaying checkbox fields within Netscape **Navigator**.*

CREATING A RADIO BUTTON

Within a form, checkboxes are ideal when the user can select more than one option. In many cases, however, the user must select one of several options. In such cases, you should use a radio-button field. Within a form, you normally place two or more radio buttons to represent a group of items from which the user can select only one at any given time. The following HTML entries will create four radio buttons:

```
How soon does your organization plan to establish a presence on the
World Wide Web? (check one)

<INPUT TYPE="radio" NAME="how_soon" VALUE="1mon"> Within one month

<INPUT TYPE="radio" NAME="how_soon" VALUE="3mon"> Within three
months

<INPUT TYPE="radio" NAME="how_soon" VALUE="6 mon"> Within six months

<INPUT TYPE="radio" NAME="how_soon" VALUE="1yr"> Within one year
```

As you can see, each of the radio buttons share the same name which, in this case, is *how_soon* (which corresponds to how soon the user needs information). When the user submits the form to the server, the browser will assign the selected value to the *how_soon* field. Figure 11.8 illustrates how Netscape *Navigator* will display the radio buttons. As the user fills in the form, the user can only select one of the four radio buttons.

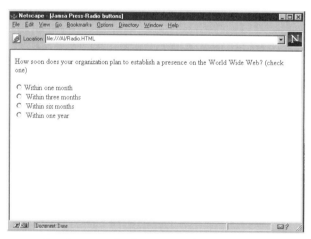

Figure 11.8 Displaying radio buttons within the Netscape **Navigator***.*

RESETTING A FORM'S DEFAULT VALUES

As a user fills in a form's fields, there may be times when the user wants to start the form again, from scratch. For such cases, you can place a reset button on the form that the user can select to restore the form's default values. To create such a button, you create a reset field, as shown in the following statement:

```
<Input TYPE="reset" VALUE="Clear Form">
```

If the user selects the reset button, the browser will restore each of the field values to the form's default settings.

SUBMITTING A FORM'S CONTENTS

When you create a form, you should place a Submit Form button on the form which makes it easy for the user to submit the completed form to the server. To create such a button, you can create a submit field, as shown in the following HTML entry:

```
<Input TYPE="submit" VALUE="Submit Form">
```

When the user selects the Submit button, the browser will encode the form's contents, as previously discussed, and will then post the form to the server. The server, in turn, will send the form to the CGI script for processing.

PLACING HIDDEN VALUES WITHIN A FIELD

Depending on a form's purpose, there may be times when you want to place hidden values on the form that the browser submits to the server. For example, you might place a hidden field named *FormVersion* on the form that tells the server which version of the form it is processing. For example, the following HTML entry creates a hidden field on a form:

```
<Input TYPE="hidden" NAME="FormVersion" VALUE="V3.1">
```

In this case, the browser will not display the field on the form. However, the browser will pass the field's value to the server when the user submits the form.

ASSIGNING A VALUE TO A FIELD

When you place a text box within a form, you may want to assign a default value to the box. To assign a value to a text or password field, you use the *VALUE* attribute. For example, the following HTML entry assigns the value Smith to the *LastName* field:

```
<INPUT TYPE="text" NAME="LastName" VALUE="Smith">
```

You can also use the *VALUE* attribute with Reset and Submit Form buttons to create a custom label that appears beside the buttons, rather than the default strings "reset" and "submit."

CHECKING A CHECKBOX OR SELECTING A RADIO BUTTON

When you use a checkbox or radio-button field, you may want to initially check one or more boxes or select a specific radio button. To do so, you use the *CHECKED* attribute. For example, the following HTML entries use the *CHECKED* attribute to select the Green radio button:

```
<INPUT TYPE ="radio" NAME="color" VALUE="red" >Red
<INPUT TYPE ="radio" NAME="color" VALUE="blue">Blue
<INPUT TYPE ="radio" NAME="color" VALUE="green" CHECKED>Green
```

In a similar way, the following HTML entries use the *CHECKED* attribute to select two checkboxes:

```
Which products or services would you like more information on?
(check all that apply)

<INPUT TYPE="checkbox" NAME="Webdev" VALUE="Webdev"> Web Site Devel-
opment

<INPUT TYPE="checkbox" NAME="Webcon" VALUE="Webcon" CHECKED> Web
Site Consulting

<INPUT TYPE="checkbox" NAME="Cuspro" VALUE="Cuspro"> Custom Program-
ming

<INPUT TYPE="checkbox" NAME="Multidevl" VALUE="Multidevel" CHECKED>
Multimedia Development
```

DEFINING THE *SIZE* OF A TEXT OR PASSWORD FIELD

The *SIZE* attribute specifies the physical size of a text or password input field. The default size is 20. The following HTML entry illustrates the use of the *SIZE* attribute:

```
<INPUT TYPE="text" NAME="firstname" SIZE=40>
```

In this case, the form will display a text field large enough to hold 40 characters, although the user can type in more than the 40 characters, causing the letters to scroll. To define the maximum number of characters a text field can hold, you must use the *MAXLENGTH* attribute discussed next.

THE *MAXLENGTH* ATTRIBUTE

The *MAXLENGTH* attribute specifies the maximum number of characters a user can type into a *TEXT* or *PASSWORD* field. The *MAXLENGTH* attribute is only valid for *TEXT* and *PASSWORD* fields. The following HTML entry uses the *MAXLENGTH* attribute to restrict a password field to 10 characters:

```
<INPUT TYPE="password" NAME="userid" SIZE=5 MAXLENGTH=10>
```

UNDERSTANDING THE *<SELECT>* TAG

Depending on a form's contents, there may be times when the user must select one or more options from a list. To create such a list, you use the *<SELECT>* and *</SELECT>* tags. Within these two tags, you create the list entries using the *<OPTION>* tag. The *<SELECT>* tag supports three attributes: *NAME*, *SIZE*, and *MULTIPLE*.

The *NAME* attribute specifies the list name. The *SIZE* attribute specifies the number of items the browser will display within a menu or scrolling list. If you set the *SIZE* attribute to 1, the browser will display the list of options as a menu list. If you do not specify the *SIZE* attribute, the browser sets the *SIZE* value to 1 by default. If you set the value of the *SIZE* attribute to 2 or more, the browser will display the options as a scrolling list. The number value defines how many items the browser will display within the scrolling list at one time.

To specify an option within a list, you use the <*OPTION*> tag. The <*OPTION*> tag supports the *SELECTED* attribute, which tells the browser to select the option by default. The following HTML elements illustrate the use of the <*OPTION*> tag to create a list:

```
Which Internet service provider do you use?
<SELECT NAME=service SIZE=5>
 <OPTION SELECTED>America Online
 <OPTION>CompuServe
 <OPTION>Microsoft Network
 <OPTION>Prodigy
 <OPTION>Local Internet Service Provider
 </SELECT>
```

As you can see, using the *SELECTED* attribute, the browser selects *America Online* by default. However, the user is free to select any one of the options. Figure 11.9 shows how these entries will appear within the Netscape *Navigator*.

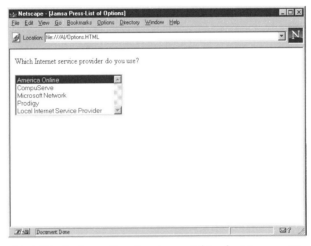

*Figure 11.9 Displaying a list of options within the Netscape **Navigator**.*

If you specify the *MULTIPLE* attribute, users can select two or more items from within the option list. If you specify the *MULTIPLE* attribute, the browser will display the options as a scrolling list, regardless of the *SIZE* attribute's value. The following HTML entries create a menu list and a scrolling list:

```
Which Internet service provider do you use?
<SELECT NAME=service MULTIPLE>
 <OPTION>America Online
 <OPTION>CompuServe
 <OPTION>Microsoft Network
 <OPTION>Prodigy
 <OPTION>Local Internet Service Provider
 </SELECT>

How would you like to receive the
```

```
information you have requested?
<SELECT NAME=receivedby SIZE=1>
  <OPTION>Sales Call
  <OPTION>E-Mail
  <OPTION>By Mail
</SELECT>
```

Figure 11.10 shows how the Netscape *Navigator* will display these two lists.

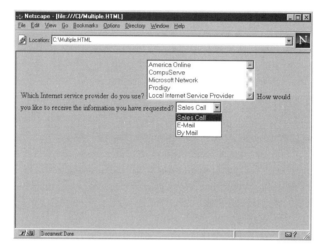

Figure 11.10 A form that contains an option menu and a scrolling list.

UNDERSTANDING THE *<TEXTAREA>* TAG

Depending on your form's purpose, the user may need to type in more than a single line of text. For example, you may place a Comments field in a form within which the user can type in several lines of text. To create a multiline text box, you can use the *<TEXTAREA>* tag. A text area provides scrollbars which let the user enter large amounts of text. The attributes for the *<TEXTAREA>* field are as follows:

- **NAME** identifies the *TEXTAREA* field

- **ROWS** indicates the number of rows the text area supports

- **COLS** indicates the number of columns (or the horizontal width) a text area supports

The following HTML entries illustrate the use of the *<TEXTAREA>* tag:

```
Is there any additional information that you would like to receive
from Digital West Media?

<TEXTAREA NAME="comments" ROWS=10 COLS=80></TEXTAREA>
```

Figure 11.11 shows how the Netscape *Navigator* will display this text area.

Figure 11.11 Displaying a <TEXTAREA> within a form.

CREATING AN INTERACTIVE FORM

By now, you should have a good understanding of how to create an HTML form. As you have learned, you can use certain tags and attributes to develop forms. The following example illustrates the use of several tags and attributes to create a form with which a user can request product information:

```
<Head><Title>Digital West Media, Inc. </Title></Head>
<Body><H1>Digital West Media, Inc. <BR> Information Request</H1>
<Form method=POST action="intrasur.pl">
<HR>
<PRE>
Name: <INPUT TYPE="text" NAME="name" SIZE=40>
Company: <INPUT TYPE="text" NAME="compname" SIZE=40>
E-mail address: <INPUT TYPE="text" NAME="email" SIZE=50>
Enter your password? <INPUT TYPE="password" NAME="password" SIZE=20>

Which products or services would you like more information on?
(check all that apply)

<INPUT TYPE="checkbox" NAME="Webdev" VALUE="Webdev"> Web Site Devel-
opment
<INPUT TYPE="checkbox" NAME="Webcon" VALUE="Webcon"> Web Site Con-
sulting
<INPUT TYPE="checkbox" NAME="Cuspro" VALUE="Cuspro"> Custom Program-
ming
<INPUT TYPE="checkbox" NAME="Multidevl" VALUE="Multidevel"> Multime-
dia Development
```

```
How soon does your organization plan to establish a presence on the
World Wide Web? (check one)

<INPUT TYPE="radio" NAME="howsoon" VALUE="1mon"> Within one month
<INPUT TYPE="radio" NAME="howsoon" VALUE="3mon"> Within three months
<INPUT TYPE="radio" NAME="howsoon" VALUE="6 mon"> Within six months
<INPUT TYPE="radio" NAME="howsoon" VALUE="1yr"> Within one year

Which Internet service provider do you use? <SELECT NAME=service
SIZE=5>
  <OPTION>America Online
  <OPTION>CompuServe
  <OPTION>Microsoft Network
  <OPTION>Prodigy
  <OPTION>Local Internet Service Provider
  </SELECT>

How would you like to receive the information you have requested?
<SELECT NAME=receivedby SIZE=1>
  <OPTION>Sales Call
  <OPTION>E-Mail
  <OPTION>By Mail
</SELECT>

Is there any additional information that you would like to receive
from Digital West Media?

<TEXTAREA NAME="comments" ROWS=10 COLS=80></TEXTAREA>
</PRE>
<Input TYPE="submit" VALUE="Send Request">
<Input TYPE="reset" VALUE="Clear Form"><p>
</Form>
</Body>
```

Figure 11.12 illustrates how this form will appear within the Netscape *Navigator*.

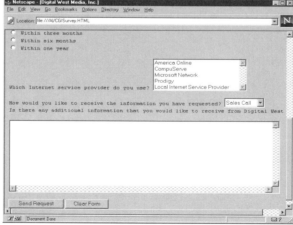

*Figure 11.12 Displaying a CGI-based survey within the Netscape **Navigator**.*

When the user submits this form, the server will send the data to the following Perl script named *intrasur.pl*:

```perl
#!/usr/local/bin/perl
#Includes cgi-lib file; if cgi-lib doesn't exist, returns malformed
#header error
do "cgi-lib.pl" || die "Fatal Error: Can't load cgi library";

#calls the subroutine in the cgi-lib.pl library
#to read in the variables from the form and set them up
#as key=value pairs in the array @in

&ReadParse;

#tells http server incoming data is text html
print "Content-type: text/html\n\n";

#returns acknowledgment of mail submission and provides a link back
print "<HTML>";
print "<HEAD><TITLE>Thank You\!</TITLE>";
print "</HEAD><BODY>";
print "<H2>Thank you\!</H2>";
print "We value your input\!";
print "<P>";
print "We will send the information you requested,\n";
print "soon as possible\n";
print "<HR>";
print "<H3>Back to the Title Page<A HREF=\"/index.html\">";
print "Digital West Media</A></H3>";
print "</BODY></HTML>";

#assigns process id to $pid
$pid=$$;

#opens up comment file for writing
open(COMMENTSFILE,">./my_comment.$pid");

#enter the form data into the file to be mailed
print COMMENTSFILE "DWMI Information Request\n";
print COMMENTSFILE "- - - - - - - - - - - - - - - - - - -\n";
print COMMENTSFILE "Customer input:\n";
print COMMENTSFILE " Name: $in{'name'}\n";
print COMMENTSFILE " Company: $in{'compname'}\n";
print COMMENTSFILE " Email: $in{'email'}\n";
print COMMENTSFILE " Password: $in{'password'}\n";
print COMMENTSFILE "- - - - - - - - - - - - - - - - - - -\n";
print COMMENTSFILE "More information on:\n";
print COMMENTSFILE " $in{'Webdev'}\n";
print COMMENTSFILE " $in{'Webcon'}\n";
print COMMENTSFILE " $in{'Cuspro'}\n";
print COMMENTSFILE " $in{'Multidevl'}\n";
print COMMENTSFILE "- - - - - - - - - - - - - - - - - - -\n";
print COMMENTSFILE " How Soon: $in{'howsoon'}\n";
print COMMENTSFILE " Provider: $in{'service'}\n";
```

```
print COMMENTSFILE " Send info: $in{'receivedby'}\n";
print COMMENTSFILE "- - - - - - - - - - - - - - - - - -\n";
print COMMENTSFILE "Comments:\n";
print COMMENTSFILE "$in{'comments'}";

#close out file to be mailed
close COMMENTSFILE;

#sends comment file as mail to user
system("mail info\@dwmi.com < ./my_comment.$pid");
system($command);

#erases temp file
unlink("./my_comment.$pid");
```

PUTTING IT ALL TOGETHER

In this chapter, you learned how to use CGI scripts to create an interactive Web page. Understanding CGI- programming concepts is difficult and often requires companies to have access to staff that is skilled in various programming languages. Even if you do not write your own interactive forms, you can use the concepts discussed in this chapter to assess ways your company can improve its intranet's capabilities. Also, you can use the concepts you learned in this chapter to guide your programming staff as they write useful, interactive forms.

In Chapter 12, you will examine issues you may face after you release the first phase of your intranet. As you will learn, providing your employees with the correct set of development tools is critical to your intranet's success. Before you continue with Chapter 12, however, make sure you understand the key following concepts:

✓ Companies must add interactive capabilities to their intranet to let employees and customers interact with various corporate databases.

✓ Most employees who provide intranet content do not need to understand CGI programming techniques.

✓ A CGI script is a program that communicates with a Web server to process or provide data.

✓ Intranet developers can write CGI scripts using a number of different programming languages, such as Perl, C++, and Java.

✓ An HTML form is similar to a standard HTML document with the addition of the HTML *<FORM>* and *</FORM>* tags and a link to a CGI script.

✓ Employees can use a set of standard CGI scripts to develop a variety of interactive HTML forms.

VISITING KEY SITES THAT DISCUSS INTRANETS

The World Wide Web is filled with hundreds of excellent and current articles on all aspects of intranets. Use the following sites as starting points for your Web exploration.

WWW FAQ

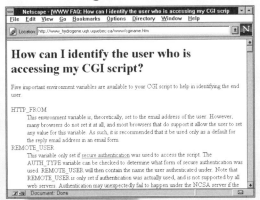

http://www_hydrogene.uqtr.uquebec.ca/www/cginame.htm

HTML AND CGI SCRIPTS

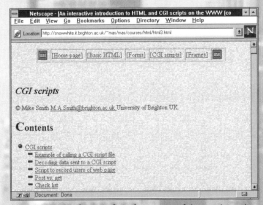

http://snowwhite.it.brighton.ac.uk/~mas/mas/courses/html/html3.html

CGI SCRIPT OUTPUT

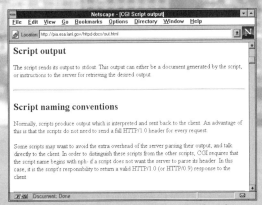

http://pia.esa.lanl.gov/httpd-docs/out.html

CGI FAQ: FORMS

http://www.dwt.co.kr/~ymji/cgi-faq/faq-forms.html

WEB/HTTPD/UNIX/NCSA

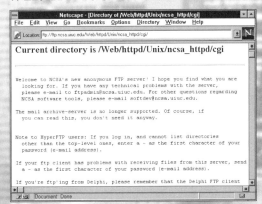

http://ftp.ncsa.uiuc.edu/Web/httpd/Unix/ncsa_httpd/cgi/

SELENA SOL'S PUBLIC DOMAIN

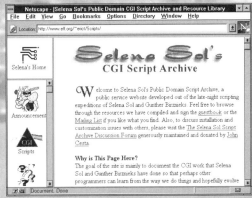

http://www.eff.org/~erict/Scripts/

CGI ENVIRONMENT VARIABLES

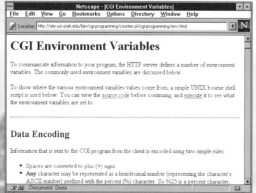

*http://ute.usi.utah.edu/bin/cgi-programming/
counter.pl/cgi-programming/env.html*

CGI SCRIPT SURVEY

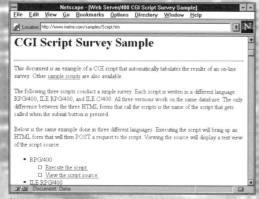

http://www.inetmi.com/samples/Script.htm

WINDOWS CGI 1.3A INTERFACE

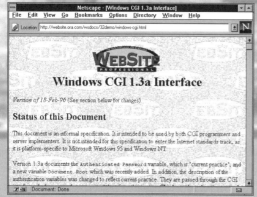

*http://website.ora.com/wsdocs/32demo/
windows-cgi.html*

WWW CGI

*http://www.ast.cam.ac.uk/%7Edrtr/cgi-
spec.html*

ANSI C LIBRARY

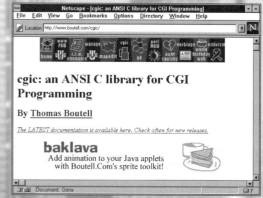

http://www.boutell.com/cgic/

CGI: CREATING FORMS

*http://www.perl.com/perl/wwwman/CGI/CGI/
creating_forms.html*

Chapter 12

Short- and Long-term Intranet Deployment Challenges

In Chapter 6, "Intranet Planning and Management," you learned how to plan for an intranet deployment. So far, all of the chapters in this book have provided you with the knowledge you need to implement the first phase of an intranet deployment. However, your real challenge is to use your intranet to bring long-lasting, positive change to your organization. Think of your intranet as a set of technologies which let users share information. An intranet may benefit your organization only after you start viewing it as part of a bigger effort—which management consultants call business re-engineering. The intranet alone cannot bring the necessary cultural change to your organization to improve teamwork or force employees to see themselves as part of a team. Instead, your employees need the vision of leaders that the intranet, along with other business tools, will, with time and effort, make them more productive.

Using an intranet, you may identify "information flows" that do not currently exist in your company. The intranet will not, however, create these information flows. Instead, you must articulate a vision of the intranet's use that will motivate employees to develop the necessary business processes and mechanisms that improve the exchange of information. In this chapter, you will learn how to work through both technological and organizational issues to benefit from the power of intranets. By the time you finish this chapter, you will understand the following key concepts:

- Companies must communicate to their employees how intranets can make them more productive and teach employees how the intranet will benefit them.

- To achieve long-term success with your intranet deployment, you must address various technological and organizational issues that face your company.

- Moving your organization toward a paperless office and connecting intranets to legacy (existing) databases are key factors to your intranet's success.

- Most intranet tools are new. In most cases, consultants can help your company implement advanced intranet features.

- Intranets comprising several Web servers are difficult to maintain and support.

- Marketing your internal Web to various divisions is the most effective way to obtain funding with which you can improve the overall effectiveness of your intranet.

- ◆ Changing an organization's culture to support collaborative efforts is the job of top management.

- ◆ Training employees to author, manage, and enhance HTML documents is crucial to mass acceptance of intranets.

- ◆ Making vendors and suppliers part of your intranet will unleash the true power of your intranet.

246

COMMUNICATING YOUR INTRANET GOALS

A description and analysis of motivational and organizational change theories are beyond the scope of this book. However, like any other change in your organization, your employees need to know how an intranet will benefit them. If it is through an improved bottom line, they need corporate leaders to tell them how an improved bottom line will help them. If your company has a culture that does not promote teamwork and collaboration, intranets will help everyone see this corporate weakness more clearly. If you, as the leader and as a manager, do not empower your employees to collaborate and share information, you may even see reduced productivity after the initial phase of intranet deployment.

What you *do not* want to happen is to entice employees to share information, but still leave all decision-making processes in the hands of a few employees in upper management. What you *do not* want to happen is for your employees to realize that they live within a bureaucratic organization that will not change with or without an intranet. If you use your intranet to streamline your business procedures, you have brought the power of the intranet to your organization.

Many management experts have praised groupware products such as Lotus *Notes*, stating how these products have benefited companies by changing the way employees work. There is no reason to believe that the implementation of groupware products and intranets will bring a positive change to every company. Some companies invest much more than their competitors in information technology, such as an intranet, but still fail to compete effectively in the marketplace. Computers alone do not, and cannot, create successful companies. Instead, corporate leaders must provide an environment that allows employees to use information technology to enhance their business practices which, in turn, will strengthen the company.

Intranets are easy to set up. However, employees and management should not expect miracles from the technology. This chapter's goal is to identify the key areas that will improve your organization's chances of bringing about long-lasting positive changes. Making intranets contribute to your business success should be part of everyone's job. Just like any other collaborative effort, everyone is part of the team and responsible for the success of the team.

DIFFERENT ASPECTS OF CHANGE

To bring meaningful change to your organization, you must actively address issues that deal with both the technological and the organizational aspects of intranets. Although the primary focus of the previous chapters has been on the technological aspect of intranets, you will soon find that it is the organizational aspect of intranets which provides companies with major challenges. Companies involved in deployment of new technologies often simplify the organizational aspects of the new technology. Also, because intranets are initially easy to set up, many companies fail to recognize the resources required to put accurate and up-to-date information on their intranets.

TECHNOLOGICAL ASPECTS OF INTRANET DEPLOYMENT

Companies such as Netscape and Microsoft are rapidly developing key intranet technologies. Many companies will soon realize that transforming a static intranet used for HTML publishing to a dynamic and interactive intranet is quite challenging. The major technological challenges facing any organization after the initial release of an intranet are:

- How to convert existing paper documents to electronic documents which employees can access electronically via the intranet.

- How to connect existing databases to the intranet for access by a wide range of computing platforms (such as Windows- and Mac-based systems).

- How to continuously enhance the intranet's features and capabilities to keep employees motivated to use the intranet.

- How to install multiple servers across various departments.

- How to install security features within the intranet, which prevent employee access to sections of your intranet that contain confidential information.

ORGANIZATIONAL ASPECTS OF INTRANET DEPLOYMENT

In addition to the above technological challenges, the following list contains several organizational issues that face companies after the initial release of an intranet:

- How to market the intranet within the organization so that all employees will support its growth.

- How to obtain additional funding that will allow you to add new capabilities to the intranet.

- How to implement an information-sharing culture within the company so that all employees will contribute to building a learning organization.

- How to merge the company's old paper-based culture with the new culture of electronic documentation to prevent the new documentation systems from becoming unmanageable.

- How to assure that the intranet's content providers update information on a regular basis.

- How to prevent one person or group from controlling (monopolizing) the intranet's content.

- How to train employees on intranet etiquette to protect the effectiveness of on-line discussion forums and other user interactions.

247

- How to make customers and vendors an integral part of the intranet and the business.

- How to measure the intranet's overall effectiveness.

By examining and working to resolve these issues, you will prepare your organization to embrace a culture of teamwork and collaboration.

UNDERSTANDING TECHNOLOGICAL CHALLENGES

As you learned in previous chapters, an intranet's technological aspects are not difficult to understand. However, intranet technology, and information technology in general, changes so fast that keeping up with the latest software and hardware solutions requires a full-time department. In this section, you will learn in detail the various technological challenges facing organizations after the initial release of an intranet, as well as some solutions to these challenges.

MOVING TOWARD A PAPERLESS OFFICE

The first issue facing companies after the initial intranet release is how to convert large numbers of existing paper documents into electronic format ready for distribution on an intranet. In previous chapters, you learned that there are many tools, such as *HTML Transit*, that can help you convert documents from most electronic formats to HTML format. Besides needing such conversion tools, users also need access to tools with which they can initially develop future documents directly in HTML.

To provide users with conversion tools that will serve them for a long-time, concentrate on deployment of tools that are free as well as tools with which users are already familiar. One such tool is Microsoft's *Internet Assistant for Microsoft Word*, which provides users with the ability to quickly convert existing *Word* documents into HTML documents. After your employees convert documents to HTML and place them on an intranet, your next challenge is to keep the documents up to date.

You may soon find that your company's initial excitement over HTML publishing will soon disappear and most employees, who originally contributed to intranet documents, will neglect updating them. Obsolete information will frustrate intranet users and encourage them to revert to their old ways of information gathering: calling people, walking to various offices, and writing memos. One way to minimize this problem is to create a database containing the published date of each document and compare that date with a stated "frequency of update" for that document. For example, assume a purchaser within your company decided to publish a list of qualified vendors on the intranet. In his or her page, the purchaser stated that the document will change every month. A database programmer, in turn, can write a program to store the document's title, date of last change, and stated *frequency of update* in a database. Each day, the program will search your intranet for documents that have passed their update due date. The program can then issue an e-mail to the document's owner that requests an update. Over the next 12 months, you will see a host of intranet products that will help organizations better manage their electronic documents.

LEGACY DATABASES

After your company converts its static documents to HTML documents, users will want to have access to their current databases using intranet technology. You will find that connecting various databases to the intranet is not as easy as you might expect. To connect your current databases to your intranet, you may need a plan to hire additional staff or to reassign your current programming staff to the task. Make sure you communicate your plans to users so that they know you are working on adding new features to your intranet. You might even post an Upcoming Features page on the intranet, which users can visit to find out your latest goals and objectives.

For your plan to integrate your legacy databases to the intranet to be realistic, you must convince management of the benefits of having a unified information-distribution system. To start, you should present your intranet as an important part of your overall deployment of information technology. You may find it difficult to get large funding for such projects if the current legacy database vendor claims that it will soon have an intranet solution. In this case, top management will probably want to wait for the outside solution. As a Webmaster or an intranet implementation team leader, you must anticipate this and plan accordingly.

In most cases, you may not be able to connect all of your legacy information systems to your intranet at one time. Instead, you should plan to connect the most important legacy databases to your intranet first. Survey employees to find out which legacy databases they want the intranet implementation team to connect to the intranet first. In most companies, employees want intranets to connect the following legacy information database systems:

- Financial reports that inform employees about project costs, product costs, and the overall financial health of the enterprise.
- Document-management systems that let employees easily submit and retrieve workflow documents.
- Human Resources information that let employees review corporate, business unit, and department missions and goals, as well as information on employee health care and benefits.

To further complicate your task, each of your legacy databases may have a group of programmers and administrators who are in charge of developing and maintaining a variety of programs. Taking a custom program from a group of programmers is a challenging task because the team that must move the software onto the intranet may start to question the technical merits of your intranet solution. Unfortunately, most companies often do not judge the overall advantages and disadvantages of various information technology solutions objectively. As you plan to migrate legacy systems onto the intranet, you must plan to achieve developer "buy in" to your intranet solution.

OUTSOURCING YOUR INTRANET DEVELOPMENT

Even if you can get the necessary funding to buy the hardware and the software you need to connect your intranet to your legacy databases, you will find out quickly that selecting the right technology is time consuming and difficult. Intranet technologies are fairly new and, in most cases, not very robust (able to adapt to a wide number of applications and problems). At first, you may find it best to get help from consultants who can tell you the tools other companies are using to develop advanced intranet applications. Outsourcing your information-technology deployment is not as easy as it may seem. Besides your need for consulting services to help you create intranet-based database applications, you may also need a consulting company to set up your initial intranet software, hardware, and primary Web site. Intranet consultants are numerous and usually familiar with how to set up a simple intranet. Most consulting companies, however, because of the newness of the applications driving the growth of the industry, have yet to design complex intranets. Today, most intranets are deployed by high-technology companies such as Sun Microsystems, who have in-house personnel capable of dealing with new technologies.

If you have a mission-critical intranet application, such as an inventory control system, you may want to obtain consulting services from at least three firms. Such complex systems need custom application programming. Often, outsourcing custom application programming can provide you with a quick solution to a specific problem. However, you need to assess the long-term requirement of such systems. In most cases, you will find that after a few months, your initial design specifications did not meet the needs of all users. To minimize such problems, you must develop a multiphase implementation plan that lets you better assess user needs over time.

Your organization must include the intranet as part of its Information Systems strategic plan. Outsourcing your information-technology needs is part of most company's long-term strategy. Therefore, if your company does not have an outsourcing policy, you may need to develop one before getting external help. By planning your outsourcing requirements, you can better communicate your needs and tasks to both the consultants and your internal staff. Make sure you have a complete blueprint that describes exactly what you expect from the outside consultants. If you want your staff to take over the project after the first phase, make sure you plan to train your staff during the first phase of the intranet's deployment. Most often, companies that need a quick solution to a problem end up hiring consultants to perform intranet programming without having a long-term maintenance and upgrade plan.

If outside programmers are writing application-specific programs for your intranets, specify the program's required functionality in detail. For example, if you outsource the development of a set of intranet-based graphs for your manufacturing data, specify to consultants the exact details of how you want the graphs to look and how you will use them. You should also provide the consultant with an idea of how often you will update the graphs and the technical level of the employee who will perform the updates. If you do not specify your requirements in detail, you may end up getting a program that is of little use after a few months . Therefore, spend time writing a complete specification before you outsource any portion of your intranet development.

USING MULTIPLE SERVERS

Having a central server is ideal for distributing information and data from one location to all employees. If you plan to have a single person, such as a Webmaster, support the central server, you will quickly find that your Webmaster cannot service all user requests. In fact, in a medium-sized company (50 employees or more), one person cannot keep up with an intranet's technological demands and also provide various departments with custom programming services. In most corporations, because of the complexity of installing and maintaining most software programs, information-technology deployments are initiated and carried out by the Information Services Department.

As your intranet becomes more complex, you will soon need multiple servers. The need for two or more servers is especially true for companies that have large numbers of divisions and business units. Because intranet technology is improving rapidly, you may soon be faced with requests from various departments that want to set up their own servers. For example, a product-development group may need to provide their team with the ability to search project-specific databases, submit forms to various databases, and use a private on-line discussion group. The Webmaster in charge of a central intranet server may find it impossible to service the group's programming requests in a timely manner. For example, Joe, a semi-technical member of the product development team decides to set up his own Web server. Now, you are faced with the task of teaching Joe about advanced features of the intranet—which may not be in your original intranet-deployment plan. But the company may ask you to help him because you now know more than Joe about intranets.

Keep in mind that the intranet's power is in its ability to distribute information throughout an enterprise. Therefore, as the main Webmaster, you must welcome such efforts and work with various departments to help them start their own servers. It is best to have various departments set up their own server using the same hardware and Web server software you are already using. In this way, you will reduce the time needed to develop the expertise necessary to run and manage an internal Web site. Figure 12.1 shows an intranet with multiple servers.

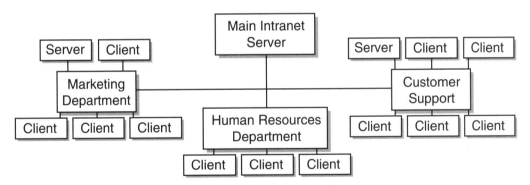

Figure 12.1 An intranet using multiple servers.

Over the next five years, installing and using a Web server will become as easy as installing and using a word processor. You should not be surprised, for example, to see Web servers become part of the Windows NT server operating system. To provide various departments with their own servers, choose server software that is easy to install and maintain. A Pentium-class machine running Windows NT server software and Microsoft's Internet Information Server is a good choice for small departments that want to set up their own servers. Another way you can provide departments with their own domain name and disk space is to use a virtual domain name (a domain name that appears to exist to users and their software, but in reality, only exists because of software that runs on your existing Web server).

To better understand the concept of a virtual domain name, consider how companies reduce hardware costs, using a *virtual servers*. As you know, a server is a program that responds to user requests. In the case of the Web, an HTTP-based server runs on a server computer. Assume, for example, that your company needs two types of Web servers, one which allows easy access and one which requires usernames and passwords. In the past, the company would have purchased two different computers to run the Web server software. Today, however, the company can run both servers on the same system—as virtual servers—which, to the user, appear as independent servers. Because the servers are somewhat independent, you can configure each server to meet your needs (perhaps making one of the servers more secure). By using virtual servers in this way, you have to purchase only one computer, on which you run each of the server programs. For more information on virtual servers, visit the site *http://www.blaze.net/wholesale.insdevs.htm.*

STANDARDIZING HARDWARE AND SOFTWARE

To avoid the need to support multiple hardware and software solutions, you might specify the server software, hardware, HTML editing tools, and browser software that your company must use. Currently, many Web sites on the Internet encourage users to use a particular browser to view their site's content. To continue to attract user visits, Internet sites must constantly upgrade their visual appeal. By requesting users to standardize their browser selection, a company can simplify its Web site development (without worrying about the idiosyncrasies of a specific browser). Within your organization, the same holds true. By standardizing browsers and other intranet tools, you will decrease the number of unexpected errors and incompatibilities. You must be willing to "just say no" to user demands for specific software. If the users want to experiment with specific software, let them do so at home. Your job is to manage and control the intranet, not to satisfy every user's software whims.

Within an enterprise, your primary goal is to disseminate various business information as fast as possible to as many employees as possible. What you do not want to do is create an environment where employees view your intranet as another business toy, rather than a serious vehicle to improve their efficiency and contribute to the bottom line. You must educate your site's content creators—their first focus should be the accuracy of the content and their second focus on the content's visual appeal.

SECURITY ISSUES

As your intranet grows, you may soon find that a large number of previously "Confidential" documents are now on your intranet. In addition to accessing sensitive documents using the intranet, employees may also want to access confidential information regarding their 401K investment portfolio or other benefits. You also may have requests from various groups that need to limit access to their pages to a specific group of employees. One Webmaster should be able to handle such requests fairly easily at first. However, as your intranet content grows, you will find it difficult for one Webmaster to satisfy the organization's various levels of security—making intranet security a full-time job. Chapter 19, "Intranet Security Issues," examines many security issues in detail.

ORGANIZATIONAL CHALLENGES

The technical challenges, in most cases, will not have a major impact on your long-term, successful deployment of intranets. Like the introduction of any other information technology to an enterprise, an intranet deployment requires good planning, implementation, and employee training. As you have learned, one feature of an intranet is its ability to initiate change within an enterprise. In the short-term, most of your effort will focus on the technical aspects of your intranet. But as time goes on, you must deal with the organizational issues that surround the use of intranets. Figure 12.2 shows how your resource mix should move over time from addressing technical issues to addressing organizational issues.

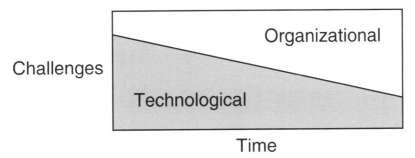

Figure 12.2 *Types of challenges facing companies deploying intranets.*

The organizational issues facing companies that deploy intranets include the following:

- How to market the intranet throughout the organization so all employees will support the intranet's content enhancement.

- How to perform a cost-benefit analysis which allows you to obtain additional funding for new intranet capabilities. You must plan for growth from the start.

- How to implement an information-sharing culture so all employees will contribute to building a learning organization.

- How to train employees to create and maintain HTML documents.

- How to update and control Intranet pages.

MARKETING YOUR INTRANET

Intranets are like most products. You must properly market the intranet to its customers for the intranet to be successful. As is the case with other new products, technology alone will not sell the product. With most new technologies, there are always early adopters who will embrace a new technology quickly and without much selling. However, most people must know what a new technology can do for them before they will use it. An intranet deployment team must have a plan to convince employees that the intranet can help them do their jobs more effectively and efficiently.

When you market your intranet, show employees the mission-critical applications that you plan to implement on the intranet. For example, most employees will readily connect to the intranet if they know they will not need to go to that old mainframe screen to print their daily reports. Employees want to view and work with mission-critical information on-line. So, plan to have at least one mission-critical application on-line within three months of your intranet deployment.

As you develop your intranet, you should "test market" new intranet applications early (letting the users try out the applications) before you commit to a full-featured implementation. As you let users try out your applications, you may learn that not all of the services you plan to provide will be popular with users. Therefore, use focus groups (groups that employ various end-users) to test your development plans. In some cases, you can obtain trial copies of new intranet applications before you purchase them. Using these trial products will give you time to assess whether the products meet employee needs.

Marketing an intranet is also necessary to convince upper management of the intranet's benefits and its contribution to the bottom line. Your first move is to find managers who are eager to use new technologies and work with them to sell your intranet to others within your company. Again, remember that the power of an intranet is at its highest when everyone uses it and contributes to the creation and exchange of content. Effective marketing of an intranet will find wide acceptance among employees and will give upper management the information they need to motivate their decision to invest in the latest intranet technologies.

FUNDING YOUR INTRANET'S GROWTH

In most organizations, the intranet's growth explodes, which requires more software, computers, and people to manage the intranet. The initial cost of setting up a simple intranet is small and may not require top-management's approval. However, to implement complex documentation-management systems, to integrate database designs, to automate workflow systems, and to implement interactive training and other advanced features requires funding and top-management's approval. To obtain the funds you need to improve your intranet's capabilities, you must convince upper-management that the intranet is part of your company's information-technology deployment.

To convince upper-management to invest the funds necessary to deploy advanced intranet technologies, you must show them the intranet's tangible benefits. Start by informing management about how the intranet is changing the way people work and communicate, and how an intranet promotes teamwork. To get funding, however, you need to connect the intranet benefits to the bottom line—which you may find a difficult task. In Chapter 15, "Return on Investments for Intranets," you will learn how to perform return-on-investment techniques that will show you how to communicate with your managers using financial terms.

The easiest way to get funding for an advanced documentation-management system is to show your top management how an on-line system will eliminate the need to hire additional staff within the document-control department as the organization grows. It is always easier to tie information-technology benefits to reduction in overhead cost than to productivity improvements.

CREATING AN INFORMATION-SHARING CULTURE

Most companies assume that technology alone will change their organization's culture and will better prepare the enterprise to face competition. As you have learned, intranets are only a component of change. An intranet facilitates information sharing, but it does not guarantee it. Upper management's involvement in unleashing the intranet's full potential is critical and necessary. It is only through upper management's commitment to identify and document work processes that an intranet can significantly improve a company's bottom line.

As you have learned, a powerful feature of intranet content is an employee's ability to find information quickly and, possibly more important, to find out which employees are experts in a specific topic. Unfortunately, most employees are not ready to put what they know and what they do on an intranet. The best way to promote letting employees learn about each other's skills is to ask everyone to put their resume on-line. An on-line internal resume does not need to match exactly what an employee might put on a traditional resume. Instead, an intranet-based resume might contain an employee's areas of expertise, educational background, areas of interest, and some personal information.

Using a search engine, employees can quickly find other employees who have the knowledge they need. Companies should not require all employees to have a personal page during the intranet's initial phase. Instead, you might start by placing the resumes of the company's new hires on-line. In addition, managers might ask their employees to provide an on-line resume as part of a company-wide knowledge collection effort.

INTEGRATING TOTAL QUALITY MANAGEMENT INTO AN INTRANET

After you migrate your company's work processes to the intranet, it is up to managers and employees to follow procedures to improve productivity and teamwork. Intranets cannot enforce adherence to work procedures. Management should not assume that because employees have a new tool, employees will change their attitudes toward customers, top management, or shareholders. Instead, managers should view the intranet as one more tool they can use in their quest for total quality management (TQM).

Before an organization will commit to quality using intranets, the CEO and upper-management must commit to a TQM philosophy. TQM provides a means of creating a system that promotes, supports, and enables quality management in all aspects of an organization. Organizations must integrate quality considerations into management's way of thinking. TQM and the successful deployment of intranets are large-scale organizational changes, which upper management must drive. Intranet deployment, along with the drive for TQM implementation, is not a program that upper management can delegate. If a CEO views quality solely as a function that occurs within the organization, TQM will not work. A CEO must view the features that intranets offer as key tools for the organization to use to achieve their quality initiatives.

Distributing information, such as customer satisfaction results, on an intranet may have a negative impact among employees if they feel they are not empowered to change their work processes. With distribution of information, everyone in a company can listen to and participate in a constructive dialog with others to improve the way work gets done. If upper-management informs employees about problems, it must also let the employees act upon the information. Corporate leaders must set an example by questioning the content of the information employees place on intranets and promote a culture that lets employees question content as well. In other words, achieving TQM requires teamwork.

TRAINING EMPLOYEES TO CREATE INTRANET-BASED DOCUMENTS

If you want employees to contribute content to the intranet, you need to train them how and why to share information with others. Because people who often set up intranets are technically competent, they assume that everyone in the organization should be to able to write HTML documents manually without training.

Without training, you will have an organization that still depends on a few people to share information. Can you imagine, if you had only one person in each department who knew how to use a word processor, and who had to write all of the e-mail correspondence and documents for everyone in the group. Without training people how to write HTML documents, and providing the right tools to do so, you run the risk of depending on only a few people within your organization to create HTML documents.

Immediately after you set up your intranet, start working with your training department. To start, prepare a questionnaire to survey the training users need and want. Often, people who deal with the technical aspects of intranets do not think comprehensive training on various aspects of the intranet is needed. Unlike word processors, even if you provide people with HTML authoring tools, you still need to teach employees about HTML document design concepts.

Most users are familiar with the steps they must perform to create a word-processing document. However, because HTML provides people with the ability to link one document to another, employees may end up using these features to create HTML documents that are not user friendly, which causes users to become confused or lost while reading the documents. Often, rather than telling the author what they do not like about the on-line document, users instead print the pages and place them in a binder for use—which defeats the purpose of having an intranet and an on-line information distribution system.

TRAIN PEOPLE USING THE TOOLS THEY ALREADY KNOW

If you decide to provide users with HTML authoring tools, use tools that they already know. Therefore, start your training using Microsoft *Internet Assistant for Microsoft Word*. Because *Internet Assistant for Microsoft Word* is an add-on program, users only need to learn the new capabilities that the add-on program provides, which is simpler than training your employees how to use a new word processor. As you work, you will find that most users do not like to create HTML documents using the HTML tags discussed in Chapters 7 through 9.

After the user's initial training phase is complete, sample a group of users and determine if the tools you have provided satisfy their needs. You may learn that many users find creating HTML documents difficult. In this case, you might need to increase your training effort or train one person in each department to assume the responsibility of training the department's staff.

What you need to realize is that learning a new way of writing documents is not easy. Our previous educational backgrounds did not prepare us for the world of intranets and on-line information. Even with all the hype about the Internet, only a small segment of the population actually places content onto the Internet. Within that small segment, there are an unlimited number of ways that people use the HTML linking capabilities to create content. Therefore, you must be patient and work continuously with employees to help them improve their HTML authoring skills. In summary, perform the following steps to help employees to author high-impact HTML documents:

- Conduct a survey to assess user training needs and wants.
- Train users how to develop HTML content.
- Provide users with HTML authoring tools that complement what they already know, for example, *Internet Assistant for Microsoft Word*.
- Review the design and flow of your intranet's content.
- Provide HTML authors with feedback on ways they can improve their site's ease of use.

As you learned in Chapter 3, Human Resources departments often take the lead in providing information that is well suited for use on an intranet. Specifically, the Human Resources department must champion the effort to eliminate the distribution of paper manuals, reports, and procedures. To start the elimination of paper manuals, Human Resources departments must perform the following steps:

- Avoid sending employees printed flyers informing them of upcoming corporate events.
- Put all corporate policy and employee manuals on-line.
- Provide incentives for people who use the Web to locate information rather than calling the Human Resources department and asking for forms and procedures that are on-line.
- Reduce the staffing in the Human Resources department by reassigning employees as intranet trainers and content creators.

UPDATING AND CONTROLLING INTRANET CONTENT

By now, you have learned that HTML content creation is not difficult. With document creation, however, also comes the responsibility of keeping the content current. Therefore, one of the major challenges organizations must face is how to transition from paper-based systems to computer-based systems, while keeping information up to date. In Chapter 11, you learned about various documentation-based applications that let you put sophisticated document-management systems in place on your intranet. However, unless you develop a plan to eliminate paper-based document-management systems, most of your efforts to move documents to the intranet may fail.

Whenever you have two systems that provide the same functions, people can use one or both. Most people will use the system they know how to use. It is not a matter of what system is better or which will provide the organization with longer lasting benefits. It is often a matter of familiarity with a given set of tools. If employees are not sure that they can get all of their documentation needs from your intranet, they will go back to the paper-based documentation system. What you must do is to move away from your strict requirements about how employees can release documents on your intranets. Currently, most organizations require several signatures on a document before they will allow company-wide distribution of the document. To motivate users to use the intranet, you might try to reduce the levels of bureaucracy users must go through to post information. Figure 12.3 shows how you might move your current control of paper-based documentation toward a lesser, yet sufficient, documentation control method.

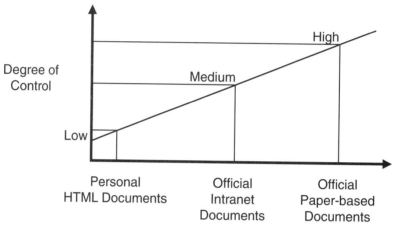

Figure 12.3 Control requirements of intranet documents versus traditional documents.

AUTOMATING HTML AUTHORING

After you establish a policy for the initial distribution of intranet documents, you must develop a set of guidelines that clearly specifies who is responsible for updating their content. Inaccurate information on an intranet greatly reduces its effectiveness. For example, incorrect product pricing information will cause a design group to use the wrong pricing information in a product proposal, which could seriously reduce profit margins. After employees lose confidence in the accuracy of the on-line information, they will revert to calling people to find information. Unfortunately, many people tend to ignore the need to update information, both in electronic and traditional print forms. That is because most people find satisfaction in creating new documents and procedures. However, updating the same document over and over again is tedious and without much self-gratification.

In some cases, your intranet will contain information that employees must update daily, weekly, or monthly. To help keep this information current, you must find out ways you can automate the process. For example, many employees have data in spreadsheets that they store within documents on their disk. In Chapter 8, you learned how to convert spreadsheet data into an HTML document. The process you learned is a manual process and does not lend itself to routine HTML reporting applications. To help users automate the task of converting spreadsheet data to HTML, consider these steps:

- Determine if you can train users to write simple spreadsheet macros that convert the data to an HTML format automatically.

- Have a staff programmer or consultant write advanced spreadsheet macros that allow users to convert several reports to HTML format automatically.

- Determine if you can write a simple program, for example, in Visual Basic, that will allow you to convert spreadsheet data into HTML format automatically.

259

DOCUMENT RATING SYSTEM

Besides helping your users to create HTML documents automatically, you also must work with employees to establish a rating system that will help users determine if a document's content is out of date. To establish such a system, you must first create an HTML document template that requires the document creator to specify information about the document at the top of each page. For example, you might require that employees specify the information listed in Table 12.1 at the top of each page.

Name of the Field	Description	Example
Title of the document	One line of text	List of HMO Doctors
Page Owner	Specifies the current owner of the page	James Soltani
Type of document	Official, Unofficial, Personal	Official
Original published date	Date	1/1/97
Last time modified	Date	3/1/97
Frequency of update	Weekly, Monthly, as Needed	As Needed
Confidential Document	Confidentiality status of documents	Confidential
Update Flag	Green, Yellow, Red	Yellow

Table 12.1 An example of fields specifying information about an HTML document.

The entries in Table 12.1 indicate that the document contains a "List of HMO Doctors" and that list is an official document that James Soltani will update monthly. Note the Update Flag field that informs users about the importance of the document's content, if the content is out of date. If, for example, you visited this page on 6/1/97, you would have noticed that the information contained on the page is out of date; the last update occurred on 3/1/97. The three flag conditions, which you can use within your documents, are defined as follows:

- A Red flag indicates that users should call the owner if content is not up-to-date. You should not use the content in this case because it is absolutely essential that you use up-to-date information.

- A Yellow flag indicates that users can still use the information, but that they may want to call the page owner and find out why the information on the page is not current.

- A Green flag indicates that the information on that page does not directly affect an organization's business processes. Therefore, users can use the content of this information without concern about its accuracy.

260

Figure 12.4 shows a sample HTML page with the appropriate document information at the top of the page.

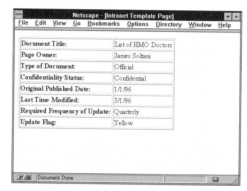

Figure 12.4 Required information for every intranet HTML page.

Your implementation of document ranking systems may seem difficult at first. However, its benefits will far outlast any of its downsides. At first, employees may not fully understand how to use your ranking system. But over time, you can work with users and create a table to guide employees on how to use the ranking system.

Besides ranking documents, you should create a logo that clearly states if the content of a page is the official position or policy of your organization. The logo may direct users to more carefully read the document's content. Also, documents should clearly indicate if the content of the page is confidential and proprietary. As you have learned, security issues concerning intranets are primarily affected by employees copying internal documents and then making the documents available to the outside world. As part of your intranet implementation plan, you must inform employees that it is important that they do not copy and take the content of your intranet beyond the scope of the company.

MANAGING DOCUMENT LINKS

In a traditional document-management system, documents often reference one another. In most cases, authors list the applicable references at the top of each new document. Because the document-control staff monitors the release of new documents, users must have confidence that they can find the listed reference documents in document-control storage cabinets. Intranets, unfortunately, create a situation where most document-control organizations cannot easily control the accuracy of links in documents.

HTML document developers use links freely and, in many cases, without checking the accuracy of those links. Even if employees test the initial accuracy of their document links, it is difficult to maintain and check the accuracy of those links after the document's release. If you have ever hit a broken link while surfing the Web, you know that it can be frustrating. People depend on links within a Web document. Today, however, there are a few mechanisms developers can use to maintain the accuracy of document links.

Employees must understand that others are linking to their pages, so they cannot freely move the location of their documents. Employees must view the organization as one unit. Again, you might use a document-ranking system to manage this problem. If, for example, a user sets a location flag to red, the user is telling other employees that the document's location will not change.

LIMITING THE POWER OF ONE ORGANIZATION TO SHAPE AN INTRANET

As you have learned, your organization may need to support various Web servers that belong to various departments. What this model of information distribution does is limit the power of one person or any one team in shaping your intranet's future. Thus, your internal Web may soon model itself after the Internet (fostering an information free for all). You must deal with such control issues early to let employees know what they can and cannot expect from the intranet.

The power of an intranet is mainly due to its ability to distribute information within an organization. If you limit this process, you will limit the effectiveness of your intranet. Over time, you will find that users from two distinct camps will argue over your information controls. One camp will want total document control. The other camp will want to make your intranet a place where employees can avoid dealing with bureaucratic systems that have become part of many companies.

In the first case, all documents and Web requests will come through a Webmaster, or an intranet team, before they are distributed on the intranet. This practice provides total control over the information flow and distribution. By controlling information in this way, you deal better with broken links and other issues that relate to standards conformance. This model, shown in Figure 12.5, resembles the traditional model of information distribution systems.

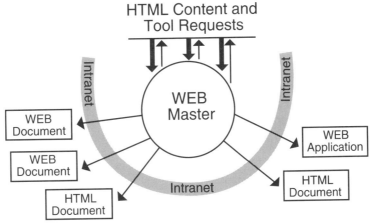

Figure 12.5 Maintaining an intranet through a centrally controlled system.

In a centrally controlled intranet information-distribution model, an organization must predict the growth of its intranet and staff to properly address employee needs. In an organization of about 500 people, a traditional document-control department may require as many as five to ten people to handle the organization's document-management needs. The number of documents that employees will put on an intranet could easily be more than ten times the number of documents that employees will release using a traditional document-control system. Employees will not distribute most of their reports, project plans, and other temporary documents through a traditional documentation-management system simply because the procedures involved in releasing such documents are too demanding.

As you have learned, HTML authoring and intranet document publishing is easy. Therefore, employees will publish more through intranets than through traditional means. The opposite of having total control over intranet document publishing is having no control at all. Figure 12.6 shows the flow of information and Web development requests in such a model.

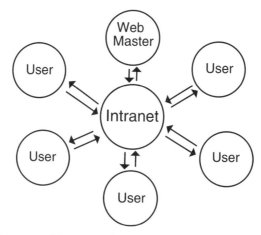

Figure 12.6 No control over the content of an intranet.

In the information-control model shown in Figure 12.6, the only control a Webmaster has is by setting policies regarding the intranet's technical aspects. The Webmaster's role in this model is very limited and is primarily that of customer support. The problem with this model is that it fosters a chaotic situation where the uncontrolled dissemination of information may eventually take over the intranet itself. You cannot afford to let this happen. There are some interesting organization and technological design ideas that will come out of such a system. But in the long term, such a system will severely limit the effectiveness of your intranet.

A model that will bring some control to your intranet, while maintaining the freedom that comes with intranets, is to give department managers responsibility for controlling the management of their own intranet site. In this model, department managers can set guidelines for their employees concerning content of their intranet documents. Managers can authorize their departments to purchase Web hardware and software following a set of guidelines set forth by a team responsible for improving the effectiveness of an intranet. Figure 12.7 shows such a model that distributes the control of intranet sites.

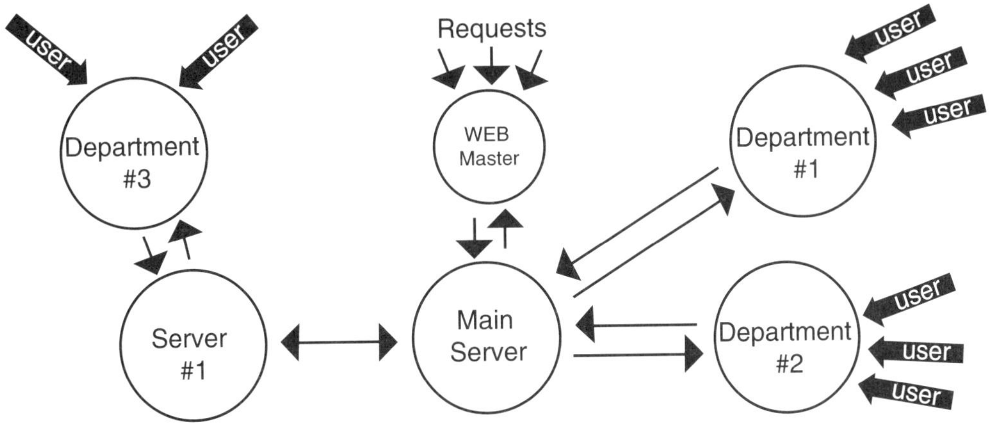

Figure 12.7 Distributive control of intranets.

In this model, managers also take responsibility for keeping their documents up to date. The model assumes that managers want to make the intranet a part of their business practices. If managers believe in setting work processes and providing excellent service to their internal customers, they will support such a system. If, on the other hand, department managers do not think that intranets can affect the company's bottom line, they will leave the control of their intranet content to others. In such cases, employees often will not update their intranet documents, and you will end up with a chaotic situation in which no one is responsible.

The implementation of an intranet is a major change for any organization. Although change is not easy, people are more inclined to change their behavior when leaders have a clear sense of direction, involve employees in developing that direction, and are able to demonstrate how the intranet will positively affect their employees' well being. Managers can work with their employees to show them that intranets can free them from the routine parts of their job so they can spend more time learning and developing new ideas for the corporation. The following lists the benefits of a distributed model of intranet control in an organization:

- You will tap into the knowledge of everyone in your organization if you make them a part of the problem, as well as a part of the solution—developing a team-based organization.

- You will limit the power of any one Webmaster to dictate the intranet's form and function.

- You will increase the number of stakeholders willing to help your intranet change your business processes. This will empower various departments to create their own information database and to eventually work with outside customers and vendors.

INTRANET NETIQUETTE

To create a truly virtual and collaborative workplace within your organization, you must provide your employees with advanced tools which foster collaboration. These tools must provide employees with the ability to establish various discussion groups and control access to those discussion groups. After you create the discussion groups, you must write policies that promote open discussion behavior while respecting each participant's opinion. Like the world outside of a corporation, a company is comprised of employees of different races, religions, and backgrounds. Within discussion groups, you must be willing to police interactions.

As you continue with your intranet implementation plan, formulate an Intranet Code of Behavior that informs employees what the corporation expects of them as they contribute to and use the intranet. As you implement threaded discussion forums, you will soon find that you need a moderator for each forum. A moderator should have the ability to immediately delete inappropriate messages that other members of the conference may find offensive. Your intranet moderators should participate in setting the Intranet Code of Behavior. In addition, if you plan to connect your intranet to the Internet, you may need to address the following issues:

- Should employees have access to all Internet sites during work hours?
- Can employees visit any Internet site during non-work hours?
- Can employees access various financial sites during their work hours to deal with their retirement accounts?
- Can employees download various controversial content from the Internet?
- Can employees use their e-mail for non-work related purposes?

Some of these issues are difficult to address, but you must address them to avoid embarrassing situations in the future. Employees do not know what an organization expects of them if it is not listed in an official document. An Intranet Code of Behavior should be part of your employee manual.

VENDORS AND SUPPLIERS AS PARTNERS

Making vendors and customers an integral part of your intranet demonstrates the true power of an intranet. A corporation exists to serve its customers. The activities of a corporation do not matter if they are not directly concerned with customer needs and wants. As you expand your intranet's capabilities, you will soon find that various departments now directly communicate with customers—which may be against your current policy of dealing with customers. For example, a software group may decide to start a discussion group on their intranet site so customers can provide them with ideas on how to improve the product and service of the software group. Currently, most organizations depend on their central customer-support group to deal with customers.

In cases for which a department wants to communicate directly with customers and suppliers, a company must write policies that define the information each department can and cannot share with customers. Again, a department manager should take the responsibility for making sure that his or her group members are communicating with customers without giving out confidential information or setting unrealistic expectations. But, without making your customer an integral part of your business practice, you lose an avenue to compete more effectively in the marketplace.

In addition to customers, you may also open your intranet to your vendors. Again, if you believe that your success in the marketplace depends on the ability of your vendors to provide you with high-quality goods and services, you should let your vendors better understand how they can affect your business. For example, assume your company inspects all incoming products and makes charts and reports on their findings. By making this information available to your vendors, they too can see how they perform. You can also show your vendors how they compare with other competing products and services that you receive.

MEASURING INTRANET EFFECTIVENESS

The goal of effective management of your intranet deployment is to improve the overall productivity of your enterprise. Measuring how intranets can and will affect the competitiveness of your company is not an easy task. What you must realize is that an intranet is not a short-term fix for most of your corporate ills. As you have learned, many intranet issues that you will deal with in the long-term will affect the way you run your business. You also must realize that an intranet can change your business practices. It is, however, up to a company's management to learn from these changes and work to develop products faster and more efficiently to have success in the marketplace.

It will take a few years before researchers can fully quantify the effect of intranets on a corporation's bottom line. In the meantime, you can establish an organization that thrives on collaboration and teamwork through the use of an intranet. Successful companies primarily depend on cross-functional teams to reduce time-to-market. Cross-functional teams are at the heart of any large-scale quality program. The success of these teams depends on the structure of the team and the collaborative tools available to the team. Intranets will bring the necessary tools to your cross-functional teams to create a long-lasting, positive change to your organization. In Chapter 15, you will learn how to perform return-on-investment techniques to better quantify the effectiveness of your intranet.

BUILDING THE CORPORATE INTRANET

Ryan Bernard of WordMark Associates has written an excellent whitepaper titled *Building the Corporate Intranet.* The paper examines ways you can incorporate Web technology into an organization to advance the organization's strategic goals. For information on downloading this paper, send an e-mail message to *wordmark@webcom.com* or visit the WordMark Web site at *http://www.wordmark.com* as shown in Figure 12.8.

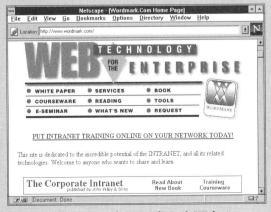

Figure 12.8 The WordMark Web site.

PUTTING IT ALL TOGETHER

In this chapter, you have learned that your intranet's long-term success depends on managing both technological and organizational issues. In most cases, in the beginning, intranet-deployment teams spend their time primarily on technological issues. In the long-run, however, organizational issues far outweigh the technological issues. Distributing quality content is the key to a high-quality intranet. Various department managers must act as intranet-deployment champions and lead their staff to distribute their knowledge on the company's intranet. By doing so, department managers can better measure the intranet's effectiveness on the overall productivity of their groups.

With intranets comes responsibility for proper conduct regarding the content of one's document or opinion in discussion groups. Companies must work with their employees to develop guidelines that specify how employees should react to situations that may cause unwanted stress. These issues primarily deal with the human aspect of running any organization. Intranets may reveal various hidden cultures in your organization that in the past you did not have to deal with. In Chapter 13, you will examine tools you can immediately put to use on your intranet. Before you move on to Chapter 13, however, make sure you understand the following key concepts:

- ✓ Top management must communicate to employees how intranets can make the employees more productive.
- ✓ Companies must address issues that deal with the technological and the organizational aspects of intranets.
- ✓ Providing users with document-management systems and access to various corporate databases are key factors in an intranet's long-term success.
- ✓ Distributing the management of an intranet to departments will increase the organization's participation in developing and enhancing intranet content.
- ✓ Successful marketing of an intranet will focus the implementation of intranets around user needs rather than the intranet's technological capabilities.
- ✓ Creating a culture based on information sharing may be the most challenging aspect affecting an intranet's long-term success.
- ✓ An intranet deployment strategy must place employee training at its center.
- ✓ Developing policies that will inform employees what they can and cannot expect from an intranet will avoid employee frustrations and embarrassments.

VISITING KEY SITES THAT DISCUSS INTRANETS

The World Wide Web is filled with hundreds of excellent and current articles on all aspects of intranets. Use the following sites as starting points for your Web exploration.

GOING MISSION CRITICAL

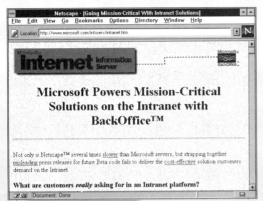

http://www.microsoft.com/infoserv/intranet.htm

THE INTRANET POST

http://www.inet2001.com/post/

267

MPI INTRANET

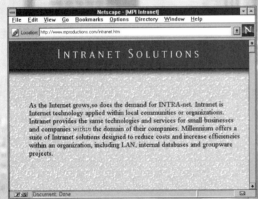

http://www.mproductions.com/intranet.htm

INTRANET DESIGN

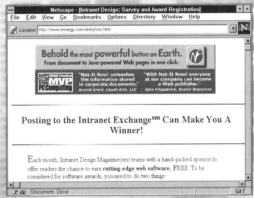

http://www.innergy.com/entryform.html

INTERLINK COMMUNICATION SYSTEMS

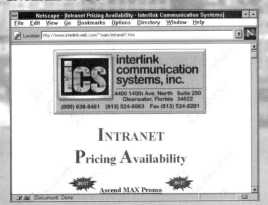

http://www.interlink.web.com/˜main/
intranet1.htm

INTRANET WORLD

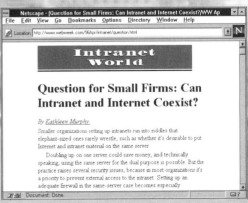

http://www.webweek.com/96Apr/intranet/
question.html

IMPLEMENTING AN INTRANET

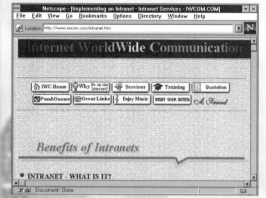

http://www.iwcom.com/intranet.htm

BBN ON THE WORLD WIDE WEB

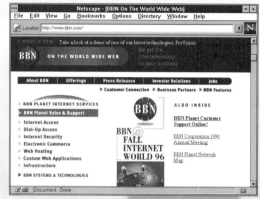

http://www.bbn.com/

IBM INTRANET

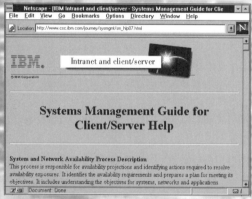

http://www.csc.ibm.com/journey/sysmgmt/
sm_hlp07.html

INFORMIX

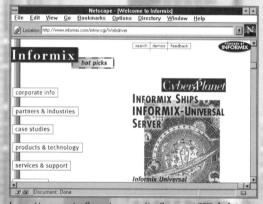

http://www.informix.com/infnx.cgi/Webdriver

INTERNET&INTANET PERFORMANCE

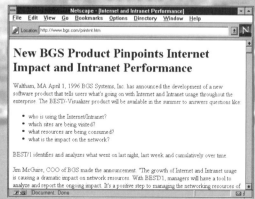

http://www.bgs.com/printrnt.htm

DOMINANCE OF THE INTRANET

http://www.lpilease.com/column.htm

Chapter 13

Ready-to-Use Intranet Tools

As you learned in Chapter 12, various technological and organizational issues can block your successful implementation of a company-wide intranet. The concepts you have learned in Chapter 12 may lead you to wonder if there are tools you can use to resolve such organizational and technological issues. In this chapter, you will learn about a variety of advanced tools that can help you quickly bring real functionality to your Web site.

As you will learn, many tools try to provide turnkey solutions to your intranets. After you learn about various tools in this chapter, you must make a strategic decision regarding purchasing turnkey solutions or developing your own applications internally. In Chapter 15, "Return on Investment for Intranets," you will learn how to perform a return-on-investment analysis to help you deal with such issues. By the time you finish this chapter, you will understand the following key concepts:

- ♦ To help you get your intranet up and running quickly, you can implement ready-to-use search engines, discussion-group software, document-management systems, and workflow applications.

- ♦ To help users locate information on your intranets quickly and efficiently, you should immediately implement a ready-to-use search engine.

- ♦ Using discussion-group software, users can collaborate on product development, as well as other corporate-wide, cross-functional team efforts.

- ♦ Various document-management systems provide employees with extensive document search, submission, and retrieval features. Think of a document-management system as an automated librarian that helps users locate, check out, and later, check in documents.

- ♦ Workflow products let users use intranets to manage complex business practices.

- ♦ High-end intranet product suites combine search, document-management, discussion group, and workflow applications in an integrated package.

- ♦ You must carefully evaluate the information-technology resources you require today and, in the long term, before you develop intranet applications internally or outsource the application development.

The ready-to-use tools this chapter discusses will enable you to solve most of the technological issues that you will face in the future. However, these tools alone cannot solve the organizational issues that you may face as your intranet becomes an integral part of your company's information system. Most intranet products are new and, in some cases, not fully tested by corporate users. As you select an advanced intranet tool, it is important that you obtain comparative data between products and determine which of the vendors has a better track record for delivering solid products. After you review product features, also try to obtain a trial version of such products and test drive them before purchasing the product.

CATEGORIZING ADVANCED READY-TO-GO PRODUCTS

After their initial intranet deployment, many companies find that their original static HTML pages do not maintain employees' interest or desire to use the intranet. As you have learned, you must add advanced capabilities to your intranet on a regular basis which continually increase the intranet's functionality. Such advanced intranet capabilities include the following:

- Search engine tools that help users locate the information they need quickly and efficiently.

- Discussion-group software that fosters collaboration.

- Document-management tools that help users locate documents, manage revisions, and notify document creators when the document requires an update.

- Workflow document tools that help users automate current processes.

- Integrated tools that let users perform common tasks using a "suite" of related software programs.

UNDERSTANDING SEARCH TOOLS

Most of you have probably used on-line help facilities within various Microsoft applications such as *Word, Excel,* or *PowerPoint.* On-line search tools let you find information about specific topics quickly and efficiently. For example, while working on a *Word* document, you can use the on-line Help topics to learn about all of *Word's* features. Just as these on-line help engines help users find information about specific aspects of their programs, Internet search engines have also become an integral part of the Internet. Today, experienced Web surfers start their searches for information at specific Web sites that provide search engines. Using these search engines, users can quickly locate sites that discuss the topics they desire. Today, the Internet's most popular search engines include *AltaVista, Excite, InfoSeek, Lycos, WebCrawler,* and *Yahoo.*

- AltaVista   *http://www.altavista.com*
- Excite   *http://excite.com/*
- Infoseek   *http://www.infoseek.com*
- Lycos   *http://www.lycos.com/*
- WebCrawler   *http://www.webcrawler.com*
- Yahoo   *http://www.yahoo.com*

As discussed, search engines provide users with the ability to search HTML documents across the Web for documents that contain the user's desired topic. Most search engines scan the Internet-based documents on a regular basis and store information about each document within the search engine's local database. For example, the AltaVista search engine indexes about 30 million Web documents which reside on 275,600 servers, and 4 million articles from 14,000 Usenet newsgroups. Internet users access the AltaVista site more than 18 million times a day. Figure 13.1 shows the AltaVista Web site.

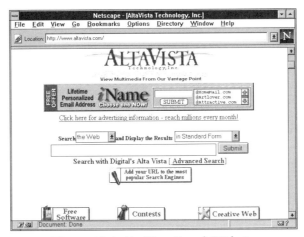

Figure 13.1 AltaVista Search Web site.

To find information available on the Internet using AltaVista, users type in the topic they are looking for (within the site's submit box), and then click their mouse on the submit button. AltaVista, in turn, queries its database and brings a brief description of all Internet sites, along with their URL, that closely match the content of the query text. For example, if you search for "Jamsa Press," AltaVista brings back 115 documents that best match the query, sorted by the site's probability of containing the information you need. In this case, the first site listed corresponds to the Jamsa Press Web site at *http://www.jamsa.com.* Figure 13.2 shows the AltaVista search results.

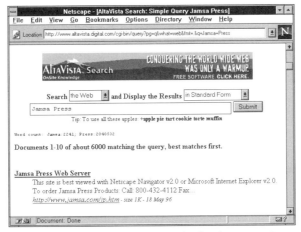

Figure 13.2 The AltaVista search results for the Jamsa Press query.

If you have your own Web site, you can add it to AltaVista's database. To add your site, you submit the site's URL using AltaVista's on-line Submit URL page. After you submit a URL for a site, AltaVista immediately retrieves the content of that site and adds it to the content of the AltaVista database. Most Intranet search engine technologies are similar to AltaVista's search technology, but most are not as advanced.

As you have learned, besides placing HTML documents on their Web sites, many companies use documents in Adobe PDF (portable document format) format. Most Web search engines, including AltaVista, do not search the content of PDF files. However, if your intranet makes extensive use of PDF files, you will need a search engine that supports the PDF format. The following sections discuss search engines that are capable of searching the contents of intranet PDF files.

INTRANET SEARCH ENGINES

Across the Web, users make extensive use of search engines to locate the information they need. As the number of documents on your intranet grows, users will need a search engine to locate content quickly. In this section, you will learn about various intranet tools that have features and capabilities matching the best Internet search engines. The intranet search engines you will learn about in this chapter include:

- *Excite for Web Servers* (EWS) from Excite Inc.
- *topicSearch* from Verity, Inc.
- *LiveLink Search* from Open Text Corporation
- The *WebSite* built-in search engine from O'Reilly & Associates, Inc.

EXCITE FOR WEB SERVERS FEATURES

As most of you know, Excite is a popular search site on the Internet. *Excite for Web Servers* (*EWS*) is a software program many companies use on their local Internet and intranet sites. You can use *EWS* to help employees locate specific content on your intranets. *EWS* does not require you to have a document database for your intranet HTML pages because *EWS* has built in all of the functionality you need in an intranet search utility. Excite Inc. currently provides this software free of charge for both Internet and intranet use. If you need product support and want to get free upgrades, however, you must pay about $1,000 a year for maintenance. *EWS* is available for both Unix and Windows NT platforms.

EWS uses a concept-based search to index and find relevant information within a collection of intranet pages. *EWS* also classifies its query results into groups that have specific characteristics. For example, if you search for "insurance" using *EWS*, the program will classify those HTML documents that refer to health insurance and those that refer to life insurance into separate categories. Besides grouping documents by subject, *EWS* also summarizes and lists the information content of each relevant page.

The only drawback to using *EWS* for your intranet is that, at this time, *EWS* only supports ASCII and HTML documents. As you have learned, your employees may generate PDF documents and publish them on intranets. However, Excite plans to add PDF search capability into *EWS* in the near future. To learn more about how other companies are using *EWS*, visit Excite's Internet Web site at *http://www.excite.com*. At this Web site, you will find a large number of private and public organizations that have selected *EWS* as their primary search engine. Figure 13.3 shows an *EWS* Web site in action.

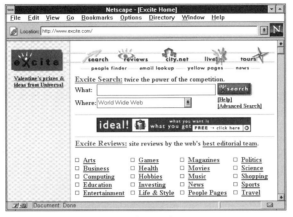

Figure 13.3 *Excite for Web Servers in action.*

The *EWS* installation and configuration is extremely easy. As you learned in previous chapters, you should obtain a trial version of various intranet tools before deciding to purchase them. *EWS* is a good product and one that you can download and test drive before making your final decision on what is the best search engine for your intranet.

TOPICSEARCH FEATURES

For a mid-range search engine, you may want to look at the capabilities of *topicSearch* by Verity, Inc. This search engine is available for both the Unix and Windows NT platform. Verity has targeted its search engine toward small businesses and the intranet publishing market. You can download a free copy of basic *topicSearch* free of charge from Verity's Web site at *http://www.verity.com/*. The basic search engine is capable of searching HTML and ASCII text documents. As you have learned, many of your intranets may be in PDF format. To support PDF documents, you must purchase the advanced version of Verity *topicSearch*, which sells for about $4,000. Figure 13.4 shows the Verity Web site.

Figure 13.4 *You can locate information on* **topicSearch** *at the Verity Web site.*

LiveLink Search Features

As you have learned, search engines are a necessary tool for any intranet. In a previous section, you learned about *Excite Web Server*, a free, low-end search engine. In this section, you will learn about *LiveLink Search* from Open Text Corporation. Unlike *EWS*, *LiveLink Search* is not a free product—it is a high-end product that can search the content of a variety of document types, such as PDF.

LiveLink Search is part of *LiveLink's* suite of intranet applications. You will learn about other components of the *LiveLink* suite later in this chapter. To use the *LiveLink* suite of intranet products, you must purchase either the *LiveLink Search* engine or the *LiveLink Library*, which is a document-management system. The *LiveLink* suite supports Windows NT and various Unix platforms.

LiveLink Search supports more than 40 different file formats, such as PDF, *Microsoft Word*, *WordPerfect*, HTML, and ASCII files of any size. Like other advanced search engines, such as AltaVista, users can query information using full-text or Boolean search techniques. Figure 13.5 shows a sample *LiveLink Search* result located on OpenText's Internet Web site at *http:// www.livelink.com*.

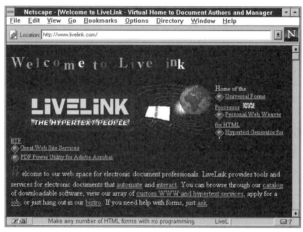

*Figure 13.5 A sample **LiveLink Search** result.*

You can also purchase *LiveLink Spider* as an optional tool to enhance *LiveLink Search*. A Web *spider* (or Web crawler) is a software that examines an intranet (or the Internet's) contents and constantly updates the search engine's content database. As you learned in previous chapters, within an enterprise, employees constantly create new intranet content or update existing content. To make new and updated information available to employees, the spider examines the documents and regularly updates the search database. Low-end search engines may not have this capability. If your search engine does not use a spider to update the content database, you must run indexing programs on a regular basis to update the content of your intranet.

WebSite Professional's Built-in Search Features

Besides standalone search engines, some Web servers, such as *WebSite Professional*, have a built-in search capability. As you learned in Chapter 5, *WebSite Professional* is an easy-to-install Web server. *WebSite's* built-in search engine lets employees search the intranet for content using a CGI program called *WebFind*. To create a database for *WebFind*, you first index your intranet content using a special program named *WebIndex*. After you index the intranet's content, users can search the index using the *WebFind* interface. As you have learned, *WebSite Professional* is a great product that sells for about $500 and runs on the Windows NT and Windows 95 platforms.

In the near future, other Web server developers will probably integrate search engines into their Web servers. If you are looking for a low-end search engine, *WebFind* or one of the free intranet search engines such as *EWS* will do the job. However, if you want to provide your users with advanced search engines, you must go with a high-end search engine, such as *LiveLink Search*.

UNDERSTANDING GROUP DISCUSSION TOOLS

After you implement a search tool capable of retrieving HTML pages, you must provide a way for employees to engage in electronic discussions to collaborate on ways to improve your business processes and to solve various issues. If you have used an Internet newsgroup, you are probably familiar with the concept of discussion-group applications. In general, discussion-group products provide a group of people with the ability to engage in various business and social discussions using electronic bulletin boards. Newsgroups and electronic chat rooms have become the most popular applications of the Internet and on-line services, such as America Online. Most companies use e-mail to let their employees collaborate and share information. Although an e-mail tool has many uses, it cannot efficiently let large numbers of users participate in resolving issues and sharing information . Think of e-mail as a one-to-one or one-to-many electronic application tool. Group-discussion software is a many-to-many electronic application tool. Using discussion-group products, product-development teams can engage in valuable on-line discussions to solve problems quickly.

Internet and intranet experts believe that discussion groups must be a part of every Internet and intranet site. Using a discussion-group product, your employees can learn from others by reading information exchanges between employees. For example, by connecting to the Human Resource department's Web site, an employee can use the discussion-group bulletin board to ask a question about his or her 401K retirement plan. Other employees will read the department's response to this question and learn more about their 401K plan. Figure 13.6 illustrates a discussion that contains questions and answers regarding intranets.

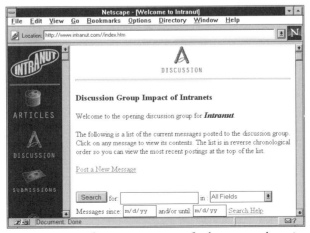

Figure 13.6 Using a discussion group to find answers about intranets.

INTRANET DISCUSSION-GROUP TOOLS

Another beneficiary of discussion-group products are product-development groups. Product-development groups often communicate various issues to one another on a daily basis. Each member of a product team cannot assume which members know or don't know information about a specific issue facing the team. By using a discussion-group tool, team members can share ideas and resolve issues, without leaving any of the team members out of the discussion. The discussion-group products that you will examine in this section include:

- *Allaire Forums*, from Allaire Corporation

- *AltaVista, Forum V2.0*, from Digital Equipment Corporation

- *WebBoard*, from O'Reilly & Associates

- *WWWBoard* freeware, written by Matt Wright

- *LiveLink Project Collaboration*, from Open Text Corporation

ALLAIRE FORUMS FEATURES

Allaire Forums is a threaded discussion product that lets intranet users share information by connecting (threading) related topic discussions. The product also provides an integrated-message feature that lets users automatically send private e-mail replies to another user after reading that user's message within a thread. Using *Allaire Forums*, an intranet system administrator can control access to various discussion groups. The product also provides a built-in search engine with which users can find messages by posted author, date, or topic keywords. You can download *Allaire Forums* free of charge and test drive it to see if fits your needs. Figure 13.7 shows a *Forums* discussion page.

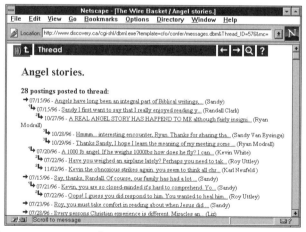

*Figure 13.7 A sample Internet site, **Allaire Forums** in action.*

Allaire Forums sells for about $800 and runs on Windows NT and Windows 95 Web server platforms. This message-exchange product is really a *Cold Fusion* application. *Cold Fusion* is a Web application development platform, also developed by Allaire Corporation, for Windows 95 and

Windows NT. Intranet developers can use *Cold Fusion* to integrate various corporate databases into their intranet. Developers can also use *Cold Fusion* to create threaded discussion-groups, or other groupware applications from the ground up. You do not need C/C++, Visual Basic, Delphi, or other traditional application programming languages to use *Cold Fusion*. If you already own *Cold Fusion*, you can purchase *Allaire Forums* for about $400. Figure 13.8 illustrates the Allaire Corporation Web site at *http://www.allaire.com*.

Figure13.8 *The Allaire Corporation Web site.*

ALTAVISTA FORUM V2.0 FEATURES

The people who brought the Web surfers one of the best search engines on the Internet are slowly getting into the intranet market. *AltaVista Forum V2.0* is a full-featured discussion-group product. Like *Allaire Forums*, *AltaVista Forum* lets users search for content, subject, and other message attributes. In addition, the software lets you send e-mail notifications to users and alert them when members of a discussion forum have added messages to that forum. System administrators can assign various levels of access to each employee to restrict which discussion-group information is available to everyone in an organization.

A powerful feature of *AltaVista Forum V2.0* is its ability to feed news to a discussion group from various sources on the Internet. For example, if you are a member of a team developing a particular software application, you can use the software to filter the news from various Internet sources and feed the news into your software-development discussion group on your intranet.

Another interesting feature of *AltaVista Forum V2.0* is its built-in polling capability, which lets team members register their opinions regarding specific topics which the software then posts to the discussion groups. Such polling helps team members establish a consensus or arrive at conclusions, even if members reside at distant geographical locations. You can install *AltaVista Forum V2.0* on both Unix and Windows NT platforms. This product also runs under popular Web servers such as those developed by Netscape and Microsoft. Figure 13.9 illustrates the *AltaVista Forum V2.0* discussion-group software.

*Figure 13.9 The **AltaVista Forum V2.0** discussion-group software.*

WebBoard Features

WebBoard is a Windows-based messaging system from O'Reilly & Associates, Inc. To use *WebBoard*, your Web server must fully support the Windows Common Gateway Interface, Win-CGI. Like *AltaVista Forum* and *Allaire Forums*, *WebBoard* lets you set various levels of access control for each conference: administrator, moderator, user, and guest. As discussed, it's important that you evaluate various intranet discussion-group products based on their capabilities. *WebBoard*, for example, lets a moderator delete questionable messages from a conference. As you learned in previous chapters, you cannot assume that all users know how to treat and respect others on an electronic conferencing forum—thus, a moderator's ability to delete entries is essential.

WebBoard, like the last two discussion-group products, displays messages in a threaded form. It also lets you use its built-in search capability to find specific messages on various conferences. You can view and modify the raw data in *WebBoard's* database using *Microsoft Access*. In the near future, the company plans to make *WebBoard's* database compatible with *Microsoft SQL Server*. Figure 13.10 shows a sample Internet site using *WebBoard*.

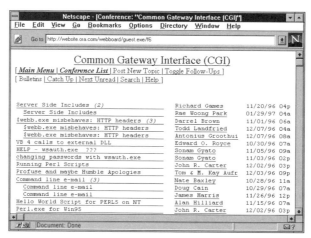

*Figure 13.10 A sample Internet site using **WebBoard**.*

You can purchase *WebBoard* for about $150, which makes *WebBoard* an affordable intranet solution. You can also download an evaluation copy of *WebBoard* from O'Reilly's Internet Web site at *http://www.ora.com*.

WWWBOARD FEATURES

For those who love Unix, Matt Wright has written *WWWBoard*, using Perl. This freeware discussion-group application runs on any Unix machine that has Perl installed. *WWWBoard* is not a commercially supported product and is not as easy as other such products to install and maintain. However, if you are a savvy Unix person, this product can provide your company with a basic discussion-group application. With a little hacking (programming), you can also port Perl scripts to other computer platforms.

Figure 13.11 shows a *WWWBoard* demo page. To download *WWWBoard*, visit *http://worldwidemart.com/scripts/wwwboard.shtml*.

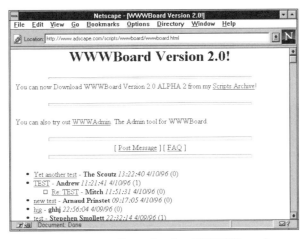

Figure 13.11 Downloading WWWBoard.

LIVELINK PROJECT COLLABORATION FEATURES

Like other components of the *LiveLink* intranet suite of applications, *LiveLink Project Collaboration* is a high-end discussion-group product. In addition to common discussion-group features, this product also provides users with the ability to assign tasks and track task completion. Think of *LiveLink Project Collaboration* as a virtual place where members of a team can discuss and track all aspects of a project.

For example, in this virtual place, you will find folders for various project documents, lists of tasks that define team-member responsibilities, and workflow maps that relate to each project. Figure 13.12 shows project workspace with *LiveLink Project Collaboration*.

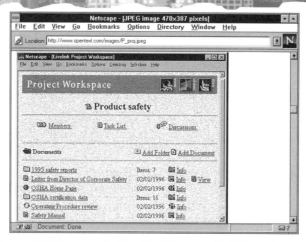

*Figure 13.12 A sample **LiveLink Project Collaboration** page.*

If you have participated in a team project, you know how difficult it can be to keep track of project tasks on a regular basis. Today, most organizations assign a team leader to each project to assure that a project stays on track. Often, a team leader publishes minutes of team meetings and publishes new tasks to team members via e-mail. The problem with this method of communication is that keeping track of action items is difficult and time consuming. Therefore, by examining the content of team meeting minutes, it is very difficult to determine if and why a project completion may be in trouble.

The project tracking features built into *LiveLink Project Collaboration* may prove invaluable for teams that want to finish their project on time and within budget. Figure 13.13 shows how *LiveLink Project Collaboration* displays a list of project tasks.

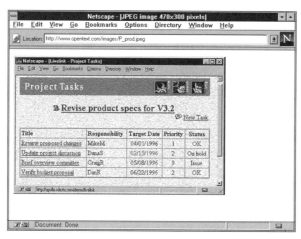

*Figure 13.13 A sample **LiveLink Project** tasks page.*

Besides these advanced features, *LiveLink Project Collaboration* also provides users with the ability to post, read, and reply to messages in a virtual project-conference space. Like other components of *LiveLink, Project Collaboration* runs on both Window NT and Unix platforms.

UNDERSTANDING DOCUMENT-MANAGEMENT TOOLS

Recently, many discussion-group products have started to integrate some document-management capabilities. The idea is that discussion-group products should make teams more effective. Teams often collaborate throughout a product's development. Intranet markets will soon place discussion-group products into two sub-categories: those that provide document-management capabilities and those that do not.

Group-discussion products will also provide employees with the capability to search and view official electronic documents. The storage location of these documents may or may not be on your actual Web server. If your company already has a dedicated document server, you must write or purchase the appropriate tool to connect it to your intranet. As you learned in the previous chapter, if employees have to deal with several systems that serve the same purpose, they normally use the one with which they are familiar, not necessarily the one that is most advanced.

As you have learned, a primary intranet goal is to create a paperless organization. In so doing, you provide employees with more time to create products and to service customers, as opposed to handling paper. Intranets are the vehicle for achieving this noble goal. The tools you use for document management on your intranet are similar to, but more advanced than, intranet search tools. Intranet search tools do not manage documents, they simply index document content and let the user search the content.

Document-management systems perform the complex task of keeping track of every document, from the moment that employees publish it, to the moment the document is no longer useful and you decide to destroy it. Document-management systems use a database to track document changes. As you learned in Chapter 12, "Short- and Long-Term Intranet Deployment Challenges," you must divide your intranet documents into two types: those for which you track changes, and those that you do not. A product specification is an example of a controlled document that team members may need to check out, update, and check back in. On the other hand, an employee's personal page is not a controlled document—only one person will manage and update the page.

INTRANET DOCUMENT-MANAGEMENT TOOLS

Currently, there are few products on the market that software companies have developed from the ground up for intranets. Document-management products are fairly complex to develop and software developers often base them on proprietary database, server, and client applications. Document-management products are often expensive and require a dedicated staff to maintain. However, in the near future, vendors of legacy document-management systems will move aggressively to offer complete intranet tools, which will provide you with more software choices. The document-management products you will examine in this section include:

- *LiveLink Library* from OpenText Corporation
- *Accelera* from Documentum, Inc.

LIVELINK LIBRARY

Like *LiveLink Search, LiveLink Library* is part of the complete and integrated intranet solution from OpenText Corporation. *LiveLink Library* is a document-management product that provides you with the capability to:

- Check documents in and out of a central repository.

- Control document revisions and track the document's change history.

- Access older versions of a document (backup versions).

- Develop a hierarchical structure, such as folders, to organize document storage.

- Convert over 40 file formats to HTML for document viewing using a Web browser.

- Manage documents in their native format, such as Microsoft *Word*.

- Search document content for keywords.

- Set multi-level permissions for document viewing and editing.

The above list of features makes *LiveLink Library* the most advanced intranet document-management product on the market today. Figure 13.14 shows a page from the *LiveLink Library* located on OpenText's Internet Web site.

Figure 13.14 A sample LiveLink Library page.

If you already have a legacy document-management system, you may want to compare its capabilities to those of *LiveLink Library*. If you plan to move to an enterprise-wide intranet document-management solution, consult with your current document-management software vendor regarding their future product offerings. You may find that your current document-management software vendor plans to enhance its product so your company's employees can access documents through a Web browser. If your current vendor plans to stay with a proprietary solution, and you are thinking of updating your current document-management system, you should consider *LiveLink Library*.

LiveLink Library is available for both Unix and Windows NT platforms and currently sells for approximately $20,000. As part of the basic *LiveLink Intranet Suite*, you can get either *LiveLink Search* or *LiveLink Library*. After you have purchased the basic *LiveLink* package, you can later add components to it. You will learn more about other *LiveLink* intranet components later in this chapter.

ACCELERA

As you have learned, document management is a task that, today, most companies perform manually. Intranet technology will accelerate a company's move to deploy a better document-management system. In addition to intranet-based document-management systems, companies use a variety of other proprietary document-management systems to organize and distribute information throughout their organizations. One of the leading companies in the client–server document-management market is Documentum, Inc. The first intranet-based product from Documentum, Inc. is called *Accelera*.

By using *Accelera*, employees can search and query a document repository database called Docbase, to locate documents with a Web browser. *Accelera* lets users view Docbase documents regardless of the document's stored format. Documents in Docbase can range from HTML to PDF to word processing documents, such as Microsoft *Word*. Like *LiveLink Library*, *Accelera* automatically converts the content of Docbase documents into HTML. *Accelera* also lets users place frequently used documents in a personal folder to reduce the time they spend searching for documents. *Accelera* sells for about $20,000 per server. You can use this product with various HTTP servers from vendors such as Netscape and Microsoft. *Accelera* is available for both Unix and Windows NT platforms. For more information on *Accelera*, visit the Documentum Web site at *http://www.documentum.com/accelera.htm*, as shown in Figure 13.15.

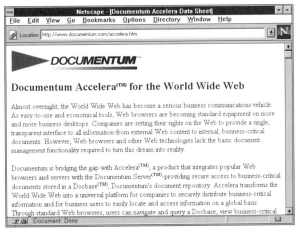

Figure 13.15 The Documentum, Inc. Web site.

UNDERSTANDING WORKFLOW TOOLS

Workflow products are an extension of document-management products. Workflow products let users process documents electronically, without wasting time filling out paperwork or moving through various bureaucratic channels. For example, assume you want to buy capital equipment (machinery with a high dollar cost), such as a $100,000 machine. At many companies, you probably need permission from you immediate supervisor, your supervisor's manager, and your unit's vice president, as well as your purchasing coordinator. Most often, however, you must go through several rounds of negotiation and discussion before you get everyone to agree that you need the capital equipment. Using a workflow document, you can initiate your capital-purchase requirement, write what you need, and why, using a memo. Then, you can send the memo electronically to the people who must review and approve your purchase.

As you have learned, a powerful feature of the *LiveLink Project Collaboration* intranet tool is its ability to provide integrated workflow within a collaborative environment. Workflow programs streamline the flow of documents between organizations and members of a team, thereby reducing the time it takes to develop various products and business processes. Workflow programs are probably the most complicated intranet application programs. These products require sophisticated mapping features that will let users create new information flows.

In a traditional document-control system, a user initiates the release of a new document, and then relies on the staff within the document-control department to get approval for the document. In large organizations, this manual process could take as many as 3-to-4 weeks. Often, the people who must review and sign documents do not respond promptly, which frustrates both the document's originators, as well as the document-control department staff. Workflow programs, on the other hand, provide features that will help people respond to document content and arrive at a decision quickly.

INTRANET WORKFLOW TOOLS

Besides technological issues, companies also consider the organizational effects related to the deployment of advanced intranet tools. Your deployment of workflow products will require that your company train both your current document-control staff, as well as team members from various project teams, on how to use these advanced tools. Unlike search engines and discussion-group tools, workflow products will replace an existing system for performing a specific task. If the tools do not have all of the necessary features employees need to get their jobs done, employees may show resistance to fully embracing intranet workflow tools. In this section, you will examine the following workflow products:

- *SamePage*, from WebFlow Corporation

- *Action Metro 1.1*, from Action Technologies, Inc.

- *LiveLink Workflow*, from Open Text Corporation

SAMEPAGE FEATURES

SamePage is a Web-based workflow program for the Unix and Windows NT platforms. WebFlow Corporation is positioning *SamePage* not only as a workflow product, but also as a new category of intranet-based products that let team members collaborate on a project using a virtual meeting room. In the near future, most of the advanced intranet discussion-group products will integrate workflow products. The goal of products such as *SamePage* is to help team members solve issues quickly and effectively. WebFlow Corporation calls *SamePage* the first of a new category of products called Intranet Work Processors.

Instead of flowing documents from one person to another person, or one department to another department, *SamePage* provides users with the ability to collaborate on project plans, specifications, and various contracts at the same time. *SamePage* lets a team start its collaborative work on a document by breaking document information such as paragraphs, pictures, and tables, into objects. Then, *SamePage* lets users comment and collaborate on those objects. Object comments may include hypertext links, text, and images. As shown in Figure 13.16, using *SamePage*, a marketing group can discuss issues on-line and assign tasks to different team members.

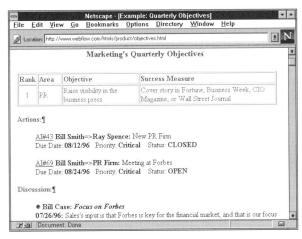

Figure 13.16 SamePage in action.

SamePage is a new product which you should deploy as a pilot project to determine how it fits your overall intranet strategy. The product may bring significant changes to the way your product teams collaborate on projects. *SamePage* costs about $3,500 for a 10-user system.

ACTIONWORKS METRO 1.1 FEATURES

ActionWorks Metro is another intranet workflow program that provides a ready-to-use application program for various departments within an organization. *ActionWorks Metro* provides users with a set of easy-to-use electronic forms that are really applications which perform different workflow tasks. Each of these applications serves a different department within an organization. After employees use an initial form, *ActionWorks Metro* starts a process that takes the form from one person to the next person following a given flow specified by the form. For example, Figure 13.17 shows a form, called ActionItem, that an employee can use to initiate an action item workflow.

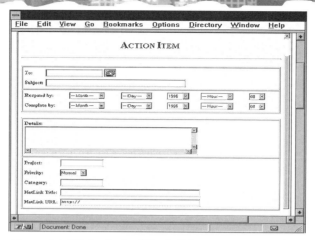

Figure 13.17 An ActionWorks Metro action item form.

ActionWorks Metro provides users with three basic Web-based forms: initiation forms, status-and-interaction forms, and work-list forms. Using an initiation form, an employee starts a workflow. For example, an employee can launch an initiation form to get approval for a travel request. *ActionWorks Metro* provides a set of ready-to-use forms and also lets you create your own. For example, the Time Off Request form lets an employee submit vacation and floating holiday requests to a Human Resources department. Using status-and-interaction forms, employees can follow and track their requests and reply to requests from other employees. In addition, by using these forms, employees can also review the history of various workflow forms. *ActionWorks Metro's* third type of forms are workbox-list forms, which let a team track the various action items that result from regular team meetings.

Before you purchase this product, download a trial version from the Action Technologies Web Site at *http://www.actiontech.com*. There are two basic options for purchasing *ActionWorks Metro*. With the first option, you can purchase *Metro ActionItem* with a 30-user license for about $250. After testing *Metro ActionItem*, you may want to purchase the complete *Metro Application Center*, which comprises 22 different applications, for about $3,000.

After becoming familiar with various *ActionWorks Metro* applications, you may want to develop your own applications. To do so, you can purchase a *Metro* Developer's Kit for about $10,000. Again, you should first use *Metro's* basic *ActionItem* application before you decide to purchase this scaleable intranet workflow product. To run *ActionWorks Metro*, you must have a Windows NT platform with Microsoft *SQL Server*, and Netscape *Commerce Server*.

LiveLink Workflow Features

Another part of *LiveLink's* intranet application suite is *LiveLink Workflow*. Like other *LiveLink* components, *LiveLink Workflow* is a high-end intranet product. A powerful feature of *LiveLink Workflow* is its graphical mapping utility, which lets users graphically create, modify, and manage various types of workflow processes. *LiveLink Workflow* supports serial, parallel, and other looping types of workflow routing. In addition, users can assign conditional branching to multiple points along a workflow process. Figure 13.18 shows a *LiveLink Workflow* process in action.

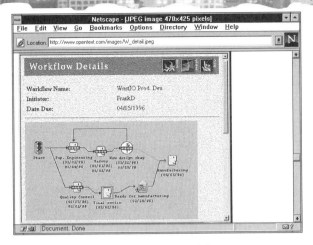

Figure 13.18 LiveLink Workflow in action.

LiveLink Workflow also provides users with the ability to review the status of various workflow processes and different stages of a flow. In addition, the software can automatically inform group members about the status of their action items and various workflow processes. As you have learned, you can run *LiveLink* products on both Unix and Windows NT platforms.

PUTTING IT ALL TOGETHER

As you have learned, basic intranets provide organizations with the ability to distribute static information to employees, vendors, and customers. Advanced intranets, as well as Internet sites, provide users with the ability to interact with database information, search for information, and engage in collaborative efforts via group-discussion software. After you release your intranet, you will discover many hidden pockets of knowledge within your organization.

In this chapter, you learned that discussion-group products let team members share their ideas and engage in collaborative efforts—even if the team members are physically located around the world. Intranet collaboration tools make employees feel that they belong to a team where everyone's input is valued. Many products, such as *SamePage*, now refer to a new breed of products that they call "Intranet Work Processors."

Intranet Work Processors will move us away from the word processor mentality which, in some ways, promotes individualism. Often, one team member writes a memo, a proposal, or a project plan and distributes it to everyone else working on the project. The information flows serially from one person to another without much collaboration taking place. Team meetings become the place where members of a team finally collaborate on their work. Team meetings, however, require everyone working on a project to be available at the same time and, in many cases, physically present during the meeting. This process does not work well in most cases. Intranet Work Processors will shift the way we think about collaboration—letting team members truly function as a team.

In this chapter, you learned several concepts that will let you deploy intranet work processors within your organization. In Chapter 14, you will examine how Microsoft's new *FrontPage* software simplifies your Web page creation. Before you continue with Chapter 14, however, make sure you have learned the following key concepts:

✓ By deploying advanced intranet applications, you will make your intranet an integrated part of your business practices.

✓ There are four groups of advanced intranet tools available in the market today: search engines, discussion-group software, document-management systems, and workflow products.

✓ Search engines let users locate specific information on your intranet quickly.

✓ Discussion-group products are available for many platforms and can vary in their features and cost of deployment. If you are familiar with Unix, you can obtain free software, from various Internet sites, that provides basic discussion-group tools.

✓ Many intranet-based document-management systems are on the market today. Most document-management systems are rooted in proprietary technologies. These products are more complex than search and discussion-group products and the cost can range as high as $15,000.

✓ A workflow program can be an extension of a document-management system. Workflow programs are also complicated and require you to train employees how to use them to increase their productivity. You can purchase inexpensive workflow programs, such as *Metro*, to test whether such software fits the way you run your business.

✓ Advanced intranet programs can prove expensive, but may pay for themselves quickly—if you deploy them properly. Integrated products, such as *LiveLink Intranet Suite*, are best-suited for large organizations with large information-technology budgets.

✓ Before you develop advanced intranet applications internally, evaluate other options carefully. In the near future, many vendors will introduce a variety of new intranet applications that may make your internally-developed applications obsolete.

VISITING KEY SITES THAT DISCUSS INTRANETS

The World Wide Web is filled with hundreds of excellent and current articles on all aspects of intranets. Use the following sites as starting points for your Web exploration.

W3.COM

http://www.w3.com/

WELCOME TO FREELOADER, INC.

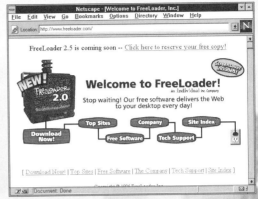

http://www.freeloader.com

THE NCSA HOME PAGE

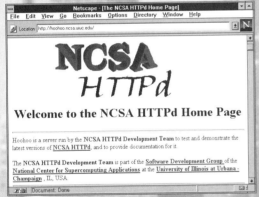

http://hoohoo.ncsa.uiuc.edu/

WEB COMPUTER

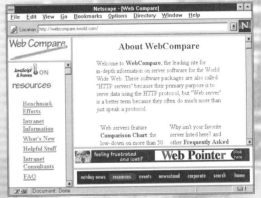

http://webcompara.iworld.com/

QUAL COMM

http://www.qualcomm.com/

CUTE FTP

http://www.cuteftp.com/

Novell: GroupWise

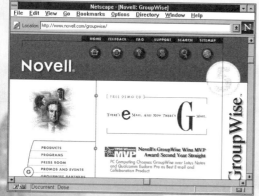

http://www.novell.com/groupwise/

The Vocal Tec

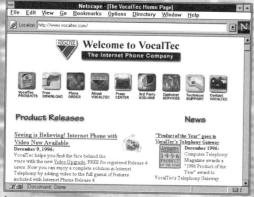

http://www.vocaltec.com/

WebBoard Central

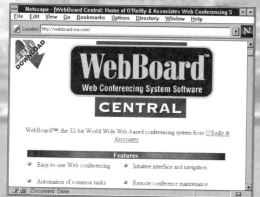

http://webboard.ora.com/

Paradox 7

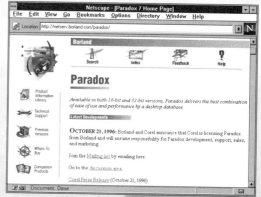

http://netserv.borland.com/paradox/

Connectix Corporation

http://www.connectix.com/

IRC Chat client mIRC

http://www.mirc.co.uk/

Chapter 14

Web Publishing Using FrontPage 97

As you learned in Chapter 13, to bring advanced functionality to your intranet, you may need to install various ready-to-run applications, such as search engines or discussion-group software. You have also learned that you will need various HTML authoring tools to help you create HTML documents.

In this chapter you will learn about *FrontPage 97* (or *FrontPage)*, which is an integrated intranet processing tool from Microsoft that can help you easily set up a basic intranet with interactive features without requiring any programming skill. So, you may find yourself asking, "If deploying intranets is so easy, why did I have to learn about HTML, CGI scripts, Web servers, search engines, discussion-group software, and a host of intranet concepts?" The answer is that you must understand intranet fundamentals, before you can assess your organization's needs.

In Chapters 7 and 8, you learned how to create HTML documents. In Chapter 11, you learned about CGI scripts and how non-technical users find writing CGI scripts difficult. In Chapter 12, you examined the issues facing organizations that want to implement distributed intranets. In this chapter, you will examine a new tool that will simplify your intranet development. Microsoft's *FrontPage* is an integrated set of programs that let you focus on your intranet's content. *FrontPage* combines advanced Web-authoring tools with site-management utilities. By the time you finish this chapter, you will understand the following key concepts:

- Employees need Web-authoring tools to help them create state-of-the-art content for your intranet.

- *FrontPage* is an integrated Web-management tool for both small and large organizations.

- The *FrontPage* development environment runs under Windows, but you can transfer its output to servers running Unix.

- Building a basic, yet dynamic, intranet using *FrontPage* will take most users only a few hours.

- *FrontPage Explorer* helps users move content to and from a *FrontPage*-based Web site.

UNDERSTANDING THE NEED FOR INTEGRATED WEB AUTHORING TOOLS

By now, you have learned that to deploy an intranet, you must have a set of software applications. These software applications include Web server software, HTML-authoring tools, and programming software. Besides these basic development tools, you must purchase or write additional software applications, such as a search engine or discussion-group software. Regardless of an organization's size, learning about various intranet application tools is difficult and time consuming. Thus, companies must have Web-publishing tools which provide the following features:

- Built-in HTML authoring tools

- Support for visual site-management operations (lets you view linked documents, broken links, and so on)

- Plug-ins that simplify the creation of dynamic content

- Include a built-in server that will work closely with the plug-in tools

- A set of templates and Wizards that assist users (of all levels of expertise) in creating Web pages

- Support for features that let teams collaborate on content development

- Support for database operations

- Various levels of security

- Minimal user training and associated costs

DECENTRALIZED CONTENT CREATION AND DISTRIBUTION

As you have learned, the power of an intranet is its ability to create an environment where departments can create and maintain their own Web content. By distributing content creation throughout its departments, an organization will increase the number of stakeholders who will care about the intranet's effectiveness. Distributing control of an intranet to various departments might seem like a bad idea at first. However, over time you will learn that a distribution of information enables organizations to tap into each employee's knowledge base.

Distributing the creation and maintenance of your intranet's content can become quite challenging if you must support many different intranet applications. As the number of applications on your intranet grows, so do your management concerns. For each application, you must be concerned with version control (Are you using the latest version of a product?), training, and maintenance. In addition to consuming much of your time, managing multiple applications can also consume much of your budget.

To reduce financial and management costs, most organizations opt to standardize their desktop productivity software applications, such as Microsoft *Office*. As you will learn in this chapter, standardization brought Microsoft *Office* to corporate desktop computers and is driving companies to standardize their selection of Web-publishing tools in integrated environments.

WEB PUBLISHERS NEED NOT BE PROGRAMMERS

After an organization decentralizes the creation and maintenance of its intranet content, more non-technical users will need Web-publishing tools that require little or no programming knowledge. As you have learned in previous chapters, employees who want to publish content must know HTML basics. With only limited HTML knowledge in hand, most employees, even those with no programming background, can use Web-publishing tools, such as *FrontPage*. As departments implement their own servers, they will eventually need to set up search engines and discussion-group software at their site. Using an integrated Web-publishing program that offers these features helps non-technical users get their intranet pages up and running quickly.

Eventually, as companies deploy advanced intranet applications, such as workflow and document-management systems, the companies must make a large investment in a skilled programming staff. To simplify the management of such complex applications, most organizations will centralize their deployment—allowing their departments to manage less complex applications.

UNDERSTANDING FRONTPAGE COMPONENTS

In previous chapters, you learned about various HTML authoring tools, such as *Internet Assistant for Microsoft Word*. Unlike standalone HTML authoring tools, search tools, or group-discussion products, *FrontPage* includes all of these components in one software package. The basic components of *FrontPage* are divided into two parts: the client side and the server side. The client-side software provides the tools users need to author both static and dynamic HTML pages, as well as tools clients can use to perform search and discussion-group operations.

The server-side tools include the *FrontPage Personal Web Server* and server plug-ins that make the client-side components server independent. For specifics on *FrontPage*, visit the Microsoft Web site at *http://www.microsoft.com/frontpage/*.

Figure 14.1 Information on FrontPage.

UNDERSTANDING FRONTPAGE "WEBS"

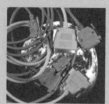

To build a Web site, you must use a variety of files which range from HTML documents to images to CGI scripts. Within *FrontPage*, a "Web" is a collection of files and folders that you can open, edit, and test. Throughout this chapter, we will use double-quoted "Web" to reference a collection of *FrontPage* folders and files. In contrast, the word Web without quotes corresponds to the World Wide Web. Assume, for example, that you are using *FrontPage* to create intranet pages for the City of Las Vegas. To organize your documents, you would store them in a folder (a *FrontPage* "Web") named Vegas. Later, when you need to edit the documents, you simply start *FrontPage* and open the Vegas "Web."

The *FrontPage* architecture provides an ideal environment for users to create and test Web pages that they can later migrate to larger Web servers. If you do not have a Web server, you can use the *FrontPage Personal Web Server* to run a small intranet. The *FrontPage Personal Web Server* is really a development Web server which users should use to test their Web pages before they migrate the pages to your company's primary Web server.

FRONTPAGE CLIENT-SIDE TOOLS

The *FrontPage* client-side tools provide all the features you need to author an entire Web site. You use various client-side tools to develop pages that belong to an intranet Web. A *FrontPage* Web consists of one or more HTML pages with or without links. Using *FrontPage*, you can view the links to various pages within the "Web," (we've enclosed your *FrontPage* "Web" within quotes to distinguish it from the World Wide Web) as well as the external links. As shown in Figure 14.2, the *FrontPage* client-side tools include five programs: *FrontPage Explorer, FrontPage Editor, FrontPage TCP_IP Test, Personal Web Server,* and *Server Administrator.*

*Figure 14.2 The five components of the **FrontPage** client-side tools.*

To begin building your "Web," you run *FrontPage Explorer*, within which you can view a "Web" or run other *FrontPage* programs, such as the *FrontPage Editor*. In general, *FrontPage Explorer* provides a framework that holds together client-side tools. Figure 14.3 shows a "Web" within the *FrontPage Explorer*.

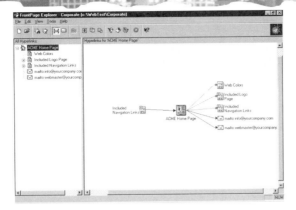

Figure 14.3 A "Web" within the FrontPage Explorer.

As you will learn, the *FrontPage Explorer* and *Editor* work together closely. While the *FrontPage Explorer* tracks a "Web's" pages and links associated with those pages, the *FrontPage Editor* is the program within which you will edit the pages. Although you can use the *FrontPage Editor* as a stand-alone HTML editor, you must use the *FrontPage Explorer* to update a "Web's" content if you want the *FrontPage Explorer* to track the corresponding links.

Within *FrontPage Explorer*, the main screen has two sections: the Link View section and the Outline View section. By dragging the window frame, you can adjust the screen area you allocate to each section. From within this main screen, you can open, create, or delete an entire "Web." You can also import HTML or ASCII files for use by the "Web," or delete documents the "Web" no longer requires.

CREATING A FRONTPAGE "WEB"

To create a "Web," select the File menu New option and choose FrontPage Web option. *FrontPage*, in turn, as shown in Figure 14.4, will display a dialog box that contains the names of templates with which you can build a "Web" quickly. As you will learn, the *FrontPage* templates are a powerful feature and are ideal for users who are creating their first pages or need to get a working "Web" up and running with minimal time and effort.

Figure 14.4 The FrontPage "Web" templates

For now, select the Personal Web template. Then, type in the name of a server on which *FrontPage* will store your files, or, simply type in the complete pathname of a directory on your disk within which you want *FrontPage* to store your "Web" files. For now, type in the location *C:\WebTest*. In addition, type in the name you want *FrontPage* to use for your Web. Again, for now, type in the name *MyWeb* and press ENTER. *FrontPage*, in turn, will create your new "Web" displaying a visual view of the "Web," within the *FrontPage Explorer* window, as shown in Figure 14.5.

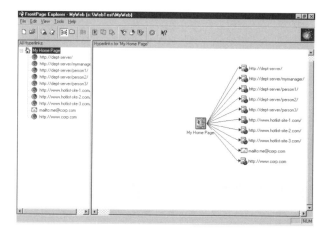

*Figure 14.5 Creating a new "Web" using the **FrontPage Explorer**.*

As you can see, using the Personal Web template, *FrontPage* creates a homepage document with links to related documents, each of which you can edit using the *FrontPage Editor*. To start the *FrontPage Editor*, you can simply double-click your mouse on the My Home Page document icon. *FrontPage*, in turn, will start its *Editor*, as shown in Figure 14.6.

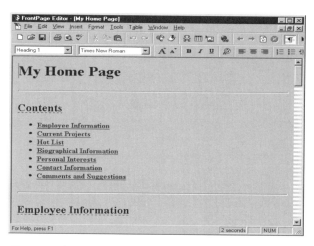

*Figure 14.6 A homepage within the **FrontPage Editor**.*

The My Home Page document contains several pages of text that you can edit to customize the information about yourself. For example, you can begin by changing the text My Home Page to contain your name.

Next, scroll down to the page titled Employee Information and type in your job title and a brief description of your job. Continue your editing process by scrolling through the remainder of the document and updating the content.

The *FrontPage Editor* uses many of the icons and menus you should recognize from other Microsoft programs. As you will learn, *FrontPage Editor* makes authoring HTML pages extremely easy. To add text to a page, you simply type the text and then use a style or other attributes to format the text, just as you would within a word processor.

As you have learned, HTML authoring tools are not 100 percent WYSIWYG capable. However, *FrontPage* comes very close. *FrontPage* supports tables and many other HTML 3.0 features. After you are content with your changes to the document, select the File menu Save option to save your edits. Then, use the File menu Exit option to exit the *FrontPage Editor*. After *FrontPage* saves your document to disk, it will return you the *FrontPage Editor*.

DISPLAYING YOUR FRONTPAGE "WEB"

To display your newly created FrontPage "Web," start your browser, such as the Netscape *Navigator* or Microsoft *Internet Explorer*. Within the address field, type the pathname to the *index.html* file that contains your "Web."

For example, if you used the names specified in the previous example, you would type the address *file:///c:\WebTest\MyWeb\index.htm*l. Figure 14.7 illustrates how the Microsoft *Internet Explorer* will display the *FrontPage* "Web."

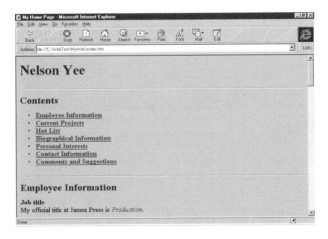

*Figure 14.7 Displaying the **FrontPage** "Web" within the Microsoft **Internet Explorer**.*

EDITING DOCUMENT LINKS WITHIN YOUR FRONTPAGE "WEB"

If you return to the *FrontPage Explorer*, you will see that the your "Web" contains links to many other documents. To remove a link, simply click your mouse on the link and select the File menu Delete option. To change a link's URL, select the Tools menu Verify Hyperlinks option. *FrontPage* will display the Verify Hyperlinks dialog box, as shown in Figure14.8.

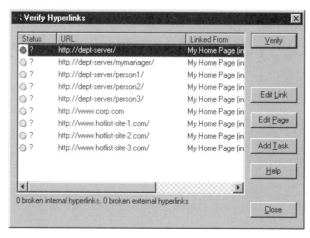

***Figure 14.8** The Verify Hyperlinks dialog box.*

Within the dialog box, click your mouse on the link you want to update and then click on the Edit Link button. *FrontPage* will display the Edit Link dialog box, as shown in Figure 14.9, within which you can change the link's URL.

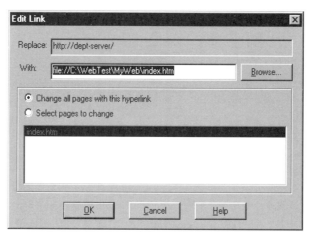

***Figure 14.9** The Edit Link dialog box.*

After you update the link, click on OK to exit the Edit Link dialog box and then click on Close to exit the Verify Hyperlinks dialog box.

FRONTPAGE CREATES YOUR HTML DOCUMENTS

To create "Web" pages, *FrontPage* must create HTML documents. Within the *FrontPage Editor*, you can select the View menu HTML option to display the document's HTML entries, as shown in Figure 14.10.

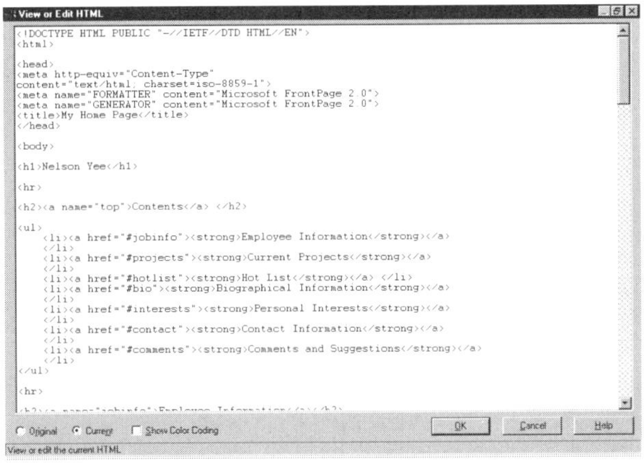

*Figure 14.10 Displaying your "Web's" HTML entries within the **FrontPage Editor**.*

FRONTPAGE SERVER-SIDE TOOLS

As you have learned, using the *FrontPage Personal Web Server*, users can develop and test their own Web content. To run an intranet, you will need a full-featured, high-performance Web server—not the *FrontPage Personal Web Server*. The *FrontPage* server-side tools include a set of CGI-executable files which let the automated features of the *FrontPage* client-side tools work on various Web servers. These server-side extensions support *Personal Web Server*, O'Reilly's *WebSite*, the Netscape *Communication Server*, and the Microsoft *Internet Information Server*.

If your organization already has an intranet and you want to make the *FrontPage* client-side tools available to various groups within your organization, you must make sure that Microsoft has released the server extensions for your particular Web server. You can find the latest list of available server extensions from Microsoft's Web site (*http://www.microsoft.com*). In addition, you will also need TCP/IP-compliant software with *Winsock* version 1.1, or later, running on each of your *FrontPage* development machines. Both Windows 95 and Windows NT provide built-in TCP/IP software.

THE HARDWARE YOU NEED TO USE FRONTPAGE

FrontPage runs on any Intel-based machines running Windows 95 or Windows NT. To run various *FrontPage* client-side tools, you will need a 486, or higher, processor. If you plan to use *FrontPage* as a department Web server, a 486 processor will work fine. However, for larger groups, you will need a Pentium-class machine. *FrontPage* requires about 15Mb of hard disk space. However, to provide room for a large "Web," you should reserve at least 500Mb. Also, you will need at least 16Mb of RAM to run *FrontPage*. For your server system, you should use at least 32Mb of RAM.

BUILDING AN INTRANET USING FRONTPAGE

As you have learned throughout this book, building an intranet requires planning, training, and a collection of software. If you have a large organization, and can put together a team which will have adequate programming skills, you may want to use *FrontPage* to create and deploy your central intranet site. However, if you are a small company, or a department with limited access to a staff with programming skills, you will definitely want to use *FrontPage* to create your intranet. In the previous section, you used *FrontPage* to create a personal "Web." In the following section, you will use a *FrontPage* template to create a corporate "Web."

USING FRONTPAGE EDITOR

To create a corporate "Web" using *FrontPage*, select the File menu New option and choose FrontPage Web. *FrontPage*, in turn, will display a dialog box that contains a list of templates. Select the Corporate Presence Wizard. Next, you must type in the location at which you want *FrontPage* to store your "Web" documents. For now, using the pathname *C:\WebTest* and the "Web" name *Corporate*, *FrontPage* will start a Wizard (software program) that will get you started.

The Wizard will prompt you for information about yourself and possibly your company, as shown in Figure 14.11.

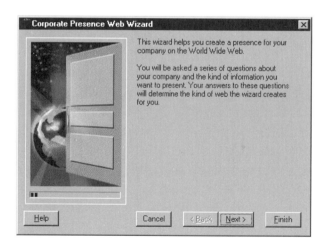

Figure 14.11 Using a **FrontPage** *Wizard.*

When the Wizard completes, the *FrontPage Explorer* will display your corporate "Web," as shown in Figure 14.12.

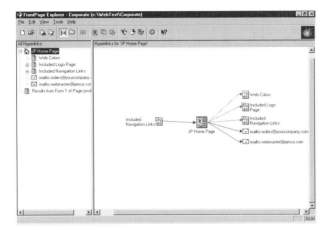

Figure 14.12 *The corporate "Web" within the* **FrontPage Explorer**.

As before, double click your mouse on the Home Page document to edit your pages. The *FrontPage Editor*, in turn, will display your document's content, as shown in Figure 14.13.

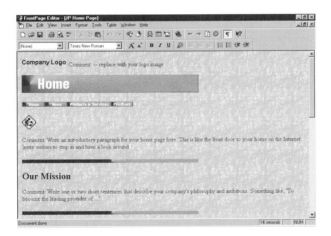

Figure 14.13 *The corporate "Web" document within the* **FrontPage Editor**.

Within the *FrontPage Editor*, edit the document's contents to customize the document to suit your needs. Then, use the File menu Save option to save your edits. To later view your "Web," start your browser and type in the address, *file:///c:\WebTest\Corporate\index.html*, as shown in Figure 14.14.

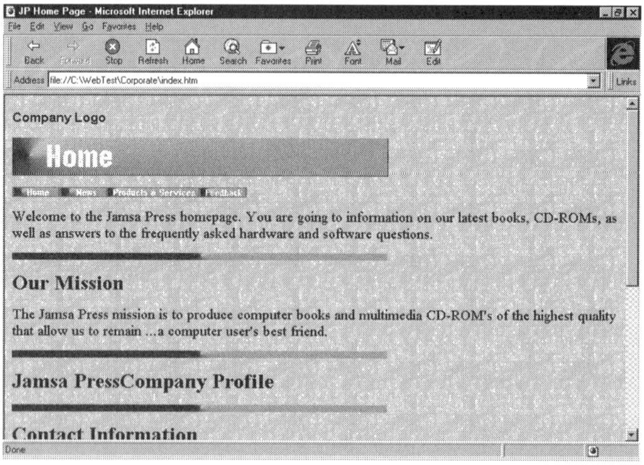

Figure 14.14 *Viewing the corporate "Web" within the Microsoft Internet Explorer.*

USING FRONTPAGE WITH OTHER TOOLS

In this chapter, you have learned how quickly you can create an intranet using *FrontPage*. However, if you already have an intranet and you want to use *FrontPage* to manage the Web's content, you must first install the *FrontPage* server extensions on your existing server. The *FrontPage* server extensions automatically gather the information that *FrontPage Explorer* needs to manage a site. After you install the server extensions, you select the *FrontPage Explorer* Tools menu Recalculate Links option to direct *FrontPage* to gather information about your site's links. Using this technique, Web authors can use other authoring tools to add pages to an existing *FrontPage* "Web."

Even though *FrontPage* provides many WebBots that eliminate your need to write most CGI scripts, Web developers may still need to write custom CGI programs. For example, *FrontPage* does not provide a WebBot with which you can connect your intranet to a database. To do so, you need a custom program. Within the *FrontPage Editor*, an author can apply a custom CGI script to any of a page's dynamic elements.

PUTTING IT ALL TOGETHER

FrontPage is an integrated Web-authoring package which sets the standard for a new generation of tools that will help Web authors, who possess few or no programming skills, develop advanced intranets. *FrontPage* significantly reduces the cost associated with deploying an intranet. For small organizations that do not require a highly-advanced intranet, *FrontPage* is a great Web-publishing tool. In addition, small departments within a larger corporation can also benefit from using this product.

You will find that most people will enjoy working with *FrontPage* to develop intranet content. The key to your successful deployment of *FrontPage* is to select a powerful server that supports the *FrontPage* server extensions. In Chapter 15, you will learn how to determine the potential return on your intranet investment by calculating your intranet's ROI. Before you continue with Chapter 15, however, make sure you have learned the following key concepts:

- ✓ Organizations need Web-publishing tools that will enable all of their employees to contribute to intranet content.

- ✓ *FrontPage* is the first integrated Web-publishing tool. It consists of an HTML editor, a Web-authoring tool, a personal Web server, and a set of server extensions.

- ✓ *FrontPage* is ideal for Webmasters who work in small companies and for departments of large companies that manage their own Web server.

- ✓ *FrontPage* provides an extensive set of Wizards with which you can build a Web site from scratch.

- ✓ The *FrontPage Editor* is a powerful HTML authoring tool that lets users quickly include dynamic elements into an HTML page.

VISITING KEY SITES THAT DISCUSS INTRANETS

The World Wide Web is filled with hundreds of excellent and current articles on all aspects of intranets. Use the following sites as starting points for your Web exploration.

ı WORLD

http://tips.iworld.com/_noframes.shtml/—
/publishing/FrontPage.html

WEBPC

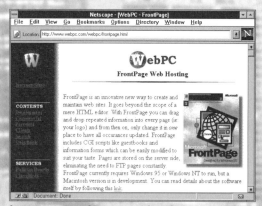

http://www.webpc.com/webpc/frontpage.html

FRONTPAGE

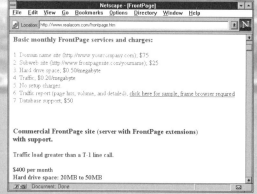

http://www.realacom.com/frontpage.htm

FRONT PAGE VIRTUAL WEB

http://web.mindspring.com/prod-svc/web/—
fp.virtual.html

FRONTPAGE

http://c2com/cgi/ploptory

LOTUS INTERNOTES VS MICROSOFT-
FRONTPAGE

http://www.carrington.com/iwpvsfp.htm

Chapter 15

Return on Investment for Intranets

Throughout this book, you have learned about many of the valuable uses of an intranet. From increasing the speed of communications and reducing the amount of printed material, to enhancing product development and creating a culture of collaboration, an intranet will certainly improve your bottom line. But, by how much? As with any commitment to new machinery or technology, business managers must be able to answer the question, "What is the return on investment (ROI)?" By analyzing the ROI, the savvy manager can project the potential benefits of a significant investment and track results against expectations. More importantly, managers can use financial terms to compare and contrast alternate investments.

The media has led small and large companies to believe that deploying intranets is fairly easy and inexpensive. For the most part, the media's claim is correct. However, eventually companies must add advanced intranet applications to enhance the capabilities of their internal Webs. As you have learned, deploying advanced intranet applications requires careful planning and the availability of resources and funds. To help those faced with the challenging task of selling the concept of the intranet to the rest of a corporation, this chapter examines the various costs and benefits of an intranet from a financial perspective. By the time you finish this chapter, you will learn the following key concepts:

- ◆ Calculating an ROI requires you to employ several basic accounting principles.

- ◆ ROI is a universal method of measuring the benefit of any capital expenditure.

- ◆ A reliable ROI analysis depends on a thorough examination of the potential income and expenses an investment will generate.

- ◆ Due to ambiguity (unknowns) that surround the intangible costs and benefits of deploying a new information technology, measuring ROI for an intranet is challenging.

- ◆ Every benefit is either tangible or intangible and quantifiable or unquantifiable.

- ◆ Intranet benefits take two forms: savings from costs you avoid and returns (income) from efficiencies you create.

- ◆ To determine a reliable ROI, you must include the cost of every piece of software and hardware you need for the intranet.

- ◆ From a "low" ROI of around 200 percent to a "high" ROI of over 2,000 percent, most intranets promise excellent returns on your investment.

THE NEED FOR *ROI* ANALYSIS

Calculating ROI requires a thorough investigation of costs and benefits. Completing an ROI analysis will help you better understand the intricacies of measuring information technology. The analysis will give you a more analytical measurement on which to base your decision about implementing your intranet. If you must obtain permission from your company's upper-management to install an intranet, preparing a systematic ROI analysis will greatly improve your chances of convincing the decision makers of the intranet's rewards.

In Chapter 5, you learned about hardware equipment and software applications that companies must have to deploy intranets. In general, the startup costs of intranet systems are not high. However, as you add a variety of advanced applications (and you will need to), your company may quickly face costs of thousands of dollars both in terms of the initial purchases and continuously thereafter for application support. To obtain approval from upper management to purchase expensive software applications, you must show the costs and benefits these applications will provide your company over time.

In Chapter 12, you learned that your success in getting support for an intranet deployment depends on your ability to market such systems. Marketing a product or a service inside a company is similar to marketing a product or service outside the company. You must show how the product will benefit the buyer. In Chapters 3 and 4, you learned how intranets benefit various parts of an organization. To analyze the intranet's ROI, you must take an inventory of all the activities that you think the intranet's deployment will affect. You must understand the cost associated with the distribution of information through traditional means (such as memos, catalogs, and handbooks). Your search for cost information may take you into unfriendly territory. Departments, within an enterprise, may not know how much it costs to run their operations and may take offense at your asking.

As you have learned, many companies initially use intranets to facilitate the activities of the Human Resource Department. So, review what you have learned in Chapter 3 and list all of the responsibilities and activities your Human Resource Department performs. Then, consult with those individuals to determine how an intranet can improve their function. Only then can you know the intranet's potential benefits. You must repeat this exercise for various departments and perform an accurate ROI analysis for each.

UNDERSTANDING *ROI*

To perform an ROI analysis for an intranet, you first must evaluate factors that effect the ROI of any investment. You express an ROI as a percentage of the benefits an investment will generate. In the simplest terms, you calculate these benefits by dividing both costs avoided and income generated from the investment by the investment's cost. Consider the following ROI formula:

$$\frac{Savings + Income}{Investment\ Cost} = ROI$$

For example, if adding a $1-million airplane to an airline's fleet generates $100,000 of additional income, the airplane's ROI is 10 percent ($100,000 / $1,000,000 = 10%). Once again, the components of an ROI are:

- Investment costs—how much money you must invest
- Savings—how much money you will save after the investment is in place
- Income—how much money the investment will generate

CAPITALIZING OR DEPRECIATING YOUR INVESTMENT COSTS

To understand ROI, you must first understand investment costs. The initial outlay for a piece of machinery, for example, is obviously the investment cost. In most cases, you will project that the investment will last for a specific number of years. Therefore, you can amortize the cost over these years by annually subtracting an amount called *depreciation*. For example, you know that a five-year-old car is worth less than its original purchase price because its owner has consumed some of the useful life of the car. The car has now *depreciated*. In their financial statements, companies subtract depreciation from their taxable income to reduce taxes—a very good thing! This tax break is the government's way to encourage investment.

Several methods are available for you to use when you calculate depreciation, such as straight-line, accelerated, and sum-of-the-years'-digits methods. The specific differences among these methods are not important now, simply note that you can choose an appropriate method for any type of investment. The following table illustrates the depreciation of a $100,000 printing press, with a life-expectancy of 10 years, using the straight-line method. Assume the press was purchased on January 1st and will have no value in ten years. Then, you can determine the press' value on December 31 of each year. The straight-line method subtracts an equal amount of depreciation each year. You can calculate this amount by dividing the purchase price by the investment's useful life ($100,000 / 10 = $10,000 = $10 K).

Year 1	Year 2	Year 3	Year 4	Year 5	Year 6	Year 7	Year 8	Year 9	Year 10
$90K	$80K	$70K	$60K	$50K	$40K	$30K	$20K	$10K	$0

By examining the item's value (straight) trend-line, shown in Figure 15.1, you can see why accountants refer to this method as straight-line depreciation. In this example, you will deduct $10,000 of depreciation each year from your profit and loss statement.

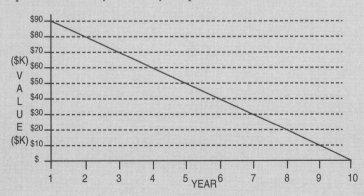

Figure 15.1 An item's value applying the straight-line depreciation method.

Another important concept you need to consider when investing in capital equipment is *capitalization*. You can capitalize expenditures that extend the useful life of an investment. Capitalizing these new costs (new investments) means adding the costs to the denominator (bottom) of the ROI formula.

For example, consider a travel bus tour company. The money the company spends on gasoline does not extend the useful life of the bus. Therefore, it is simply an expense the company records during the current accounting period. If, on the other hand, the owner overhauls the engine and is able to drive the bus for eight more years, he can capitalize the cost of the overhaul. In other words, rather than taking the cost of the overhaul as a current expense, the owner can depreciate the expense over a period of years, taking a part of the expense each year. Because capitalizing expenses effects the company's tax liability, it is wise to consult a certified public accountant or other tax professional to understand the finer points of this procedure.

Because your company must periodically upgrade hardware, such as hard disks, memory, and various software applications, the concept of capitalization will affect your cost of maintaining an intranet.

Understanding Savings

If an investment lets your organization avoid costs that you are currently incurring, the investment, in essence, generates income. As you calculate your ROI, you count these avoided costs toward the benefits the investment creates. For example, consider a company that installs an automated telephone system. If the phone system eliminates the company's need for an operator to answer and direct incoming calls, the company can tally the salary costs of the operator as "income" the automated system creates. As you will discover, calculating the cost savings of an intranet is not always a straight forward task.

Understanding Income

Without diverging too far into the accounting field, you will want to know some basics like the difference between revenue and income. Revenues are total receipts. Income is what is left after you subtract the expenses you incur in generating the revenue. Youngsters around the world provide a perfect example. When your daughter opens a lemonade stand and counts $10 at the end of a hot day, she has $10 in revenue. After reimbursing you $4 for cups and lemonade mix, she now has $6 in income.

The impact these terms have on calculating ROI is clear. The income figure that accountants use in the numerator (the top part of the ROI equation) is the remainder of the revenues minus costs. Using the airplane example from earlier in this chapter, assume the new plane actually generates $300,000 in revenue. After you subtract $200,000 in personnel costs, maintenance, supplies, and insurance, the remaining income is $100,000. By adding savings to revenues minus costs, you have the net benefits of the intranet.

THE ROI FORMULA PART TWO

With your new understanding of ROI components, you can now understand the advanced version of the ROI formula. The numerator and denominator of the ROI equation are more accurately shown below:

$$\frac{Savings + Income - Expenses - Depreciation}{Depreciated\ Investment\ Cost} = ROI$$

The hypothetical scenario that follows puts all the pieces of the ROI together. Using the printing press example previously discussed, Tables 15.1, 15.2, and 15.3 itemize the financial effects the press has had on the company:

Benefit Year 1	Category	Description
$25,000	Savings	New machine uses only one operator instead of two
$95,000	Revenue	Proceeds from printed document sales for the year
$ 5,000	Savings	New press needs less maintenance than the old press
$125,000	**Total financial benefits**	

Table 15.1 Total benefits for year one.

Cost Year 1	Category	Description
$25,000	Cost	Salary for one operator only
$55,000	Expenses	Material costs (paper) for printing projects
$ 3,000	Expenses	Maintenance
$10,000	Expenses	Depreciation
$93,000	**Total financial Costs**	

Table 15.2 Total costs for year one.

Benefit Year 1	Category	Description
$100,000	Investment	Initial purchase price
$ 10,000	Depreciation	Subtract depreciation for year one
$90,000	**Total depreciated investment**	

Table 15.3 Total depreciated investment for year one.

After you apply the numbers from Tables 15.1, 15.2, and 15.3 to the ROI formula you will get:

$$(125,000 - 93,000) / 90,000 = 0.36 \text{ or } 36\%$$

In this case, the printing press delivers a 36 percent return on investment during year one. To further develop your understanding of the ROI equation, you must now calculate the ROI during year five. To do this, assume that the benefits in year five total $130,000 and the costs amount to $97,000. From the press' depreciation table previously shown, you can see the press is now worth $50,000. The ROI during year five is shown below:

$$(130,000 - 97,000) / 50,000 = 0.66 \text{ or } 66\%$$

As you can see, because the investment is increasingly less valuable (in financial terms), and the benefits remain steady, the ROI grows dramatically. The results here are just the same as if the company bought a used printer for $50,000 in year five.

While these numbers are fairly simple, you can see the power of the ROI formula. By calculating the net benefits and dividing by the current financial value of the investment, you can see the return it generates. You must realize that the merit of your ROI analysis rests in the accuracy of your calculations. As the saying goes, "Garbage in—garbage out." If you estimate amounts too broadly or omit significant items, your results are worthless. It is a good idea to collaborate with others as you construct the spreadsheets you will use to calculate an ROI. Double check each line item in the formula, as well as the method that you used to calculate it. Try to uncover every factor that may affect ROI and carefully compute its best estimate.

MEASURING INFORMATION TECHNOLOGY

Now that you know the mechanics of calculating ROI and the importance of proceeding carefully, it is appropriate to talk about some of the challenges and terms involved in measuring information technology. Since the first forms of information technology were used to automate processes, financial benefits were relatively easy to calculate. For instance, a company might have installed an electronic device to run a machine which replaced workers. Or, a company may have installed a PC to replace a bookkeeper's journal entries. Today, information technology provides management with data it can use to make strategic decisions. These benefits are not only much more advanced, they are also much more difficult to pinpoint.

Because a company's financial investment for an information technology tool can be high, performing a cost–benefit analysis is important. Unfortunately, such evaluations are not always accurate or thorough. Often, an evaluation is not performed at all. Reasons companies fail to accurately measure information technology tools include:

- The accurate estimation of costs and benefits is difficult
- The system's true costs and benefits may not be clear for quite some time

- The system's evaluation may require months or years of careful study after the initial implementation

- The senior executives may be uncomfortable with and suspect of information technology

- The costs of not proceeding with an information technology investment are equally difficult to estimate

- The type of measurement preferred often varies depending on the person responsible for the evaluation (such as the Chief Financial Officer, a board member, or MIS Director)

These obstacles often make measurement of information technology more qualitative than quantitative. After simply creating a generalized estimate of costs and a brief narrative description of some of the technology's benefits, companies often install expensive new information technology systems. It is one company among dozens that insists upon a thorough financial cost–benefit analysis prior to the intranet's implementation.

CONCEPTS AND TERMINOLOGY

Mathematically speaking, calculating an ROI is easy. However, the process of identifying costs and benefits is difficult. After you know your costs and benefits, calculating an ROI involves no more than simple addition, subtraction, and division. To help you classify and define intranet costs and benefits, the following sections present several key concepts and terms.

DEFINING HARD COSTS

For an intranet, your hard costs include hardware and software. Hard costs are easy to understand and pinpoint. They are predictable estimates for easy-to -detect costs. Any number of vendors can quote (to the penny) the purchase price of any piece of computer equipment or software. The costs of installing the hardware or software are also hard costs. Within an acceptable percentage of variance, the cost of installing software on a server or installing a browser on 50 desktop computers is easy to estimate. The issue is not whether the estimate is 100 percent accurate, it is simply that these costs are more concrete, and therefore more measurable.

DEFINING SOFT COSTS

Soft costs are costs for intangible objects, such as training or inefficiency during the user's learning period. Soft costs may be easy to understand, but are more difficult to pinpoint. While you can identify soft costs, their values are not concrete. For example, it is difficult to estimate how long it will take employees to learn a new technology or to become as proficient as they are now with an existing technology. More importantly, you probably want to know how much time it will take for users to exceed their current proficiency level. Such learning time not only costs the company a portion of the individual's salary, but may also temporarily affect the entire organization's output.

DEFINING BENEFITS

To determine the ROI of an information technology, you must first understand the types of benefits that an enterprise will gain by deploying such technologies. Table 15.4 defines the various benefit types.

Types of Benefits	Description
Tangible	Tangible benefits are those that directly affect the company's bottom line. You can objectively say that these benefits generate profits.
Intangible	Intangible benefits are those that indirectly affect the company's bottom line. They may or may not generate profits.
Quantifiable	Benefits that you can easily measure and quantify.
Unquantifiable	Benefits that you cannot easily measure or quantify.

Table 15.4 *Definition of various intranet benefits.*

Every benefit is either tangible or intangible and quantifiable or unquantifiable. Figure 15.2 shows the four possibilities in a two-by-two matrix.

	Quantifiable	*Unquantifiable*
Tangible	(1) Software replaces two bookkeepers	(2) Obtaining more accurate research data
Intangible	(3) Improved employee satisfaction	(4) Improved reputation as a good corporate citizen

Figure 15.2 *Classification of tangible and intangible benefits.*

The numbers in each cell represent the cell's order of importance to you as you calculate an ROI. Assume that you are using the ROI of an intranet to convince your company to invest in the technology. Each type of benefit will provide you with ammunition for your debate. Benefits that fit Category 1 (tangible/quantifiable) are the most important for you to uncover and report. You can also use Category 2 (tangible/unquantifiable) entries if you can make reasonable estimates of the benefits. Since unquantifiable means that you cannot readily and objectively apply a value to the benefit, you obviously must choose your numbers carefully. But, as long as the number is reasonable and conservative, it can contribute to the ROI formula. Category 3 (intangible/quantifiable) entries are valuable for discussing the qualitative (feel good) benefits the technology will provide.

Descriptions of these benefits are an added bonus that make the ROI number easier for managers to accept. Likewise, Category 4 (intangible/unquantifiable) entries can be useful for the thoroughness reporting them implies.

Do not make the mistake of starting your analysis with Categories 3 and 4. Instead, do the hard work required to discover and report Categories 1 and 2. Realize that the ROI formula is based on accounting principles that rely on numbers. After an initial ROI calculation , you can move on to more subjective matters for additional support.

INTRANET BENEFITS: THE ROI NUMERATOR

In calculating the ROI numerator, you must define the benefits an intranet offers. These benefits take two forms: savings from costs avoided and returns from efficiencies created. Costs avoided are fairly obvious. If a cost is no longer necessary due to the intranet's implementation, your company has saved money and you can count the cost as a benefit of the intranet. Similarly, if a job can be completed faster due to the intranet's implementation, your company has saved money which you can also count as a benefit of the intranet. (Remember, the time-honored business equation, "time equals money!") Returns from efficiencies created are the profits that your company may see from putting time saved to good use.

COSTS AVOIDED

As you have already learned, an intranet is a "virtual" printing house inside your company. Many of the advantages an intranet provides are in the form of electronic publishing. A company can place virtually anything that it prints and distributes on paper onto the company's internal Web sites and, in turn, reduce printing costs. Also, by using electronic documents, readers can complete and electronically return materials that require responses. A driving force in business, over the last several decades, has been the paperless office. An intranet may provide the most significant step toward that elusive vision.

PRINTING COSTS

Anyone with access to a computer can retrieve and send information electronically, avoiding the costs of hard-copies. The most obvious costs are paper and ink. Reducing the amount of money spent on paper and ink (toner, ribbons, print cartridges, and so on) for internal use is one way to cut costs without reducing customer service. Expensive stationery and laser printers rarely provide any value-added benefits for "widget" builders. Why not use the money saved for more widget research and development?

In addition, electronic publishing provides other cost savings. When companies professionally print large quantities of expensive materials (such as an employee benefits handbook), companies often order extra copies because reprinting small quantities is costly. When a company uses intranet publishing, the company can create exactly enough copies, with no waste! Whether you have one employee or one-thousand-and-one, each employee views the same on-line copy! In addition, document errors and out-of-date information are much easier and less costly to correct. If you have ever thrown out stacks of incorrect or out-dated material, you know how costly such waste is to your company. With intranet publishing, you eliminate such waste.

OTHER COSTS

As you calculate your cost savings, do not forget that you must store all those boxes of paper and toner cartridges. When hard copies arrive at someone's office, they also must be filed or stored. By storing information on-line, you can reduce your space requirements for supplies and files. In addition, you must consider your distribution expenses (postage, shipping, and courier costs can be significant). As you already know, facsimile machines have nearly wiped out the need to send most short documents by mail. Likewise, an intranet allows you to send any length document to everyone in just seconds! Another communications expense is travel. In the future, many companies will rely on their intranet to eliminate the need to travel to distant meetings. When you consider the cost of airfare, cabs, hotels, and meals, each trip your company avoids can save several hundred dollars per person.

ELECTRONIC PUBLISHING USING INTRANETS

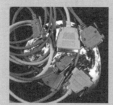

For many, the cost reductions from implementing an intranet may sound too good to be true. The following is a list of items that are good candidates to electronically publish on your intranet. Certainly, you will think of more that are specific to your company.

- Corporate mission/goals/vision (by dept.)
- Biographies of top executives
- Description of the company's industry
- Organization chart
- HR forms/performance review measures
- Employee benefits/forms/documentation
- Employee policies/handbook
- Job postings
- Job training opportunities/classes
- Product pricing/information/updates
- Catalogs/sales guides/order forms
- Employee newsletter(s)

- Employee directory/home pages
- Company calendar/events/holidays
- Company performance measures
- Balance sheet and income statement
- Major competitors/competitive market data
- Training manuals
- Company approved vendors/suppliers
- Frequently asked questions
- Press releases
- Sales forecasts/updates
- Cost savings tips
- Periodic reports (by department)

SUMMING UP COST SAVINGS

By collecting data on how much money your company will save by publishing corporate information on the intranet, you will have made a good start on calculating ROI benefits. Looking for this data will take time and effort. Your departments may not have each item of printed material budgeted separately. In that case, you will have to approximate a figure. The best type of figure to use, if it is available, is a figure that represents a per-employee expenditure (such as a benefits manual that costs the company $10 to produce). You can also use "industry norms" for estimated costs—you might research these costs using industry-specific journals. Using a spreadsheet, itemize and total all the costs your company can avoid by using an intranet to publish materials. You have now completed the first step in calculating an ROI.

EFFICIENCIES CREATED

While the most important advantage of an intranet is its ability to disseminate information across many platforms, the ease of which users can access the information is the intranet's next most crucial advantage. Employees (and customers or vendors, if permitted access) can find information on an intranet almost instantaneously. As you have learned, an intranet makes finding information intuitive and quick. For example, the Human Resource Department homepage is the obvious place for an employee to look for benefit information. Hyperlinks make finding a document or report a simple mouse-click operation. Users can examine lists and categories of data with sub-lists and sub-categories in minutes. If the user does not know where to begin a search for information, the user can use a search engine to pinpoint the data.

Every minute that an intranet saves employees contributes to greater employee productivity. Do not forget that when workers cannot find data on their own, they often resort to asking other workers for help. This disruption raises the price the business pays for information retrieval. The intranet is an information technology solution that not only shortens the time between the request for information and its delivery, but also reduces the number of people involved in delivering the information.

FILLING OUT A TRAVEL FORM

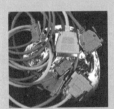

To better understand how an intranet can save employee time, consider the simple example of a manager completing a travel form.

Without an Intranet—A manager wants to be reimbursed for travel expenses. The manager searches through a file (or files) for the proper form, copies it, completes it, and drops it off at the accounting office (Total time: 25 minutes). Accounting personnel sees that the form is outdated, copies the data to a new form, and returns the material to the manager (Time required: 25 minutes). The manager completes the new form and returns it to accounting (Time required: 10 minutes). It has taken an hour of personnel time to file the proper form.

With an Intranet—A manager wants to be reimbursed for travel expenses. The manager searches through the intranet for a form, completes it, and transmits it to the accounting office (Time required: 15 minutes).

When considering the ROI for an intranet implementation, it is important that you realize how much value there is in saving time. Indeed, time may be a company's most precious resource. If the intranet can save employees minutes when they submit a simple form, think about the cumulative hours the intranet can save if employees use it to complete daily and weekly reports, to find information, and to broadcast announcements to workgroups. The intranet lets team members conduct on-line brainstorming sessions without having a face-to-face meeting, which will save multiple employees considerable time.

In the past, a search for specialized information required employees to inspect documents, ask questions of the document authors, visit the company library, and possibly exchange several memos or faxes. With an intranet search engine, an employee can locate information on a topic within seconds. Instead of spending hours or days looking for information, employees using an intranet may spend minutes, and find much more information in the process!

PUTTING EFFICIENCIES TO GOOD USE

Using the time they save, employees can, at the very least, start their next task at hand. Most likely, you will not find workers with too little to do! Little by little, as the intranet speeds up tasks, employees will find "extra" time. By putting this time to good use, even if it is only 15 minutes, the company is poised to see extraordinary results. For instance, suppose someone in marketing has enough extra time to make a phone call to an engineer in research and development. A friendly inquiry about a current project may be all it takes to spur a conversation that leads to a new idea. The engineer and marketer may discover that what was once a problem to one customer has now become an advantage.

Think about the prospect of your company's sales staff being able to make just one more call per week. That single solicitation may become the next big contract. And, if the customer becomes a long-term buyer, the life-time rewards of that one sales call are immense.

MEASURING THE VALUE OF EXTRA TIME

As you can see, the value of the extra time an intranet creates is potentially quite high. From the seemingly small but important value of a courtesy call to a client, to the infinite value of a major sales call, the ROI formula should reflect the value of extra time in some way. But how? At a minimum, the value of extra time is proportionate to the cost of the worker's salary. If an hour of the secretary's time is saved, it is worth at least one hour of her salary. If the salesperson can spend an extra day per month on sales calls, the value cannot be less than one day's salary. While the value could be much more, it certainly could not be worth less. Later, in specific business scenarios, this chapter will show you steps you can use to calculate the value of extra time.

COSTS INCURRED

Another step you must perform, to define the net income for the ROI formula, is to estimate the various expenses you will incur on a regular basis as you operate your intranet. This section examines several typical costs. You may think that some of these costs are unnecessary. In some cases (the smallest applications), they may be. In others (the largest applications), you should not ignore the costs. Do not get hung-up on these figures. Whether you believe an estimate is 25 percent lower or higher will make little difference in the final analysis. Including a large item or not including a large item, however, will make a significant difference. Avoid overestimating your ROI by including benefits that are debatable. You will find that underestimating leaves room to reasonably round up, while overestimating puts the entire analysis in a suspicious light. The most common expenses for deployment of an intranet include:

- **System Personnel**: A *system administrator* keeps the intranet running, installs new equipment, upgrades desktop computers, and maintains system security. While current staff may be able to absorb these responsibilities, a new position may be necessary for larger installations. As the organization's workers increase their use of the intranet, they will soon see the need for customized software or applications. An *application administrator* has an assignment much like that of the system administrator, except that the application administrator focuses on software. In addition to managing existing software, the application administrator may need to write custom applications.

- **Training**: To start, your system and application administrators must attend classes and certification programs to stay on the cutting edge of the technology. And, although intranets are easy to use and instinctive in their design, you should provide your users with ongoing instruction on ways they can maximize the benefits of the system. Such user training may occur using your staff as trainers or using out-of-house trainers. In either case, your company will incur training costs.

- **Post Installation Planning:** Because an intranet is an evolving system, your company should put in place a cross-functional team that continuously guides the intranet's development. While these team members are making plans, they are not accomplishing their regular assignments. You must count a cost, based on these employees' salaries, as an expense.

- **Authoring**: An intranet is only as useful as the information it makes available. Your company should encourage each employee (possibly in some controlled way) to put information on the internal Web. When employees are authoring such information, they are not performing their regular tasks. You must count a cost, based on the employee's salary, as an expense.

- **Miscellaneous Hardware and Software:** During each year, you must make a budget allowance for anticipated and unexpected hardware and software expenses.

Create a spreadsheet for each year of your proforma analysis (assuming you are performing a multi-year projection) and include the above expenses. You may include additional expenses you deem appropriate. After you total the costs avoided, estimate the benefits of efficiencies created, and total the expenses incurred, you will have the information for the ROI numerator (net benefits):

Cost Avoided + Efficiencies Created - Cost Incurred(Including Depreciation) = Net Benefit

or

Saving + Revenue - Costs - Depreciation = Net Income

INTRANET INVESTMENT: THE *ROI* DENOMINATOR

An intranet investment consists primarily of hardware and software. This discussion assumes that the company has an existing network. While there may be some debate as to whether each piece of software is needed or whether the hardware is sufficient, your goal is to include everything reasonable in order to determine the most reliable ROI. Each company situation is different. In fact, some companies may have enough surplus equipment to start a small intranet with no hardware costs and can then download free software from Internet sites. While this is possible, a full analysis using retail prices is the most honest approach to calculating an ROI. The investment costs for an intranet include:

- **Pre-Installation Planning**: The company should formulate a cross-functional team to design the intranet and its uses. While these team members are defining the intranet plans, they are not accomplishing their regular assignments. You must count a cost, based on each employee's salary, as an expense.

- **Hardware:** The intranet will require at least one server computer with adequate hard disk space and speed to house the Web sites. Servers will require replacement or expansion during the life of the intranet. In addition, you may require additional servers which serve as security firewalls (See Chapter 19).

- **Software:** The intranet will require server software, as well as client software (browsers), firewall software, HTML-authoring tools, collaborative groupware, a document-management system, a search engine, and more, depending on your company's needs.

- **Installation:** The company must physically set up each server and install the proper software. Likewise, the company may need to install software on each user's system. One or more skilled technicians may spend many hours completing this work.

- **Depreciation:** As discussed, you must subtract an amount of depreciation from the investment each year.

To finalize your calculation of the ROI denominator, total the costs incurred for the original investment and any subsequent years and then subtract depreciation. Because of the volatility of hardware and software prices, you may want to consult a technician to determine your needs. Then, contact a vendor for current retail prices. In summary, you calculate the ROI denominator as follows:

$$Costs - Depreciation = Depreciated\ Investment\ Costs$$

SAMPLE *ROI* ANALYSES

By using hypothetical companies, the following examples detail a ROI analysis. Each company is an electronics or technology industry. While both implementations may be small (100 and 500 employees), the numbers are analogous to a larger company installing an intranet for a single division or operating unit. Each company's intranet installation was projected over five years to analyze ROI trends. Many benefits and costs are projected to rise due to increased usage or five percent inflation. The results of each analysis are discussed in the last section of this chapter.

Scenario A–100 Employee Company

The first scenario profiles a company of 100 employees. A detailed explanation of each benefit or cost line-item follows its listing.

RIO Numerator

As you have learned, the ROI numerator represents the net benefits of the intranet deployment. The following 10 items are a combination of costs avoided, efficiencies created, and expenses incurred that result in the ROI numerator for a 100 employee company intranet installation. Refer to Figure 15.3 as you read these items to further understand their function.

B	C (% of Co.)	D (Salary/Hr.)	J (Year 1)	L (Year 2)	N (Year 3)	P (Year 4)	R (Year 5)	T
Annual Savings	% of Co.	Salary/Hr.	Year 1	Year 2	Year 3	Year 4	Year 5	
Salary - Executives	10%	$56.17	29,208	46,004	64,407	84,539	106,517	
Salary - HR	2%	$21.11	2,195	3,457	4,840	6,354	8,006	
Salary - Marketing	10%	$23.99	12,475	19,648	27,508	36,101	45,490	
Salary - MIS	10	$20.63	10,728	16,895	23,650	31,044	39,125	
Salary - Engineering	20	$26.39	27,446	43,228	60,528	79,430	100,090	
Salary - Secretarial	8	$14.89	6,194	9,759	13,661	17,930	22,589	
Salary - Production (50%)	20	$12.86	13,374	17,550	22,105	23,213	24,383	Total Annual
Communications savings			4,000	5,000	6,250	7,813	9,766	Savings
Total			105,620	161,541	222,950	286,423	355,964	1,132,499
Annual Expenses								
System administrator			25,000	26,250	55,125	57,881	60,775	
Application developer				26,250	27,563	57,881	60,775	
Administrator training			2,400	2,640	2,904	3,194	3,514	
User training costs			1,500	1,650	1,815	1,997	2,196	
Post-installation planning				3,938	4,134	4,341	4,558	
Salary Authoring costs - HR	20% of 2%		1,317	1,383	1,452	1,525	1,601	
Authoring costs - Marketing	20% of 10%		7,485	7,859	8,252	8,664	9,098	
Authoring costs 4 - MIS	20% of 10%		6,437	6,758	7,095	7,451	7,825	
Authoring costs 5 - Eng.	20% of 20%		16,467	17,291	18,158	19,063	20,018	
Misc. soft-/hardware			3,000	3,000	3,000	3,000	3,000	Total Annual
Depreciation			11,660	13,160	14,900	14,900	16,900	Expenses
Total			75,266	110,179	144,399	179,898	190,261	700,001

Sheet10 / Sheet11 / Sheet12 / Sheet13 / Sheet14 / Sheet15 / Sheet16

23

Figure 15.3 ROI numerator for the 100 employee company.

- **Salary Savings:** This item constitutes the money a company has saved by making employees more efficient through the use of the intranet. The company was divided into seven basic employee categories. The categories (executives, human resources, marketing, MIS, engineering, secretarial, and production) let the analysis attach percentages to the number of employees in each category. A national salary survey was used to find the average salary for a worker in each grouping. Next, an assumption was made as to the amount of time that the intranet might save each worker during a typical week. Finally, these factors were multiplied together to find the dollar value of time saved for the company during a given year. The equation is as follows:

Percent of Company x Number of Employees x Hourly Salary x
Number of Hours Saved Per Week x 52 weeks

For Executives in the first year, the savings was

$$Year\ 1 = (10\% \times 100) \times (\$56.17 \times 1) \times 52 = \$29,208$$

An alternate process, though possibly less precise, is to take the company's actual salary expenditures and divide by the number of employees to find a per employee average wage. You can then use this average wage with the average time saved.

In both Scenario A and B, all categories except that of production workers are projected to save one hour per week (or 12 minutes per day) throughout the first year. In each successive year, employees are assumed to find the intranet more useful, and therefore save more time. As such, the analysis increases the time savings by one-half hour per week to a total of three hours per week in year five.

As for production workers, the analysis assumes 50 percent will not use the intranet. Some production workers, assigned more manual duties, may not need to use the intranet frequently. Though ideally this is not true, it is a more conservative approach. The analysis calculates the production workers' intranet-generated time savings differently than it does for other workers. The analysis projects production workers would save 1.0 hour per week in year 1, 1.25 hours per week in year 2, and 1.5 hours per week in years 3 through 5. Since some production workers are not included in the analysis, there are actually 80 users in the 100 employee company and 390 workers in the 500 employee company.

- **Communications Savings:** This number represents an amount of money the company will save on printed material, travel, telephone, and courier costs per employee during the year. While this number is difficult to put in such simple terms, you must determine a more accurate estimate on a case-by-case basis. For the purposes of this analysis, a modest figure of $50 per person was chosen with that amount rising by 25 percent per year.

- **System Administrator Costs:** At an annual salary of $50,000 per year, years 1 and 2 are allocated a part-time administrator. Years 3 through 5 use a full-time administrator.

- **Application Administrator/Developer:** At an annual salary of $50,000 per year, years 2 and 3 are allocated a half-time developer. Years 4 and 5 use a full-time developer.

- **Administrator/Developer Training:** Training is estimated at $100 per person per month rising at 10 percent per year.

- **User Training Costs:** In a classroom, 10 users receive two hours of instruction. Instructor costs are estimated at $150 per class. All users receive two hours of classroom experience each year. Average cost per user is $15.

- **Post-Installation Planning Costs:** Estimates are based on a team of five, working 15 hours each. Estimated hourly salary cost of $50 per person.

- **Salary Authoring Costs:** The analysis estimates these costs in the same way as it estimates salary savings, substituting the number of hours spent for the number of hours saved.

- **Miscellaneous Hardware and Software:** Unplanned equipment and software needs are estimated at $3,000 per year.

- **Depreciation:** Multiply each previous year's total investment by 0.5 (50 percent) because of the rapid rate of replacement for high-tech equipment.

ROI DENOMINATOR

The ROI denominator represents the net investment of the intranet deployment. The following 14 items are a combination of investment costs incurred and depreciation that result in the ROI denominator for a 100 employee company intranet installation. Refer to Figure 15.4 as you read these items to further understand their function.

Investment Expenses	Initial Investment	Year 1	Year 2	Year 3	Year 4	Year 5	Total Investment Expenses
Pre-installation planning costs	5,000						
Server	3,000						
Server software	1,000						
Client software	3,920						
Installation costs	3,800						
Additional/replacement servers			6,000		9,000		
HTML authoring software		1,200	1,200	1,200	1,200	1,200	
Intranet software updates			6,900		7,900		
Collaborative software		1,800		1,800		1,800	
Database connectivity tools	400						
Doc. management system			6,500		6,500		
Search tools	4,500		4,500		4,500		
Firewall server							
Firewall software	1,700		1,700		1,700		
Total	23,320	3,000	26,800	3,000	30,800	3,000	89,920
Net Savings		30,354	51,363	78,551	106,526	165,703	
Depreciated Investment Costs		14,660	28,300	16,400	32,300	18,400	
Yearly ROI		207%	181%	479%	330%	901%	393%

Figure 15.4 ROI denominator for Scenario A.

- **Pre-Installation Planning:** Estimates are based on a team of five working 20 hours each, with an average hourly salary of $50 per person. Net $5,000.

- **Server:** Estimate is based on a Pentium NT 200Hz, 32Mb RAM, 2Gb SCSI hard drive at $3,000.

- **Server Software:** The Web server software is estimated to cost $1,000.

- **Client Software:** The Netscape *Navigator* browser is estimated at $49 per desktop.

- **Installation:** The estimate is based on 40 hours at $95 per hour (an average of three client installations per hour plus the server installation).

- **Additional/Replacement Servers:** Year 2: Replace original server PC and purchase one additional. Year 4: Replace both server PCs and purchase an additional one. Use original price as a basis, though technology innovations promise higher performance units.

- **HTML Authoring Software:** Purchase software for 25 percent of desktops each year beginning in Year 2. Cost is estimated at $60 per copy.

- **Intranet Software Upgrades:** Replacement software for each server and client in years 2 and 4. Estimates are based on original prices of $1,000 and $49.

- **Collaborative Software:** Estimated at $1,800 to be purchased in years 1, 3, and 5.

- **Database Connectivity Tools:** Estimated at $400.

- **Document-Management System:** Estimated at $6,500, to be purchased in years 2 and 4.

- **Search Engine:** Estimated at $4,500 to be purchased in years 1, 3, and 5.

- **Firewall Server and Software:** Because the application is relatively small, no separate server is required. Firewall software can run on the Web servers and is estimated to cost $1,700. Software should be replaced in years 2 and 4.

- **Depreciation:** As already discussed, the amount of depreciation is subtracted from the investment each year. Given the rapid rate of replacement and technical innovation, the total investment is depreciated 50 percent per year. The denominator of the ROI formula is then 0.5 times the previous year's total investment plus the current year's total investment. Although different interpretations (especially by accountants) as to the finer details of calculating depreciation may exist, the most important point is to consistently follow a basic convention such as the one just described.

SCENARIO B – 500 EMPLOYEE COMPANY

Scenario B is a company of 500 employees. The analysis of the benefit and cost line items are the same as those previously discussed, although the analysis has made adjustments for the larger number of users. The ROI formula for the 500 employee company is calculated exactly the same as was done for the 100 employee company. For this reason, these costs are explained in less detail below.

ROI NUMERATOR

As you have learned, the ROI numerator represents the net benefits of the intranet deployment. The following ten items are a combination of costs avoided, efficiencies created, and expenses incurred that result in the ROI numerator for a 500 employee company intranet installation. Refer to Figure 15.5 as you read these items to further understand their function.

Intranet ROI

	B	C	D	J	L	N	P	R	T
2	**Annual Savings**	% of Co.	Salary/Hr.	**Year 1**	**Year 2**	**Year 3**	**Year 4**	**Year 5**	
3	Salary - Executives	3%	$56.17	**43,813**	69,007	96,611	126,809	159,775	
4	Salary - HR	1%	$21.11	5,489	8,642	12,100	15,886	20,015	
5	Salary - Marketing	12%	$23.99	74,849	117,889	165,048	216,606	272,938	
6	Salary - MIS	10%	$20.63	53,638	84,474	118,248	155,220	195,624	
7	Salary - Engineering	15%	$26.39	102,921	162,104	226,980	297,863	375,336	
8	Salary - Secretarial	4%	$14.89	15,486	24,398	34,154	44,824	56,472	Total
9	Salary - Production (50%)	28%	$12.86	93,621	122,850	154,736	162,490	170,680	Annual
10	Communications savings			19,500	24,375	30,469	38,086	47,607	Savings
11	**Total**			**409,315**	**613,739**	**838,346**	**1,057,783**	**1,298,447**	4,217,630
12	**Annual Expenses**								
13	System administrator			50,000	52,500	55,125	57,881	60,775	
14	Application developer			0	26,250	55,125	57,881	60,775	
15	Administrator training			2,400	5,280	5,808	6,389	7,028	
16	User training costs			5,850	6,435	7,079	7,786	8,565	
17	Post-installation planning			0	7,875	8,269	8,682	9,116	
18	Salary Authoring costs - HR	20% of 1%		3,293	3,457	3,630	3,813	4,003	
19	Authoring costs - Marketing	20% of 12%		44,909	47,156	49,514	51,985	54,588	
20	Authoring costs 4 - MIS	20% of 10%		32,183	33,790	35,474	37,253	39,125	
21	Authoring costs 5 - Eng.	20% of 15%		61,753	64,841	68,094	71,487	75,067	Total
22	Misc. soft-/hardware			6,000	6,000	6,000	6,000	6,000	Annual
23	Depreciation			35,980	39,805	33,655	33,655	38,655	Savings
24	**Total**			**242,368**	**293,389**	**327,773**	**342,813**	**363,697**	1,570,039

Sheet7 / Sheet8 / Sheet9 / Sheet10 / Sheet11 / Sheet12 / Sheet13 / She

Figure 15.5 ROI numerator for the 500 employee company.

- **Salary Savings:** In a company of 500 employees, the number of personnel within each classification is different. For instance, the company of 100 has 10 percent of its employees in the offices while the company of 500 has only 3 percent.
- **Communications Savings:** For the purposes of this analysis, a modest figure of $50 per person was chosen. That amount rises by 25 percent per year.
- **System Administrator Costs:** Annual salary of $50,000 per year.
- **Application Administrator/Developer:** At an annual salary of $50,000 per year, year 2 is allocated a half-time developer. Years 3 through 5 use a full-time developer.
- **Administrator/Developer training:** Estimated at $100 per person per month, rising at 10 percent per year.
- **User Training Costs:** Average cost per user is $15.
- **Post-Installation Planning Costs:** Estimates are based on a team of 10 people working 15 hours each. Estimated hourly salary cost of $50 per person.
- **Salary Authoring Costs:** These costs are calculated in the same way as salary savings were previously calculated. Simply substitute the number of hours spent for number of hours saved.
- **Miscellaneous Hardware and Software:** The analysis estimates unplanned equipment and software needs at $6,000 per year.
- **Depreciation:** Multiply each previous year's total investment by 0.5 (50 percent) to depreciate the investment because of the rapid rate of replacement for high-tech equipment.

ROI Denominator

The ROI denominator represents the net investment of the intranet deployment. The following 14 items are a combination of investment costs incurred and depreciation that result in the ROI denominator for a 500 employee company intranet installation. Refer to Figure 15.6 as you read these items to further understand their function.

	B	I	J	L	N	P	R	T	U
25			Year 1	Year 2	Year 3	Year 4	Year 5		
26	**Investment Expenses**	**Initial Investment**							
27	Pre-installation planning costs	20,000							
28	Server	9,000							
29	Server software	1,000							
30	Client software	19,110							
31	Installation costs	14,250							
32	Additional/replacement servers			18,000		27,000			
33	HTML authoring software		5,850	5,850	5,850	5,850	5,850		
34	Intranet software updates			21,110		22,110			
35	Collaborative software		1,800		1,800				
36	Database connectivity tools	400							
37	Doc. management system			6,500		6,500			
38	Search tools	4,500		4,500		4,500			
39	Firewall server	2,000		2,000		2,000		Total Investment	
40	Firewall software	1,700		1,700		1,700		Expenses	
41	Total	71,960	7,650	59,660	7,650	69,660	5,850	222,430	
43	*Net Savings*		166,948	320,350	510,573	714,970	934,750		
44	*Depreciated Investment Costs*		43,830	63,485	37,480	73,485	40,680	Ave. ROI	
46	*Yearly ROI*		383%	505%	1362%	973%	2298%	1023%	

Figure 15.6 ROI denominator for the 500 employee company.

- **Pre-Installation Planning:** Estimates are based on a team of 10 working 40 hours each, with an average hourly salary of $50 per person.

- **Server:** Pentium Pro NT 200Hz, 128Mb DRAM, 8Gb SCSI hard drive with RAID technology estimated to cost $9,000.

- **Server Software:** Web Server estimated to cost $1,000.

- **Client Software:** The Netscape *Navigator* browser estimated at $49 per desktop.

- **Installation:** The estimate is based on 150 hours at $95 per hour (average three client installations per hour plus the server installation).

- **Additional/Replacement Servers:** Year 2: Replace original server and purchase one additional. Year 4: Replace both servers and purchase an additional one. Use original price as a basis, though technology innovations promise higher performance units.

- **HTML Authoring Software:** Purchase software for 25 percent of desktops each year beginning in year 2. Cost is estimated at $60 per copy.

- **Intranet Software Upgrades:** The estimate is based on replacement software for each server and client in years 2 and 4. Original prices of $1,000 and $49.

- **Collaborative Software:** Estimated at $1,800 to be purchased in years 1, 3, and 5.

- **Database Connectivity Tools:** Estimated at $400.

- **Document Management System:** Estimated at $6,500 to be purchased in years 2 and 4.

- **Search Engine:** Estimated at $4,500 to be purchased in year 1, 3, and 5.

- **Firewall Server and Software:** Firewall servers estimated to cost $2,000 are purchased in years 1, 3, and 5. Firewall software is estimated to cost $1,700 in the same three years.

- **Depreciation:** Calculated as above.

THE RESULTS

It is hard to categorize the results shown in Scenario A and B in any other way than extraordinary! From a low of around 200 percent to an ROI of over 2,000 percent, an intranet promises to be an incredibly productive tool. Table 15.5 summarizes the results of the ROI analyses.

	Yr. 1	Yr. 2	Yr. 3	Yr. 4	Yr. 5
Company of 100	207%	181%	479%	330%	901%
Company of 500	383%	505%	1,362%	973%	2,298%

Table 15.5 *Results of proforma ROI analyses.*

This basic, but powerful, method used to calculate the intranet's financial merit indicates highly positive rewards. You can make a very strong case for the potential returns from intranet use. When you consider the enormous rewards that companies can obtain from putting efficiencies to good use (an area that was only estimated to be worth a proportion of an employee's salary), even greater returns are possible. Also, since many companies are familiar with computer technology and may have Information Systems resources available, companies may further reduce numerous costs. Figure 15.7 depicts the result of ROI analyses graphically.

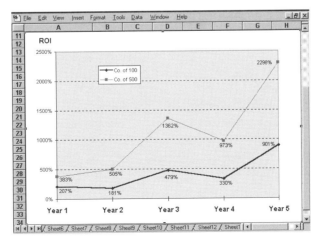

Figure 15.7 *Graphical representation intranet ROI analysis.*

REAL-WORLD ROIs

Across the Web, companies are experiencing huge returns on their intranet investments. In fact, most companies find that within 10 to 12 weeks they have fully covered their costs! The site *http://cgi.netscape.com/cgi-bin/roi_reg.cgi* discusses the returns several companies have experienced on their intranet investments, as shown in Figures 15.8a through 15.8d.

Figure 15.8a *Cadence Designs Systems, Inc. 1,766%.*

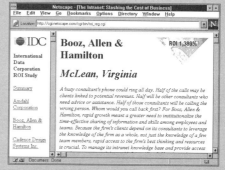

Figure 15.8b *Booz, Allen & Hamilton 1,389%.*

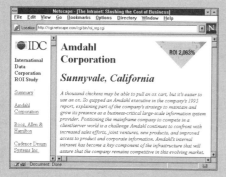

Figure 15.8c *Amdahl Corporation 2,063%.*

Figure 15.8d *Silicon Graphics, Inc. 1,427%.*

PUTTING IT ALL TOGETHER

An intranet is an extremely useful tool for business. As industries move to obtain sustainable competitive advantages through the control of resources, and the management of information, the intranet remains a cost effective information technology solution. Any enterprise considering various technologies to increase internal connectivity must consider the intranet as a low-cost undertaking with high-return potential.

This chapter's ROI analysis for intranets indicates a high rate of return for the use of this technology. You may argue that this chapter makes many assumptions. However, the basic premise still holds regarding fundamental benefits of intranets. Even if you argue that the ROI analyses are off by a factor of 10, the intranet's ROI still results in 20 to 200 percent increases. In Chapter 16, you will learn about the basic components and benefits of integrated groupware products such as Lotus *Notes*. As you read through Chapter 16, remember that concepts you learned in this chapter apply to the deployment of other information technologies as well. Before you continue with Chapter 16, however, make sure you understand the following key concepts:

327

✓ An intranet enhances existing computer architecture, allowing a local- or wide-area network to perform better than before.

✓ Intranets reduce costs, enhance productivity, and promote information exchange—three universal success factors.

✓ Intranets have proven themselves as a valuable business tool and will continue to do so in the future.

✓ Depending on their size and intranet use, companies should expect an intranet to generate an ROI between 200 and 2,000 percent.

✓ Because an intranet is only as useful as the information it makes available, businesses must promote the widespread use of their intranet resources.

✓ To maximize the use of their intranet, companies must encourage employees to use the intranet as a daily tool, and not simply for an occasional reference.

✓ When businesses with sustainable competitive advantages implement intranets to manage information and its human capital, they will find the intranet magnifies these advantages.

VISITING KEY SITES THAT DISCUSS INTRANETS

The World Wide Web is filled with hundreds of excellent and current articles on all aspects of intranets. Use the following sites as starting points for your Web exploration.

INTERNET IT INFORMER

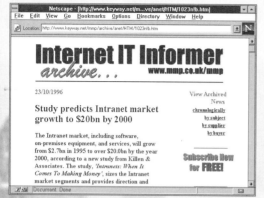

*http://www.keyway.net/mmp/archive/anet/—
HTM/1023n!b.htm*

ROI REPORTACCESS

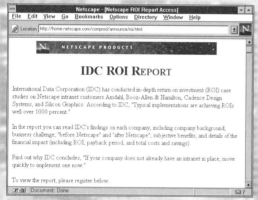

*http://home.netscape.com/comprod/announce—
/roi.html*

INTRANET DESIGN & DEPLOYMENT

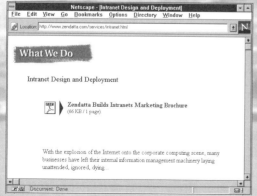

http://www.zendatta.com/services/intranet.html

INTERNET MARKETING DISCUSSION

*http://www.i-m.com/i-m/hyper/inet—
markrting-archive/0012.html*

CASH IN ON THE INTRANET EXPLOSION

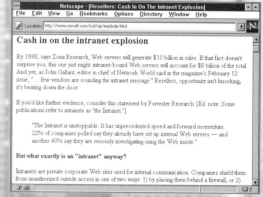

http://www.novell.com/icd/nip/explode.html

INTECO

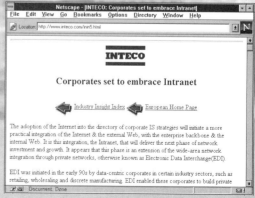

http://www.inteco.com/inin5.html

Chapter 16

Intranets Versus Groupware

329

As you have learned in previous chapters, intranets are groupware solutions based on the Internet's open standards. It is important for you to understand that the intranet model of group collaboration is not new. Since 1989, Lotus *Notes*, from Lotus Corporation (which is now a subsidiary of IBM), has set the standard for information sharing and collaboration within organizations. *Notes* is a proprietary client-server software program that supports group-communication, e-mail, group discussion, database replication, and an application development environment. Currently, *Notes* is under attack by a host of intranet solutions that are ready to challenge its market dominance. Today, stock analysts wrestle with the question of whether or not the $3.3 billion that IBM paid to acquire *Notes* was money well spent. The answer to their question depends on whether *Notes* can satisfy the information sharing needs of corporations around the globe.

Before you start your intranet deployment, you should know what features Lotus *Notes* has to offer. To many people, the debate over *Notes* versus intranets sounds much like the debate over Macs and PCs. Proponents of each technology want you to believe that the competing system does not have a chance of dominating the market. But as you will learn in this chapter, the future holds room for *Notes* and a variety of groupware products. Someday, you might even find yourself using a software program titled something like *IntraNotes*: a software product based on a marriage between intranets and *Notes*. This chapter examines Lotus *Notes* in detail. By the time you finish this chapter, you will understand the following key concepts:

- Lotus *Notes* has been under development for over 11 years and has more than 3 million licensed users.

- Lotus *Notes* provides a highly-integrated environment with high-end, proven groupware products.

- Lotus *Notes* provides an easy way to create, add, and search information stored in its proprietary database.

- When you compare Lotus *Notes* and intranets, you will find that both have distinct advantages and disadvantages.

- To support open standards, Lotus *Notes* is changing its future strategy to move away from its proprietary technologies.

- There are other groupware products, such as Microsoft *Exchange*, that compete with Lotus *Notes* and other intranet products.

- In the future, the question will be not whether Lotus *Notes* will survive but, rather, how Lotus *Notes* and intranets can learn to coexist.

GETTING TO KNOW LOTUS NOTES

In 1985, Lotus Corporation began developing Lotus *Notes* (or simply, *Notes*). After its introduction in 1989, *Notes* quickly received rave reviews from companies that needed a software product to bring groups of people together, electronically. *Groupware* is software that lets groups of people share information within an enterprise. Currently, *Notes* is the industry's dominant client-server groupware product. As shown in Figure 16.1, Lotus designed *Notes* to manage information for groups of people targeting *Notes* as an information manager. *Notes* manages corporate information by collecting and storing it in central storage locations called servers.

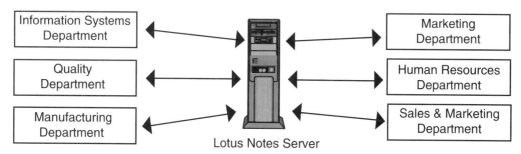

Figure 16.1 Lotus Notes provides access to many groups of people.

Notes provides clients with software for e-mail, discussion groups, workflow management, electronic conferencing, and multilevel security in an integrated proprietary environment. (Lotus does not publish "open" protocols which makes it easier for other software developers to write programs that interact with *Notes*.) Like intranets, *Notes* users can access data across different computer platforms which include Windows, Mac, OS/2, and Unix. *Notes* works both on local- and wide-area networks. Over 1,000 third-party products are available for *Notes* from over 500 different independent *Notes* developers. Lotus *Notes* provides an integrated suite of applications that simplify content management.

LOTUS NOTES FEATURES

Notes provides a graphical user interface within which users can easily read, write, and create new database documents. The basic element of a *Notes* database is a document. A document may contain a variety of objects including text, spreadsheet data, and graphical images. For example, an e-mail message is a document. Lotus *Notes* lets users move their desktop spreadsheets and word processing files to a shared database. Each *Notes* database holds related sets of documents. Using its search function, *Notes* can easily search and retrieve information from within a database. The *Notes* database manages documents, unlike a traditional database organization which uses table-based data.

Notes supports the use of different types of databases, such as discussion databases and customer-tracking databases. In general, each group of related topics has its own database. For example, as shown in Figure 16.2, a company might place a product-specification database and a marketing database on the same server.

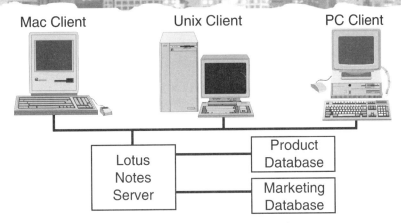

Figure 16.2 Two Lotus **Notes** databases on the same server.

Using forms (or templates), users place documents into a *Notes* database. After inserting data into the database, users then create views with which they display and organize the information. Users can sort database documents by date or topic. *Notes* provides a search utility with which users can easily find information. As shown in Figure 16.3, users may store documents in various databases that reside on different servers. In addition, users can also create local databases on their own local hard drive.

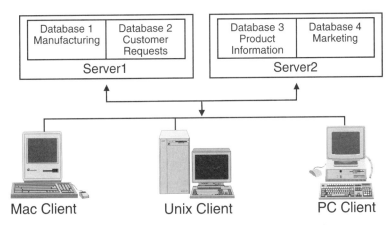

Figure 16.3 **Notes** supports multiple servers and databases.

FINDING INFORMATION IN A NOTES DATABASE

When a user opens a database, *Notes* will list the documents the database contains and will display a tag next to each unread document. Users can sort database documents by date or topic. As briefly discussed, *Notes* also provides a built-in search utility that lets users search database documents by content. *Notes* also lets users search multiple databases. Depending on a document's contents, users may need to move the document from one database to another, as shown in Figure 16.4. As you will learn, *Notes* provides the ability to automatically replicate information on multiple servers.

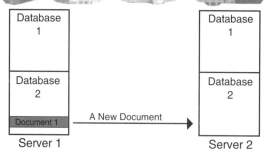

Figure 16.4 Notes makes it easy to transfer documents from one database to another.

CREATING DOCUMENTS IN NOTES

To create (and edit) a database document in *Notes*, you use a *form* to compose the document's contents. In *Notes*, a form is a template that displays document information in a specific way. A form contains a number of fields. Composing a document within *Notes* is similar to writing an e-mail message. You fill out a form, and then place text, objects, tables, and graphics within the body of the form. A *Notes* document may also contain icons that link one document to another document—much like an HTML hyperlink. You can also attach an object to a document or embed the data as an OLE object. As you will learn, OLE objects let you include data objects (such as audio clips or spreadsheet data and graphs) within a document. For example, using OLE, a user might integrate a presentation the user created using Lotus *Freelance*, a presentation software package similar to *PowerPoint*, within a *Notes* document. By making the document available to other users, each of the company's sales staff can access a database to get the latest sales presentation.

UNDERSTANDING OLE

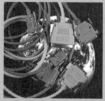

OLE (object linking and embedding) is a technology developed by Microsoft to provide a standard way for programs to include information within documents. Technically, OLE defines a set of specific rules (or protocols) that programs use to link or embed an object, such as a spreadsheet graph within another document, or a word processing document. For more information on OLE, visit the site at *http://www.r2m.com/windev/OLE.html*, shown in Figure 16.5.

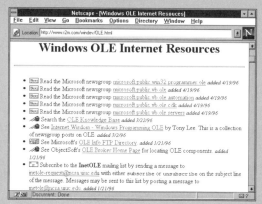

Figure 16.5 Information on object linking and embedding.

USING NOTES E-MAIL

Besides letting users share information via databases, *Notes* lets users exchange information using its integrated e-mail capability. Lotus *Notes* provides users with the ability to direct the flow of an e-mail automatically and, hence, to create a workflow system. As you have learned, a *workflow system* routes information electronically from one worker to the next. For example, one employee might create a document that requests travel approval. At the top of the document, the employee can place the name of everyone who must approve travel. *Notes* can route the e-mail message from one user to the next (within the intranet or to a user on the Internet) until each user on the approval list has approved or declined the travel.

REMOTE ACCESS AND DATABASE REPLICATION

As you have learned, as employees travel (or if employees work outside the company), they need a way to access the company's internal networks. In the case of an intranet, a remote employee can access the network through an Internet firewall. As shown in Figure 16.6, Lotus *Notes* users can access a *Notes* server using a modem and a phone line.

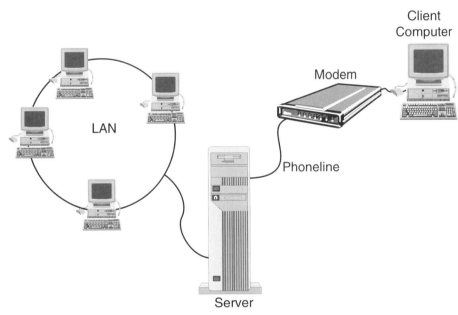

*Figure 16.6 Remote access to a **Notes** server.*

After a remote user connects to a *Notes* server, the user might place a replica (copy) of the database on a local hard drive. In this way, the user is not continuously connected to the *Notes* server (possibly incurring long distance phone charges) while working. Using the *Notes* database replication feature, a user can work with a database replica on his or her system when away from the office. The next time the user connects to the network server, *Notes* will automatically synchronize the two database copies, and ensure that the changes a user makes in one database will appear in every other replica. Figure 16.7 illustrates the replication feature.

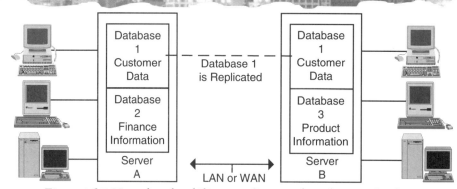

Figure 16.7 Notes has the ability to replicate and synchronize databases.

Rather than copying a complete database to their system, *Notes* lets users place only selected documents on local hard disks. To simplify this process, users can create a document that directs *Notes* to automatically call several servers and download specific information.

DESIGNING A DATABASE IN NOTES

As you have learned, *Notes* stores all user documents in databases. By sharing documents, users can employ a database as a discussion area. For example, a group of marketers might use database documents to discuss a new product marketing campaign. *Notes* databases not only contain the information that the users need, but also an interface which provides users with access to the information.

Unlike conventional databases, designing a *Notes* database is fast and easy. *Notes* lets authorized users design and customize databases to meet their specific needs. To help users design databases, *Notes* provides many database templates which give users a good starting point for developing a database. These database templates provide a skeleton which does not contain any documents, but does have built-in fields.

Each *Notes* database uses one or more forms, each of which specifies a document template. For example, a discussion-group database might use a main-topic form, a response form, and a reply-to-response form. Users can easily modify these standard forms to add additional fields. For example, using the discussion main-topic form, a user might add a Vote field, which recipients could use to vote on a new marketing campaign. As shown in Figure 16.8, a *Notes* document can contain many custom features.

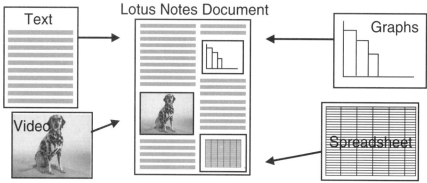

*Figure 16.8 You can customize your **Notes** document to meet your requirements.*

Users do not have to be on a *Notes* server to design your database. Instead, users can design database on their own local machines and later place the databases on a *Notes* server. Users can only use a database if they have access. As you will learn, *Notes* provides multilevel security.

NOTES' SECURITY FEATURES

Notes supports multiple levels of security which lets you fine-tune your database access. Most companies have multiple organizations with specific security needs. For example, if you are a Human Resource manager and have just started an electronic newsletter on your intranet, you may not want other employees to add content to your newsletter. You will, however, want all employees to be able to read the newsletter.

Notes lets database administrators restrict databases to certain groups or individuals. Before a user can login to a *Notes* server and access documents, the user must obtain a *Notes* ID. Later, when the user tries to access documents, *Notes* uses the ID to verify the user has access to the database. *Notes* provides the following security levels:

- **Manager Level**: *Notes* lets manager-level users create a database and add or delete other users from the database's access control list (the list that tells *Notes* which users can access the database and each user's level of access).

- **Designer Level**: *Notes* lets designer-level users modify the database layout. For example, a designer-level user might add fields to a database form.

- **Editor Level**: *Notes* lets editor-level users create, read, and update database contents.

- **Author Level**: *Notes* lets author-level users read and modify the contents of existing documents, but does not allow author-level users to create new documents.

- **Reader Level**: *Notes* lets reader-level users read database documents.

- **Depositor Level**: *Notes* lets depositor-level users place documents within a database.

Notes multilevel security feature is one of its strongest features. A large number of organizations have used *Notes* successfully to protect very sensitive data. In contrast, good security for an intranet, although attainable, can be very difficult to set up properly. When new network designers add new components to an intranet, such as a new server or new home pages, the designers must revalidate the intranet's security to ensure they have not introduced a hole or back door into the intranet. With *Notes*, users specifically indicate their desired security level which leaves much less to chance. The next section covers other differences between *Notes* and intranet-based solutions in greater detail.

NOTES VERSUS INTRANETS

Rarely a day goes by without someone writing about intranets and their effect on *Notes*. Today, the big question for those using or considering *Notes* is whether intranet technology will replace *Notes*. As it turns out, replacing *Notes* is perhaps too strong a proposition. In the history of technological breakthroughs, only a few new innovations have effectively replaced an older technology. Moreover, Lotus *Notes* is a perfect solution for many users. But for many others, an intranet-based implementation may be more ideal. In the following sections, you will learn how to determine whether an intranet or *Notes* will best meet your needs. For an excellent article regarding Notes and intranets, visit *http://WWW.LOTUS.COM/corpcomm/29a6.htm*, as shown in Figure 16.9.

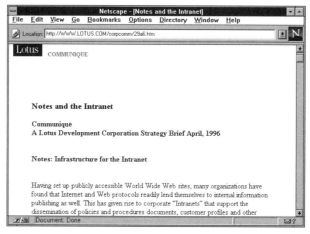

Figure 16.9 An excellent article on Notes and intranets.

ADVANTAGES OF NOTES OVER INTRANETS

In the past seven years, *Notes* has done a great job of providing organizations with a framework for transforming their traditional organizational structure into a network-based structure. Today, intranets are transforming the masses. The advantages of *Notes* over internally developed intranets are:

- Unlike intranets, *Notes* tracks document revisions automatically. In contrast, most intranets pass the task of revising and maintaining documents to the user. In some organizations, each department assigns one team member the task of updating and maintaining document revisions. Even with this approach, keeping track of thousands of documents on an intranet can be quite challenging.

- *Notes'* multilevel security feature is better than intranet-based packages on the market. You must weigh these security features heavily when you decide whether to use *Notes* or an intranet. If departments want levels of document security, you may find current intranet products don't quite meet your needs.

- *Notes* provides users with the ability to design new databases quickly.

- *Notes* has a suite of ready-to-run workflow tools.

- *Notes* replicates and synchronizes the content of different databases, which is extremely useful for people who must frequently work on the road. Currently, there are few intranet products in the market that can do this.

- Managing content under *Notes* is easy.

- If you must have each of the *Notes* features on your intranet, your Webmaster must either develop similar features or buy multiple products. Your Webmaster may have a difficult time integrating the various products to produce a comparable intranet product.

- *Notes* is a mature product. Lotus has spent over a decade developing and perfecting *Notes*, and now IBM's money is backing its continued development.

As the old saying goes, you do not get anything for free. Lotus has spent years perfecting *Notes* features. IBM paid $3.3 billion dollars for *Notes*, which makes it a pretty safe bet that customers won't see free versions of *Notes* on the Web. But, a similar old saying reminds us that you get what you pay for and, in the case of Notes, you are paying for some outstanding features. The following section examines advantages intranets provide over *Notes*.

Advantages of Intranets over Notes

Just as *Notes* provides several advantages over intranets, *Notes* is not without its disadvantages. The following list briefly summarizes several advantages that intranets hold over *Notes*.

- *Notes* is expensive. As you know, you can get Web browsers for free, or for a very low price (less than $40 per client). *Notes Express* costs about $100 per client, and a full version of *Notes* costs around $200.

- Selecting *Notes* locks your company into the Lotus/IBM proprietary technology—which, to many, is a very significant disadvantage.

- To develop applications under *Notes*, your programmers must use a *Notes* database and convert your existing legacy applications.

- Intranet technologies are improving and changing much faster than *Notes*. Currently, a "virtual army" of programmers are developing software for intranets. With *Notes*, you have only IBM.

- When you use *Notes*, you tie your company to one company's view of groupware. With an intranet, you can select any combination of vendor products that meet your needs.

- Intranets are scaleable, which means after you set up your intranet, you can add more features without much difficulty or cost. *Notes*, on the other hand, may prove harder to scale because it offers fewer software solutions.

Cost of Notes

Notes server software costs about $600, with client copies ranging from $55 to $225 (for the full client software, which includes the application development environment). An intranet Web server, however, costs about $300 with mostly free client software.

338

In most cases, the initial investment *Notes* requires is not the factor that moves companies towards intranet-based solutions. The real factor is the hidden cost of training and application development. To traverse an intranet, most employees can use the same techniques they use to surf the Web. Therefore, intranet users require little training, which is not the case for *Notes* users.

Training programmers and developers to support *Notes* is another major issue companies must face. For example, to convert a company's legacy systems to *Notes*, a company must hire people who are familiar with the *Notes* implementation. *Notes* developers are in demand and, consequently, can charge higher than average rates for their services. Your current Information Systems department may not be able to develop *Notes'* applications without receiving training themselves. Therefore, you must either hire outside consultants or train your own programmers.

Using Internet technology, intranet programmers can use an open-standard architecture. Therefore, the knowledge they gain from one project is often applicable to a wide range of company needs. Also, as you look for programmers and developers, you will find a much larger group already conversant with Internet applications who can provide your company with intranet-based solutions.

As you have learned, calculating your return on investment (ROI) for your use of information technology is not as easy as it sounds. The debate over the cost of *Notes* versus intranets will only increase over the next few years. There are, however, signs that intranets are already forcing Lotus to lower the cost of *Notes'* clients and servers.

You may want to look at a study done by the Lotus corporation on the issue of cost of ownership for *Notes* versus intranets. The Lotus study, which surveyed 100 information-technology managers who were deploying intranet applications, concludes that implementation of Lotus *Notes* applications takes less time than intranets and that intranets must improve their collaboration facilities. You can find this study at *http://parter.netscape.com/comprod/at_work/press_clippings/computer_world_2.html*, as shown in Figure 16.10.

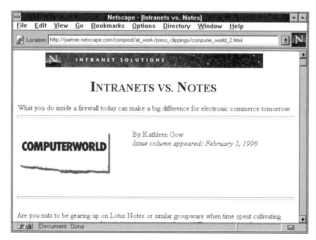

Figure 16.10 The cost of Notes versus intranets.

CHOOSING NOTES OR AN INTRANET

In reality, comparing *Notes* and intranets is much like comparing apples and oranges. *Notes* and intranets complement one another. Unfortunately, based on costs, you must probably choose one or the other. Which of these two technologies you should deploy in your organization depends upon your needs. *Notes* is a mature product that offers an outstanding integrated set of tools. Intranets are based on the open standard of the Internet. You have to assess your needs before committing to either of these solutions.

Notes is well suited to support workflow-based applications as well as collaboration among a small group. On the other hand, intranets provide good solutions for bringing information to the masses. If the members of an organization have to communicate with people in other parts of the world, there is a good chance that not everyone uses *Notes* clients.

Both *Notes* and intranets are based on the client–server model and provide users with the ability to link related documents. If you need an information browsing tool, intranets are the best and the least expensive alternative. Intranets will let you provide browsing capabilities to your organization via products most users already know how to use. If you have a specific and focused application development tool, intranets are the clear choice. If you need an integrated data-management system, then *Notes* is a better choice.

Lotus is a complete proprietary architecture that provides you with a set of tools which could prove difficult to implement within an intranet environment. Companies that need only e-mail and access to discussion group databases can buy a low-end version of *Notes*, but clients will lose the real benefit of full-fledged *Notes*.

CRITERIA FOR SELECTING LOTUS NOTES

As you evaluate your company's information sharing needs, you might lean toward implementing a Lotus *Notes* solution based on the following criteria:

- You need a highly-integrated tool.

- You need multiple levels of security.

- You need support for database replication.

- You need support for workflow processing.

- You must limit data management and application support to only a few people in the organization.

- You need a complex document-management system.

CRITERIA FOR SELECTING AN INTRANET

As you evaluate your company's information sharing needs, you might lean toward implementing an *intranet* solution based on the following criteria:

- You must electronically publish and distribute documents.

- Document creation and maintenance occurs within various organizations spread throughout your company.

- The Web's e-mail and conferencing tools currently satisfy your collaboration needs.

- Your users must be in charge of their own document management—which consists primarily of "unofficial" documents.

- Your applications require that you develop sophisticated custom intranet applications.

- You can wait for advanced intranet solutions to come to the market.

LOOKING AT THE FUTURE OF LOTUS NOTES

If Lotus *Notes* does not dominate the groupware-application market, its proprietary architecture could lose against the open standard of intranets. However, *Notes* is becoming more Web-like. Lotus has finally acknowledged that the future belongs to open systems. The new *InterNotes Web Publisher*, which is an integral part of *Notes Release 4*, will provide *Notes* users with the ability to automatically communicate to *Notes* servers using a Web browser. In addition, *InterNotes Web Publisher* lets current *Notes* users translate their *Notes* documents to Web pages. The software converts table, text, and images to HyperText documents while preserving the *Notes* hyperlinks. The key features of *InterNotes Web Publisher* include:

- Using a Web browser, users can fill out *Notes* documents and forms and submit them to a *Notes* database.

- *Internotes Web Publisher* automatically converts *Notes* documents, forms, views, and attachments into HTML.

- Users can use their Web browser to search *Notes'* databases.

- *Internotes Web Publisher* supports Windows NT, Windows 95, and the OS/2 platforms.

Lotus has also released its *InterNotes News Note* server application, which lets *Notes* users access intranet and Internet newsgroups from within *Notes* without having to run TCP/IP. For more information on *InterNotes Web Publisher*, visit *http:/www.internotes.lotus.com/*, as shown in Figure 16.11.

Figure 16.11 Information on InterNotes Web Publisher.

But Lotus is going even further to embrace the open standards of Internet technology and soon will offer a new server that supports the following Internet protocols: TCP/IP, HTTP, POP3, SMTP, and HTML. This server, named *Domino II*, will provide the replication capabilities of the current *Notes* server to intranet browsers. The server will also provide intranet developers with an integrated HTML publishing tool and database application capabilities. For more information on the *Domino II* server, visit *http://domino.lotus.com/*, as shown in Figure 16.12.

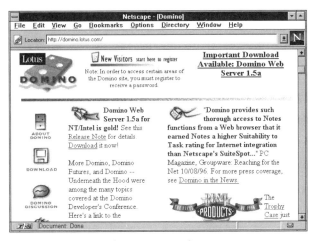

*Figure 16.12 Information on the **Domino II** server.*

Netscape and other Internet server developers will probably have servers that offer replication capability in 1997 or 1998. For now, the Lotus *Domino II* has a good lead over all existing servers. Netscape's acquisition of Collabra, a maker of groupware products, indicates Netscape's intention to capture the groupware market. For users, the result of competition among large software manufacturers is lower prices and more groupware products for their companies.

In the next few years, proprietary and open-system collaboration products will merge to provide users with a uniform, easy-to-use set of groupware solutions. At that time, if you are a *Notes* user, you will not need to panic and convert immediately to intranet solutions. Instead, both intranets and *Notes* will probably provide features that complement each other nicely. Today, your task is to review the checklists in the previous sections and pick the right technology for your needs. As you will learn in the next section, there are other groupware products that have several, but not all, of the features of Lotus *Notes*.

Other Groupware Products

Even though *Notes* has the dominant share of the proprietary groupware products, other groupware products in the market compete directly with *Notes* (and intranets). After Lotus released *Notes* in 1989, many companies soon realized the power of groupware products and set out to develop their own proprietary products. However, only a few such products have been able to compete with *Notes* and capture a small share of the proprietary-groupware market. Two of these products, *GroupWise* from Novell Corporation and *Exchange* from Microsoft, provide several *Notes*-like functions. The third product, *SAP*, provides sophisticated business application software plus workflow capabilities.

GROUPWISE FROM NOVELL CORPORATION

According to Novell, currently over five million *GroupWise* clients are installed worldwide. *GroupWise* is an integrated e-mail, calendar, group-scheduling, and task-management messaging system. *GroupWise* also includes support for basic workflow processing. *GroupWise* supports Windows, MS-DOS, Mac, and Unix clients. *GroupWise* clients can even run on an 80386/33Mhz IBM-compatible machine. Novell is positioning the latest version, *GroupWise XTD*, in the middle of full-featured e-mail communication products such as Microsoft *Exchange*, and full-fledged groupware products such as *Notes*. *GroupWise XTD* offers the following capabilities:

- Support for mail messages, group scheduling, task assignments, and phone messages.

- Native e-mail-based threaded discussion.

- Integrated document management.

- A graphical authoring tool with which users can define workflow routing.

- Full message tracking to help users monitor the progress of routed messages.

The proprietary architecture of *GroupWise*, like *Notes*, will come under heavy scrutiny from those that want to deploy their organizations with open systems. As the price of *Notes* continues to drop, *GroupWise* will have a difficult time competing.

EXCHANGE FROM MICROSOFT CORPORATION

Since the introduction of *Notes* in 1989, Microsoft has had difficulty coming out with a solid product to compete with *Notes*. However, with the release of Windows 95, Microsoft has built the first piece of its groupware solution. Microsoft *Exchange* is an e-mail system, built into the operating system, that can send and receive e-mail messages to LAN-based or Internet-based e-mail servers. This is a significant plus for *Exchange* users because these built-in e-mail features work just as well for the Internet as for an intranet. *Exchange* also provides users with the ability to automatically book meetings and manage appointments and tasks using the *Schedule+* group-scheduling and personal-calendar software. Figure 16.13 shows a screen shot of Microsoft *Schedule+*.

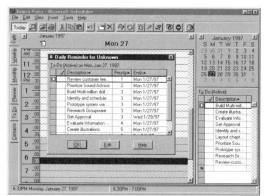

*Figure 16.13 A screen capture of Microsoft **Schedule+**.*

The growth of intranets is suddenly making Microsoft a very serious contender in the battle for groupware dominance. As you have learned in previous chapters, Microsoft has a broad offering of intranet products. In the future, Microsoft will integrate groupware features into its existing products. As a result, Microsoft will probably win the battle for enterprise groupware.

SAP AND INTRANETS

In the past few months, several articles in popular magazines have included groupware products, such as *Notes,* in their discussions of business applications, and software products such as SAP in their discussions of intranets. SAP is an integrated suite of client-server business-application products. A group of IBM software developers founded SAP (Systems, Applications, and Products in Data Processing) in 1972 in Waldorf, Germany. SAP currently holds more than 30 percent of the worldwide client–server enterprise applications software market. More than 6,000 companies in over 40 countries use different components of the SAP suite of software products. The primary use of this business-application software is for manufacturing, finance, sales and distribution, human resources, and documents. Figure 16.14 shows the different capabilities of SAP client-server business software applications.

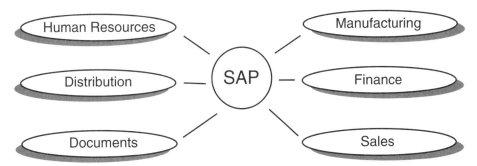

Figure 16.14 Components of SAP.

In several popular business journals, experts have predicted business application software makers will also come under the attack of intranets. However, as you have learned in previous chapters, the primary use of intranets today is the distribution of content. Most intranets are not yet sophisticated enough to take on the mission-critical applications of large companies. Software from companies such as SAP and Oracle Corporation provide high-end business application client–server software. SAP runs on both Unix and NT machines, using commercially available databases like those from companies such as Oracle and Informix.

In addition, there are still many factors that benefit the legacy mission-critical programs that have been developed by IBM, Digital, and SAP. These legacy business application systems can handle large numbers of transactions per second, and they have reliable hardware and software. Large companies need to know that the company providing them with their mission-critical system will be around in the long-term to protect their hardware and software investments. In contrast, most companies may not care whether or not their on-line documentation systems are available due to hardware and software problems. However, they will not stand for down-time on their business software solutions. The following Figure 16.15 shows the road map for intranet solution for the next 10 years.

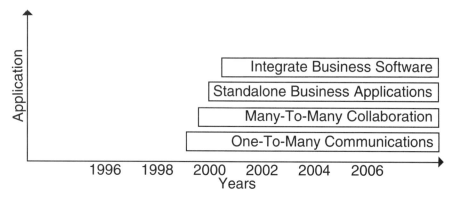

Figure 16.15 *Deployment of intranet applications.*

INFORMATION ON COLLABORATION APPLICATIONS

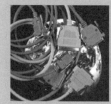

Over the next year, as intranet use becomes more widespread, the use of programs that help users collaborate on projects will grow at a rapid pace. Today, there are a variety of software vendors who have or are developing a range of groupware products. For more information on these products, visit *http://www-sloan.mit.edu/15.967/group09/collab.html* shown in Figure 16.16.

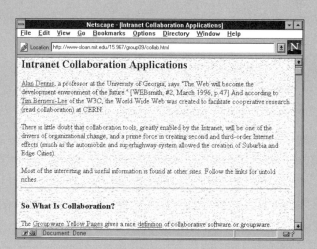

Figure 16.16 *Information on collaboration applications.*

Putting It All Together

Before you decide on your in-house collaboration environment, you must evaluate the choices closely. With *Notes*, you commit to a proprietary solution which has high up-front costs, but provides an excellent track record. With an intranet, you opt for an easy-to-use, ubiquitous approach which you can expand almost limitlessly. In many ways, the technology for any type of in-house collaboration environment is still very immature. New techniques, products, and the issues which surround them are just recently coming to scrutiny. As you develop a solution for your specific business, you may find it useful to reassess the market's offerings frequently. Your migration plan should include periodic reviews of current technology. It will likely be the case where a required feature may be missing today, but solve all your problems tomorrow.

345

This chapter has given you a framework to assist you in evaluating whether your company should select a proprietary groupware product or a Web-based intranet. In Chapter 17, you will examine several key networking concepts you should understand as you prepare to implement or expand your intranet. Before you continue with Chapter 17, however, make sure you understand the following key concepts:

- ✓ Lotus *Notes* has a successful history of providing a highly integrated and proven environment for over 3 million licensed users.

- ✓ You can quickly customize a database with Lotus *Notes*, as well as easily create, add, and search for information.

- ✓ Lotus *Notes* has advantages over today's intranet solutions with features such as built-in security and version control for documents.

- ✓ To respond to competition from intranet-based solutions, Lotus *Notes* is changing its future strategy to move toward open-standard technologies. *InterNotes Web Publisher* combines Web compatibility with *Notes* functionality.

- ✓ Other groupware products such as *GroupWise* from Novell Corporation and *Exchange* from Microsoft provide several *Notes*-like functions.

- ✓ Both groupware products and intranet-based solutions are evolving closer to one another. Soon, you should expect to see a rush of additional features and capabilities for both groupware and intranet products.

Visiting Key Sites That Discuss Intranets

The World Wide Web is filled with hundreds of excellent and current articles on all aspects of intranets. Use the following sites as starting points for your Web exploration.

INTRANET AS GROUPWARE

http://www.4expertise.com/minicat/
sx010011.htm

COLLABORATION APPLICATIONS

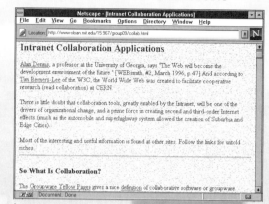

http://www-sloan.mit.edu/15.967/group09/
collab.html

INTRANET RESEARCH LINKS

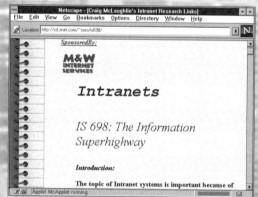

http://sd.znet.com/~zoro/is698/

INFORMATION AND CONSULTING

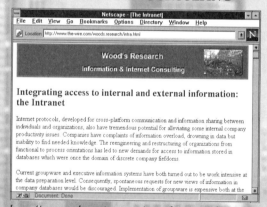

http://www.the-wire.com/woods.research/
intra.html

WHY AN INTRANET FOR ICP

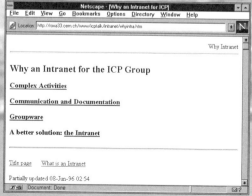

http://roxa33.cern.ch/www/icptalk/intranet/
whyintra.htm

COST BENEFITS

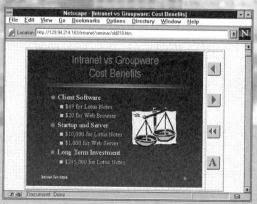

http://129.94.214.163/intranet/seminar/
sld018.htm

Chapter 17

Networking Computers

As you learned in Chapter 5, intranets are based on Internet technology. Your first step in setting up an intranet is to build a computer network. A computer network lets computers, which are connected via a physical or a wireless connection, communicate with each other. This chapter will discuss the components of a computer network in detail, and how intranets fit into existing computer networks. As you have learned, computer networks usually fall into two categories: local area networks (LANs) and wide area networks (WANs). This chapter primarily focuses on LANs because most companies start with a LAN intranet and eventually move to WAN intranets.

At first, you may find networking concepts difficult to understand. That's because most people have not had a chance to review networking terminology and share their understanding of how computer networks function. For most people, it has become fairly easy to talk about the types of PCs that users might need for home or business, how much memory the system should have, its modem speed, and so on. Most people, however, use computer networks without really knowing how the network works. Computer networks, in some ways, work like telephone lines, relying on switches and central traffic-management stations that make connections between telephones possible. Just as you are unaware of "behind the scenes operations" that let you place a phone call, you are probably unaware of the operations your network performs for you.

This chapter's goal is to familiarize you with networking concepts, so you can better evaluate your intranet's future needs. By understanding the concepts this chapter presents, you can read and understand information on a wide range of network products. By the time you finish this chapter, you will understand the following key concepts:

- A computer network consists of two or more connected computers.

- Computers transfer data using two communication switching techniques: circuit switching and packet switching.

- Network designers configure computer networks in various network topologies, such as the bus or star configurations.

- Computer networks use repeaters, bridges, routers, and gateways to transfer data between computers reliably and efficiently.

- Networks consist of layers of hardware and software. Each layer builds on the layer beneath it to perform a specific task.

- The ISO/OSI (International Standards Organization/Open Systems Interconnect) network model describes networks as layers of functionality.

NETWORKS AND INTERNETS

As you have learned, a computer network consists of two or more computers that are connected to each other using cables and other network devices that handle the flow of data. When you connect two or more computers together, you form a network. Later, if you conncct one network to another, you form an *internetwork* or an *internet,* for short. The Internet that you hear about each day is the largest internetwork in the world. Just like the Internet, you can set up various networks within your organization (such as a sales network and production network). Later, if you connect these networks, you create an internet.

Network technology enables employees to use resources located on computers on different networks without understanding the technology difference behind each of these networks. Figure 17.1 shows the relationship between networks and internetworks (internets).

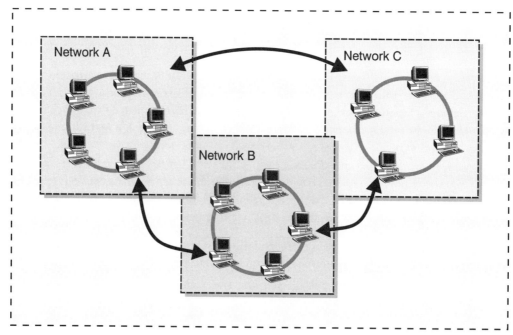

Figure 17.1 The relationship between networks and internetworks (internets).

UNDERSTANDING SIMPLEX AND DUPLEX COMMUNICATION

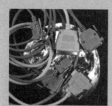

Computers connected to the network use different methods to transfer data, usually over physical cables (or wires). Networking professionals use three terms to describe these methods of data transfer: simplex, half-duplex, and full-duplex communications. In simplex communication, data flows from one computer to another in only one direction. Half-duplex communication lets data flow between two computers in two directions, but only in one direction at a time. In full-duplex communication, data flows in both directions simultaneously. Figure 17.2 shows these methods of data transfer between computers.

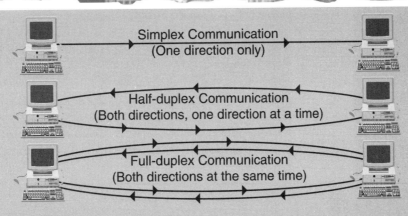

Figure 17.2 Methods of data flow between two computers.

Modems, for example, use half-duplex communication. In other words, the modem can send and receive information. However, the modem can only send or receive at a specific time. The modem cannot receive information while it is transferring data. If you have an external modem, you can watch the modem's transfer and receive lights to determine the modem's current operation. For information on simplex and duplex communication methods, visit the site at *http://www.tafe.sa.edu.au/institutes/torrens-valley/programs/eit/datacoms/ res.htm#trans*, as shown in Figure 17.3.

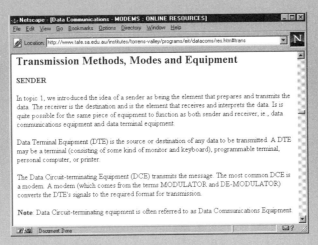

Figure 17.3 Information on simplex and duplex communication.

COMMUNICATION SWITCHING

Through the use of *communication switching*, computer networks allow computers to transfer data using shared lines of communication (such as a cable). Communication switching works similar to telephone switching networks. A telephone switching network eliminates the need to connect a wire between your telephone and every telephone you may ever call. Instead, the phone company connects your phone (and everyone else's phone) to a set of switches. When you place a phone call, the switches create the connection between two phones. Without a telephone switching network, if you needed to call 1,000 different people, you would need to connect 1,000 lines to your phone. In a similar way, computer networks rely on communication switches. Networks use two common methods of communication switching to transfer data: circuit switching and packet switching.

In circuit switching, the switches create a single, unbroken path between devices that want to communicate. Figure 17.4 illustrates examples of a circuit switch. Because the circuit switch requires a physical connection between two devices, no other devices can use the physical lines until the two communicating devices are done.

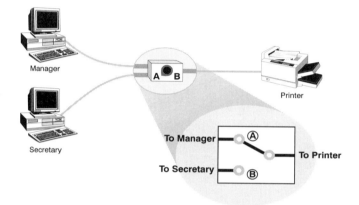

Figure 17.4 A circuit switching network.

Most computer networks, including the Internet, don't use circuit switching. They use a technique called packet switching. In packet switching, programs break data into small pieces, called packets, and then transmit the packets between computers. Packets are a piece of data that adheres to a standard set of rules (protocols) that define their size and format. Unlike circuit switching, in a packet-switched network, data can flow along multiple paths, as shown in Figure 17.5.

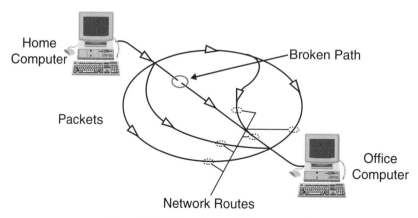

Figure 17.5 A packet switching network.

In packet-switched networks, breaking one path does not prevent the data from reaching its destination. Instead, the packet will simply find a different path. Each packet must contain its destination address. As the packet travels from one computer to another, each computer examines the packet's address and routes the packet to its next intermediate hop or directly to the destination. The Internet is a packet-switched network. Think of a packet in a packet-switched network as a traveler flying from New York to Los Angeles. Depending on the available flights, the traveler may be able to fly nonstop (the packet was lucky enough to get a direct connection). In most cases, however, the traveler must stop at airports along the way (possibly in Dallas, Salt Lake, or Denver). In a similar way, a packet may visit several computers as it travels across the Internet.

For more information on packet- and circuit-switched networks, visit the Web site at *http://www.lidoorg.com/traditio.htm*, shown in Figure 17.6.

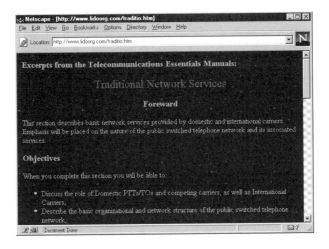

Figure 17.6 Information on packet- and circuit-switched networks.

INTRANET CONSTRUCTION

If your company does not have a network, the first thing you must decide as you plan to build an intranet is to select a network configuration. Your selection of a particular network configuration depends on your short- and long-term computing needs. You must keep in mind that an intranet is just one application that you may run on your network. Thus, you must determine the various applications for which you will use your network. Then, you must determine if you need a wide-area or a local-area network. You must also determine the number of computers you plan to connect to your network, how much you can spend on the network, the level of network performance you need, and your security requirements.

To build a network, you first choose the network topology—which defines how you will physically connect the computers together. Then, you select the network equipment with which you will implement (connect) the topology. In Chapter 5, "Understanding Intranet Components," you learned about network operating systems, server hardware and software, and the client hardware and software that you can use to build an intranet. You also briefly learned about network topologies. In the following sections, you will learn more about the network topologies and the issues that you must consider when selecting one.

NETWORK TOPOLOGIES

You can connect computers together in many ways to form a network. Network professionals refer to the arrangement of computers in a network as the *network topology*. By understanding common network topologies, you can better compare different arrangements of network computers. Each of the three most common topologies—star, ring, and bus—has unique strengths and weaknesses. Selecting the right topology for your intranet is important, because rearranging computers from one topology to another is difficult and expensive. By understanding network topologies, you can better decide how to plan the installation of your intranet so you can easily expand it in the future.

BUS TOPOLOGY

The bus topology is probably the simplest network arrangement. A bus topology uses a single transmission medium called a bus. Network professionals also refer to the bus topology as a chain, because it chains computers together. Each computer on the bus has a unique address that identifies it on the network. You can think of network addresses like telephone numbers. Your telephone number identifies your phone within a telephone network. In a similar way, a computer's address on the bus distinguishes that computer from another. Figure 17.7 shows a computer network that uses the bus topology.

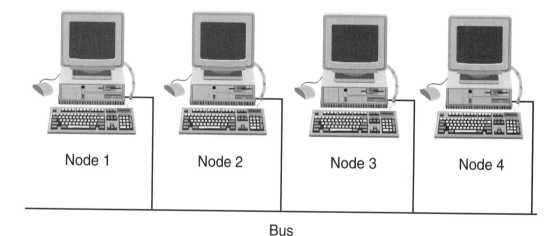

Figure 17.7 A bus topology.

In a bus topology, you can connect computers using a coaxial cable similar to the wire you use to connect your TV to the cable TV outlet. Network professionals often use RG-58 A/U coaxial cable to connect computers. This type of wire has excellent electrical properties. In most cases, the coaxial cable is not one long length of cable, but many short strands that use T-connectors to join together ends of the cable. In addition, T-connectors let the cable branch off in a third direction to connect other computers to the network. Figure 17.8 illustrates a T-connector.

Figure 17.8 A network cable T-connector.

You must use special hardware to terminate both ends of the coaxial cable so a signal traveling to the end of the bus does not bounce back to the other end of the cable, thus appearing as a repeat data transmission. As shown in Figure 17.9, the bus termination absorbs signals at the end of a bus wire and prevents signals from bouncing back.

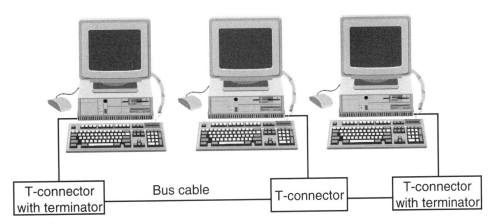

Figure 17.9 You must terminate both ends of a bus cable.

As the data travels down the bus cable, each computer examines the data to determine which computer the information is for. After examining the data (based on rules defined by the network protocol), the computer either receives the data being sent to it, or ignores data intended for another computer. Provided the computers are in close proximity to one another, a bus network is inexpensive and easy to install. To build a computer based on the bus topology, you simply connect a cable from one computer to the next, and eventually terminate the cable at both ends.

The problem with bus topology is that if the bus cable breaks at any point along the entire bus, the computers on one side of the break will not only lose contact with those on the other side, but the break will cause each side to lose its termination. The loss of termination will cause the signals to reflect and corrupt data on the bus. In addition to cable problems, if one computer's network card becomes bad and begins to send noisy signals on the bus, the errant signals can cause the entire network to function improperly.

If you choose the bus topology as your network configuration, you are also limited to the number of computers that you can attach to the bus. This is because as the signal travels along the cable, the signal becomes weaker. If you must add more computers to the network, you must use special network equipment called a repeater, which strengthens the signal at fixed locations along the bus. You will learn more about the repeater and other network equipment later in this chapter. Because it uses a minimal amount of wire and minimal special hardware, a bus-topology network is inexpensive and relatively easy to install.

STAR NETWORK TOPOLOGY

In a star topology, the network computers connect to a central system, which network professionals call the *hub* or *concentrator*, as shown in Figure 17.10.

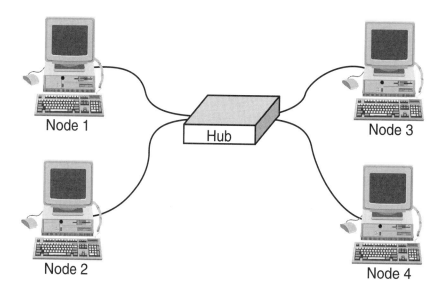

Figure 17.10 A star topology.

In a star topology, data packets travel from each node to the central hub. The central hub, in turn, re-transmits the packets to their destination address. A hub usually provides between 8 and 48 inputs, which controls the number of computers you can connect to the hub.

Network professionals refer to each computer on a network as a *node*. A node can be a client, a server, or both. In a hub system, there are no direct connections between computers. Instead, all computers connect to each other through the hub. Each node connects to a hub using a single cable. Depending on the number of computers you need to connect using a star topology, you may need to use multiple hubs. Figure 17.11 shows a computer network that uses multiple hubs.

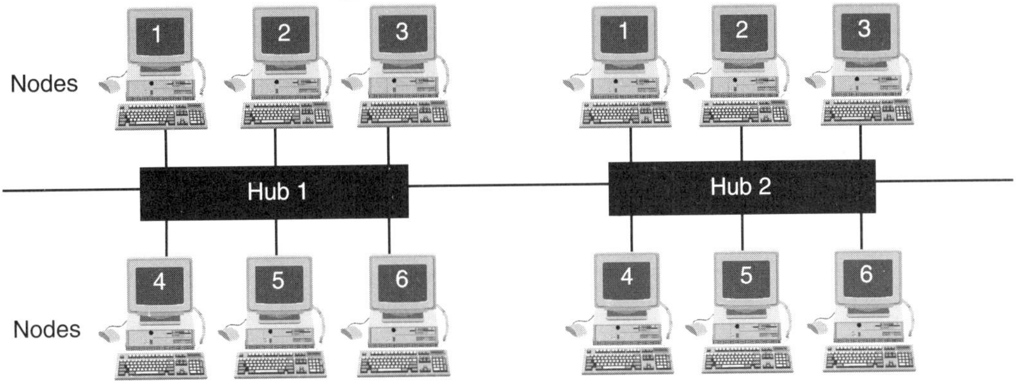

Figure 17.11 A star topology with multiple hubs.

Because each computer connects to a hub using a single cable, a star topology uses more networking cable than a bus topology. In a star topology, the central hub itself also represents an additional cost that is not required for a bus topology. For a star topology, you can use either unshielded, twisted pair (UTP) wire, or shielded, twisted pair (STP) wire. The unshielded and shielded, twisted pair wires appear similar (although slightly larger) to the wires that connect your household telephone to the plastic wall jacks. The price of shielded, twisted pair wire is often double that of the unshielded wire. To save costs, many network designers use unshielded, twisted pair cables for star-topology networks. However, if the distance (length of the wire) from the hub to each node exceeds 110 meters, you must use the higher-quality shielded, twisted pair wire. You should also use shielded, twisted pair cable in environments where there is high levels of electromagnetic interference (EMI) or radio frequency interference (RFI) present.

Because the benefits of a star-topology network often outweigh the higher costs associated with the hub and additional wiring, the star topology is becoming the defacto choice among network designers. The major advantage of the star topology is that a communication breakdown between any computer and the hub does not affect any other node on the network, because each node has its own connection to the hub. In addition, because each data packet must travel through the hub, you can use special hubs that let you monitor the status of all of connected nodes. Using special software, you make dynamic changes in the way the hub connects to each node, thereby increasing the reliability of your network. The disadvantage of the star topology is that if the central hub breaks, your whole network will go down.

RING NETWORK TOPOLOGY

In a ring topology, the network has no end connection, which means the network forms a continuous (an unbroken, but necessarily circular) ring through which data travels from one node to another. Figure 17.12 shows a computer network based a ring topology.

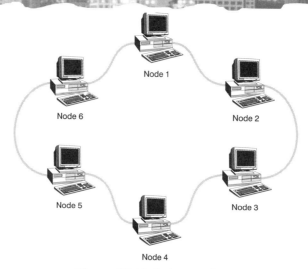

Figure 17.12 A ring topology.

On a ring topology, you can travel from any point on the network and eventually return to your starting point because in ring topology, data flows in only one direction. A ring topology transmits data from node to node around the ring. Each node receives the data signal, analyzes the data, and if the message is for another node, passes the data to the next node on the ring. Using the ring topology, you can connect more nodes to the network than you can using the other two topologies because, as each node examines the data, it also reconditions (cleans) and amplifies the data signal before sending it to the next computer. Therefore, there is less signal loss as data travels from one node to another on the ring topology than the bus and star topologies.

Network designers often use ring topology to design networks that cover a large geographic location where implementation of star topology is difficult. Unlike the star, a ring topology requires an unbroken path between all computers on the network. A break anywhere in the ring will cause all network communications to stop. Network designers sometimes guard against failures through the implementation of a backup signal path. Another weakness of ring topology is that because data passes through every computer on the network, users can eavesdrop on the data circulating throughout the ring.

SELECTING THE RIGHT NETWORK TOPOLOGY

As you have learned, your selection of a network topology is very important. The network topology is the foundation of your network. It is something that you cannot easily change after you have built your network. It is important that you consider the number of nodes you need today, and the number you will need in the next two to five years. The cost of implementing each network topology is dependent on the cost of network interface cards. A network interface card is a special add-on board you install in your computer that connects the computer to the network. You need a network card for each node. Table 17.1 summarize the features of the three network topologies.

Features	Bus	Star	Ring
Typical Expense	Low	Medium	High
Availability of Components	Good	Excellent	Good
Reliability	Good	Excellent	Excellent
Geographical Coverage Ability	Poor	Good	Excellent
Ease of Troubleshooting	Poor	Excellent	Good
Ease of Relocating a Node	Poor	Good	Good
Network Node Capacity	Low	Medium	High

Table 17.1 Comparison of the three network topologies.

The cost of network components increases as you migrate from bus, to star, to ring topologies. When you purchase network components, however, you should be skeptical of low prices when it appears that the cost of star topology is lower than bus topology. On average, network interface cards for PCs sell for about $60 to $100 for bus topology, and from $80 to $145 for star topology. There are also network interface cards that feature combinations of connectors for both bus and star topologies that sell for about $90 to $150. Network designers call this type of card a *combo* card. You can use a combo card when you have a small bus network that you expect to eventually reconfigure into a star network.

The cost of ring topology network interface cards generally start at about $190. This is partially attributed to licensing costs that board manufacturers have to pay to IBM for developing the technology behind this type of network configuration.

As you learned in previous chapters, you must also consider what is the right type of cabling for your network. Bus topology networks commonly use coaxial cable, which should be RG-58 A/U cable. For star networks, you must use unshielded, twisted pair or shielded, twisted pair category 5 cable. Network professionals sometimes refer to category 5 cable as Cat 5, which is the rating cable manufacturers specify for the cable's resistance to interference and the cable's transmission property. If you want to build a star network, you must use at least a Cat 5 cable. Any rating below 5 may affect data integrity, especially at higher transfer rates.

The quality of a star-network's hub (or concentrator) also makes a difference in your network's overall reliability. An eight-port hub sells for about $350. A port is simply a jack where the cable from a node attaches to a hub. Inexpensive hubs often use lower-quality parts and can greatly impact the performance of your network. As you learned, hubs are the main components of star networks. While the hub remains functional, a star topology has several advantages over a ring or a bus topology. When the hub fails, however, the cost to resolve the problem can be significant (both in time and money).

In brief, the star topology is the most widely used network topology. As you have learned, initial installation of a star topology requires more cabling and will cost more than bus or ring topologies. It is, however, a more reliable topology which you can manage from a central location and modify nodes as needed, easily and efficiently.

NETWORK TOPOLOGIES VERSUS NETWORK TECHNOLOGIES

By now, you know the basic differences among the three types of network topologies: bus, star, and ring. Many people use the term topology when they are really referring to a specific *network technology*. The two most popular network technologies are Ethernet and IBM Token Ring. Network professionals also refer to network technologies as network architecture. Network technologies establish some of the rules for how computers exchange data across a network.

358

In 1973, a team of researchers at Xerox Palo Alto Research Center (PARC), led by Bob Metcalf, developed the Ethernet technology. You can configure an Ethernet network in either a star or a bus topology. Typically, if you use coaxial cable as the transmission medium, you will configure the network as a bus. If you use twisted-pair wiring for the transmission medium, you will normally configure the network as a star.

On an Ethernet network, each node listens for network traffic on the bus before transmitting data. If a node hears another node talking (transmitting data) on the bus, that node waits until the other node is finished before it transmits data. Despite rules for transmitting data, two nodes often try to transmit data at the same time. If this happens, a data collision occurs, which corrupts the information. When a collision occurs, the Ethernet collision-detection system requires that the transmitting nodes stop transmitting and that the nodes must each wait a random period of time before they try to send their data again.

The IBM Token Ring network is an interesting mix of topologies. As the name implies, IBM developed the token ring technology, a hybrid (mix) of star and ring topologies. It uses a star technology with an IBM device called a Multi-station Access Unit (MAU) as its central hub. IBM Token Ring networks, however, also use a ring topology. Each computer on the network uses two cables to connect with the hub. The computer transmits data to the hub on one line and receives data from the hub on the other. Therefore, an IBM Token Ring network forms a contiguous ring in the shape of a star. Figure 17.13 shows a computer network in an IBM Token Ring topology arrangement.

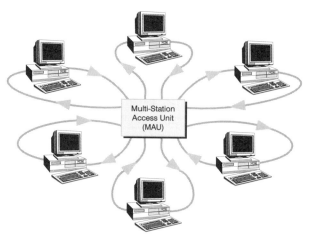

Figure 17.13 Data flow in an IBM Token Ring network.

IBM Token Ring technology solves the data-collision problem of Ethernet network technology by requiring nodes to obtain permission from the network before they can transmit data. To obtain permission to transmit, a node must grab a special data packet called a token. Think of a token as a permission slip. If the token is not used by any node on the network, the token is available and a node can grab it and use it to transmit data. One permission token travels endlessly around the ring in one direction, waiting for a node to use it. Because there is only one token, only one node can transmit data at any given time so collisions do not occur.

359

CONNECTING TWO OR MORE COMPUTER NETWORKS TOGETHER

Like the Internet, you may connect several computer networks in your company together to create an internetwork. Such internetworks do not take the form of any particular network topology, such as star or ring, or any network technologies, such as Ethernet or IBM Token Ring.

To connect various computer networks together (to create an internetwork), you use special network devices called repeaters, bridges, routers, and gateways. Using these network devices, you can extend your connections within a local-area network, or create a wide-area network.

UNDERSTANDING SIGNAL ATTENUATION

As signals travel through network media (cables and wires), they become weaker. Think about what happens if you drop a pebble into a swimming pool. You will notice that the wave ripples become smaller as they travel farther away from where you dropped the pebble. In networking and other electronic signal media, such as a computer circuit board, the signals will lose their strength and also their characteristics as they travel from connector to connector or network equipment to network equipment. Engineers refer to this weakening of signals as *attenuation*. Network designers use special networking devices called repeaters to amplify network data.

REPEATERS

Network designers use repeaters to connect two segments of a network together. As its name implies, a repeater copies or repeats signals that it receives. A repeater, however, amplifies and rebuilds the characteristics of signals before retransmitting them. By doing so, a repeater increases the size of a long waveform it receives (without changing its frequency). Network designers use repeaters so they can increase the distance between adjacent network computers. Figure 17.14 shows a repeater that connects two segments of a network.

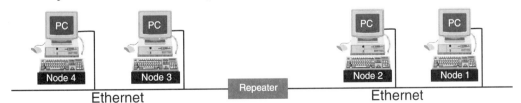

Figure 17.14 A network repeater.

Long-haul networks may contain many repeaters. Ethernets often use repeaters to extend the length of the bus cable within a local-area network. Companies, such as Lantronix, make a variety of multiport Ethernet repeaters for a variety of network configurations. A 4-port Lantronix repeater sells for about $1,000.

NETWORK MEDIUM

Network designers often use repeaters to amplify the thin coaxial Ethernet cable. You can use four different Ethernet media to build an Ethernet network: thin coax, thick wire, unshielded twisted wire, and fiber optics. Network professionals refer to thin coax cable wire as 10BASE2 Ethernet. This type of wire costs less than thick wire. Network designers often use 10BASE2 for low-cost network topologies, such as the bus topology. Using a 10BASE2 cable, you can make a bus topology about 190 meters long before needing a repeater.

Network designers often use thick wire to create Ethernet backbones (the primary cables to which the thinner PC-to-network cables connect). Network professionals refer to thick wire backbone as 10BASE5 Ethernet backbone. The 10BASE5 cables can be up to 500 meters long, and can have about 100 nodes attached. Network backbones often take the form of a bus topology. You should keep the distance between nodes at least three meters apart to prevent the signal from adjacent nodes from interfering with one another.

As you learned previously, twisted pair wires are similar to those you use to connect your telephone to the wall jack. Twisted pair wires have various transmission rate capabilities. Network professionals refer to unshielded, twisted pair cable as 10BASE-T medium. For example, twisted pair Level 5 wire can transmit data at a rate of close to 100 Megabits per second (100Mbps). If you need a network medium with a bandwidth of less than 5Mbps, you can use Level 1 wire.

The most expensive network medium, among the four, is fiber optic. Network designers use fiber optic lines to connect offices that are up to two kilometers apart. Fiber optic cable also performs well in areas where electromagnetic interference is present.

USING A BRIDGE TO CONNECT NETWORKS

If you have two separate computer networks that use the same network technology, such as two Ethernet networks that you want to connect, you can use a network bridge. A bridge is more than a repeater. The main function of a bridge is to keep the network traffic on one side of a network. For example, assume a bridge connects two networks: Leftside and Rightside. When the bridge receives a packet from the Leftside, it compares the destination address of the packet with the address of the node on its left side. If the destination address of the packet is on the same side as the origin, in this case the same as Leftside, the bridge drops the packet and does not allow it to go to the Rightside. If the destination address of the packet is a on different side than its source address, the bridge lets the packet cross to the other network.

In a computer network, a bridge acts as a traffic cop at busy intersections. By doing so, the bridge localizes the network traffic and does not let packets move to another network if they cannot prove they must cross the bridge. Network professionals also refer to bridges as a "stop-and-forward" device. Figure 17.15 shows a bridge connecting two segments of a network.

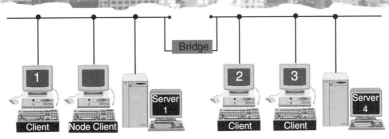

Figure 17.15 *A network bridge.*

Using a Bridge to Improve Network Performance

A network bridge does more than connect segments of a network. A network bridge provides network designers with the ability to improve the performance, reliability, and security of their networks. As you learned in previous sections, the more nodes you connect to a network, the more data collisions occur (because more nodes try to access the network at the same time).

You can use a bridge to improve network performance problems that result from heavy traffic and data collisions. A bridge can divide a crowded local area network into smaller network segments, as shown in Figure 17.15. By localizing the traffic on each segment, the bridge in Figure 17.15 reduces the overall network traffic.

Using a Bridge to Improve Reliability

Network designers also use bridges to improve their network reliability by dividing large networks into smaller segments. As you learned, a faulty cable or node can bring down an entire ring or bus network. By segmenting (partitioning) a single local-area network into multiple smaller networks, connected by a bridge, network designers reduce the impact of a faulty cable or node on the entire network. Consider the previous network example, shown in Figure 17.15. If the cable between nodes 2 and 3 breaks, only nodes on the Leftside segment will go down. Without the bridge, a fault between nodes 2 and 3 will bring down the entire network.

Using a Bridge to Improve Security

As you have learned, in bus and ring topology, data passes through each computer on the network. Any network user can use a special electronic device, called a network analyzer, to intercept and examine data packets on the network. You can also use software to analyze network data.

Network professionals often use network analyzers to troubleshoot network problems. Network programmers use network analyzers to debug network programs. These are legitimate reasons for monitoring network traffic. However, a network analyzer can present network administrators with security problems if unauthorized people use it.

Network designers can use a bridge to divide the entire network into secured and unsecured segments. For example, if a company's top executives are all located in the same area, and do not want anyone outside their immediate area to have access to their network data, a network designer can use a bridge to separate the executive computers from the rest of the network. In so doing, the bridge can restrict unauthorized users from tapping into the confidential data that travels between the executive's computers.

A NETWORK ROUTER

The function of a router is similar to a bridge. Network designers use routers to transfer, or route, data between networks that use different network technologies. For example, a network designer can use a router to connect an Ethernet network to an IBM Token Ring network. Because the Internet comprises various networks that use many different network technologies, routers are an integral part of the Internet. A router has an address on the network; a bridge does not—which is the key difference between a router and a bridge. Figure 17.16 shows a router connecting an Ethernet network to an IBM Token Ring network.

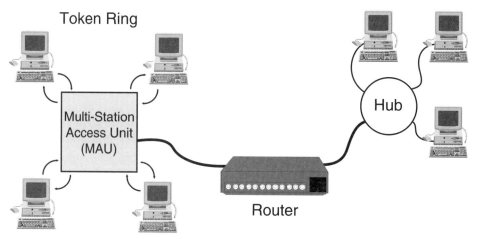

Figure 17.16 A router connecting two different networks.

Using the addressing capability of routers, nodes on a network can send packets destined for another network to a router. The router, in turn, will transfer the packet to the other network. To manage network traffic, Network designers also use routers to segment large sections of a LAN to smaller segments, called subnets.

To route data, routers commonly use *routing tables*, which are similar to a lookup database. Using a routing table, routers can look up the correct path (or best route) from the packet's current location to any destination on the network. Depending on the network's requirements, a designer can implement routing tables as static or dynamic. With a static routing table, the network administrator must manually update the table. Network software automatically updates dynamic routing tables. The advantage of dynamic routing tables is that, should part of the network get bogged down with a lot of traffic, the network software can update the routing tables to route packets around the current bottleneck.

Many people refer to routers as gateways. A *gateway* is a generic term that can refer to three types of network entities: you can refer to a router as a gateway; a gateway is also the entity that translates data from one network protocol to another; and network professionals refer to an application gateway as a gateway. Application gateways translate data that specific programs use. The most common type of application gateway is one that an e-mail application uses. For example, you can use MCI *Mail* to send e-mail to someone on a private company's local-area network in another state. Your e-mail message might travel from MCI *Mail* to the Internet and from the Internet to the destination local-area network. At each interconnection, an application gateway would translate the message into a format suitable for further transmission.

Understanding Network Architectures

If you have programmed computers in the past, you may know that by defining and maintaining the interface between code and modules (the parameter list), you can make extensive changes within a module without affecting any other code module in your program. Network designers build networks using similar principles. The term network architecture refers to the network's modular format and design structure. The term describes how network developers piece together network components to build the network.

Today, most computer networks, including the Internet, are based on a network-design model called the Reference Model of Open Systems Interconnection (OSI). As you may know, in an *open system*, the design or features of the system are not proprietary. The network professionals who developed the OSI model derived the model from a proposal by the International Standards Organization (ISO). Network literature commonly refers to the OSI model as the ISO/OSI model. In an ISO/OSI model of network architecture, various functional layers perform specific network operations. The ISO/OSI model is a design guide and not a specification. Figure 17.17 shows various layers of the ISO/OSI network model.

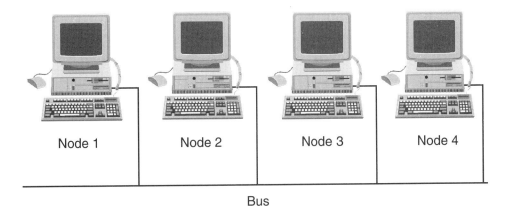

Node 1   Node 2   Node 3   Node 4

Bus

Figure 17.17 ISO/OSI model of network architecture.

As you may have noticed, each layer of the ISO/OSI network model uses a different unit of data. For example, the application, presentation, session, and transport layers usually identify a unit of data as a message. The network layer identifies each unit of data as a packet. The data-link layer refers to a unit of data as a frame. The physical layer sees all data as bits—binary data representing either a 1 or a 0. As the data moves from one layer to the next, the network software translates the data into the correct format. The advantage of a layered computer network architecture is that network designers can use a variety of hardware and software components to build a network. Although network designers may use hardware and software from a variety of vendors, the standard protocols that govern the flow of data between different network layers ensure the hardware and software communicate correctly.

UNDERSTANDING THE PHYSICAL LAYER

The physical layer transmits data through the network's communication channels. The physical layer includes the physical elements (hardware), such as the cables and connectors that define the network technology (Ethernet and IBM Token Ring), which in turn defines the parameter for data transfer. The physical layer also determines whether data transfers use a simplex, half-duplex, or full-duplex mode of communication. In addition, the physical layer contains details about a network's topology. With all these low-level details as part of the physical layer design, network designers can create the higher layers (data-link, network, session, transport, presentation, and application layers) without considering network topologies.

A network-interface card lets you connect computers together using twisted-pair wiring like telephone wiring, or coaxial cable like cable TV wiring. The physical layer of a network determines the electrical and mechanical aspect of network communication channels.

UNDERSTANDING THE DATA-LINK LAYER

As you learned before, a protocol is a set of rules for all data transmissions, transmitted and received, over a network. Each computer on a network contains one or more technology-specific network cards that connect the computer to the network. Some computers, like engineering Unix machines and high-end computers, have built-in network cards. When computers send data across the network, the data flows from one network card to another. Each network card has a unique network address.

In a layered network model, your network card represents the link layer, often called the data-link layer. The link layer sits between the physical layer and the network layer. In other words, network interface cards represent the link between the physical layer (the cable) and network software. The Ethernet provides a set of link-layer protocols that hide the physical implementation of a network from the network layer. Because of the link layer, protocols in the network layer are not affected whether the network uses Ethernet network technology or other network technologies, such as IBM Token Ring. Remember, network-interface cards are technology specific. You must use an Ethernet interface card if you want to connect your computer to an Ethernet network and a token ring interface card if you use an IBM Token Ring network.

When the data-link layer formats raw bits, network professionals usually call the resulting units of data a *frame*. The data frame's content depends on the underlying network technology (the physical layer). Thus, the network layer does not care how the link layer creates the frames. By design, data frames provide error checking capabilities. You should understand that the primary purpose or function of the link layer is to prevent data corruption (many people assume that formatting data into frames is the primary purpose of the link layer). Figure 17.18 shows the content of an Ethernet data frame.

64 Bits	48 Bits	48 Bits	16 Bits	368-12,000 Bits	32 Bits
Preamble	Destination Address	Source Address	Frame Type	Frame Data	Cyclic Redundancy Check (CRC)

Figure 17.18 *The content of an Ethernet data frame.*

UNDERSTANDING THE NETWORK LAYER

As you have learned, each data packet in a packet-switched network contains both a destination and a source address for routing purposes. The network layer determines the route or the path that data follows to reach its destination. The network layer handles network traffic, congestion, and transfer rates (speed) across the network medium. The network layer uses bridges and routers to manage the flow of data on the network. Both Internet Protocol (IP) and Novell corporation's *NetWare* Internetwork Packet Exchange (IPX) operate at the network layer.

UNDERSTANDING THE TRANSPORT LAYER

The function of the transport layer is to provide the reliable transfer of data between computers on a network. The transport layer separates the application layer (where the network programs run) from the layers that deal primarily with the transmission of the data. The TCP protocol (from TCP/IP) is a transport-layer protocol. Application programs use this protocol to send data to a network layer. Not all application programs go through TCP to get to network layer protocols. SPX is *NetWare's* transport-layer protocol. Like TCP, SPX provides reliable data transmission on a *NetWare*-based network.

The transport layer provides reliable data transmission by breaking, or fragmenting, the data it receives from the session layer into the smaller pieces that the network layer requires. On the receiving end, the transport layer must reassemble the fragmented data so the transport layer's design greatly impacts the quantity of packets that flow through the network. In other words, the transport layer produces the packet traffic that the network layer must manage.

UNDERSTANDING THE SESSION LAYER

On most computer networks, you must login (enter your user name and password) each time you want to use any network service. Network professionals refer to each login as a network session. The session layer, for each login session, negotiates and establishes connections between processes or applications between different nodes. Network professionals refer to the process of setting up a session as *binding*. In addition, the session layer authenticates both ends of a connection. This means the session layer requires each end of the connection to prove who they are.

Both ends of a connection must establish their authorization to use a specified connection or session. The Internet eliminates the need for a session layer. Although in most cases you must login to use the Internet, the software that authorizes users is not part of the network-software design. On the Internet, the transport-layer protocols include many functions that the session layer normally handles. In short, the session layer establishes and manages connections between users and network applications.

UNDERSTANDING THE PRESENTATION LAYER

The presentation layer contains common functions that the network repeatedly uses during network communication. These common functions include the network's interface to printers, video displays, and file formats. A presentation layer typically includes many data conversion routines. The presentation layer, for example, might make a computer's use of multiple file formats transparent to a network application. Internet networks do not include a standard presentation layer, so application programs perform most presentation-layer functions.

Often, the layers below the presentation layer perform functions to guarantee correct network operations. The presentation layer provides useful but non-essential network services. The presentation layer might also provide communication services, such as encrypting data and compressing data. The purpose of the data encryption is security. On a network, encryption transforms intelligible data into something unintelligible prior to transmission. At the receiving end of the connection, the presentation layer must decipher the transmission and transform the data back into usable information.

Like data encryption, data compression involves conversion of data. Users compress data to reduce its size rather than hide its meaning. Unlike encryption, the methods of decoding compressed data are available throughout the network. By compressing data near the top network, the presentation layer reduces the amount of data that the network must transport. Therefore, efficient data compression in the presentation layer can increase overall network performance.

UNDERSTANDING THE APPLICATION LAYER

The application layer contains all the details related to specific applications or computer programs written by programmers for network users. Most TCP/IP-based software suites provide users with standard networking applications, such as FTP and Telnet. As you have learned, FTP lets you connect to other computers on a network to transfer files. Likewise, the Telnet program lets you login to a remote computer. Another example of a network-wide application is e-mail. Web browsers are also application-layer programs.

PUTTING IT ALL TOGETHER

At first, network terminology may seem difficult to understand but, in general, network concepts are easier to understand than other computing concepts, such as advanced programming techniques. This chapter introduced you to the various physical components of a network, such as cable types, repeaters, routers, and bridges. The functions these network components perform are well defined by networking professionals. You can use the information you learned in this chapter as fundamental knowledge to build your first network or to enhance the performance of your existing network.

Understanding of the ISO/OSI network model will also help you choose various network components to improve your network performance. You don't have to write network programs to design a high-performance network. You must, however, know what is behind a network technology so you can select various network applications that bring the true power of your intranet to everyone in your company. In Chapter 18, you will take a closer look at the TCP/IP network protocol. Before you move on to Chapter 18, make sure you understand the following key concepts:

367

✓ When you connect two or more networks, you form an internetwork, or an internet. The Internet is the world's largest internetwork.

✓ To transfer data, networks use two common methods of communications switching: circuit switching and packet switching.

✓ There are many ways you can connect computers together to form a network. A network's topology lets you compare different arrangements of network computers. The three most common network topologies are the star, ring, and bus.

✓ To connect various computer networks (to create an internetwork), you use special network devices, such as repeaters, bridges, routers, and gateways.

✓ A repeater amplifies and rebuilds the characteristics of a signal before re-transmitting the signal to an adjacent node.

✓ The main function of a bridge is to keep the network traffic in one segment of a network. You can use a network bridge to improve performance, increase reliability, and enhance the security of a network.

✓ The functions of a router are similar to a bridge. A router, however, filters the data between segments of computer networks.

✓ Most computer networks, including the Internet, are based on a network-design model that network literature calls the ISO/OSI model. This model describes networks as layers of functionality. Each layer performs a well-defined function and uses one or more protocols to perform its function.

✓ The physical layer transmits data through the network's communication channels. The physical layer includes the physical elements (hardware) such as the cables and connectors that define the network technology (Ethernet or IBM Token Ring).

✓ The primary purpose or function of the link layer is to detect data-transmission errors.

✓ The network layer determines the route data follows to each network destination.

✓ The transport layer delivers data between applications on host computers.

✓ The session layer is the user's interface to the network.

✓ The presentation layer contains common functions that the network repeatedly uses during network communication. Common functions include the network's interface to printers, video displays, and file formats.

✓ The application layer consists of network application programs.

VISITING KEY SITES THAT DISCUSS INTRANETS

The World Wide Web is filled with hundreds of excellent and current articles on all aspects of intranets. Use the following sites as starting points for your Web exploration.

CISCO CONNECTION ONLINE

http://www.cisco.com/

SYBASE, INC.

http://www.sybase.com/

WEB ACCESS

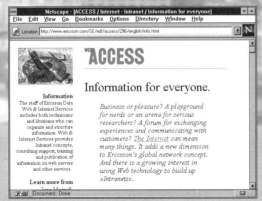

http://www.ericsson.com/SE/edit/access/296/
english/info.html

NETSCAPE NEWS SERVER 2.01

http://www.netscape.com/comprod/server

PINE INFORMATION CENTER

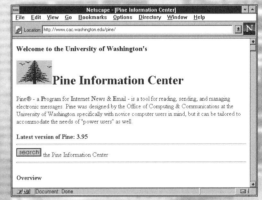

http://www.cac.washington.edu/pine/

APACHE HTTP SERVER PROJECT

http://apache.org/

IBM RS/6000 Software

http://www.austin.ibm.com/software/OS/

SCO Free Unix System

http://www.sco.com

FreeBSD Inc.

http://www.freebsd.org/

IBM OS/2 Warp Server

http://www.software.ibm.com/os/warp-server/index.html

Linux Information

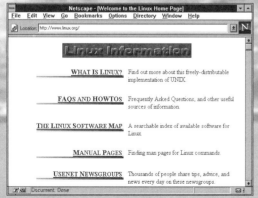

http://www.linux.org/

Microsoft Products

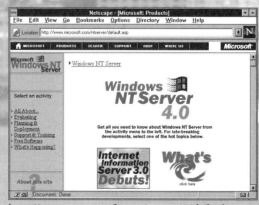

http://www.microsoft.com/ntserver/default.asp

Chapter 18

Getting to Know TCP/IP

371

In previous chapters, you learned various aspects of network computing and that your network must support the TCP/IP protocol. This chapter will give you a detailed description of the TCP/IP protocol and how it lets one computer communicate with another computer through the various networks that make up the Internet. For most of you, it is not essential that you examine TCP/IP in the level of detail presented here. Instead, you should use this chapter to gain a general understanding of TCP/IP's inner workings. By the time you finish this chapter, you will understand the following key concepts:

- ◆ The TCP/IP protocol suite is a collection of protocols that work together to communicate information across the Internet.

- ◆ The TCP/IP network model uses components from the ISO/OSI network model.

- ◆ A protocol stack refers to the vertical order in which protocols appear in a layered network.

- ◆ When your programs transmit data to a remote host on the Internet, the data flows down the protocol stack and across the network. At its destination, the data flows up the protocol stack to the destination program on the remote host computer.

- ◆ The TCP/IP network layer manages data delivery between host computers on the network.

- ◆ A 32-bit IP address identifies a specific network and a specific computer within that network.

- ◆ A TCP/IP protocol port represents a network application address within a host computer.

UNDERSTANDING THE IMPORTANCE OF THE *TCP/IP PROTOCOLS*

As you have learned, protocols are rules which define how software programs communicate. Network protocols manage the flow of information between two programs running on the same or different computers (such as the communication between a Web browser and a server). The TCP/IP protocol suite manages all the information that moves across your intranet, as well as the information that flows across the Internet.

As it turns out, the TCP/IP protocol suite is actually a collection of multiple protocols, each of which transfers data across the network using a different format and different options, such as error checking. Depending on which program you use on your intranet, one of a variety of protocols within the TCP/IP suite will likely transmit information across the network.

TCP is an acronym for Transport Control Protocol. Likewise, IP stands for Internet Protocol. However, when you combine these two acronyms (TCP/IP), they represent more than just the two protocols. For this reason, the term *TCP/IP* often confuses TCP/IP newcomers.

DEFINING THE *TCP/IP* PROTOCOL SUITE

The Internet, as well as your intranet, relies on a collection of protocols called the TCP/IP protocol suite. A *protocol suite* is a collection (a set) of complementary and cooperative protocols. The TCP/IP protocol suite includes the Transport Control Protocol and the Internet Protocol, as well as other protocols. All of these protocols work together to communicate information across the Internet.

Table 18.1 lists the commonly used TCP/IP protocols.

Protocol	Purpose
IP	The Internet Protocol is a network-layer protocol that moves data between host computers.
TCP	The Transport Control Protocol is a transport-layer protocol that moves data between applications.
UDP	The User Datagram Protocol is another transport-layer protocol. UDP also moves data between applications; however, UDP is less complex (and less reliable) than TCP.
ICMP	The Internet Control Message Protocol carries network error messages and reports other conditions that require attention by network software.

Table 18.1 Commonly used TCP/IP protocols.

The terms *network-layer* and *transport-layer* refer to a specific type of functionality found within what is known as the ISO/OSI network model. For more information on the TCP/IP protocol suite, visit the site at *http://kafka.unic.ca/~svanmoss/FA345/TCP.IP.HTML*, shown in Figure 18.1.

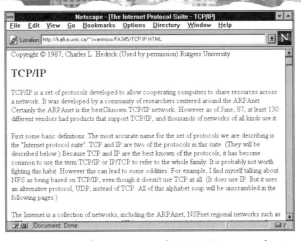

Figure 18.1 *Information on the TCP/IP protocol suite.*

UNDERSTANDING LAYERING

The ISO/OSI model uses layers to organize a network into well-defined, functional modules. Network designers use the model's descriptions of these layers to build real networks. In a layered network, each module (or layer) provides specific functionality or services to its adjacent layers. In addition, each layer shields layers above it from lower-level implementation details. In other words, each layer interfaces with only the next layer in the network. Figure 18.2 shows the layers in the ISO/OSI network model. Later in this chapter, you will learn the importance of each layer and how each relates to the TCP/IP protocol.

7	Application Layer
6	Presentation Layer
5	Session Layer
4	Transport Layer
3	Network Layer
2	Data-Link Layer
1	Physical Layer

Figure 18.2 *Network layers in the ISO/OSI network model.*

DEFINING A PROTOCOL STACK

As you learned in the previous section, the ISO/OSI network model divides networks into layers, each of which performs a very specific function. Within each layer, the ISO/OSI model associates protocols that define the layer's functionality. For example, the network layer, which manages data delivery across the Internet, contains the Internet Protocol, which moves data between host computers.

As shown in Figure 18.3, the ISO/OSI model represents a network as a vertical stack of modules or layers. Because the model associates at least one protocol with each layer, you can say the model stacks protocols on top of each other. The term *protocol stack* comes from this concept of networks as vertical layers and stacked protocols.

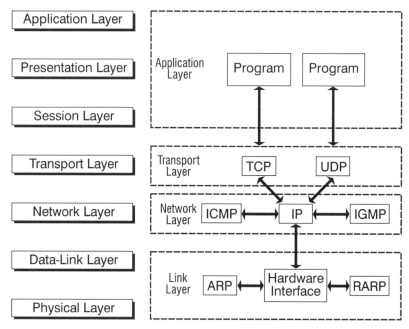

Figure 18.3 The ISO/OSI model and protocol stack.

UNDERSTANDING THE DATA FLOW

As previously mentioned, the TCP/IP protocol suite moves information across the network. Because the TCP/IP protocol suite provides a collection of cooperative protocols, you can think of your data as flowing from one layer to another and from one protocol to the next. As you can see in Figure 18.3, the top layer in the ISO/OSI model is the application layer. The physical layer at the bottom consists of the network transmission lines. As your data moves through the protocol stack, your data flows from the application layer down to the physical layer and across the network. When your data arrives at its physical destination, your data flows up through the protocol stack toward the destination application.

EXPLORING THE TCP/IP PROTOCOL STACK

The ISO/OSI reference model defines seven functional layers for network designs. However, the ISO/OSI reference model is merely a guide—not a design in and of itself. For example, the TCP/IP network design uses only five of the ISO/OSI protocols in its respective network layers. Figure 18.4 shows the TCP/IP network model.

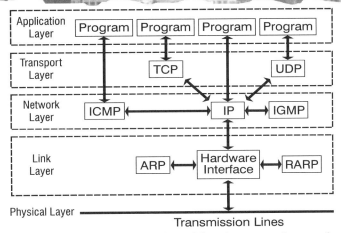

Figure 18.4 *TCP/IP network model with associated protocols.*

In Figure 18.4, the lines with arrows show possible avenues of communications between the various network software and hardware modules. For example, to communicate with the transport layer, your applications talk to the User Datagram Protocol (UDP) and Transport Control Protocol (TCP) modules. To communicate with the network layer, your applications talk to the Internet Control Message Protocol (ICMP) or Internet Protocol (IP) software modules. However, your data must flow through the IP module to reach the network hardware regardless of which route your data takes from the application layer to the network layer. The following sections examine how data moves through the protocol stack. You will start with the bottom layer (the physical layer) and work upward to the top layer (the application layer).

Understanding the Physical Layer

The physical layer in a TCP/IP network is identical to the ISO/OSI model and includes the transmission media that carries network data. This media is usually some type of twisted-pair or coaxial cable.

Understanding the Link Layer

As you saw in Figure 18.4, the link layer includes a hardware interface and two protocol modules: the Address Resolution Protocol (ARP) and the Reverse Address Resolution Protocol (RARP). In the following sections, you will learn more about these protocols. For now, simply note that the link layer uses these two protocols to resolve addresses. The link layer, which the ISO/OSI model calls the data-link layer, sits between the physical layer and the network layer. As its name implies, the link layer links the physical layer to the network layer.

As shown in Figure 18.5, the link layer handles the exchange of data between the physical layer and the network layer. More specifically, in the TCP/IP protocol suite, the link layer sends and receives data for the network layer's IP module. Besides performing a specific function, each layer in a layered network hides network implementation details from the layers above it. Thus, another purpose of the link layer is to hide the network's physical implementation from the network layer. When the link layer does its job, protocols in the network layer are not affected whether the network uses Ethernet technology or IBM Token Ring technology. The network layer simply passes data to the link layer, which then handles all further data transmission.

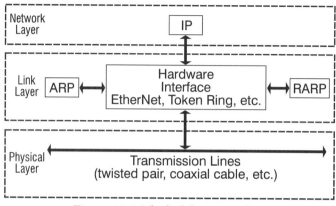

Figure 18.5 The link layer interface.

MORE TCP/IP TERMS

To understand the remaining layers of the TCP/IP protocol, you must understand several key terms. These terms define the differences between the two TCP/IP transport protocols: the User Datagram Protocol (UDP) and the Transport Control Protocol (TCP). Furthermore, these terms describe protocol characteristics related to network connections, protocol reliability, and data services.

NETWORK CONNECTIONS

Network connections are either *connection-oriented* or *connectionless*. A connection-oriented protocol must establish a connection with another application before any communication can occur. For example, when you use a telephone to communicate with someone, you dial a telephone number and wait for someone to answer. You cannot talk or communicate with anyone until someone picks up the telephone at the other end of your call. In the same way, a connection-oriented protocol cannot communicate or transport data until it establishes a connection. The Transport Control Protocol is a connection-oriented protocol.

A connectionless protocol does not establish a connection before transmitting messages. As a result, each message that uses a connectionless protocol must contain all delivery information. For example, when you mail a letter to someone, you must write a complete address on the envelope. You do not personally deliver the letter. Instead, the postal service delivers it for you. In the same way, each message transmitted by a connectionless protocol contains a complete and accurate address for delivery. A connectionless protocol passes the message to the next layer in the protocol stack and depends on the network for delivery. The User Datagram Protocol and the Internet Protocol are connectionless protocols.

UNDERSTANDING PROTOCOL RELIABILITY

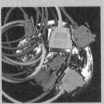

Protocols are either *reliable* or *unreliable*. When your data passes through a reliable protocol, the protocol guarantees delivery of that data. Typically, reliable delivery includes several features. First, to ensure data delivery, the protocol exchanges acknowledgment messages between communicating applications. Second, to ensure delivery of valid data, a reliable protocol includes one or more checksums with each transmission. A checksum is a number that the sending and receiving computers compute independently based on the contents of the data. If the receiving computer's checksum does not match the checksum computed by the sending computer, the data is invalid due to a transmission error. The Transport Control Protocol is a reliable protocol that uses checksums, acknowledgment messages, and other techniques to help ensure reliable data delivery.

In contrast, an unreliable protocol does not ensure data delivery. The protocol will try to deliver the data but does not guarantee success. More significantly, an unreliable transport protocol does not notify the sending application when the delivery effort fails.

Both the User Datagram Protocol and the Internet Protocol are unreliable protocols. You may wonder why anyone would ever use an unreliable protocol. The answer is cost. An unreliable protocol is much simpler to design, implement, and use. Cost, in terms of complexity and network bandwidth, is significantly lower with an unreliable protocol. Understand that an unreliable protocol can perform reliable data delivery. Good network applications are designed with added reliability features.

PROTOCOL DATA

Two basic types of data services exist within the TCP/IP protocol suite: a byte-stream service and a datagram service. A protocol that uses a byte-stream service transmits information as a series of bytes. In other words, the protocol treats the data as a single serial stream of bytes, regardless of the data length and the number of transmissions required to send or receive all the data. In addition, when an application uses a byte-stream protocol to send data, the protocol guarantees that the other end of the connection will receive the data in the same order as the transmission sequence. The Transport Control Protocol is a byte-stream protocol.

In contrast, a protocol that uses datagrams transmits information as self-contained units of information. In other words, the protocol transmits each datagram independently—a datagram is not dependent on any other datagram. When the protocol transmits multiple datagrams to the same destination, the datagrams may not arrive in the same order as they were transmitted. If the receiving application requires sequential data, the application must collate the data after it all arrives. The User Datagram Protocol and the Internet Protocol use datagrams to deliver data.

VIRTUAL CIRCUITS

A *virtual circuit* is a connection that appears to be a dedicated point-to-point link. For example, if you place a phone call between New York and Los Angeles, your connection is a virtual circuit. In reality, the telephone company will route your call through many switches in several cities. In other words, you don't have a dedicated wire running between the two telephones.

In many cases, your programs will require a point-to-point connection or virtual circuit. For example, if you want to transfer a file from a remote host computer outside your intranet to your local system, you will probably want to establish a virtual circuit. You do not want to wait for a lot of individual datagrams to deliver the file a few bytes at a time—because the datagrams (and bytes) might arrive in the wrong order. Within the TCP/IP protocol suite, the Transport Control Protocol provides a virtual circuit for network communications; the User Datagram Protocol and Internet Protocol do not.

Table 18.2 summarizes the various characteristics of the Transport Control Protocol (TCP), User Datagram Protocol (UDP), and Internet Protocol (IP).

Characteristic	TCP	UDP	IP
Connection-oriented	X		
Connectionless		X	X
Reliable	X		
Unreliable		X	X
Byte-stream	X		
Datagram		X	X
Virtual circuit	X		

Table 18.2 Summary of protocol characteristics.

UNDERSTANDING INTERNET ADDRESSES

An Internet address is an IP address. Most users, and even much Internet literature, associate IP addresses with host computers. However, you should understand that a computer on the Internet does not really have an IP address. Instead, the IP address is assigned to each Ethernet interface card within the computer. Your computer may have several Ethernet interface cards, each with a unique IP address. For simplicity, you can normally associate an IP address with a host computer. But keep in mind that the interface card (not the host computer) actually owns the IP address.

UNDERSTANDING DOTTED-DECIMAL NOTATION

An IP address is a number which is 32 bits (or 4 bytes) wide. You can represent an IP address in several ways, but most people are used to seeing the dotted-decimal notation. *Dotted-decimal notation* conveniently represents each IP address as a series of decimal numbers separated by periods (or dots). For example, the following numbers are equivalent representations of the same IP address:

IP address as a binary number:	10000110 00011000 00001000 01000010
IP address as a decimal number:	2,249,721,922 (or-2,045,245,374)
IP address as a hexadecimal number:	0x86180842
IP address in dotted-decimal notation:	134.24.8.66

The 32-bit IP address encodes (combines) a network number and a host number (an interface number). As you know, the Internet consists of thousands of interconnected networks. To distinguish one network from another, the Internet Network Information Center (InterNIC) ensures each network has a unique network identifier. As originally designed, the high-order byte (that is, the leftmost number) in an IP address identifies the network number, and the lower three bytes identify the host computer (interface). For example, in the IP address 134.24.8.66, the ID number is 134.

In general, Internet software interprets a field with all 1's as "all." An address field that contains all 1's represents a broadcast address (or, in other words, a message destined for all computers on the network). Normally, Internet software interprets a field with all 0's as "this." In other words, an address field with all 0's would represent "this" network and "this" host computer. The Internet reserves these two addresses (all 1's and all 0's) for these purposes only.

UNDERSTANDING ADDRESS CLASSES

As you know, the original address-encoding scheme used the high-order byte for a network ID number. As a result, users could interconnect only 255 networks. (Remember, the Internet reserves all 1's for broadcast messages.) To overcome this address space limitation, Internet professionals devised a simple but effective encoding scheme. IP addresses no longer use the high-order byte for a network number. Instead, IP addresses use the high-order bits in the high-order byte to identify an *address class*. The address class specifies how many bytes the address uses for the network ID number. The class-encoding scheme sounds much more complicated than it really is. As you read the following paragraphs, refer to Table 18.3. This table will help you understand how the Internet's address-encoding scheme works.

Class	High-Order Bits	Bytes Available for a Network ID
A	0 _ _ _ _	1
B	1 0 _ _ _	2
C	1 1 0 _ _	3
D	1 1 1 0 _	(Used for multicasting)
E	1 1 1 1 0	(Reserved for future use)

Table 18.3 IP address classes.

As you have already learned, a TCP/IP network requires every network interface card on the same physical network to have the same network ID number, but a unique host ID number. By taking a closer look at how classes expand Internet address space, you will understand how network designers can balance the number of networks supported by the Internet against the number of host computers within each network.

DEFINING A CLASS A ADDRESS

If you refer to Table 18.3, you can see that a Class A address uses a maximum of one byte for the class type and network ID. This leaves three bytes for host ID numbers:

1 Bit	7 Bits	24 Bits

| 0 | Network ID | Host ID |

Class A Address

In Table 18.3, you can also see that Class A addresses use one of the high-order bits for class encoding. As a result, only seven bits of the high-order byte are available for network ID numbers. This means the Internet can interconnect only 127 networks with Class A addresses (seven bits can represent 128 unique values, but all 0's is a reserved address). However, because networks with a Class A address use 24 bits for host address space, each such network can theoretically attach 16,777,216 hosts. Therefore, only those few networks that need to attach more than 65,536 hosts use Class A addresses.

DEFINING A CLASS B ADDRESS

As shown in Table 18.3, Class B addresses use a maximum of two bytes for the class type and network ID. This leaves two bytes for host ID numbers:

2 Bits	14 Bits	16 Bits

| 1 | 0 | Network ID | Host ID |

Class B Address

After you subtract the two high-order bits used for class encoding, 14 bits are available for network ID numbers. As a result, the Internet can connect 16,384 networks with Class B addresses. Using 16 bits for the host identifier, each network with a Class B address can theoretically attach up to 65,536 hosts. Networks that need to attach more than 65,536 host computers require a Class A address. The InterNIC reserves Class B addresses for networks that expect to attach at least 256 host computers.

DEFINING A CLASS C ADDRESS

Class C addresses use a maximum of three bytes for the class type and network ID. This leaves one byte for host ID numbers:

3 Bits	21 Bits	8 Bits

| 1 | 1 | 0 | Network ID | Host ID |

Class C Address

After you subtract the three high-order bits used for the class encoding, you have 21 bits available for network ID numbers. As a result, the Internet can connect a staggering 2,097,152 individual networks that use Class C addresses. However, because Class C addresses have only eight bits available for host ID numbers, the Internet limits each of these networks to less than 256 host computers. In other words, small networks use Class C addresses.

DEFINING CLASS D AND E ADDRESSES

The InterNIC uses the D Class for multicast addresses. A multicast address represents a group of Internet host computers. In other words, multicasting delivers messages to one or more host computers. The InterNIC is reserving Class E addresses for future use.

ADDING UP THE NUMBERS

Compare the Internet address space with and without class encoding. With the original addressing scheme (using one byte for network IDs and three bytes for host identifiers), the Internet could connect over four billion computers. However, as previously mentioned, all these computers would be part of a mere 255 networks. Using the class-encoding scheme, the Internet reduced the potential number of host computers by approximately ten percent. However, the class-encoding scheme increased the number of potential networks from 255 to more than two million. In other words, by using the class-encoding scheme, the Internet sacrificed a few individual host computer addresses to gain a tremendous number of individual network identifiers.

UNDERSTANDING SUBNET ADDRESSES

InterNIC assigns all network ID numbers and ensures their uniqueness. Within each network, the network administrator assigns host (interface) ID numbers. Consequently, network administrators have significant flexibility when they set up their networks. Network administrators can use their network's host address space any way they want as long as they identify each network interface with a unique address. A network administrator can subdivide his or her network's host address space to effectively create a local network of networks. For example, assume a network administrator is responsible for an Internet network that uses a Class B address. As discussed, the network administrator has 16 bits available for host ID numbers. The network administrator can subdivide these 16 bits into two bytes, using one byte as a network ID number and one as a host ID number. By doing so, the network administrator creates a *subnet*.

Theoretically, this network administrator could create a subnet of 254 interconnected networks, each with 254 hosts (not 256, because the values containing all 1's and all 0's are reserved). Typically, network administrators use subnet addresses to let a single Internet address span more than one physical network. Systems attached to other networks send packets to the Internet address. Within subnetworks, however, internal routers will use the subnet addresses to route data to the correct physical address. In other words, networks use subnet addresses internally. Other networks use the normal Internet address.

For more information on InterNIC, visit the Web site at *http://rs.internic.net*, shown in Figure 18.6.

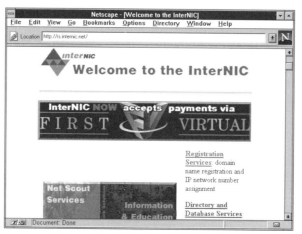

Figure 18.6 The InterNIC Web site.

UNDERSTANDING THE INTERNET ADDRESS PROTOCOLS

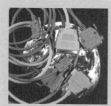

As previously shown in Figure 18.4, the link layer includes two address protocols: the Address Resolution protocol (ARP) and the Reverse Address Resolution Protocol (RARP). In the preceding section, you examined IP addresses on the Internet. The previous section did not discuss the difference between an IP address and the address used by the link layer.

As you have learned, Ethernet addresses (at the physical level) are six bytes wide, compared to IP addresses which are four bytes wide. All data transmitted across a network using Ethernet technology must use Ethernet data frames. As you may recall, an Ethernet interface card scans the frames on the network looking for its Ethernet address. The interface cards do not acknowledge IP addresses.

In other words, TCP/IP protocols only work with IP addresses and Ethernet frames only work with Ethernet addresses. In order to convert or translate the two different address types, the Internet uses the Address Resolution Protocol (ARP) and the Reverse Address Resolution Protocol (RARP). The ARP and RARP exist to resolve addresses. For example, they translate an IP address into a link layer address and vice versa. Figure 18.7 shows the basic function of each protocol.

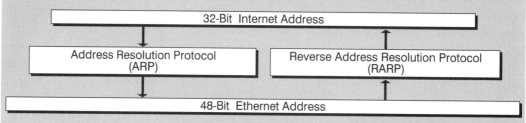

Figure 18.7 Address resolution protocols convert IP and link-layer addresses.

UNDERSTANDING THE *IP DATAGRAM*

As previously discussed, the Internet Protocol (IP) is the delivery system for the TCP/IP protocol suite and the entire Internet, including your intranet. The Internet Protocol uses unreliable, connectionless datagrams to deliver information across a TCP/IP network. You can refer to such datagrams as *IP datagrams*. TCP/IP networks transmit all application data across the Internet as IP datagrams. Each IP datagram includes an IP header and the actual data.

DEFINING AN *IP PACKET*

Internet literature may refer to an IP datagram as an *IP packet*—the terms are synonymous. This seemingly casual use of multiple names for the same unit of data may mislead you. For example, you have learned that multiple protocols such as IP and UDP use datagrams. However, you should also understand that an IP datagram and a UDP datagram are not the same.

As you have learned, a datagram is a self-contained unit of data. In contrast, a byte stream represents data as a continuous data flow. The term *datagram* specifies a type of delivery service. That is, a protocol uses datagrams or a byte-stream. A particular datagram type, such as an IP datagram or a UDP datagram, specifies the datagram's format and contents.

The term *packet* is a generic term that refers to a unit of unidentified data. When you use the term *IP packet*, for example, you specify a unit of IP data. In other words, packet refers to the data. Datagram refers to the delivery service.

UNDERSTANDING THE *IP HEADER*

As you have learned, a TCP/IP network encapsulates nearly all information that flows across the Internet within an IP datagram. The encapsulation creates an IP datagram that includes an IP header and data. The network software always creates an IP header in multiples of 32-bit words, even if it must pad (include additional zeros within) the IP header. The IP header includes all information necessary to deliver the data encapsulated within the IP datagram.

IDENTIFYING INFORMATION IN AN *IP HEADER*

As you might expect, an IP header includes a lot of information because IP is the delivery system for the entire Internet. However, despite its importance and the amount of information it contains, an IP header only consumes 20 bytes of storage space. In fact, unless special IP header options are present, an IP header will always be 20 bytes wide. Figure 18.8 shows an IP datagram with the fields in the IP header identified.

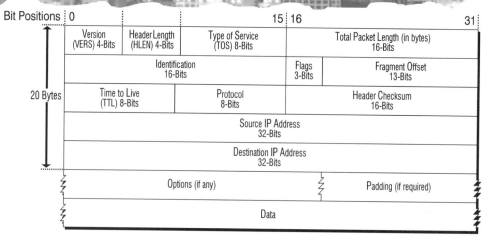

Figure 18.8 *The structure of an IP datagram showing the fields in the IP header.*

Although Figure 18.8 shows the header structure in layers, you should understand that the header is simply a serial stream of data at least 20 bytes long. Table 18.4 briefly describes each field in the IP header.

Data Field	Purpose
Version	Version of the Internet Protocol that created the datagram
Header length	Length of the IP header in 32-bit words
Type of Service	Used to set transmission performance and delivery priorities. The various bits within the Type of Service field are used to indicate precedence, delay, throughput, reliability, and cost. Most Internet software does not widely support this field.
Packet Length	This 16-bit field specifies the length of the entire IP packet, including the IP header, in bytes.
Identification	Used to reassemble fragments of datagrams that were broken into smaller pieces.
Flags	Used with the Identification field to reassemble fragments.
Fragment Offset	Used with the Identification field to reassemble fragments.
Time-to-Live	Used to prevent a packet from wandering the Internet forever. This field is decremented by 1 every time the packet is processed by a router. Once it reaches 0, the packet is destroyed.
Protocol	Indicates which protocol created the data encapsulated within the packet. A value of 6 indicates TCP. A value of 17 indicates UDP.

Table 18.4 *Summary of IP header fields. (continued on the next page)*

Data Field	Purpose
Header checksum	The checksum of the IP header fields only, not the data. This is used to detect transmission errors, whereupon the receiving host discards the IP datagram.
Source IP address	The IP address of the sending host.
Destination IP address	The IP address of the receiving host. If this field were all 1's, the message would be sent to all hosts.
Options	This 8-bit field allows network professionals to test and debug network applications.

Table 18.4 Summary of IP header fields. (continued from previous page)

UNDERSTANDING FRAGMENTATION

Network technologies such as Ethernet specify a maximum transfer unit (MTU). The MTU defines the maximum packet size that the network can transmit. When an application transmits a packet larger than the underlying network's MTU, the network software automatically breaks the packet into smaller chunks and transmits the data as multiple packets. The IP header's fragmentation-related fields, such as Identification, Flags, and Fragment Offset, are updated to indicate that the packet is a fragment and in what order it should be reassembled.

When the destination host receives the fragmented IP packets, a *reassembly timer* is started. All fragments must arrive before the timer expires, otherwise the host will discard all the fragments as invalid. Because fragmentation and reassembly occur between the network and link layers of your network, the process is normally transparent. You normally do not need to do anything special because the network protocols handle fragmentation and reassembly for you automatically.

UNDERSTANDING IP ROUTING

Each section of this chapter has progressively taken you deeper and deeper in your exploration of the TCP/IP protocol suite. In exploring the link layer, the network layer, Internet addresses, associated protocols, and datagrams, you have traveled to the heart of TCP/IP. You now have the essential knowledge you need to pull back and begin to view the big picture as you continue your tour of the TCP/IP protocol stack. You have learned that IP is the Internet delivery system. You have learned a lot of related information about the IP datagrams. You know that delivery of such datagrams is the means by which application data and protocol information move across the Internet. The key to delivering IP datagrams is the IP routing table.

An *IP routing table* stores addresses for selected destinations on the network. In other words, network software can search a routing table to find the best way to reach a specific destination. Routing protocols manage all routing table entries. However, these protocols are not a direct part of TCP/IP.

UNDERSTANDING ROUTING TABLE ENTRIES

A routing table is a list of the addresses in neighboring networks. When a host computer receives a packet, the IP module consults the routing table to determine if the destination address is listed in the table. If the destination address is listed, the packet is sent directly to that network. Otherwise, the packet is sent to another network which is on the way to the final destination. The routing table maintains information on these "indirect" routes.

Each routing table entry includes the following three fields: Network, Gateway, and Flags. The first two fields contain network ID numbers. The Flags field identifies networks that directly connect to the owner of the routing table. The Gateway field identifies a router on a path that leads to the network identified in the Network field. However, the router may not directly connect to the destination network. In other words, routing tables only show the next hop along the path to a particular destination.

UNDERSTANDING THE TRANSPORT LAYER

Up to this point, you have learned how the IP layer delivers data between host computers. The rest of this chapter explains how the transport layer delivers data between applications. In many ways, the transport protocol's responsibilities are similar to those of the IP module. Conceptually, much of what you learned about the IP datagram and the IP header also applies to the transport protocols. As you know, TCP/IP includes two transport protocols: the Transport Control Protocol (TCP) and the User Datagram Protocol (UDP). The Transport Control Protocol is a connection-oriented protocol that uses a reliable byte-stream to send and receive data. The Transport Control Protocol provides a virtual circuit for network communications. The User Datagram Protocol is an unreliable, connectionless protocol that uses datagrams to send and receive data.

In TCP/IP terminology, a port is like an IP address except that TCP/IP associates a port with a protocol rather than a host computer. In the same way that IP datagrams store source and destination IP addresses, transport protocols store source and destination port numbers. In short, network programs associate an Internet protocol port with a specific application and function.

As a connectionless and unreliable protocol, UDP simply deposits data at the port. UDP does not maintain a connection between the sender and receiver. In contrast, TCP is connection oriented. TCP maintains a connection while communicating. In addition, TCP can open multiple connections on the same port.

UNDERSTANDING THE USER DATAGRAM PROTOCOL

UDP is very similar to IP in that both are unreliable, connectionless protocols that use datagrams for data delivery. IP delivers data to a host computer, however, only UDP can route data to multiple destinations (network programs) on a single host. The structure of a UDP header is much simpler than that for an IP header. Figure 18.9 shows the structure of a UDP header.

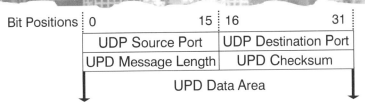

Bit Positions : 0   15 : 16   31

UDP Source Port	UDP Destination Port
UPD Message Length	UPD Checksum
UPD Data Area	

Figure 18.9 The structure of a UDP header.

UNDERSTANDING THE TRANSPORT CONTROL PROTOCOL

Other than the Internet Protocol, the Transport Control Protocol is the most commonly used protocol in the TCP/IP protocol suite. Like the User Datagram Protocol, TCP transports data between the network and application layers. However, TCP is much more complex than UDP because it offers a reliable byte-stream, connection-oriented data delivery service. In other words, TCP ensures that delivery occurs and that the destination application receives the data in the correct sequence. In contrast, UDP doesn't guarantee datagram delivery. Nor does UDP ensure that datagrams arrive in proper sequence.

ENSURING RELIABILITY

To ensure reliability and byte-stream sequencing, TCP uses *acknowledgments*. After the destination end of a TCP connection receives a transmission, the destination end transmits an acknowledgment message to the transmitting end. In short, to the sender, the acknowledgment says, "Yes, I got your message." Each time the transmitting end of a connection sends a message, TCP starts a timer. If the timer expires before the TCP module receives an acknowledgment, TCP automatically re-transmits the unacknowledged data.

To improve message throughput, TCP does not send a message and then wait until it receives an acknowledgment before transmitting another. Instead, TCP uses a concept called a *sliding window*, which lets TCP transmit several messages before it waits for an acknowledgment.

DEFINING A TCP MESSAGE

You can refer to each package, or unit of TCP data, as a TCP message or TCP segment. Both terms are correct and widely used in Internet literature. However, for reasons discussed in the following paragraphs, you might want to use the term *segment*. Remember, TCP treats data as a single, unbroken, serial stream of data. However, TCP must use IP datagrams for delivery. Luckily, your programs can treat TCP data as a continuous byte stream, ignoring IP datagrams.

Whenever you see the term *TCP message*, you may want to substitute the term *TCP segment*. By doing so, you will acknowledge the fact that each TCP message that an IP datagram delivers is really only one segment of the TCP byte stream. A TCP segment consists of a TCP header, TCP options, and the data that the segment transports. Figure 18.10 shows the structure of a TCP segment.

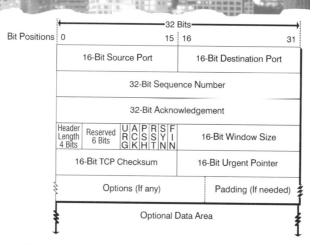

Figure 18.10 *TCP segment (or message) structure.*

Although Figure 18.10 shows the TCP header structure in layers, you should understand that the header is simply a serial stream of data at least 20 bytes long. Table 18.5 briefly describes each field in the TCP header.

Data Field	Purpose
Source Port	Identifies the protocol port of the sending application.
Destination Port	Identifies the protocol port of the receiving application.
Sequence Number	Identifies the first byte of data in the data area of the TCP segment.
Ack Number	Identifies the next byte of data that the sender expects from the data stream.
Header Length	Specifies the length of the TCP header in 32-bit words.
URG Flag	Tells the receiving TCP module that the Urgent Pointer field points to urgent data.
ACK Flag	Tells the receiving TCP module that the Acknowledgment Number field contains a valid acknowledgment number.
PSH Flag	Tells the receiving TCP module to immediately send the data to the destination application.
RST Flag	Asks the receiving TCP module to reset the TCP connection.
SYN Flag	Tells the receiving TCP module to synchronize sequence numbers.

Table 18.5 *The purpose of the TCP header data fields. (continued on next page)*

Data Field	Purpose
FIN Flag	Tells the receiving TCP module that the sender has finished sending data.
Window Size	Tells the receiving TCP module the number of bytes that the sender is willing to accept.
TCP Checksum	Helps the receiving TCP module detect data corruption.
Urgent Pointer	Points to the last byte of urgent data in the TCP data area.
Options	Usually used with the Maximum Segment Size option, which advertises the largest segment that the TCP module expects to receive.

Table 18.5 *The purpose of the TCP header data fields. (continued from previous page)*

ESTABLISHING A *TCP CONNECTION*

To ensure data reliability and byte-stream ordering, TCP sends and receives acknowledgments. To accomplish these operations, TCP must have some method of identifying the transmitted data. Likewise, the network must somehow synchronize the receiving end of the TCP connection with the sending end. In other words, both ends of the TCP connection need to know when they can start transmitting data. They also need to know how to identify the sender's data. For example, suppose a TCP module receives a corrupted data packet. The receiving TCP module needs a way to tell the sending TCP module which packet to resend. To establish a TCP connection, both ends of the connection must negotiate and agree to use packet identification information that the other end understands.

Likewise, as part of this synchronization process, both ends of the TCP connection must establish some system for acknowledging messages. Otherwise, miscommunication may occur. To establish and terminate connections, as well as to send and receive acknowledgments, the TCP header uses the Sequence Number, Acknowledgment Number, and Flags fields. Each time your program wants to use TCP to transport data, your program transmits a request for a TCP connection to your host computer's transport layer. Next, the TCP module in your host's transport layer sends a TCP message with a Synchronization (SYN) flag to the remote port to which your program wants to connect.

The Synchronization flag tells the receiving (or server-side) TCP module that a client program wants to establish a TCP connection. Along with the Synchronization flag, the message also includes a 32-bit *sequence number* that the sending TCP module stores in the Sequence Number field. The server-side TCP module replies with a TCP segment that includes an Acknowledgment (ACK) flag and an *acknowledgment number*.

Programs close TCP connections using a two-way handshake. Either end of a TCP connection can initiate the close of the connection. To close a connection, one side of the connection sends a message with the Finished (FIN) flag set. Upon receiving the FIN message, the receiving end responds with a message containing the FIN flag set. Both sides follow by shutting down the connection. Keep in mind that because TCP has full-duplex capability, it is possible to close one side down while the other continues to be active.

APPLICATION LAYER

The application layer is most familiar to programmers who write software that needs to communicate over the network. The application layer is program-specific and contains all the details about a specific application. In other words, the application layer is designed as a programmer designs his program. As you have learned, a programmer can design a program to communicate over the network simply by sending information down the protocol stack.

PUTTING IT ALL TOGETHER

In this chapter, you learned that the TCP/IP protocol suite is a collection of cooperative protocols; the protocols in the TCP/IP protocol suite coordinate to deliver data across the TCP/IP networks that comprise the Internet, as well as across your own intranet. You also learned that the network layer and the Internet Protocol deliver data between host computers on the Internet. In addition, the transport layer and the transport protocols deliver data between applications. In Chapter 19, you will examine intranet security issues. Before you continue with Chapter 19, however, make sure you understand the following key concepts:

- ✓ The TCP/IP protocol suite is a collection of protocols that work together to communicate information across the Internet.

- ✓ A protocol stack refers to the vertical order in which protocols appear in a layered network.

- ✓ The TCP/IP protocol stack consists of all the protocols in the TCP/IP protocol suite.

- ✓ When your programs transmit data to a remote host on the Internet, your data flows down the protocol stack and across the network. At its destination, your data flows up the protocol stack to the destination program on the remote host computer.

- ✓ You can replace the link layer (the network interface card) with different network technologies and not affect existing TCP/IP applications.

- ✓ Reliable protocols guarantee data delivery; unreliable protocols do not.

- ✓ A byte stream delivers data as a single, serial stream of data. A datagram delivers data as individual, self-contained units of data.

✓ The TCP/IP network layer manages data delivery between host computers on the network.

✓ The TCP/IP address protocols translate packet addresses between IP addresses and link-layer data-frame addresses.

✓ Routing tables identify the next destination address (or hop) in the path to any destination on the Internet.

✓ A TCP/IP protocol port represents a network application address within a host computer.

✓ Transport protocols use protocol ports to talk to applications.

✓ TCP uses full-duplex communication, which requires TCP modules to terminate data flow in both directions before closing a TCP connection.

VISITING KEY SITES THAT DISCUSS INTRANETS

The World Wide Web is filled with hundreds of excellent and current articles on all aspects of intranets. Use the following sites as starting points for your Web exploration.

PLUGGED IN COMMUNICATIONS

http://www.plugged.net.au/pi/intranet.html

US ROBOTICS

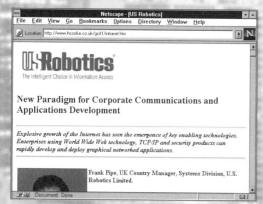

http://www.hcooke.co.uk/gcit1/intranet.htm

PC/TCP NETWORK SOFTWARE

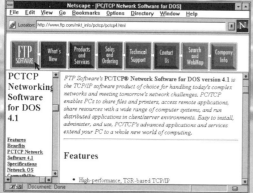

http://www.ftp.com/mkt_info/pctcp/pctcp4.html

ATTACHMATE

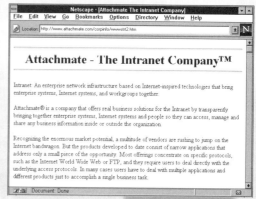

http://www.attachmate.com/corpinfo/
wwwstrt2.htm

INTRANET WORLD

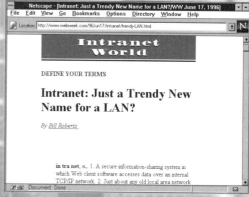

http://www.webweek.com/96Jun17/intranet/
trendy-LAN.html

CRT 1.1.4

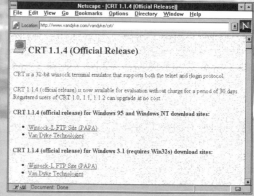

http://www.vandyke.com/vandyke/crt/

Chapter 19

Intranet Security Issues

When users discuss intranets, security issues frequently surface. The Internet (and intranets) is structured in a way that information often flows freely, without adequate safeguards. This allows information to flow directly from your intranet to the desktops of users who can harm your business. Your office may have a security policy that lets some individuals access specific parts of the building. In addition, your system may have further restrictions that apply to specific high-security offices, such as the CEO's office, Human Resources, Finance, or even the nurse's office. In such cases, your company may accomplish its security in a variety of ways. For example, people with access to these areas may use a special key or ID card and visitors to the areas may require an escort.

As you create your intranet, you must define a security policy which restricts user access to various locations on your site. The security techniques this chapter describes protect your intranet from external and internal unauthorized visitors. You may use the security techniques to protect high-security intranet documents, granting access to only those users who need to know the document's contents.

Despite your efforts to develop a comprehensive security plan, you must be prepared to deal with the possibility of someone gaining unauthorized access to information on your intranet. Security breaks have happened before and will happen again. This chapter will identify some steps you can take to prevent most accidental intrusions. You will also learn some of the tricks hackers have used to gain access into an otherwise well-protected network. By the time you finish this chapter, you will understand the following key concepts:

- You must design security into your network.

- A *firewall* is a system of hardware and software designed to protect your network from unauthorized access.

- A router can filter out and reject packets coming into your network.

- You can use firewalls within your network to enforce security between departments inside your company.

- A firewall cannot prevent computer viruses from entering your network.

- Before you design a firewall, you must develop a security plan outlining the type of access your employees and outsiders should have.

- The three main types of firewalls are network-level, application-level, and circuit-level firewalls.

- The three most popular firewall architectures are the dual-homed host firewall, the screened-host firewall, and the screened-subnet firewall.

- If programmers do not design and implement CGI scripts with security in mind, CGI scripts may open your system to security threats.

- Users should encrypt files before sending confidential data across the Internet.

- Users can encrypt information in several ways, including link encryption, document encryption, the secure-socket layer (SSL), and secure HTTP (S-HTTP).

- Across the Internet, hackers have several well-established ways to break into your network.

THE DIFFERENT FORMS OF SECURITY

The Internet's original developers designed it to be resistant to network attacks in the form of equipment breakdowns, broken cabling, and power outages. Unfortunately, the Internet today needs additional technology to prevent attacks against user privacy and company security. Luckily, you can buy a variety of hardware and software solutions which will help you protect your networks.

WHAT IS A BASTION HOST?

 As you read literature about firewalls, you may encounter the term *bastion host*. In general, a bastion host is a computer specially fortified against network attacks. Network designers place bastion host computers on a network as a first line of network defense. A bastion host is the "choke point" of all communications that lead in and out of your intranet. By centralizing access through one computer, you can easily manage network security and configure the appropriate software for that one machine.

PROTECTING AGAINST EXTERNAL INTRUSION

Most companies provide their employees with access to the Internet long before they provide intranet access. Thus, by the time they implement their intranet, they must make the connection through a firewall. A *firewall* is a collection of hardware and software that interconnects two or more networks and, at the same time, provides a central location for managing security. A firewall typically consists of a bastion host—a computer that is fortified against network attacks. As shown in Figure 19.1, the bastion host can be any computer you already own and is sometimes referred to as a server.

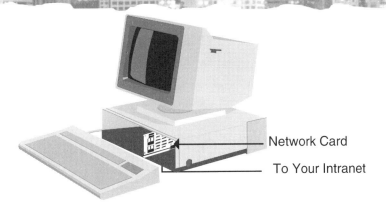

Network Card

To Your Intranet

Figure 19.1 You can designate any PC you already own as a bastion host.

In addition to traditional firewall hardware and software, you may want to use a piece of equipment known as a *router*. As you have learned, a router is a special device which filters out data packets based on criteria that you specify. You can also implement a router using an existing PC or Unix computer. Figure 19.2 shows how a router passes certain packets and rejects others.

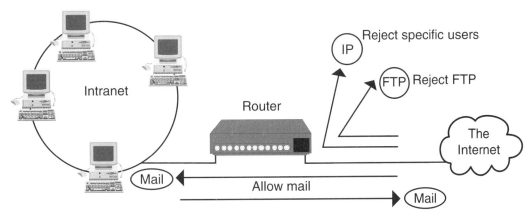

Figure 19.2 A router is a device which filters packets.

As you will learn later in this chapter, by properly configuring a firewall using a combination of bastion hosts and routers, you can achieve reasonable security against Internet users.

PROTECTING AGAINST INTRUSION BETWEEN INTERNAL DEPARTMENTS

Just as you must protect your intranet from Internet users, you may also need to protect various departments within your intranet from one another. In general, your intentions should be to protect the confidential documents your departments generate from all attacks. In most cases, you probably focus more on protecting your documents against malicious attacks from outside your intranet than from within. Regardless of your internal security concerns, you will find that firewalls provide as much security as you need. What's more, the firewalls that protect you against Internet users are similar to the firewalls you use to protect your documents internally. For example, Figure 19.3 illustrates a simple configuration that uses one host computer with three network cards to protect three departments from each other's casual intrusion.

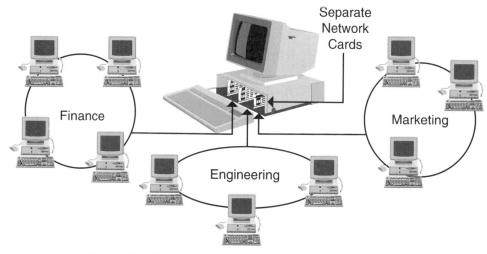

Figure 19.3 Using a host computer to protect several intranets.

SENDING PRIVATE INFORMATION ACROSS THE INTERNET

In addition to protecting one network from another, you must maintain the confidentiality of information you send across networks. For example, imagine that one doctor sends confidential medical data to another doctor. In this case, it does not matter whether the two doctors share the same intranet within one hospital, or whether they are in two distant hospitals communicating over the Internet. The network transmission must keep the patient's medical data confidential and unavailable for public viewing. To protect documents that traverse networks, you must consider a variety of encryption options. Later in this chapter, you will learn some ways you can effectively encrypt information.

UNDERSTANDING FIREWALLS

As you have learned, a firewall is a system that controls access between two networks. Normally, you install a firewall between your intranet and the Internet as a way to prevent the rest of the world from accessing your private intranet. Do not think of a firewall as a single piece of equipment or one do-it-all software program. Instead, think of a firewall as a comprehensive way to achieve maximum network privacy, while minimizing the inconvenience authorized users experience.

In the safest sense, you can create the ultimate firewall by not connecting your network to the Internet. For example, all you need in many intranet installations is an internal network for groupware collaboration. In such cases, you can physically isolate your computer network from the rest of the world.

KEEPING YOUR INTRANET ISOLATED

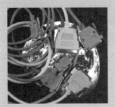

The best way to prevent outsiders from gaining access to your intranet is to physically isolate your intranet from the Internet. In simple terms, networks are connected by cables. To isolate your network, just make sure that your intranet cable never connects to your Internet cable!

By connecting two sets of cables, one for your intranet and the other for the Internet, you can provide your employees access to both the internal and external networks. For example, as shown in Figure 19.4, an employee's client computer can use a switch box to flip between the two networks.

397

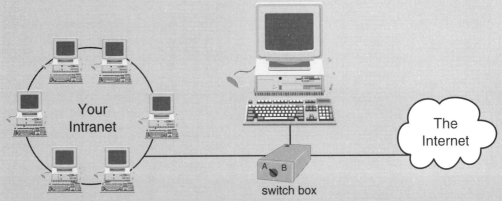

Figure 19.4 Using a switch box to select separate networks.

Figure 19.5 shows a configuration within which the computer has two separate network cards installed—each isolated from each other and switchable through software.

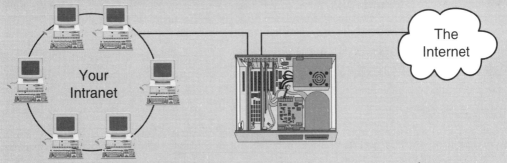

Figure 19.5 Using two network cards to access separate networks.

HOW TO BE ISOLATED BUT NOT UNREACHABLE

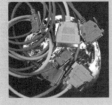

Throughout this book, you have learned how a company intranet is a valuable employee tool. However, if your intranet is isolated from the Internet, you make it much more difficult for off-site employees to benefit from your intranet. Therefore, companies normally provide employees throughout the world with access to the intranet via a direct Internet connection. However, despite the reasonable effectiveness of a well-designed firewall, you may decide that your security concerns make a direct connection to the Internet completely out of the question.

To provide remote employees with access to your intranet, you have several alternatives. First, employees who are on the road or are working from home can call a special phone number which connects them to your intranet server. Such users can use an ordinary modem and, typically, the point-to-point protocol (PPP) to communicate using TCP/IP. As you learned in Chapter 1, PPP is a common method PCs use to communicate via modems. In this situation, you should provide a password account for the caller, or a callback mechanism which dials a pre-established phone number for each employee who tries to dial into the system. In other words, the callback method lets the caller dial into the system and enter a password. Next, the office computer hangs up and immediately calls the pre-established phone number to reconnect the call. Figure 19.6 shows how a callback process increases security by reducing the number of locations from which a user can actually connect to a system.

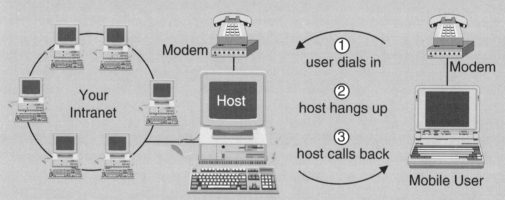

Figure 19.6 How a callback system works.

If multiple buildings need to share the same intranet, you may want to consider using a private underground cable to make the physical connection. Other options you can use to increase security include scrambled satellite transmissions and dedicated phone lines. Granted, such security solutions become substantially more expensive than using the Internet's "public" connection, especially if you need to connect several geographically dispersed locations—but they do increase your system's security.

WHAT A FIREWALL CANNOT DO

Even without a connection to the Internet, your organization is susceptible to unauthorized access. For example, voice mail is probably the security threat you consider least today. However, imagine the damage a company might incur should someone learn the CEO's voice-mail password. In such a case, an outsider could dial into the voice mail system (which is frequently managed by a third-party firm) and listen to confidential information. To reduce the opportunity for such intrusions, your company should formulate a policy that requires frequent password changes and even place limits on the length and number of voice-mail message recordings your system will record.

For example, disgruntled employees, including those who have been recently laid off, can be a serious security threat. Such employees can leak anything from source code to company strategies to the outside. In addition, casual business conversations, overheard in a restaurant or other public place, may lead to a compromise in security. In short, your business already has security issues to deal with. Obviously, a firewall cannot solve these specific problems. Hopefully, your company already has a security policy, which you can extend to include firewall issues.

Finally, a firewall cannot keep viruses out of your network. Viruses are a growing and very serious security threat. You must prevent viruses from entering your intranet from Internet users who upload files to your server. To protect your system, you must run anti-virus software on a regular basis.

399

FIREWALL DESIGN DECISIONS

The need for a firewall implies that you have a need to connect your intranet to the outside world—the Internet. By assessing the types of communications you expect to cross between your intranet and the Internet, you can formulate a specific firewall design. Some of the questions you must ask include:

- Do you want Internet-based users to upload or download files to or from the company server?
- Are there particular users (such as competitors) for which you want to deny all access?
- Will your company publish a Web page?
- Will your site provide *telnet* support to Internet users?
- Should your company's intranet users have unrestricted Web access?
- Do you need statistics on who is trying to access your system through the firewall?
- Will you have a dedicated staff to monitor firewall security?
- What is the worst case scenario should an attacker break into your intranet?
- Do users need to connect to geographically dispersed intranets?

UNDERSTANDING THE THREE TYPES OF FIREWALLS

As you will learn, to meet the needs of a wide range of users, there are three types of firewalls: *network level, application level,* and *circuit level* firewalls. Each firewall type uses a somewhat different approach to protecting your intranet. After you have determined your firewall needs based on the questions presented in the previous section, you should carefully consider each firewall. By understanding the type of protection you need, you can better design your firewall.

Keep in mind that most firewalls support some level of encryption, which means you can send data from your intranet, through the firewall, encrypt it, and send it to the Internet. Likewise, encrypted data can come in from the Internet, and your firewall can decrypt the data before it reaches your intranet. Figure 19.7 illustrates the process of firewall encryption. Using such encryption, you connect geographically dispersed intranets through the Internet without worrying about someone intercepting and reading your data. Likewise, your company's mobile employees can also use encryption when they dial into your system (perhaps via the Internet) to access private intranet files.

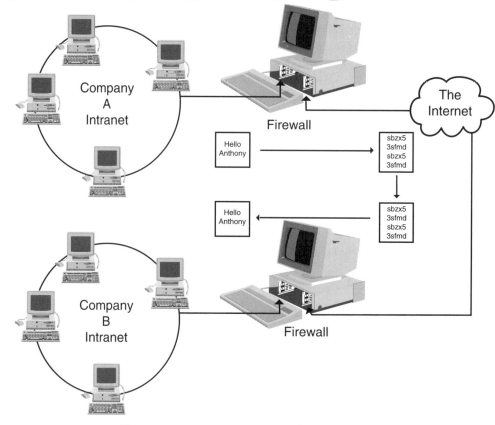

Figure 19.7 Using an encryption feature of firewalls.

NETWORK-LEVEL FIREWALLS

A network-level firewall is typically a router or special computer which examines packet addresses, and then decides whether to pass the packet through or to block the packet from entering the intranet. As you have learned, packets contain the sender's and recipient's IP address, along with a variety of other information about the packet.

You might, for example, configure your network-level firewall or router to block all messages from a specific competitor's site. Normally, you block packets using a file that contains the IP addresses of sites whose target or destination packets the router should block. When the router sees a packet that contains a specified IP address, the router will reject the packet, preventing the packet from entering your intranet. Blocking specific sites in this way is sometimes called *blacklisting*. Normally, router software will let you blacklist an entire site, but not a specific user.

Keep in mind that a packet arriving at your router may contain an e-mail message, a request for a service such as HTTP (Web page access) or ftp (file upload and download capability), or even a telnet login request (a remote access to your computer). The network-level router recognizes and performs specific actions for each request type. For example, you can program your router to let Internet users view your Web pages, yet not allow them to use *ftp* to transfer files to or from your server. Normally, you can set up a router which will consider the following information on a per-packet basis, before deciding whether to send a packet through:

- Source address from which the data is coming
- Destination address to which the data is going
- Session protocol such as TCP, UDP, or ICMP
- Source and destination application port for the desired service
- Whether the packet is the start of a connection request

If you properly install and configure a network-level firewall, it will be very fast and transparent to users. Of course for users you have blacklisted, your router will live up to the name firewall in its effectiveness to keep out unwanted trespassers.

How Do You Use a Router?

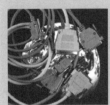 A router is a special computer which screens (filters out) specific packets based on criteria that you define. You can program criteria into your router using router-specific software. Most commercial routers are available with the software you need. In addition, router screening software for PCs and Unix computers is available to the public. To download these programs, use *ftp* to visit these sites:

- PC files: *ftp://ftp.net.ohio-state.edu/pub/kbridge*
- Unix files: *ftp://ftp.cisco.com/pub/acl-example.tar.gz*

You program a router by listing a set of rules within a router-specific file. These rules tell the router how it should handle each incoming packet. For example, you may specify a rule that blocks incoming *ftp* connections. After you have programmed your router, you simply install it between your intranet and the Internet. The router, in turn, will screen all communications between these two networks.

Application-Level Firewalls

An application-level firewall is normally a host computer running software known as a proxy server. A *proxy server* is an application that controls traffic between two networks. When you use an application-level firewall, your intranet and the Internet are not physically connected. Instead, the traffic that flows on one network never mixes with the traffic of the other because the two network cables don't touch. The job of the proxy server is to transfer an isolated copy of the packet from one network to the other network. This type of firewall effectively masks the origin of the initiating connection and protects your intranet from Internet users who may be trying to glean information about your private network.

Because proxy servers understand network protocols, you can configure the proxy server to control which services you want on your network. For example, you can direct the proxy server to allow *ftp* file downloads, but to disallow *ftp* file uploads. Proxy servers are available for a variety of services, such as HTTP access, *telnet, ftp,* and *Gopher*. You must set up a proxy server for each service you want to provide. Two popular proxy servers are the *TIS Internet Firewall Toolkit* and *SOCKS*. For information on these two proxy servers, visit the Web sites shown in Figures 19.8a and 19.8b.

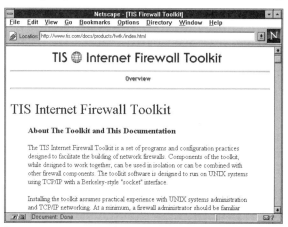

Figure 19.8a Information on TIS at http://www.tis.com/docs/products/fwtk/index.html.

Figure 19.8b Information on SOCKS at http://204.156.150.110/linux/howto/Firewall-HOWTO-8.html.

When you implement an application-level proxy server, users must use client programs that support proxy operations. Network designers developed many TCP/IP protocols, such as HTTP, with proxy support in mind. In most browsers, users can easily configure their browsers to point to the proxy server using preferences in the browser software. Unfortunately, other protocols do not readily support proxy services. In such cases, you may have to make your Internet application selections based on whether they are compatible with a common-proxy protocol. For example, applications which support the *SOCKS* proxy protocol are a good solution if you base all network access on *SOCKS*. As you set up your application-level firewall, you must also assess whether your users already have client software that supports proxy services.

Application-level firewalls provide you with the ability to audit the type and amount of traffic that is accessing your site. Because application-level firewalls make a distinct physical separation (a break) between your intranet and the Internet, they are a good choice for high-security requirements. However, because a program can analyze the packets and make decisions about access control, application-level firewalls tend to reduce network performance. If you plan to use an application-level firewall, use the fastest computer you have to host the proxy server.

CIRCUIT-LEVEL FIREWALLS

A *circuit-level firewall* is similar to an application-level firewall in that both are proxy servers. The difference is that a circuit-level firewall does not require you to use special proxy-client applications. As you learned in the previous section, application-level firewalls require special proxy software for each service, such as *ftp*, *telnet*, and HTTP.

In contrast, a circuit-level firewall creates a circuit between a client and server without requiring either application to know anything about the service. The advantage of a circuit-level firewall is that it provides service for a wide variety of protocols, whereas an application-level firewall requires an application-level proxy for each and every service. For example, if you use a circuit-level firewall for HTTP, *ftp*, or *telnet*, you don't have to do anything special or change your applications in any way; instead, you can simply run your existing software. Another benefit of circuit-level firewalls is that you work with only a single proxy server, which is easier to manage, log, and control than multiple servers. For more information on circuit-level firewalls, visit the site at *http://gows.gintic.ntu.ac.sg:8000/~ronnie/security/firewall.html#categories*, shown in Figure 19.9.

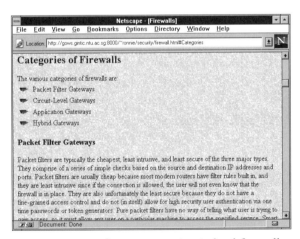

Figure 19.9 Information on circuit-level firewalls.

UNDERSTANDING FIREWALL ARCHITECTURES

As you construct your firewall, you must decide what type of traffic you will allow and not allow through your intranet. As discussed, you can choose a router which will screen selected packets, or you can use some type of proxy software that will run on your existing host computer. As it turns out, a firewall architecture may encompass both of these configurations. In other words, you can maximize your intranet's security by combining both a router and a proxy server into your firewall. The three most popular firewall architectures are the *dual-homed host firewall*, the *screened host firewall*, and the *screened subnet firewall*. The screened-host and screened-subnet firewalls use a combination of routers and proxy servers.

UNDERSTANDING DUAL-HOMED HOST FIREWALLS

A dual-homed host firewall is a simple, yet very secure configuration in which you dedicate one host computer as the dividing line between your intranet and the Internet. The host computer uses two separate network cards to connect to each network, as shown in Figure 19.10. Using a dual-home host firewall, you must disable the computer's routing capabilities so it does not "connect" the two networks. One of the drawbacks of this configuration is that it is easy to inadvertently enable internal routing.

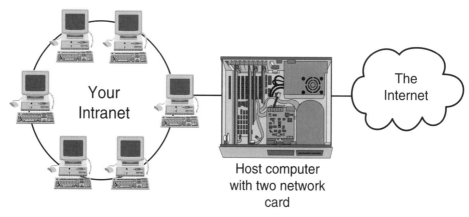

Figure 19.10 *A dual-homed host firewall.*

The dual-homed host firewall works by running either an application-level or a circuit-level proxy. As you learned earlier, proxy software controls the packet flow from one network to another. Because the host computer is dual-homed (connected to both networks), the host firewall sees both packets on both networks, which lets it run proxy software to control traffic between the two networks.

UNDERSTANDING SCREENED-HOST FIREWALLS

Many network designers consider screened-host firewalls more secure than a dual-homed host firewall. By adding a router and placing the host computer away from the Internet, you achieve a very effective and easy-to-maintain firewall. Figure 19.11 shows a screened-host firewall.

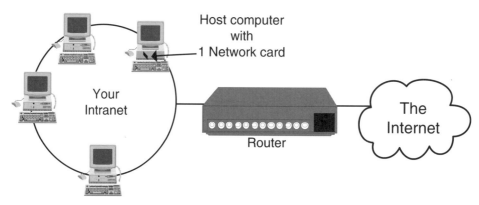

Figure 19.11 *A screened-host firewall.*

As you can see, a router connects the Internet to your intranet and, at the same time, filters the types of packets it allows through. You can configure the router so that it sees only one host computer on your intranet network. Users on your network who you want to connect to the Internet must do so through this host computer. Thus, internal users appear to have direct access to the Internet, but external user's access is restricted by the host computer.

UNDERSTANDING SCREENED-SUBNET FIREWALLS

A screened-subnet firewall architecture further isolates your intranet from the Internet by incorporating an intermediate perimeter network. Within a screened-subnet firewall, you place your host computer on the perimeter network which users can access through two separate routers. One router controls intranet traffic and the second, Internet traffic. Figure 19.12 shows a screened-subnet firewall.

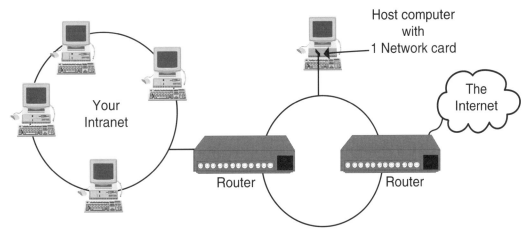

Figure 19.12 A screened-subnet firewall.

A screened-subnet firewall provides a formidable defense against attack. Because the firewall isolates the host computer on a separate network, it reduces the impact of an attack to the host computer and further minimizes the chance that your internal network will be harmed.

THE DANGERS OF CGI SCRIPTING

As you surf the Web, you will come across sites that provide two-way communications. For example, a Web page may present you with a form with empty fields. When you fill in this form and click your mouse on the form's Submit button, your browser requests the server computer to run a special program, typically a CGI (Common Gateway Interface) script, to process your form's contents. The CGI script runs on the server computer to process the form and creates the output which the server returns to the browser for display.

From a security perspective, the danger of CGI scripts is that they give users the power to make your server perform a task. Normally, the CGI process works very well, and users can use scripts to get information ranging from amortization tables to product order forms to a wide range of product information. Unfortunately, some users have found ways to go beyond the script's intended design to make it perform other operations. In some cases, attackers can actually shut down a server by sending it CGI data it was never intended to have.

If you have a server and publish interactive Web pages, you probably use CGI scripts to provide the interaction. The following sections describe several techniques you can use to make your CGI scripts resistant to tampering.

SECURING CGI SCRIPTS

A CGI script is simply a program that runs on your server in response to a user request. When the CGI script runs, it tells your server to perform specific operations based on the user's input. To evaluate a CGI script from a security perspective, you must make sure that users cannot use the CGI script to execute potentially damaging commands on your server. The following list provides important guidelines that will help you create safe CGI scripts:

- Establish a comprehensive testing policy for every new CGI script that you install on your host server.

- Expect users to enter unexpected characters. Fields in CGI forms should handle blank entries, bad characters, letters when numbers are expected, numbers when letters are expected, and hidden characters.

- Avoid letting the user enter Unix shell metacharacters, such as the *, |, \, and & characters. These characters may force your machine to perform unintended and potentially devastating actions.

- Make sure that you test for an overflowing field (one with too many characters). For example, your script may expect a nine-digit zip code, but a user may type in pages of the text from a novel.

- Test your script using a variety of browsers. Some browsers may encode special (unexpected) characters which affect your server, giving an attacker a possible backdoor into your system.

- Avoid assembling filenames based on user input. An attacker may use a pathname to gain access to your system files, such as the Unix */etc/passwd* file, within which the attacker can create unauthorized accounts on your system. For example, if your CGI script writes a log file based on a user's name, the user may enter a pathname, such as *../../../../etc/passwd*, instead of a simple name, which lets the user navigate to unauthorized directories.

- Do not pass user commands to the subprocess when your CGI script directs the server to run subprocesses.

- Use the */usr/lib/sendmail* program, instead of the */bin/mailx* or */usr/ucb/ mail* programs if your CGI script runs on a Unix machine and lets users send mail, because the */usr/lib/sendmail* program does not let the user escape to a shell as do the others.

- Remove the backup files that many script editors leave behind. Attackers know to look for these and may try to execute them.

- Assign an administrator to control access to the scripts directory. Do not let anyone else add new scripts to your system without submitting the scripts for exhaustive testing.

- Avoid storing your scripts in a directory that is accessible through *ftp*. Attackers may be able to delete your scripts or replace them with ones that they have written themselves.

How to Send Mail and Files Securely

For most users, Internet technology eased its way into their lives through e-mail. Because of its simplicity, low cost, and almost instantaneous delivery time, the ability to use e-mail to send a note or document has become a necessity for many users. Unfortunately, most users do not realize that e-mail is not automatically secure. Instead, e-mail messages can be read by anyone who has access to any one of the many servers through which e-mail travels as it makes its way to its final destination. Granted, the average person will probably not read any of your e-mail messages. But, privileged users, such as your network administrator, can go through your mail.

To reduce the probability of someone reading your e-mail, you need to consider the various encryption methods that make your e-mail unreadable by everyone but the most ardent attackers.

Do Not Send Private Messages by E-Mail

 If you are an employee within a company that has its own e-mail server, you may not be aware that every piece of e-mail that you send or receive can easily be read by other employees. The e-mail messages that flow in and out of your office go through the company's server and finally to your desktop computer. Many servers are set up to automatically backup e-mail messages. Therefore, the server may backup your e-mail on a nightly basis. Even though you may have deleted an e-mail you wrote containing a scathing description of your boss, the e-mail may reside in a backup file.

Because the server and its files are owned by your company, you are not protected by privacy laws. Your boss can read all your e-mail, personal and otherwise, and you will have to deal with the repercussions. In some cases, company encryption programs may not help you. Again, the company owns the files, including the encryption keys, and may force you to decrypt your files.

Although you are safer using an on-line service such as America Online (because your e-mail messages are stored on a remote system and not your PC), you are still at risk of having others read your e-mail. The best way to eliminate an electronic invasion of your privacy is to assume that your e-mail is much like a postcard you are sending through the U.S. Postal Service. If you do not want people reading it, encrypt it or don't send it.

ENCRYPTION METHODS

Encryption prevents others from reading your documents by "jumbling" the contents of your file in such a way that it becomes unintelligible to anyone who views it. To read the file's contents, you must have a special key. A key is a special number, much like the combination of a padlock, which the encryption hardware or software uses to encrypt and decrypt files. Just as padlock numbers have a certain number of digits, so do encryption keys. When you hear people talk about 40-bit or 128-bit keys, they are simply referring to the number of binary digits in the encryption key. The more bits in the key, the more secure the encryption and less likely an attacker can guess your key and unlock the file. However, attackers have already found ways to crack 40-bit keys.

You can introduce encryption as a way to improve your communications security in several ways: link encryption, document encryption, the use of the secure-sockets layer (SSL), and the use of secure HTTP (S-HTTP). The following sections describe these encryption methods in detail.

UNDERSTANDING PUBLIC-KEY ENCRYPTION

Public-key encryption is an encryption method in which a sender encrypts a document using two separate keys: a *public key* and a *private key*. A user gives the *public key* to other users who, in turn, use the key to encrypt a file. The original user then uses his or her own *private key* to decrypt files (encrypted with the public key).

Users with the public key can only encrypt files, not decrypt them. The private key is the only key that can decrypt the file. Therefore, the only person that can decrypt a message is the person holding the private key. The person with the private key gives users the public key which is used only to encrypt files for that user. Figure 19.13 shows how the public-key encryption process works.

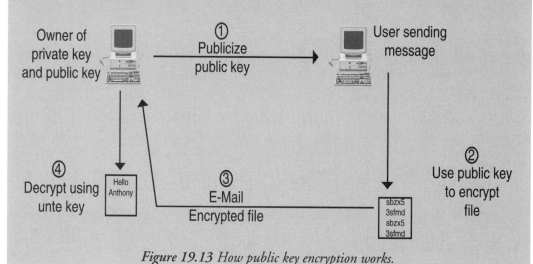

Figure 19.13 How public key encryption works.

In 1976, Whitfield Diffie and Martin Hellman described this technique in a paper entitled "New Directions in Cryptography." For more information on public-key encryption, visit the Web site at *http://uep.Ams.AMeslAb.gov/dev/charlie/pke/pke.html*, shown in Figure 19.14.

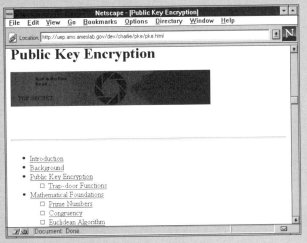

Figure 19.14 Information on public-key encryption.

UNDERSTANDING AND USING DIGITAL SIGNATURES

A *digital signature* is a technique which assures a recipient that an Internet file is truly from the person the file indicates. The use of digital signatures prevent clever programmers from forging e-mail messages. For example, a programmer who is familiar with e-mail protocols can build and send an e-mail using anyone's e-mail address, such as *BillClinton@whitehouse.gov*.

If you understand how public-key encryption works, you may already understand how a digital signature works. In public-key encryption, the sender encrypts a document using a public key, and the recipient decodes the document using a private key. With digital signature, the reverse occurs. The sender uses a private key to encrypt a signature, and the recipient decodes the signature using a public key. Because the sender is the only person who can encrypt his or her signature, only the sender can authenticate messages.

By including a digital signature and using public-key encryption with your documents, you help your recipient authenticate that the document came from you, allowing only the recipient to read your document's contents.

To obtain your own digital signature, you must register your key with a certificate authority (CA), which can attest that you are on file and that you are the only person with the key. The certificate authority can be your company or a trusted neutral party. For more information on digital signatures, visit *http://www.sevenlocks.com/DigitalSignatures.htm*, shown in Figure 19.15.

Figure 19.15 Information on digital signatures.

UNDERSTANDING LINK ENCRYPTION

Link encryption is a technique that long-haul telephone lines use to encrypt communications between two distant sites. Link encryption requires the two sites to agree on encryption keys and is commonly used between divisions of a company that have frequent communications needs. Because it requires a dedicated line and separate software to handle the encryption, link encryption is an expensive way to encrypt data. However, many of the latest generation of routers provide built-in encryption options which increase reliability and convenience, while reducing the cost for maintaining separate components. Figure 19.16 illustrates the use of link encryption.

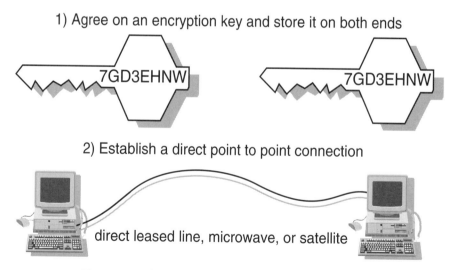

Figure 19.16 Using link encryption between two systems.

UNDERSTANDING DOCUMENT ENCRYPTION

Document encryption is a technique in which a document's sender encrypts the document which the recipient later decrypts. Document encryption places the burden of security directly on those who are involved in the communication. The major weakness of document encryption is that it adds a sometimes cumbersome additional step every time a sender and receiver exchange a document. Because of this extra step, many users prefer to save time by skipping the encryption.

The primary advantage of document encryption is that anyone with an e-mail account can use document encryption, using inexpensive or, in some cases free, software.

411

UNDERSTANDING PRETTY GOOD PRIVACY (PGP)

Pretty Good Privacy, which is often called *PGP*, is a free (for personal use) e-mail security program. Philip Zimmermann developed PGP in 1991 to support public-key encryption, digital signatures, and data compression. To obtain your own copy of PGP, visit the site *http://web.mit.edu/afs/net/mit/jis/www/pgp.html*, shown in Figure 19.17.

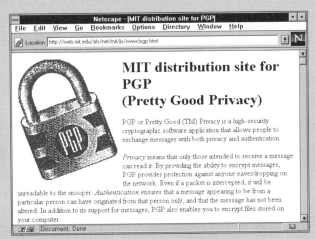

Figure 19.17 Information on PGP.

Before you send an e-mail message, you use PGP to encrypt your document. The recipient also uses PGP to decrypt the document. PGP is an excellent step toward security, and it uses a 128-bit key. In addition, PGP provides users with the option to compress the file before they send it. Besides making a document smaller, the compression further enhances the file's security because compressed files are more difficult to crack. According to the PGP documentation, it would take 3×10^{11} years for someone to break the encrypted message of a compressed file.

A commercial version of PGP, *ViaCrypt PGP*, is available for around $150. For information on *ViaCrypt PGP*, visit *http://www.dancingbear.com/PGP/VPGPPressRelease.html*, shown in Figure 19.18.

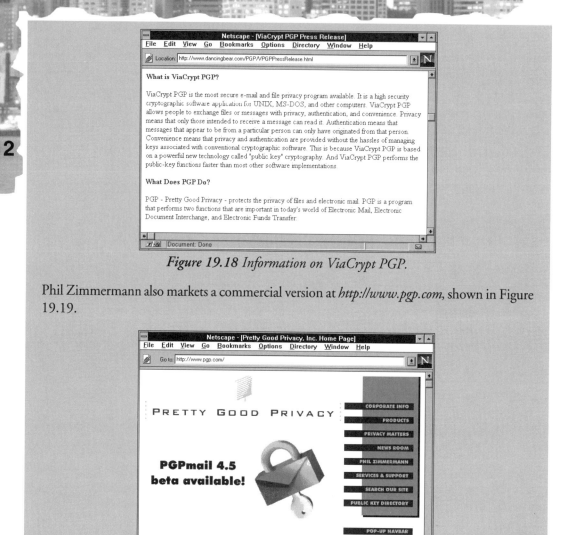

Figure 19.18 Information on ViaCrypt PGP.

Phil Zimmermann also markets a commercial version at *http://www.pgp.com*, shown in Figure 19.19.

Figure 19.19 Information on the commercial version of PGP.

UNDERSTANDING THE SECURE SOCKET LAYER (SSL)

The *Secure Socket Layer* (SSL) is a system developed by Netscape Communications that provides encryption over TCP/IP between two host computers. You can use SSL to encrypt any TCP/IP protocol, such as HTTP, *telnet*, and *ftp*. SSL works at the system level. Therefore, any user can take advantage of SSL because the SSL software automatically encrypts messages before they are put onto the network. At the recipient's end, SSL software automatically converts the messages into a readable document.

SSL is based on public-key encryption and works in two steps. First, the two computers wishing to communicate establish a special *session key* (so named because the key is valid for only the current communication session). One computer encrypts the session key and transmits the key to the other computer. Second, after both sides know the session key, the transmitting computer uses the session key to encrypt messages. After the document's transfer is complete, the recipient uses the same session key to decrypt the document. Figure 19.20 shows how Secure Socket Layers encrypt and decrypt documents.

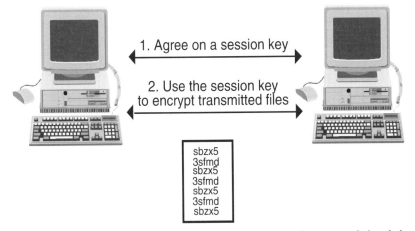

Figure 19.20 *The Secure Socket Layer encrypts and decrypts documents behind the scenes.*

For more information on SSL, visit *http//bit.csc.lsu.edu/~hendriks/ssl.html*, shown in Figure 19.21.

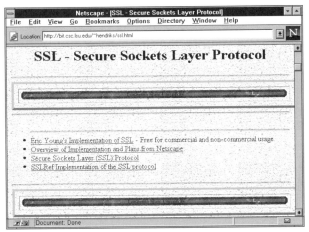

Figure 19.21 *Information on the Secure Sockets Layer.*

Understanding Secure HTTP (S-HTTP)

Secure HTTP is a protocol developed by the CommerceNet coalition which operates at the level of the HTTP protocol. S-HTTP is less widely supported than Netscape's Secure Socket Layer. Because S-HTTP works only for HTTP, it does not address security concerns for other popular protocols, such as *ftp* and *telnet*.

S-HTTP works similarly to SSL in that it requires the sender and receiver to negotiate and use a secure key. Both SSL and S-HTTP require special server and browser software to perform their encryption methods. For more information on S-HTTP, visit *http://www.eit.com/projects/s-http*, shown in Figure 19.22.

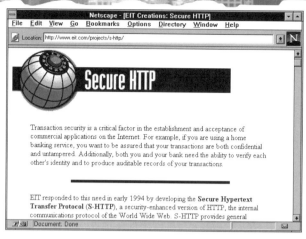

Figure 19.22 Information on S-HTTP.

LOOKING AT OTHER COMMON SECURITY THREATS

As you have learned, programmers who understand network protocols can provide a variety of threats to your network security. As you will learn, many of these security threats occur in low-level network operations, many of which you might never consider. The following sections examine some additional network threats you should consider as you implement your intranet's security policies.

PROTECTING AGAINST SOURCE-ROUTED TRAFFIC

As you have learned, network software breaks the messages it sends across a network into packets. These packets contain the text of the message as well as information that indicates the destination address. The packet's addressing information is the packet's *heading*. As the packets move across the Internet, they may follow independent routes to their ultimate destination. The packets only require that the network deliver them to the address specified within their heading. As they travel to their destination, packets will follow whatever route is available.

There is a seldom used way that applications can instruct a packet to use an explicit route to travel to its destination. For example, a sender could map a route that sends the packet from one specific computer to another, specifying each step of the way to the final computer. Encoding this road map information in a packet's heading is called *source routing*, and it is used mainly to debug networks and for some specialized applications.

Unfortunately, programmers can also use source routing to gain access into your network. They may accomplish network access by modifying a source-routed packet so that it claims to be from a computer within your network. In many cases, your router will obediently perform the packet's routing instructions and permit the packet to enter your network.

One way to combat such attacks is simply to direct your firewall to block all source-routed packets. Most commercial routers provide an option to ignore source-routed packets.

PROTECTING AGAINST *ICMP* REDIRECTS

When a router (also known as a packet switch) sends a packet to another router, it listens to see if that packet actually arrives at the specified router. Occasionally, a route may break or become overloaded. In such cases, the sending router may receive an *ICMP-redirect* message that indicates a new path the sending router should use. ICMP stands for Internet Control Message Protocol. ICMP defines the rules routers use to exchange traffic (routing information).

By writing low-level programs, attackers can forge the ICMP-redirect messages which direct routers to re-route communication traffic to some other destination. Network designers use the term *spoofing* to describe the process of tricking a router into rerouting messages in this way. Therefore, as you design your firewall, you may want to screen ICMP traffic.

PROTECTING AGAINST DENIAL OF SERVICE

In some cases, an attacker's goal is to incapacitate your network to prevent your company from receiving or sending network communications. As discussed above, by forging ICMP-redirect messages, an attacker can cause your network to lose communications. Because your network is connected to other networks and, therefore, dependent on those networks to send it information, an attacker can bring down your network indirectly. By attacking the networks which connect others to your network, it is possible for an attacker to disrupt your connection to the Internet.

Fortunately, the Internet was designed to re-route traffic around congested or damaged routers, and it is difficult for an attacker to bring down your network through an indirect approach. If it happens, you will probably lose your connection for only a few seconds.

A SECURITY CHECKLIST

If you decide to allow access to and from your intranet and the Internet, a firewall will become an inevitable addition to your network. You must design, implement, and maintain your firewall continuously for it to protect your intranet and your company's information. This chapter has given you several approaches that you can study and use as a guide in your firewall implementation. Several suggestions you should keep in mind include:

- Use a router to filter packets between your intranet and the Internet. Routers filter packets and restrict who can access your intranet.

- Use a separate host computer to act as your server.

- Use a circuit-level firewall at the host to ensure all traffic flows through a single choke point.

- Use a circuit-level firewall to define who can connect to your network and what services they can use.

- Consider implementing several different protocols to provide a further barrier. For example, you may choose to keep Novell IPX/SPX *NetWare* protocols on your intranet and to force users to connect to TCP/IP at a host computer to access the Internet.

- Make sure your CGI scripts test for unexpected input. Also, protect your scripts from *ftp* access.

- Pay special attention to log or backup files which your server may generate. These files contain valuable information for a would-be attacker.

- Encrypt any information that you deem confidential. Remember, sending information across the Internet is like sending an open postcard in the mail. Anyone can read the information as it makes its way to its final destination.

PUTTING IT ALL TOGETHER

By designing your firewall early in your intranet design, you can better respond to the inevitable issues of network security. This chapter gives you a framework from which you can start, as well as ammunition you can use, to convince those who may hesitate toward connecting your network to the rest of the world. In Chapter 20, you will examine Java, the hottest programming language used on the Web today. Before you continue with Chapter 20, however, make sure you have learned the following key concepts:

✓ Start thinking about security issues as you begin your intranet design. Use your company's existing security policy, if one exists, as your guide.

✓ A firewall can be as simple as a single router, or as complex as a system of routers and bastion hosts. Your security policy, as it relates both to outside and inside users, will help you determine the extent of your firewall.

✓ Routers provide security by filtering and rejecting packets that come into your network, based on specifications within a file that you create.

✓ You can install firewalls within your network to enforce security between departments inside your company.

✓ A highly-fortified host computer is known as a bastion host. You can run proxy software on a bastion host which isolates two networks from one another.

✓ In addition to your security concerns, you must have a method to detect and prevent computer viruses. Firewalls cannot detect computer viruses.

✓ The three main types of firewalls are network-level, application-level, and circuit-level firewalls.

✓ The three most popular firewall architectures are the dual-homed host firewall, the screened-host firewall, and the screened-subnet firewall. Because it incorporates an intermediate perimeter network to protect against threats, the screened-subnet firewall may offer the best protection.

✓ Because they can be a major security threat if they are not properly designed with security issues in mind, you must provide careful oversight of all CGI scripts.

✓ To prevent other users from intercepting and reading the confidential files you send over the Internet, you should encrypt confidential communications.

✓ Link encryption, document encryption, SSL, and S-HTTP are ways you can encrypt files. SSL, which is based on public-key encryption, works behind-the-scenes when you send and receive files between sites that support it.

✓ Attackers use several well established methods to break into your network. You can protect against most of these by using a good firewall and carefully designing CGI scripts.

VISITING KEY SITES THAT DISCUSS INTRANETS

The World Wide Web is filled with hundreds of excellent and current articles on all aspects of intranets. Use the following sites as starting points for your Web exploration.

ASCEND COMMUNICATIONS

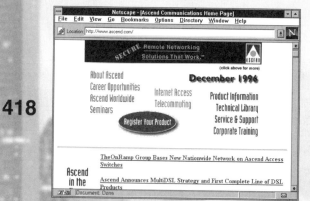

http://www.ascend.com/

THE INTRANET BOOM

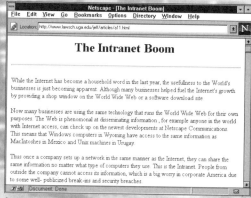

http://www.lawsch.uga.edu/jeff/articles/
a11.html

ABITEC, INC.

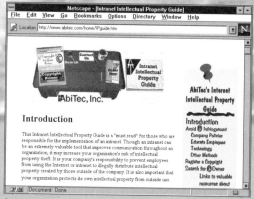

http://www.abitec.com/home/IPguide.htm

CIOS AND THE INTERNET/INTRANET

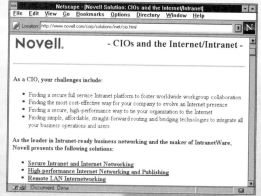

http://www.novell.com/corp/solutions/inet/
cio.html

CERT COORDINATION CENTER

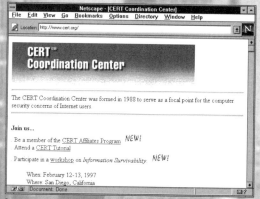

http://www.cert.org/

INTRANET PLANNING

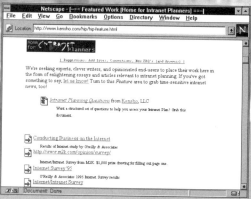

http://www.kensho.com/hip/hip-feature.html

Chapter 20

Java and Intranets

During the past year, one of the newest developments involving the Internet was the Java programming language. Java brings to the Web the ability for your browser to run special programs, from interactive 3D graphics, to custom order-entry forms, to real-time charting. To better understand how Java will impact the Web, think about all the programs you run from your PC on a regular basis. Next, imagine those programs running within a browser.

The ability for Web pages to run programs is what Java is all about. Java is a new language that is just starting to capture the imagination of the software-development community. Fortunately, your intranet is probably ready to use Java today. In this chapter, you will learn what Java is and how you can take advantage of it within your intranet. You will also experiment with simple Java *applets* (small Java applications). By the time you finish this chapter, you will understand the following key concepts:

- Java is a new programming language which lets programmers create small applications, called applets, which you can place on your Web pages.

- Java gives programmers the ability to create multimedia-based programs that integrate text, images, sounds, and video into a Web site.

- When a user visits a Web site that uses one or more Java applets, the server downloads the applets to the browser using the same techniques the server uses when downloading text and graphics. The browser, in turn, executes the applet.

- You do not need any special hardware or software to add Java applets to a Web page.

- To place a Java applet within a Web page, you use the HTML *<APPLET>* tag.

- There are many new programming environments with which programmers can create Java applets. Two of the best known Java environments are the Java Development Kit from Sun Microsystems, Inc. and Visual J++ from Microsoft.

- Java applets are platform independent, which means the same Java applet will run within a Windows-based browser, a Mac-based browser, and even a Unix-based browser.

- Because Java is a programming language, you will need a skilled programmer to develop custom applets.

- The developers at Sun Microsystems, Inc., who created Java, designed the programming language with security issues in mind. The restrictions designers placed on Java make it very difficult for programmers to create viruses using Java.

- In the near future, just-in-time (JIT) Java compilers will increase the performance of Java applets.

UNDERSTANDING THE NEED FOR JAVA

As you have learned, when you visit a Web site, the browser requests the server to download an HTML document. As the browser examines the HTML file, it will request the server to download the document's graphic files. Depending on the size of the graphics and the speed of your Internet connection, this file download process can become quite time consuming.

Initially, Web pages were static (unchanging), often described by users as a slow magazine that you had to wait to download. Because of slow download times, it was impossible for Web sites to feature animations or to take advantage of audio clips and music. Java, however, changed all that.

Java lets programmers build small programs called applets, which Web designers can place on a Web page. When a user visits the Web site, the server downloads the Java applet, just as it does the site's HTML document and graphics files. The user's browser, in turn, runs the applet. You can think of a Java applet as a program that you download from a Web site and that your browser runs. Figure 20.1, for example, shows the Netscape *Navigator* running a Java applet that spins two graphics, one of which is the Jamsa Press Dalmatian, Happy.

*Figure 20.1 Running a Java applet within the Netscape **Navigator**.*

In a similar way, Figure 20.2 illustrates a Java applet that turns the mouse pointer into an eraser. As you move the mouse pointer, it erases one image to reveal another. You might, for example, place an image of a new product on your Web site. As users erase the image, they would reveal a second image that illustrates your product's inner workings.

Figure 20.2 *The Java Eraser applet.*

Later in this chapter, you will learn how to run both of these Java applets, which are on the CD-ROM that accompanies this book.

JAVA AND COMPUTER VIRUSES

When you download programs from the Internet and run those programs on your computer, you run a very high chance of encountering a computer virus—a program written by a malicious programmer with the goal of damaging your computer's disk or the files it contains. In general, you should not download programs from the net. The only exception to this rule is when you download a program from a reputable software development company, such as Microsoft, Borland, or Netscape, and even then, do not run the programs until you examine the program files using a virus checker.

As discussed, a Java applet is a program that your browser downloads from a Web site and then runs on your computer. At first glance, running a Java applet seems to violate the rule of not downloading and running programs from the Net. However, as you will learn, to prevent programmers from creating viruses using Java, the Java developers restricted the operations that Java applets can perform on your system. For example, although a Java applet runs on your computer, the applet cannot write to a file on your disk—which is an essential operation for a computer virus. So, as you surf the Web, you can feel safe connecting to Web sites and running the Java applets they contain.

JAVA RUNS ON MULTIPLE PLATFORMS

If you think about the computers that make up the World Wide Web, you will realize that users surfing the Web may use a Windows-based system, a Mac, a Unix-based workstation, an OS/2-based PC, or some other system. One of the features that makes HTML so powerful is that it is platform independent. In other words, whether users are using a Windows-based system or a Mac, they will use the same HTML file.

Java is also platform independent. This enables programmers to create one Java applet. When a user's browser downloads and runs that applet, it does not matter if the user is Mac-based, Windows-based, or Unix-based, provided the user's browser knows how to run a Java applet.

As you know, programs are processor specific. For example, the programs a user runs under Windows contain machine code (the binary instructions the processor executes) for an Intel-based processor, such as a Pentium or 486. Likewise, the programs a user runs on a Mac contain machine code for a Motorola-based processor. Because programs are processor dependent, you cannot run machine code written for a Pentium computer on a Motorola-based system—which is why you can not run Windows-based programs on the Mac and vice versa.

However, as discussed, the same Java program will run on a Mac, Intel, or Unix-based system. That is because a Java applet does not contain machine code (the ones and zeros) that is specific to a processor. Instead, the Java applet uses virtual machine code—a generic combination of ones and zeros. When a browser downloads and runs a Java applet, the browser must first convert the Java applet's code into machine code that is specific to its processor.

For example, assume that a Windows-based user running Microsoft *Internet Explorer* downloads a Java applet. Before the *Internet Explorer* can run the applet, it converts (translates) the Java virtual machine code into Intel-based code. Likewise, assume a Mac user running Netscape *Navigator* downloads the same applet. Before *Netscape* can run the applet, it must first translate the Java virtual machine code into Motorola-specific machine code.

By using virtual machine code, Java is platform independent. The disadvantage of using machine code is that the translation time required to convert the Java virtual machine code to processor-specific machine code is lengthy, which causes the applet to run slower (as much as 20 times slower than an equivalent C/C++ program). Java virtual machine code is sometimes referred to as Java *bytecode*.

USING A JAVA-ENABLED BROWSER

As you have learned, when your browser downloads a Web page that contains a Java applet, the browser translates the applet's virtual machine code into processor-specific machine code, which it then executes. Not all browsers support Java applets. Those browsers that do not support Java will ignore the HTML *<APPLET>* tag developers use to place an applet on a Web page. Browsers that support Java are called *Java-enabled browsers*.

To run a Java applet contained on a Web page, you must use a Java-enabled browser. The latest versions of both the Netscape *Navigator* and Microsoft *Internet Explorer* are Java enabled. You can download the Netscape *Navigator* at *http://home.netscape.com*. After you install *Navigator*, you must enable it to run Java applets. To enable Java support, select the Options menu Network Preferences option. *Navigator*, in turn, will display a dialog box that contains various tabs across the top. Select the Languages tab. Within the tab, you will see a Enable Java checkbox. If this box is not checked, you should check it now. If you cannot check the box, or the checkbox does not appear, your version of the browser does not support Java. You will have to download the latest version from Netscape's Web page.

To download the Microsoft *Internet Explorer*, visit the Microsoft Web site at *http://www.microsoft.com*. After you install the *Internet Explorer*, verify that the browser has Java support enabled by selecting the File menu Properties option. The *Internet Explorer* will display the Properties dialog box. Select the Security tab. Within the Security tab you will see a checkbox labeled Enable Java Programs. Make sure the checkbox contains a checkmark.

To test drive a Java applet, visit Jamsa Press Java demo at *http://www.jamsa.com/catalog/javalib/ex.htm*. Your browser will load the Magnify applet which converts your mouse pointer into a magnifying glass. As you move the pointer, you can zoom in on an image as shown in Figure 20.3.

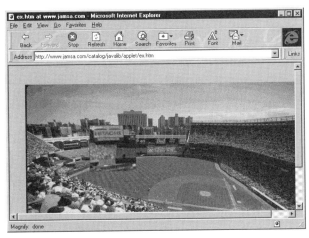

Figure 20.3 The Magnify applet at Jamsa Press.

RUNNING JAVA APPLETS FROM THE COMPANION CD-ROM

To help you better understand the use of Java applets, the companion CD-ROM that accompanies this book contains several Java applets you can run from the CD-ROM using the Netscape *Navigator* or Microsoft *Internet Explorer*. For example, to run the spinning heads applet previously shown in Figure 20.1, type in the following address within your browser and replace the drive letter D: with the drive letter that corresponds to your CD-ROM drive:

```
file:///D:\SPIN.HTML
```

Likewise, to run the Eraser applet previously shown in Figure 20.2, type in the following address:

```
file:///D:\ERASER.HTML
```

How Java Works within Your Intranet

As you have learned, the programmers at Sun originally designed Java as an Internet-based programming language. They designed applets, as special Java programs your Web browser can execute. In general, an intranet, is an in-house version of the Internet. It uses the same technologies, software, and equipment as the Internet. Whereas most sites on the Internet are controlled by other organizations, your company has control of the servers and client computers that make up your intranet. Such application control will make your intranet an ideal environment for custom applets written in Java. Using Java applets, your programming staff can quickly solve special problems that are specific to your company. Your programmers, for example, might design applets that provide a consistent user interface to company databases, documentation stores, equipment controls, and more. Because Java is platform independent, the Java custom applets your company creates will immediately run on a Mac, PC, and even a Unix workstation.

Learning More about the Java Language

Now that you have a general overview of what Java applets are, you may want to learn more about Java programming. If you have programmed with C or C++, Java will look familiar to you. In fact, many of the basic program statements are the same. To find the information you need to create your first Java programs, access the Sun Microsystems, Inc. Web site at *http://www.javasoft.com*, as shown in Figure 20.4.

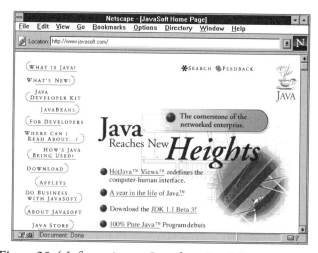

Figure 20.4 Information on Java from Sun Microsystems, Inc.

Sun's Javasoft site contains a wide range of documentation (white papers, application program interface (API) specifications, programmer's guide and sample applets). For specifics on these documents, visit *http://www.javasoft.com/doc/programmer.html*, as shown in Figure 20.5.

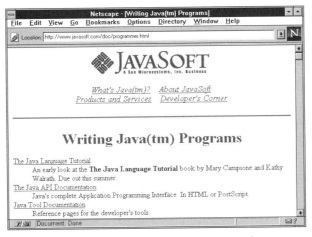

Figure 20.5 Java programming specifics.

THE JAVA DEVELOPMENT KIT

To create your own Java applet, you must use an editor to type in the Java program statements and then use a special program called the Java compiler to compile the statements. When programmers create programs using a programming language such as C or C++, the programmers must buy a compiler which may cost several hundred dollars. Sun Microsystems, Inc., however, currently gives Java away for free! Sun packages everything you need to build and test applications within a set of programs and files called the Java Development Kit or JDK.

If you are using Windows 95 or Windows NT, you can install the Java Development Kit from the CD-ROM that accompanies this book. To install the Java Development Kit, perform these steps:

1. If you are running Windows 95, select the Start menu Run option. Windows 95, in turn, will display the Run dialog box. Within the Run dialog box, type **command** and press <ENTER>.

2. If you are using Windows NT, select the Program Manager's File menu Run option. Windows NT, in turn, will display the Run dialog box. Within the Run dialog box, type **command** and press <ENTER>.

3. From the command prompt, use the following change directory command to select the root directory as your current directory:

```
C:\WINDOWS> CD \    <ENTER>
```

4. Insert the *Intranet Bible* companion CD-ROM.

5. Without changing your current drive from your hard drive, type in the program JDK102 preceded by your CD-ROM drive letter, a colon, and a back slash and then press <ENTER>. For example, if your CD-ROM drive is drive D:, you would type the following:

```
C:\> D:JDK102    <ENTER>
```

426

Note: When you install the Java Development Kit on your hard disk, the installation program will create a Java directory within your current directory. In most cases, you will want to put the Java directory within your disk's root directory. If, for some reason, you install Java in the wrong directory, simply remove the Java directory using the DELTREE command and run the JDK102 program a second time, but from the correct directory.

DOWNLOADING THE *JDK* FROM THE *INTERNET*

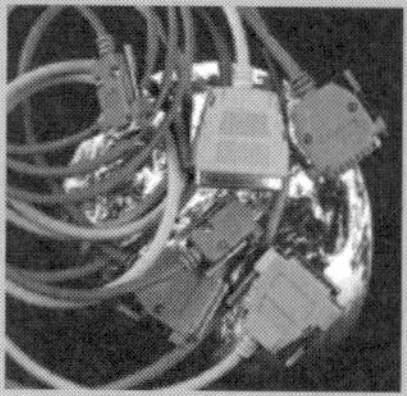

If you are using Windows 95 or Windows NT, you can install the Java Development Kit (JDK) from the companion disk that accompanied this book. If you are using a Mac or Unix-based system, you can download the JDK, for free, from Sun Microsystems at *http://www.javasoft.com/products/JDK/1.1/index.html*, as shown in Figure 20.6.

Figure 20.6 You can download the Java Development Kit from Sun Microsystems, Inc.

UNDERSTANDING THE *<APPLET>* HTML TAG

To place a Java applet within a Web page, you use the HTML *<APPLET>* and *</APPLET>* tags. Although the <APPLET> tag supports several attributes, most applets require only that you specify the applet file name (which will have the *.class* extension) and the width and height of the applet window. For example, assume that you want to place an applet named *Clock.class* that displays the current time on a Web page. Assuming the size of the clock window is 200x100 (pixels), you would use the following entry:

```
<APPLET CODE="Clock.class" WIDTH=100 HEIGHT=200></APPLET>
```

The *<APPLET>* tag *CODE* attribute tells the browser the name of the Java class. The *WIDTH* and *HEIGHT* attributes specify the applet's window size. If you are currently running either the spinning heads or eraser applets, which are provided on this book's companion CD-ROM, use the browser's Show Source option to view the contents of the HTML file. Search the HTML entries for the *<APPLET>* entry that corresponds to the Java applet. For specifics on the HTML *<APPLET>* tag, visit the site, *http://info.uibk.ac.at/info/kurs/htmlkurs/htmlref/applet.html*, shown in Figure 20.7.

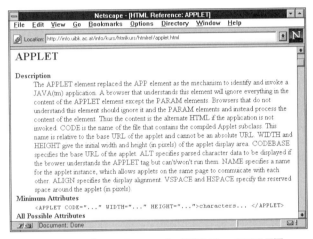

Figure 20.7 Information on the HTML <APPLET> tag.

LOOKING AT A SIMPLE JAVA APPLET

To create a Java applet, a programmer must first create a file, called the source file. The *source file* contains the Java statements that direct the applet to perform a specific operation. The following Java applet, *Hello.java*, simply displays the message **Hello, World!** within an applet window. To create this program, you must type in the statements exactly as they appear here (including matching upper and lowercase letters):

```
import java.applet.*;
import java.awt.Graphics;

public class Hello extends Applet {
  public void paint(Graphics g)
    {
      g.setColor(Color.red);
      g.drawString("Hello, World!");
    }
  }
```

In this case, you would store the Java statements within a source file named *Hello.java* (with the uppercase H in Hello). For now, it is not important that you understand how the program statements work, but rather, the steps you must perform to compile the program—which creates a file with the *.class* extension that contains the Java virtual machine code.

Using the Java Development Kit, which you installed from this book's companion CD-ROM, or which you downloaded from Sun Microsystems, Inc., you must compile your applet from the command-line prompt as shown here:

```
C:\JAVA> javac Hello.java   <ENTER>
```

If you have typed the program statements correctly, the Java compiler will successfully convert your statements into Java virtual machine code. If, however, you have mistyped the statements, the Java compiler will display one or more error messages on your screen. If the error messages occur, edit your Java source file and correct the errors (you may need to compare your file's contents closely to the previously shown statement). After you successfully compile the program, place the following *<APPLET>* tag within an HTML file named *MyApplet.HTML*:

```
<APPLET code="Hello.class" width=300 height=300></APPLET>
```

Next, within your browser, type in the following address, replacing the characters **pathname** with the directory path to the *MyApplet.HTML* file:

```
file:///c:\pathname\MyApplet.HTML
```

Your browser, in turn, will display the applet window which contains the **Hello, World!** message as shown in Figure 20.8.

*Figure 20.8 Displaying the **Hello, World!** message within an applet window.*

PUTTING YOUR JAVA APPLET ON A SERVER

To place a Java applet on your Web server, you do not need to do anything to your server. Instead, you simply need to create a Web page that uses the HTML *<APPLET>* tag to tell the browser about the applet. Normally, you will place your applet's class file within the same directory as your HTML document and its image files. For example, the following HTML file directs the browser to load the applet file *MyFirst.class* within a 100x300 window:

```
<APPLET CODE="MyFirst.class" WIDTH=100 HEIGHT=300></APPLET>
```

NEW DEVELOPMENTS IN STORE FOR JAVA

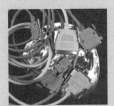

Over the next year, the next major enhancement to Java will be increased performance. As you have learned, when your browser downloads a Java applet, the server sends platform-independent Java bytecodes that the Java virtual machine within your browser interprets. Although, by using bytecodes in this way, Java applets are platform independent. They are also much slower than an equivalent program written in the C/C++ programming language. In fact, depending on the application, the Java applet can be 20 to 40 times slower than code you compiled for use on a specific platform, such as a C/C++ program you compiled for use on an Intel processor.

The increase in Java performance will come from new browser-side software called a just-in-time (JIT) compiler. Normally, your browser does not translate Java bytecodes for use on your machine until you start to run the applet. Then, before the browser can execute bytecode instructions, the browser must first translate the instructions—a slow process.

A just-in-time compiler, on the other hand, will start processing the bytecode as the browser downloads the applet, converting the code for use on your specific computer type (such an Intel or Motorola processor). In this way, the just-in-time compiler eliminates the need for the browser to translate the bytecode as the applet runs, making the Java code execute as fast as your other applications. As you might guess, each of the major compiler and IDE manufacturers, such as Borland, Microsoft, Symantec, and Metrowerks, are all developing just-in-time compilers. For more information on these companies' Java compilers, visit the Web sites shown in Figures 20.9a through 20.9d.

Figure 20.9a http://www.borland.com/— openjbuilder/

Figure 20.9b http://www.microsoft.com/— visualj/

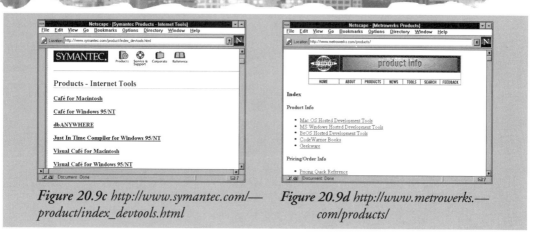

Figure 20.9c *http://www.symantec.com/— product/index_devtools.html*

Figure 20.9d *http://www.metrowerks.— com/products/*

UNDERSTANDING JAVASCRIPT

Although Java is very powerful, to create Java applets, you must be a programmer. To bridge the gap between programmers and Web-site developers, Sun Microsystems, Inc., released JavaScript. Like Perl, JavaScript is a scripting language with which designers can create interactive sites. For example, Figure 20.10 illustrates a simple loan calculator developed using JavaScript.

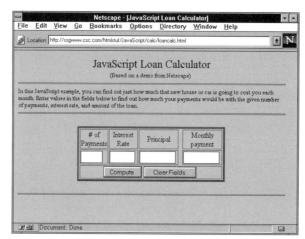

Figure 20.10 *A JavaScript-based calculator*

You can think of JavaScript as a mix of Java and HTML. You place JavaScript commands within an HTML file. Unlike Java, you do not compile JavaScript. Instead, as the browser examines the HTML file, the browser will simply execute the JavaScript entries. For example, the following HTML file, *JSDemo.HTML*, uses JavaScript to display the message **Hello, World!** within a Web page:

```
<HTML><BODY>
<SCRIPT LANGUAGE="JavaScript">
  document.write("Hello, World!");
</SCRIPT></BODY><HTML>
```

Figure 20.11 illustrates how the Netscape *Navigator* will display the JavaScript message.

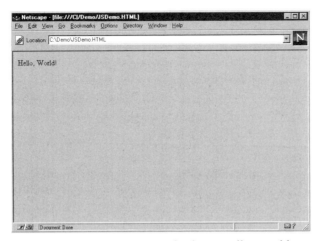

***Figure 20.11** Using JavaScript to display a Hello, World! message.*

Although this JavaScript example was quite simple, you can use JavaScript to create Web pages that are very interactive. For more information on JavaScript, visit the Web site, *http://home.netscape.com/eng/mozilla/3.0/handbook/javascript/index.html*, as shown in Figure 20.12.

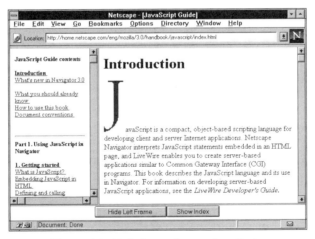

***Figure 20.12** Information on JavaScript.*

UNDERSTANDING VBSCRIPT

As you know, it does not take Microsoft long to capitalize on a good idea. After Web sites started to put JavaScript to use, Microsoft released VBScript, a scripting language based on Microsoft's very popular (and powerful) Visual Basic. Unlike JavaScript which supports most platforms, VBScript currently runs only within Windows-based browsers. However, because the majority of the users are Windows based, many Web-site developers are starting to make extensive use of VBScript. One of the reasons VBScript is so popular, is VBScript makes it very easy to use ActiveX objects. As you will learn, ActiveX is a new technology from Microsoft that, in general, makes OLE-like objects available within a Web page.

Using ActiveX, programmers create objects that you can place within a Web page. For example, a programmer might create a marquee object that scrolls text across a page, or a clock object that shows the current time, or a search-engine object with which users can quickly search a site's contents for a specific topic. Currently, there are over 2,000 ActiveX objects! In the near future, you will begin hear terms such as "active browsers" and "active servers" and possibly even "active Web." Each of these terms correspond, in some way, to use of the ActiveX objects.

432

Figure 20.13, for example, illustrates the use of the ActiveX label object, with which a Web designer can rotate text on a Web page.

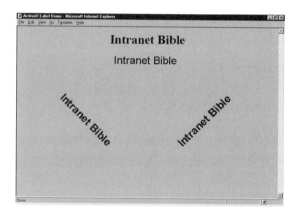

Figure 20.13 Using the ActiveX label object.

The following HTML entries use VBScript and the label object to display the rotated fonts:

```
<HTML>
<HEAD><TITLE>ActiveX Label Demo</TITLE></HEAD>
<BODY><H1 ALIGN=CENTER>Intranet Bible</H1>
<OBJECT CLASSID="clsid:99B42120-6EC7-11CF-A6C7-00AA00A47DD2"
id=MyLabel1 width=750 height=80 align=center>
<PARAM NAME="caption" VALUE="Intranet Bible">
<PARAM NAME="FontSize" VALUE=24>
</OBJECT>

<OBJECT CLASSID="clsid:99B42120-6EC7-11CF-A6C7-00AA00A47DD2"
id=MyLabel2 width=400 height=280 align=left>
<PARAM NAME="caption" VALUE="Intranet Bible">
<PARAM NAME="angle" VALUE="315">
<PARAM NAME="FontSize" Value="24">
<PARAM NAME="FontBold" Value="1">
</OBJECT>
```

```
<OBJECT CLASSID="clsid:99B42120-6EC7-11CF-A6C7-00AA00A47DD2"
id=MyLabel3 width=300 height=280 align=LEFT>
<PARAM NAME="caption" VALUE="Intranet Bible">
<PARAM NAME="angle" VALUE="45">
<PARAM NAME="FontSize" Value="24">
<PARAM NAME="FontBold" Value="1">
</OBJECT>
</BODY></HTML>
```

For more information on ActiveX, turn to the book, *ActiveX Programmer's Library*, Jamsa Press 1997. In addition, for information on VBScript, visit the Web site *http://www.microsoft.com/vbscript/ us/vbslang/vbstoc.htm*, as shown in Figure 20.14.

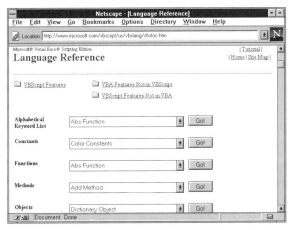

Figure 20.14 Information on VBScript.

You can also find information on ActiveX, at *http://www.microsoft.com/intdev/controls/ctrlref-f.htm*, as shown in Figure 20.15.

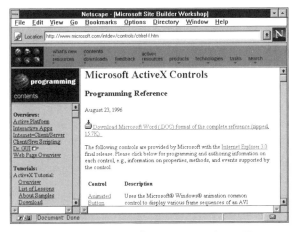

Figure 20.15 Information on ActiveX.

PUTTING IT ALL TOGETHER

In the past year, the use of the Java programming language has grown rapidly. Soon, most C/ C++ programmers will use Java for many applications. Within an intranet, Java provides an excellent tool·with which developers can create custom-programming solutions. If your company has programmers writing network-based applications, the programmers should strongly consider Java as their development tool.

Across the Web, there are many outstanding sources of information on intranets, CGI, network security, HTML, and more. Chapter 21 presents the Web addresses of some of the Web's "Best of the Best Intranet Sites." You should take time to visit each site Chapter 21 presents. Before you continue with Chapter 21, however, make sure you understand the following key concepts:

✓ Using Java, programmers can create applets which you can place on your Web pages.

✓ Java applets let you integrate multimedia into a Web site.

✓ When a user visits a Web site that contains a Java applet, the Web server downloads the applet to the browser which, in turn, executes the applet.

✓ To place a Java applet within a Web page, you use the HTML *<APPLET>* tag.

✓ Java applets are platform independent. If you create a Java applet for use within Windows, that same Java applet will run within a Mac- or Unix-based browser.

✓ Because Java is a programming language, you will need a skilled programmer to develop custom applets.

✓ The Java developers made it very difficult for programmers to create computer viruses using Java.

✓ The CD-ROM that accompanies this book contains the Java Development Kit (JDK) from Sun Microsystems, Inc., with which you can create Java applets.

VISITING KEY SITES THAT DISCUSS INTRANETS

The World Wide Web is filled with hundreds of excellent and current articles on all aspects of intranets. Use the following sites as starting points for your Web exploration.

BOARDWATCH MAGAZINE

http://www.boardwatch.com/

ORACLE CORPORATION

http://www.oracle.com/

NETSCAPE SERVER PLUG-INS

*http://home.netscape.com/comprod/server_*
central/server_add_ons.html

OBLIX, INC.

http://www.oblix.com/prodindex.html

435

JAVA INTRANET FRAMEWORK

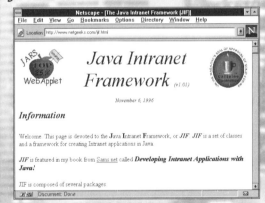

http://www.netgeeks.com/jif.html

JAVAWORLD

http://www.javaworld.com/

NC Vendors

http://www.ncworldmag.com/ncworld/
common/ncw-vendorlist.jw.html

ICC Click HR Product

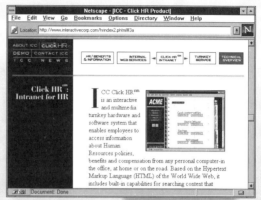

http://www.interactivecorp.com/
hrindex2.phtml#3a

BulletProof Corporation

http://www.bulletproof.com/

Home Account Network, Inc.

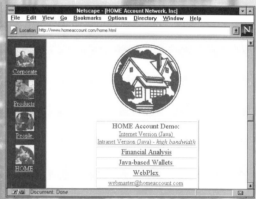

http://www.homeaccount.com/home.html

Studio J2000

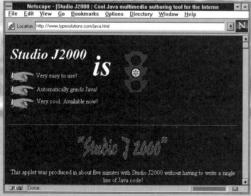

http://www.typesolutions.com/java.html

Active Software

http://www.activesw.com/

436

Chapter 21

A Guide to Essential
Intranet References

Throughout this book, you have found many Internet sites from which you can gather additional information, tools, and ideas which will help you implement different aspects of your intranet. Some essential sites you should visit on a regular basis are presented in this chapter. In many cases, the sites offer ongoing conversations among users, who, just like you, are building and improving their intranets. At other sites, you will find ready-to-run software that can provide security tools, HTML editors, graphics conversion, and much more. Rather than simply glancing at the sites this chapter presents, read this chapter while you are connected to the Web. As you read about a site, stop and visit it. The Web has a huge body of knowledge specific to intranets. With the background you have gained by reading this book, you will be quite surprised how much of the information you already know! So, connect to the Web right now and get started.

WebMaster Magazine

Figure 21.1 http://www.web-master.com

Process Software Corporation's Intranet White Paper

Figure 21.2 http://www.process.com/intranets/

The Intranet Rolls In

Figure 21.3 http://techweb.cmp.com/iw/564/64iuint.htm

PC Magazine's Internet User

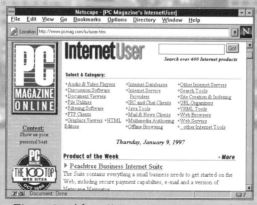

Figure 21.4 http://www.pcmag/IU/iuser.htm

GETTING YOUR COMPANY'S INTERNET STRATEGY RIGHT

Figure 21.5 http://pathfinder.com/fortune/magazine/1996/960318/infotech.html

INTRANETS: INTERNET TECHNOLOGIES DEPLOYED BEHIND THE FIREWALL FOR CORPORATE PRODUCTIVITY

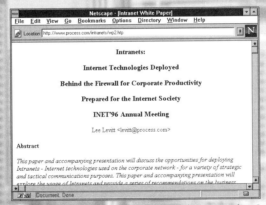

Figure 21.6 http://www.process.com/intranets/wp2.htp

THE INTRANET: A CORPORATE REVOLUTION

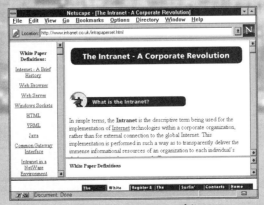

Figure 21.7 http://www.intranet.co.uk/intrapaperset.html

CORPORATE INTRANET STRATEGIES

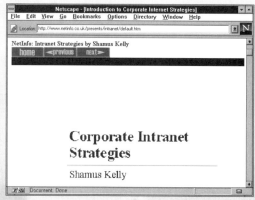

Figure 21.8 http://www.netinfo.co.uk/presents/intranet/default.htm

THE INTRANET JOURNAL - EXPERT'S CORNER

Figure 21.9 http://www.intranetjournal.com/expert.html

INTRANET SOUNDINGS

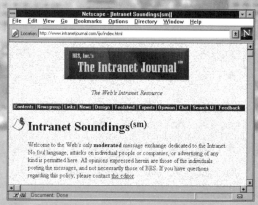

Figure 21.10 http://www.intranetjournal.com/ijx/index.html

Web Mastery Resource Lists.

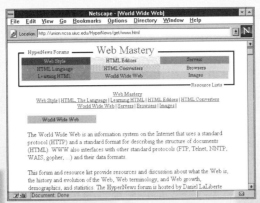

Figure 21.11 http://union.ncsa.uiuc.edu/HyperNews/get/www.html

The Intranet Journal

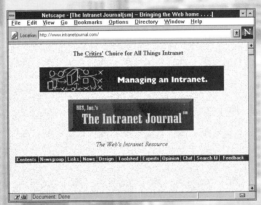

Figure 21.12 http://www.intranetjournal.com/

Intranet Solutions

Figure 21.13 http://home.netscape.com/comprod/at_work/index.html

THE WEBMASTER'S NOTEBOOK

Figure 21.14 http://www.cio.com/WebMaster/wm_notebook.html

THE COMPLETE INTRANET RESOURCE

Figure 21.15 http://www.intrack.com/intranet/

DAVID STROM'S WEB INFORMANT

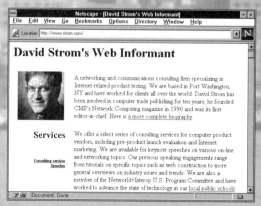

Figure 21.16 http://www.strom.com

ZONA RESEARCH'S INTRANET REPORT HIGHLIGHTS

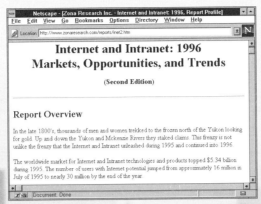

Figure 21.17 http://www.zonaresearch.com/reports/inet2.htm

INFOWEB - INTRANET RESOURCE LINKS

Figure 21.18 http://www.infoweb.com.au/toc2.htm

INTRANET JOURNAL - LINKS

Figure 21.19 http://www.intranetjournal.com

MICROSOFT INTERNET RESOURCE CENTER

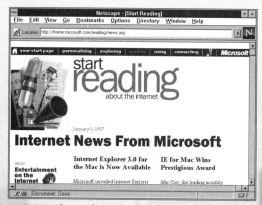

Figure 21.20 http://home.microsoft.com/reading/news.asp

INTERNET INFOCENTER

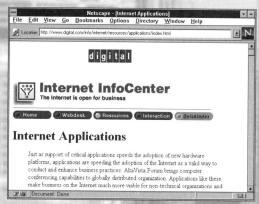

Figure 21.21 http://www.digital.com/info/internet/resources/applications/index.html

WEBREFERENCE.COM

Figure 21.22 http://webreference.com/

TECH WEB

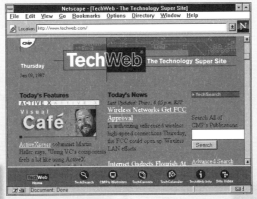

Figure 21.23 http://www.techweb.com/

SEARCH TOOLS

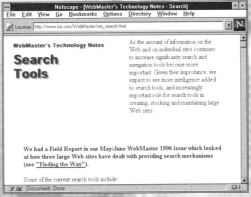

Figure 21.24 http://www.cio.com/WebMaster/wm_search.html

THE TABLE SAMPLER

Figure 21.25 http://home.netscape.com/assist/net_sites/table_sample.html

Conferencing Tools

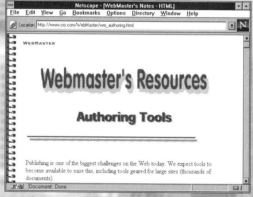

Figure 21.26 http://www.cio.com/WebMaster/wm_conferencing.html

Authoring Tools

Figure 21.27 http://www.cio.com/WebMaster/wm_authoring.html

Web Developer

Figure 21.28 http://www.webdeveloper.com/resources.html

INTRANET SOFTWARE RESOURCE

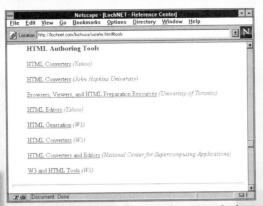

Figure 21.29 http://lochnet.com/lochusa/usrefer.htm#tools

GIF? JPEG? WHICH SHOULD YOU USE?

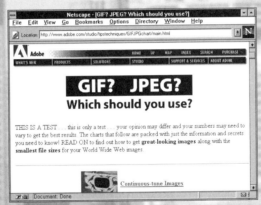

Figure 21.30 http://www.adobe.com/studio/tipstechniwues/GIFJPGchart/main.html

JOHN WARNOCK GETS ANIMATED WITH GIF!

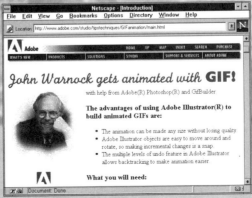

Figure 21.31 http://www.adobe.com/studio/tipstechniques/GIFanimation/main.html

THE DISCRIMINATING COLOR PALETTE

Figure 21.32 http://www.adobe.com/newsfeatures/palette/main.html

OPTIMIZING WEB GRAPHICS

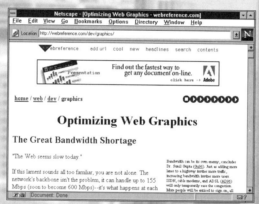

Figure 21.33 http://webreference.com/dev/graphics

JPEG AND GIF COMPARISON

Figure 21.34 http://www.dwmi.com/dw_pictures.html

How to Make an Animated GIF

Figure 21.35 http://webreference.com/dev/gifanim.html

GIF Animation on the WWW

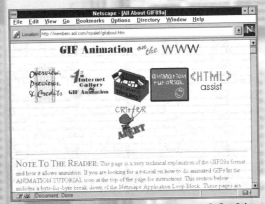

Figure 21.36 http://members.aol.com/royalef/gifabout.htm

Anthony's Icon Library

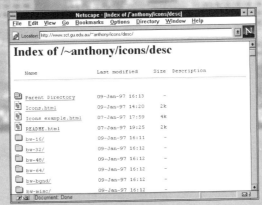

Figure 21.37 http://www.sct.gu.edu.au/~anthony/icons/desc/

WWW ICONS AND LOGOS

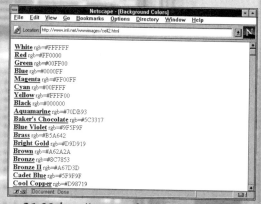

Figure 21.38 http://www-ns.rutgers.edu/doc-images/

BACKGROUND COLORS

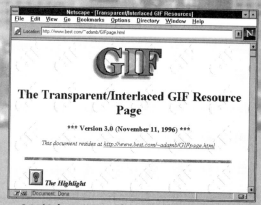

Figure 21.39 http://www.infi.net/wwwimages/cell2.html

THE TRANSPARENT/INTERLACED GIF RESOURCE PAGE

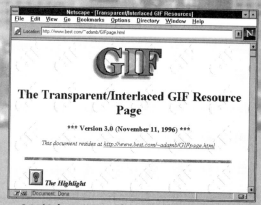

Figure 21.40 http://www.best.com/~adamb/GIFpage.html

TRANSPARENT BACKGROUND IMAGES

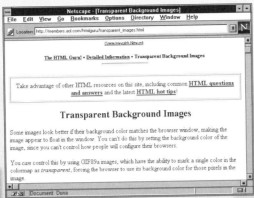

Figure 21.41 http://members.aol.com/htmlguru/transparent_images.html

CLIENT-SIDE IMAGE MAPS

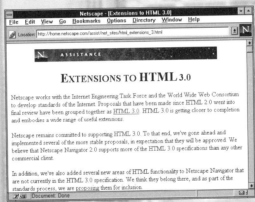

Figure 21.42 http://home.netscape.com/assist/net_sites/html_extensions_3.html

NCSA IMAGEMAP TUTORIAL

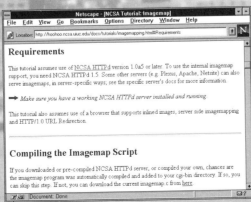

Figure 21.43 http://hoohoo.ncsa.uiuc.edu/docs/tutorials/imagemapping.html#Requirements

CLIENT-SIDE IMAGEMAP UPDATE

Figure 21.44 http://www.ihip.com

THE WEB MULTIMEDIA TOUR

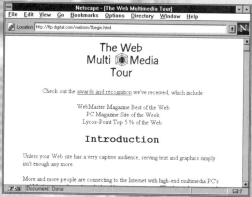

Figure 21.45 http://ftp.digital.com/webmm/fbegin.html

AUDIO SITES AND SITE LISTS

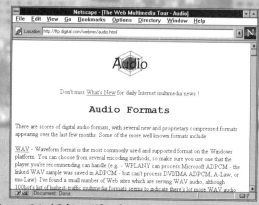

Figure 21.46 http://ftp.digital.com/webmm/audio.html

452

APPLE'S QUICKTIME VR

Figure 21.47 http://quicktime.apple.com

MACROMEDIA DIRECTOR'S SHOCKWAVE

Figure 21.48 http://www.macromedia.com/shockwave/

WEBMASTER'S TECHNOLOGY NOTES: VIDEO

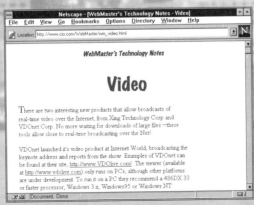

Figure 21.49 http://www.cio.com/WebMaster/wm_video.html

WEBMASTER'S TECHNOLOGY NOTES: SOUND

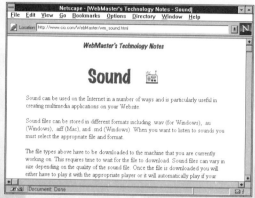

Figure 21.50 http://www.cio.com/WebMaster/wm_sound.html

WEBMASTER'S TECHNOLOGY NOTES: MULTIMEDIA

Figure 21.51 http://www.cio.com/WebMaster/wm_multimedia.html

Index

Essential Intranet References